A Good-Natured Riot

A GOOD-
NATURED

Charles K. Wolfe

RIOT *The Birth of the Grand Ole Opry*

The Country Music Foundation Press and Vanderbilt University Press

NASHVILLE

99 00 01 02 03   5 4 3 2 1

This publication is made from paper that meets
the minimum requirements of ANSI/NISO Z39.48 (R 1997)
Permanence of Paper for Printed Library Materials ∞

Frontispiece: In 1935 the cast of the Grand Ole Opry posed on the stage of the Hillsboro Theater for this group shot. The clock was set for 8:00, the time the Opry usually took to the air every Saturday night. *Bottom row, from left:* Bobby Castleman (accordion), Jack Shook, Nap Bastien, Dee Simmons, unidentified, Rabon and Alton Delmore (checked shirts), Amos Binkley, Gail Binkley, Claude Lampley, Tom Andrews, unidentified, DeFord Bailey. *Second row, seated, from left:* unidentified, Walter Liggett, Dr. Humphrey Bate, (across the fireplace) Uncle Dave Macon, George Wilkerson, Paris Pond, Robert Lunn, Sam McGee. *Third row, standing, from left:* unidentified, unidentified, Lewis Crook, Bill Etter, Herman Crook, Roy Hardison, Bert Hutcherson, Paul Warmack (in hat), Charley Arrington (with fiddle), Buster Bate (with tiple), Oscar Stone (light coat), probably Jimmy Hart, Sarie and (across the fireplace) Sally, Judge Hay, Honey Wild, Roy Hardison, Dorris Macon, unidentified, Sid Harkreader, Arthur Smith, Kirk McGee, and Oscar Albright (bass).

Library of Congress Cataloging-in-Publication Data

Wolfe, Charles K.
    A good-natured riot : the birth of the Grand Ole Opry / Charles
K. Wolfe. — 1st ed.
    p. cm.
Includes bibliographical references and index.
ISBN 0-8265-1331-X (cloth : alk. paper)
    1. Grand ole opry (Radio program) 2. Country music—History and
criticism. I. Title.
ML3524 .W64 1998
791.44'72—ddc21
                                                    98-40104
                                                    CIP
                                                    MN

*To Alcyone,
who got me started in the right direction,
and to Mary Dean,
who kept after me until I got it done*

Contents

Illustrations

Preface

On a cold day in February 1973, I walked up to the porch of Herman Crook's house on Russell Street in historic East Nashville. I had with me a notebook full of questions, a Sony cassette recorder, and a lot of curiosity. I knew that Herman and his band, the Crook Brothers, were one of the last of the authentic string bands still playing on WSM's legendary Grand Ole Opry and one of the few acts that had been on the show from the beginning. I had heard and admired the old Victor 78s that the Crook Brothers had recorded back in the 1920s, and it was hard to believe that their sound had been virtually unchanged in the years since. By 1973, the band was using a fiddle and harmonica lead and had a light skipping sound unlike any other band. Herman was featured on harmonica and the genial Ed Hyde on fiddle.

Herman had agreed to talk with me about the early days of the Grand Ole Opry. For several years I had been listening to talk about those pioneering days, but not many of the people doing the talking actually spoke from firsthand experience. More legends about the early Opry seemed available than facts. Little had been written, and the vertical files at the newly opened Country Music Foundation had only begun filling. Herman's wife invited me into their sitting room, and I got a chance to meet Herman himself, a tall, stately man with a strong sense of history. On his television rested an old framed picture of the very first group photo of the Opry cast, made in 1926 or 1927—the first such picture I had seen. Throughout the morning, Herman talked about what it was like in the days when Judge Hay was forming up what was then called the Barn Dance, and when legends like Uncle Dave Macon and Uncle Jimmy Thompson ruled the Saturday night airwaves. At the end of the interview, Herman brought out his harp, and gave me a concert of some of the old songs he used to play on the show in those days: "Put My Little Shoes Away," "Lost Train Blues," and "Amazing Grace."

At a party a couple of weeks later, I met a man named Ed Shea, then the editor of *Music City News.* He too was interested in the history of the

Opry and offered to publish an article about the Crook Brothers if I would write it up. I did, and Herman called me to tell me he was pleased. He also said I needed to talk to some of the other old-timers in the area. I was a little surprised: were there that many original members left? "Yes indeed," he said, and started rattling off names. At about the same time, I began to get letters from people who had seen my article: one was a great nephew of Uncle Jimmy Thompson asking if I would like to talk to his daughter-in-law. Another was a friend of Sam McGee's who would be happy to take me out to meet him. Soon I had a notebook full of leads, and I was off on a quest that would span some twenty years and result in this book.

What I had embarked upon was, at first, the tracing of an oral history of the world's most famous country radio show and how it got started. Stories about those days had been passed down in oral tradition through three and even four generations to the 1970s, each year leaving fewer and fewer of the veterans who knew about the Opry's history firsthand. Although the legends and myths about the show are in themselves revealing, at some point a factual body of data must be created, something with which to measure these legends.

That became my goal, and this book is my attempt to provide such a standard. The only detailed history of the early days, George Hay's little book *A Story of the Grand Ole Opry*, was colorful and engaging but full of Hay's disclaimers that he was not a historian and that he was informally writing from memory. There was a need for someone to collect the oral histories and then verify them with written or printed data from other sources.

Soon I had met and begun to interview many of these radio veterans: Sam and Kirk McGee, who rode with Uncle Dave Macon and Arthur Smith; Jack Jackson, the "Strolling Yodeller," who recorded with the Binkley Brothers and on his own; Arch and Dorris Macon, the sons of Uncle Dave; Elizabeth Hale, daughter of Theron; DeFord Bailey, the show's great harmonica soloist; and especially Alcyone Bate Beasley, the daughter of Dr. Humphrey Bate. Alcyone was especially important to the project. Not only did she sit for numerous interviews, but she also gave me references helpful in arranging to interview other subjects, opened up her huge scrapbooks, and kept urging me on when I got discouraged about the research or over the fact that few on the modern Nashville scene seemed to care about the old days. She also played me some wonderful country ragtime on her big grand piano, songs her father used to play, like "Waltz Me Around Again, Willie."

By 1975 I had met and started writing for Tony Russell, the editor of the British quarterly *Old Time Music*. Tony took early country music more

seriously than anybody I had met, and had, even that early, an encyclope-
dic knowledge of it. We routinely shared information and "discoveries"
from our research, and I kept him up to date about my Opry work. In
1975 the Opry was to celebrate its fiftieth anniversary, and Tony felt that
the event might provide a good opportunity to publish some of my
research. The result was the Old Time Music publication *The Grand Ole
Opry: The Early Years, 1925–1935*, which made its debut at Fan Fair that
year. Though it was published in England and sometimes hard to find in
the states, it received very good reviews and made its way onto numerous
bibliographies and "Selected Reading" lists. Tony's superb editing and
sense of layout made it an appealing book, and working with him showed
me how to weave interviews, newspaper data, company files, discographi-
cal data, and song histories into a readable and accurate account.

The publication of *GOOEY* (as Tony and I called it) might have been
the capstone to the research, but it was not. It attracted even more leads
and suggestions. Since my home was in the Nashville area, I could go back
and do follow-up interviews with Opry veterans, and I could see them
informally around town. At a flea market I ran into one of Arthur Smith's
sons selling old magazines, and I met the wife of Curt Poulton at a reception given by the Country Music Hall of Fame for veteran performers.
Even major Opry stars of the time, like Roy Acuff and Bill Monroe, let me
interview them about the early days. After completing dozens of interviews, many taped, I began to realize that I needed to fit them into a much
larger and complete format than I had done in *GOOEY*. Not that the earlier book contained all that many mistakes. It was just that I now had
much more detail and a much broader picture of the early Opry. Instead
of treading lightly on the decade of the 1930s, as I had done earlier, I now
felt that that decade played a crucial role in the show's survival. It deserved
as much detail as the 1920s. The season of 1939–1940 marked a natural
watershed for the show: it began its NBC network affiliation and in 1940
won national exposure through a Hollywood film. The time formed a
national watershed as well: World War II, looming on the national hori-
zon, had begun in Europe, and the last vestiges of the Depression were
dying away. It thus seemed logical to expand the scope of the book to
1940.

Some portions of this book, such as the chapter on Dr. Bate, appeared
in different form in *The Grand Ole Opry: The Early Years, 1925–1935*,
and I am grateful to Tony Russell and Old Time Music Publications for letting me further develop that material here. Most of the chapters, though,
are newly written, and most of the last half of the book is completely new.

Acknowledgments

In producing this book my greatest debt is to the many Opry pioneers who shared with me their stories and scrapbooks, and these sources are listed in the endnotes to the specific chapters. However, when I did the 1975 book, I paid homage to the "Opry originals" who were then still alive and had helped in the project. These include DeFord Bailey, Alcyone Bate Beasley, Herman and Lewis Crook, Hubert Gregory (of the Fruit Jar Drinkers), Sid Harkreader, Bert Hutcherson (of the Gully Jumpers), Sam and Kirk McGee, Dorris Macon, Grady Moore, Blythe Poteet, and Goldie Stewart (of the Possum Hunters). Sadly, each one of these originals is now gone; the last, Lewis Crook, died in 1997.

I also owe much to fellow researchers into Opry history who have, through informal conversations and published studies, helped inform and correct me. These include Bill Malone, the dean of country historians; John Rumble, of the Country Music Foundation; Danny Hatcher, formerly of the CMF; Doug Green, of Riders in the Sky; Steve Davis, who helped provide me with tapes of old records; Bill Harrison, who shared his memories of the show and its stars; Richard Blaustein, of East Tennessee State University; Marice Wolfe, in charge of Special Collections at the Jean and Alexander Heard Library at Vanderbilt; Richard Hulan, an independent researcher then affiliated with Vanderbilt; David Morton, for his research on DeFord Bailey; Paul Ritscher, for his independent and vital research into the careers of Kirk McGee and Mrs. Edna Wilson; Robert Oermann, for his early research and scholarship; Mrs. Lucy Gray, for her firsthand knowledge of the Fruit Jar Drinkers; Ronnie Pugh and Bob Pinson of the CMF; John Hartford, for sharing his own considerable collection of early Opry stories; Kyle Cantrell, current station manager of WSM; Richard Peterson of Vanderbilt for sharing long discussion about the Opry; Kyle Young, Paul Kingsbury, Chris Dickinson, and Mark Medley of the CMF staff; Danny Hatcher, formerly of the CMF; and Charles Backus of Vanderbilt University Press, for encouraging the book. Special thanks must go to Paul Kingsbury, John Rumble, and Ronnie Pugh for reading over the manuscript.

I am also indebted to the Faculty Research Committee at Middle Tennessee State University for supporting this research and this writing. Mrs. Susan Bragg and Mrs. Betty Nokes helped with the typing, and Susan Newby and Dana Park with research; David Lavery and Sarah Lavery helped transfer my archaic manuscript to diskette. Finally, I wish to acknowledge my family, who have lived with this book hanging over their heads for over twenty years: my wife, Mary Dean, and my daughters Stacey Wolfe and Cindy Wolfe Beatty.

Charles K. Wolfe
Murfreesboro, Tennessee

A Good-Natured Riot

"A Good-Natured Riot"

T HERE ARE TWO WAYS TO LOOK at the Grand Ole Opry as it emerged through its first fifteen years: as a radio show and as a collection of talented musicians. The distinction could be considered arbitrary, of course, because in the real world a show's form cannot be separated from its content. But an artificial division can be made for the purposes of study, and in the case of the Grand Ole Opry the "form" includes the complex of geographical, political, commercial, and historical factors that caused a Nashville insurance company to found and sustain a controversial radio show. It also includes the public relations genius of a young announcer named George Hay, who established and defined the scope of the show. Any notion of the program's form must include the temper of the 1920s, the time that spawned such a program, and the way in which the people of that time looked at entertainment and mass media. And the concept of form must include the city of Nashville, a city which aspired to become a center of classical culture and instead became a center of popular culture.

The content of the Opry must include a look at the musicians and their music. What was so special about this particular group of musicians that caught the imagination of the South, when similar groups of similar quality dropped into obscurity? What did these pioneering artists think they were doing with their music and with their show? Who were these legend-shrouded figures like Uncle Jimmy Thompson, Uncle Dave Macon, Dr. Humphrey Bate? Most of them are now gone, but by using modern research techniques we can reconstruct their lives, their careers, and their music. The picture that emerges is fascinating.

In this chapter and the next, we will be examining some of the aspects of the Opry's genesis and form. We will attempt to study the Opry as a single entity—a whole—and trace its direction and changes. Yet the early Opry as a whole was primarily a live radio show—a vague and amorphous thing born in a sparkling moment, that then vanished into the night, leaving only memories. And in the end, it was nothing but a collection of individuals and music. Thus for the bulk of this study we will concentrate primarily on individual musicians, with occasional side trips into relevant historical events. We cannot hope to recapture the essence of the early Opry, its wonderful music. Much of that, unrecorded in any form, is gone forever. But we can try to recapture the personalities who made the music and, hopefully, gain some fleeting hints as to the nature of that music.

Every student of the subject knows the prototype Opry story. On November 28, 1925, young George Hay sits an old white-bearded man before one of the station's newfangled carbon mikes. He lets him play a few fiddle tunes. The switchboard lights up and telegrams pour in. The old man, Uncle Jimmy Thompson, plays for an hour, and across the country listeners scramble for the earphones to their old crystal radio sets. Hay gets an idea: why not have a regular weekly show of this sort of stuff? Soon he is besieged by pickers and fiddlers of every variety: "We soon had a good-natured riot on our hands," he recalled. The show was off and running.

In many ways this story is fairly accurate. The founding of the Opry was indeed a dramatic event. But it was more dramatic, and in more complicated ways, than even George Hay remembered.

National Life and WSM

The National Life and Accident Insurance Company (originally called the Tennessee Sick and Accident Association) was founded in Nashville shortly after the turn of the century. Importantly, two of the founders, brothers Cornelius and Edward Craig, were from Giles County, in rural south-central Tennessee. The business was successful throughout the early years of the century, specializing in industrial health and accident insurance. Soon Cornelius Craig was elected president and brought his son Edwin into the company after the young man had graduated from Nashville's Vanderbilt University. In 1919 the firm made an important decision to go into the life insurance business and to place Edwin Craig at the head of this division. Both decisions were to be important later, for the life insurance move helped to redefine the company's customer appeal.

In early 1924 National Life moved into a new building located on Seventh Avenue in downtown Nashville, only a few blocks from the state capitol and on a hill commanding most of the town. By this time Edwin Craig had become fascinated by the phenomenon of radio. He had seen it grow into a nationwide fad during 1923 and was intrigued by its potential. He urged the company to start its own station and to include a studio in the new building. The company's old guard saw little in the idea, but they finally gave in to Craig and let him have what one of them later referred to as "his toy." In 1925 work began on the station, to be located on the fifth floor of the building. No expense was spared, and National Life intended, once it had committed itself, to create one of the finest stations in the country.

The station was seen not so much as a corporate investment as simply an elaborate advertisement. The company quickly associated itself with the new station's call letters: WSM stands for the slogan "We Shield Millions," capitalizing on the shield used in the company's logo since its inception. It was not at all uncommon to have one-advertiser stations in early radio; Sears's WLS in Chicago ("World's Largest Store") was perhaps the most popular station in this regard. Many other stations were owned by newspapers. Edwin Craig's own rationale for starting the station was described by Powell Stamper in *The National Life Story* (1968):

> His insight as to the potential values of the station through such collateral benefits as extending company identity, service to the community, the influence of public relations, and supporting the company's field men in their relations with both prospects and policyholders, activated his interest and support of the idea. (121)

The last reason—support for the field men—was to become vastly important later with the founding of the Opry.

With Craig in charge of the radio project, station WSM went on the air on October 5, 1925. It began broadcasting with one thousand watts of power, making it one of the two strongest stations in the South, and stronger than 85 percent of all the other broadcasting stations in the country at the time ([Nashville] *Tennessean*, October 4, 1925). For a time WSM shared its wavelength assignment (282.8 meters) with WOAN, a smaller station operating out of Lawrenceburg, Tennessee. That station was operated by James D. Vaughan, a nationally known publisher of gospel songbooks, who used the station to publicize his new gospel songs. Some of Vaughan's quartets would later become regulars on other WSM programs. Vaughan's was also the first Southern concern to issue its own phonograph records, starting in 1922, several years before any Opry performers would record. WSM also worked out an alternating schedule with two other stations in Nashville, finally giving it a schedule that featured Monday, Wednesday, and Saturday nights. (For an account of WSM's relationships with other Nashville stations, see the following chapter.)

The first program broadcast by WSM featured Tennessee Governor Austin Peay, Mayor of Nashville Hilary Howse, National Life's President Craig, and noted announcers from other parts of the country: Lambdin Kay of WSB, Atlanta; Leo Fitzpatrick of WDAF, Kansas City; and George D. Hay of WLS, Chicago. The musical entertainment schedule included several light classical pieces, some quartet singing, the dance bands of Beasley Smith and Francis Craig, assorted tenors, sopranos, and baritones, a quintet from Fisk, and a "saxophone soloist." Not a note of old-time music was played.

For the first month of operation, the mainstay of the station was Jack Keefe, a popular Nashville attorney who announced, sang, and played the piano. Keefe was responsible for broadcasting Dr. Humphrey Bate and his band, Uncle Dave Macon, and Sid Harkreader, though he did so on a rather random schedule. It was also Keefe who initiated an early "remote" broadcast from the Ryman Auditorium in early November, when many of the WSM regulars performed for the policemen's benefit. Keefe was apparently very popular, for when WSM announced, a month later, that it had hired George Hay, it had to assure audiences that Keefe would still be heard on the station. Keefe left the station a few years later and went into politics. WSM veterans have described Keefe's "real" departure from the station. One night he was "standing by" for a network feed of a talk by then-President Herbert Hoover. Just before the feed, not realizing his mike was on, Keefe grumbled aloud, "Who in the hell wants to hear Hoover?" This story has not been verified, but it has certainly become a part of Opry lore.

Other early WSM staff members included Rise Bonnie Barnhart of Atlanta, the program director who also doubled as pianist, singer, and story-hour hostess. The original engineers were Thomas Parkes of Nashville, John DeWitt, a Vanderbilt student, and Jack Montgomery, who had helped build the station and who was also a relative of fiddler Uncle Jimmy Thompson. Both DeWitt and Montgomery were to remain with the station well into the modern era.

Thus by the end of October 1925 all the basic elements for the Opry were in place: a powerful radio station located in an area rich in folk tradition; a backing company with impressive assets and (with Edwin Craig at least) a dedication to principles of commercial radio; and an eager and enthusiastic audience just learning and growing accustomed to the benefits of a new entertainment medium. What these elements needed was a catalyst, and that they got when, on November 2, 1925, WSM hired George D. Hay to manage the station.

George Dewey Hay

Though it has been widely assumed that George Hay was a Southerner, he was in fact born in Attica, Indiana, in 1895. Though only 120 miles from Chicago, Attica at the turn of the century was a surprisingly rustic place. Hay later recalled: "I used to walk two or three blocks to the edge of town and there was the beginning of some wonderful corn fields. They have 'em in the Hoosier state! I love corn." The old Hay house in Attica was on the very edge of the town, close to some of the larger farms. But Hay's father was a well-known local jeweler, remembered as a "progressive merchant" who tried all manner of advertising and promotions—including releasing balloons into the air with discount coupons in them. His mother was a Dewey, and she named her son after her maiden name. (Later stories that Hay was named after Adm. George Dewey, the hero of the Spanish-American War, are untrue.) When George was in the third grade, his father died, and his mother took the family and moved away from Attica—eventually settling in Chicago. Young George was not happy there: "I never did care too much for cobble stones, asphalt pavement, blocks upon blocks of 'flat' buildings and the terrific tempo of large cities. . . . If you say, 'Howdy neighbor,'[people] think you are as nutty as a fruit cake. I lived there for many years, against my better judgment (for you see I was a little kid and had to go there with my folks)."

Nonetheless, it was in Chicago that Hay developed his skills as a writer and soon began a career as a newspaper journalist. By 1919 he was living in Memphis and began covering the municipal court beat for the *Commercial Appeal*. He soon converted his court reporting into a humorous column called "Howdy, Judge," which revolved around dialogues between a white judge and various black defendants. These skits were written in dialect and are full of the ethnic stereotyping that characterized so much nineteenth-century vaudeville and blackface humor. The sketches proved immensely popular, and because of them George Hay, even though a young man of twenty-eight, acquired the nickname "Judge." Hay published them in book form in 1926 and apparently converted many of them into skits, which he performed with Ed McConnell during the early days of the Opry. Such skits were not all that anachronistic in the 1920s—an era that made best-selling Victrola records out of Moran and Mack's "Two Black Crows" series and made the Chicago-based "Amos 'n' Andy" a favorite radio show.

In 1922 the *Commercial Appeal* founded station WMC in Memphis, and Hay, somewhat against his will, was "elected" announcer and radio editor for the paper. Hay sensed that radio, like any other mass medium, developed its heroes through audience identification. Hay understood that his radio popularity required auditory gimmicks. He thus devised a highly stylized form of announcing that was characterized by a deep baritone "chant" introduced by the sound of a steamboat whistle. His toy steamboat whistle, which he named "Hushpuckena," was used to announce the start of WMC's "entertaining trip down the Mississippi" (from one of the first wire service stories about Hay, [Nashville] *Tennessean,* June 27, 1926.)

Hay also edited the radio page for the *Commercial Appeal,* broadcasted shows from Beale Street, and sent out press releases to papers back in Chicago, such as the *Defender.* On August 2, 1923, Hay became the first broadcaster in the U.S. to announce the death of Warren G. Harding, further establishing his validity as a newsman and announcer. It was not surprising, therefore, that the next year, in 1924, he was hired by the Sears company to announce over their new station WLS in Chicago. Hay successfully made the move and adapted his style; he traded his riverboat whistle for a more appropriate train whistle. He spoke glowingly of the "WLS Unlimited" going over "the trackless paths of the air." (The train imagery would continue to fascinate him after he came to WSM: he loved to have harmonica wizard DeFord Bailey play train imitations, and for years he had microphones placed at a crossing in south Nashville to broadcast the daily passing of the Pan American.)

By now, still in Chicago, he was referring to himself simply as "the solemn old Judge," and his popularity in 1925 was such that regular WLS artists who recorded hired Hay to introduce them on record. Thus Hay is heard blowing his whistle, chanting "WLS, Chi-ca-go," and introducing the musicians on 1925 recordings by popular singers Ford & Glenn and dance-band leader Art Kahn. Hay worked at WLS as an all-purpose announcer and was present when the station inaugurated its famous Barn Dance program in April 1924. Contrary to popular belief, Hay did not start the Barn Dance program but was only an announcer. He was, however, deeply impressed by the success of the program and by the way it attracted such a large, loyal, and primarily rural audience. He had been impressed earlier with this sort of music when, as a cub reporter in Memphis, he had visited a backwoods community in Arkansas shortly after World War I; there he had attended a country hoedown in a log cabin near Mammoth Springs. Hay now saw this same spirit being successfully fitted to the new medium of radio, as throughout 1924 and 1925 the WLS

Barn Dance became the first totally successful radio show featuring old-time music.

Later in 1924 Hay was awarded a gold cup by the magazine *Radio Digest* for being the most popular announcer in the nation; the winner of the award had been determined by votes of radio fans around the country. It is important to note that at this point in his career, while Hay was an announcer of the WLS Barn Dance, he was by no means associated exclusively with that program or with country music. He was simply a successful and innovative announcer who had captured the imaginations of thousands of Americans.

On October 5, 1925, Hay was invited as a guest of honor to the ceremonies opening WSM, where he must have greatly impressed the owners of the station. As noted earlier, National Life had set up WSM as a deluxe station, and they were prepared to spare no expense in making it nationally known as quickly as possible. Thus it was natural that they should go after one of the leading announcers in the country. There is no indication in the newspaper releases of the time that WSM pursued Hay because he was an expert in barn dance programs, nor was he hired with the intention that he start a country music show. WSM probably offered Hay the job because he had just been awarded the *Radio Digest* cup and because he was already known to many Tennesseans through his work in Memphis. Hay, for his part, saw the move as a step up: he was moving from merely being an announcer in Chicago to "radio director in charge" of the entire station in Nashville. He would be free to craft the new station's actual image and to develop his own line of programming. The fact that Hay had had considerable experience in dealing with the rural audiences of the Sears station, WLS, was not lost on the National Life executives, who were becoming very interested in rural and working-class customers.

Hay accepted the new job on November 2, 1925, and arrived in Nashville to take over a week later. What he found was a station that was directing its programming at the varied and rather sophisticated tastes of Nashville itself. Some traditional music was occasionally heard, but a great deal of the fare was light or semi-classical music, dance bands, and ladies' string trios. Given the potential of WSM's broadcast range, which on good nights could actually reach both coasts, Hay knew that a much vaster audience than the Nashville urban area lay within range and demanded a reconsideration of programming. According to the early show historian Don Cummings, not long after Hay arrived he told Eva Thompson Jones that he wasn't entirely satisfied with the programming direction of the station and asked for suggestions.

Hay soon decided to act on his instinct and to try to expand the audience appeal to include the rural South. He himself changed whistles again, going back to the kind of steamboat whistle he had used in Memphis. This whistle he named "Old Hickory" in honor of Nashville's hero Andrew Jackson. (Later he changed it back to its original "Hushpuckena," perhaps originating from the town of the same name in north Mississippi). He noted with interest the appeal of hillbilly artists like Dr. Bate, Uncle Dave Macon, and Sid Harkreader as they played on WSM. (Documentary evidence shows that at least these three musicians had appeared on WSM well before Hay arrived in town.) Thus when, on November 28, 1925, Hay sat Uncle Jimmy Thompson down before the WSM microphones, he should not have been as surprised at the response as he says he was. True, telegrams and phone calls poured into the station, many requesting special numbers. But this same syndrome had already occurred at almost every other station that tried programming old-time music in these early days; it had happened with WLS in 1924, with WSB in Atlanta in 1923, and with several other stations. It was a "vox populi" phenomenon, with the stations being apologetic about broadcasting such music but caving in to public demand. Hay had seen some of this firsthand at WLS and must have been aware of this sort of possible reaction. He had also had time to note the kind of response Dr. Bate and Uncle Dave Macon had gotten for their playing. Audience reaction to Uncle Jimmy was probably more dramatic and more extensive, but it was part of a pattern. Probably the main effect of the November 28 program was to confirm to Hay that WSM's audience for old-time music existed in the mid-South as much as it did for WSB's in the Deep South and for WLS's in the Midwest. He might have exaggerated his surprise at the response for two reasons. First, it was a good story and could be dramatized effectively in press releases; second, it could help convince a reluctant National Life and a skeptical Nashville that old-time music filled a definite need for "the people."

Uncle Jimmy played on November 28 without being formally scheduled through newspaper listings or announcements. (The November 28 date is verified only through a December 26 *Tennessean* story, which mentions that Uncle Jimmy had made his first WSM appearance almost one month earlier.) The Barn Dance program was thus not formally established on that night, though Uncle Jimmy returned the next week to play again. In neither case did Hay bill it, through the newspapers, as any sort of special old-time program. Probably during December the idea for such a program was taking shape in Hay's head. It may have been during this time that Hay told Obed Pickard's brother that "he was going to start something like the *National Barn Dance* in Chicago and expected to do better because the people were real and genuine and the people really were playing what they were raised on." This quote, presuming it is accurate, gives us our clearest notion yet of what Hay was planning to do with the Barn Dance.

Whatever the case, Hay's formal announcement of the establishment of a regular program devoted to old-time music and to be aired on Saturday nights came late in December 1925 when the station announced: "Because of this recent revival in the popularity of the old familiar tunes, WSM has arranged to have an hour or two every Saturday night, starting Saturday, December 26." (*Tennessean*, December 27, 1925). The Grand Ole Opry (then called the Barn Dance), as a deliberately structured old-time music show broadcast regularly over WSM, would thus have to date from December 1925.

Hay and Folk Music

None of this, though, tells us much about Hay's real motives for starting the Barn Dance program. What was his own personal attitude toward old-time music? How did he see such music functioning in his world of 1925? Was he aware of the scholarly renaissance and popular interest in folk song books, represented most visibly by Carl Sandburg's *American Songbag* and the poet's own singing career—all of which developed in Chicago during the time Hay was there? Did he turn to old-time music simply because it was proving popular across the South and the nation as a whole during the mid-1920s? Or did he go to it, like Henry Ford, out of a genuine idealism about the music's ability to reflect and sustain traditional American values? Or was he simply pragmatic, going to the music because he felt it would attract the kind of audience National Life wanted to sell insurance to? Since virtually all the statements we have from Hay are in the nature of press releases or public posture statements, it is hard to determine what he actually thought about the music. But certain patterns do emerge, even from the public statements.

Contemporaneous newspaper accounts of the early Opry are rich in what rhetoricians today would call "attitude," and most of them reflect the stately romanticism of Hay's own writing. Certainly they were supplied to the newspapers by the stations and were probably written by Hay himself. (In fact, there are several such press releases that are almost identical to later writings by Hay; and, in any event, as station manager Hay had to approve these releases.) Judging from this publicity, Hay originally favored airing the music because it was so popular and so commercially successful. He suggests as much in his first public statement about old-time music, in a December 27, 1925, release announcing upcoming performances by Uncles Jimmy Thompson and Dave Macon:

> Old tunes like old lovers are the best, at least judging from the applause which the new Saturday night feature at Station WSM receives from its listeners in all parts of the country; jazz has not completely turned the tables on such tunes as "Pop Goes the Weasel" and "Turkey in the Straw." America may not be swinging its partners at a neighbor's barn dance but it seems to have the habit of clamping on its ear phones and patting its feet as gaily as it ever did when old-time fiddlers got to swing.

Clearly, the public was demanding the old-time tunes. But the proper citizens of Nashville still resented the idea of having hillbilly music on their new station, and two months later (*Tennessean*, February 26, 1926) the tone of Hay's press release had become more apologetic: "Much has been said for and against the old-time tunes but the fact remains they are taking the country by storm. There is some delightful little folk strain that brings us back to the soil, which runs through each of the numbers." The appeal of the music could not be denied. Like jazz, its appeal was emotive, but, to many, unlike jazz it played on the healthy and natural, as opposed to base, emotions. But in this early announcement of Hay's, popularity is the central defense of the music. This was made evident in an interview with Hay published in the July 7, 1929, issue of the *Knoxville News-Sentinel*. Here Hay stresses the number of musicians who come to the show wanting to play, and he concludes by saying: "There are so many we just can't stop. In fact, we've been expecting that each year would be the last of this series. But we can't give it up. There's too much of a demand for the old folks and their tunes."

But if these accounts suggest that Hay started the Opry primarily because the people demanded it, other evidence hints that he saw the music in more philosophic terms. At first Hay seemed to make no clear distinction between "old-time tunes" and "folk tunes": the former he seemed to see as any older, nineteenth century, pre–jazz-age music, with its appeal not so much to cultural geography as to simple nostalgia. This philosophy was apparent when the early Saturday-night programs contained band music, barbershop quartets, bird imitators, even musical saws, acts that were "old-time" mainly by virtue of their nostalgia content. But gradually Hay began to focus his definition of what he meant when he said, "Keep it down to earth." He began to use the term *folk* to describe some of his musicians: Uncle Dave, in an April 1926 story (*Tennessean*), sang "folk-songs" which seemed "to strike home." Even the February 1926 story cited above mentions a "folk strain" that "brings us all back to the soil." A year later a release refers to the fact that "the old time tunes of the Tennessee hills are presented the way they were handed down through the generations" (*Tennessean*, November 27, 1927). The 1929 *Knoxville News-Sentinel* story insists that "the songs they play—and at times sing—are known only to the backwoods region from which they come. They're the American folk tunes of Tennessee." A 1931 story by Hay refers to "old hill-billy tunes, as they are called" that "have been handed down through many generations. . . . Of course, the tunes are distinctly elemental in construction" (*Nashville Banner*, February 22, 1931).

But Hay's vision of himself as a preserver of American folk culture did not really emerge fully until after the Opry had become an established institution. In his own little book, written in the mid-1940s, he stresses this idealistic motive for starting the show. "Radio station WSM," he writes, "discovered something very fundamental when it tapped the vein of American folk music which lay smoldering and in small flames for about three hundred years." Later he echoes the familiar Henry Ford philosophy of folk music reflecting basic American values. "After all, we try to keep the Opry 'homey.' . . . Many of our geniuses come from simple folk who adhere to the fundamental principles of honesty included in the Ten Commandments. The Grand Ole Opry expresses these qualities which come to us from these good people." Hay asserts that he had perceived the value of traditional music as early as 1919, when he made his trip into the Arkansas Ozarks. Perhaps so, but his posture in the earliest days of the Opry was to maintain hillbilly music simply because it was popular; the idealistic underpinning came after the program had established itself.

From his references to "Turkey in the Straw" and "Pop Goes the Weasel," it might seem that Hay had a rather superficial notion of what real folk music was. That might have been true originally, but his years of experience in working with musicians on the show—who, before 1930, were nearly all amateur musicians and native Southerners—soon taught him a great deal about the folk transmission process. Evidence suggests, in fact, that Hay understood the full dimension of Southern folk tradition better than did most of the respectable "academic" folklorists of the day. Scholars like Cecil Sharp, for instance, allowed into the folk canon only those songs passed exclusively by oral tradition down through generations and emphasized only the vocal music. Modern folklorists are just beginning to appreciate the full extent to which popular Tin Pan Alley music of the nineteenth century got into oral tradition in the South. But Hay understood this. "The line of demarcation between the old popular tunes and folk tunes is indeed slight," he wrote in his history. Later, as cowboy singers and barbershop quartets crowded onto the Opry, Hay expanded his definition of "folk" music to include folk music from areas outside the South; "any folk tune is okay," he said.

His notion of folk music would expand even further during the 1940s, as the Opry became more commercial and began using more composed songs. During this time the show was often introduced as featuring genuine folk music or "music in the folk tradition." This became especially noticeable in the early '40s after NBC began broadcasting an Opry segment nationwide, and when the Armed Forces Radio Services (AFRS) began to syndicate the show to a nationwide audience. The term *folk* could make the music more acceptable to a mainstream audience. It certainly had better connotations than the adjectives *hillbilly* or *old-time*.

Whatever he personally thought about the music, Hay sensed that it was very popular with Southern audiences and sought ways to exploit this popularity. Others who had exploited the music had done so by creating hillbilly stereotypes. In California the group called the Beverly Hill Billies were "discovered" rusticating up in the mountains; in Washington, D.C., Al Hopkins and His Hill Billies dressed in overalls; in Atlanta a sophisticated jazz-tinged fiddler named Clayton McMichen was made lead fiddler in a band called the Skillet Lickers and participated in skits about moonshine and "revenooers." Thus by the late 1920s, Hay had plenty of patterns to follow as he began image-building for his Opry musicians.

It is interesting to trace Hay's deliberate attempt to "rusticate" the show. Very few of the program's regular members originally fit the hillbilly stereotype (nor, in fact, did most of the successful country entertainers of the 1920s). Many of them worked in Nashville at lower- and middle-class trades. Others were farmers from the Davidson County, Middle Tennessee area, perhaps of the soil but hardly cut off from the world. They were not professionals by any means (except Uncle Dave), but few of them were naive hill folk preserving an exclusive and rare heritage. That is, until Hay began building the Opry image. An important first step was his renaming the Barn Dance the Grand Ole Opry in 1927. Unlike the rather neutral term "Barn Dance," "Grand Ole Opry" suggested a deliberate rustic burlesque of formal and classical music.

Hay also came up with colorful names for the Opry bands; Paul Warmack's band became the Gully Jumpers, and the Binkley Brothers string
band became the Binkley Brothers Dixie Clodhoppers. In fact, Kirk McGee
recalled that the Judge kept a list of "colorful" names in his desk drawer,
and when a new band signed on, he chose one from the list. (He never tried
it with the McGee Brothers since the name itself already had cornball connotations.) He also devised tag lines to be associated with each performer:
DeFord Bailey, "the harmonica wizard"; Sam and Kirk McGee, "from
sunny Tennessee"; Uncle Dave Macon, "the Dixie Dewdrop."

He also changed the physical appearance of the show, once it became
popular enough to attract sizable live audiences. Early photos of the Opry
players—of Dr. Bate in 1925, for instance, or the one of the entire cast
made in 1928—show them dressed in business suits. But the picture of Dr.
Bate made in 1933 shows him in a cornfield dressed in overalls, and the
next Opry group shot shows most of the gang in hats and overalls. Alcyone Bate Beasley, daughter of Dr. Humphrey Bate, recalled that she hardly
ever saw anyone not in a suit on the early programs, and that the costumes
came in when the groups started touring and playing frequently before live
audiences.

In addition to creating images through names and visuals, Hay began
to stress the hillbilly image in print in the late 1920s. The July 1929
Knoxville News-Sentinel interview with Hay, which was probably syndicated nationally, stated that "every one of the 'talent' is from the back
country," and the music represents "the unique entertainment that only the
Tennessee mountaineers can afford." Hay went out of his way to stress the
genuine picturesque qualities of Uncle Jimmy Thompson and Uncle Bunt
Stephens. Ironically, the greatest push toward rustication came in the early
1930s, when some of the Opry's genuine traditional musicians were being
replaced by full-time professionals. Also influencing this move to promote
a rural hillbilly image was the beginning of Opry tour groups and the
increasing movement toward appealing to the live studio audience as well
as the radio audience. By 1935 the image of the Opry as a rustic hillbilly
show was well entrenched.

The Opry's First Year

Part of the image of the Opry that Hay fostered was that the show
was completely informal and improvised, that every Saturday night a
bunch of good ole boys would bring their fiddles and banjos into the big

city and sit around picking tunes. In 1931, for instance, Hay talked about "the informality with which the program is presented. It is a distinctly human affair which may be termed a big get-together party of those who listen in. Messages have been announced which have brought old friends and even members of families together after absences of many many years" (*Nashville Banner*, February 22, 1931). By some standards, the Opry was informal and loosely structured; indeed, radio historians such as Eric Barnouw report that any sort of ad-lib was virtually banished from NBC by early 1927. Despite its image of informality, as early as January 1926, during the earliest weeks of the Barn Dance, the program was fairly tightly structured, at least to the point of knowing what artist would be on at what time and for what duration. The programs were mapped out well enough in advance that Hay was able to provide to the two Nashville papers a detailed preview of the coming week's programs for publication in Sunday's papers. These preview columns are among the best documentary sources for information about the shows and artists and form the basis for much of the following discussion.

The chart reproduced here, then, shows exactly who was scheduled to play on the Saturday night "barn dance program" during each week of the year 1926. Something that becomes immediately evident is that the program was not initially confined to old-time music. In fact, the term "barn dance" seems to have been used as a general descriptive term for elements on the Saturday night program, rather than the name of the program itself. In news listings in early 1926, the show is sometimes referred to simply as "the Saturday night program," "general good time and barn dance party" (January 9), a program that "includes barn dance features" (May 7), and as late as September, "the popular and barn dance program" (September 4, 11). These titles indicate that the makeup of the show remained in flux throughout most of the year. Though hillbilly music was emphasized often, the Saturday night program featured popular music of all types. For instance, the jazz bands of Dutch Erhart and Harry Bailey, as well as a Dixieland combo called the Blue Grass Serenaders (from Gallatin), appeared often. Other band appearances included the Castle Heights Military Academy Orchestra and the Saxophone Sextette from the Tennessee Industrial School. Popular tenors like Jack Eagan, Marshall Polk, and Little Jack Little provided some of the vocal fare, and popular pianists like Doc Byrd Jr., the Wandering Pianist, provided some of the instrumentals. Happy Jack Haines and announcer Jack Keefe often played and sang as well. Hawaiian music was very much in evidence, with groups like Fields and Martin and the Silver String Hawaiians, and barbershop and gospel quartets often appeared.

Table 1. 1926 Opry Log

KEY: UJT = Uncle Jimmy Thompson; UDM = Uncle Dave Macon; Bate = Dr. Humphrey Bate and his old-time band; DfB = DeFord Bailey; OP = Obed Pickard.

An underlined name indicates first appearance on the program. Numbers in parentheses indicate the time length of each artist's segment of the program. For instance, Bandy (1) means that Bandy was scheduled to play one hour. For obscure artists instrumentation is given: (bj) = banjo; (f) = fiddle; (Fh) = French harp (harmonica); (g) = guitar; (haw. g) = Hawiian guitar; (1,½, etc.) = one or portions of an hour; (v) = vocals. All names are verbatim as in the source. For details about individual musicians, see appendix 2, "The Opry Roster."

January

2: Happy Jack Haines, Bate (1)

9: UJT, Charlie the French Harp King ("general good times and barn dance party")

16: UJT, Gallatin Blue Grass Serenaders (entire show: 2 hours).

23: Wild Cat Tom's fiddlers (1), Happy Jack Haines (1), Nolen Dawson and barn dance team, UJT (1) (Opposite on WDAD this night: Bate [2]).

30: Dixie Volunteers (dir. by Tom Ridings), UJT, Jack Eagan (v), Bate, Fulton Mitchell (f).

February

6: UJT, J. Crook, Wm. Baker (f) with Mrs. Neil Clark, Bate.

13: UJT, M.G. Smith (f) and W.L. Totty (banjo), Chesterfield Four (vocal).

20: UJT (1), Wild Cat Tom's Fiddlers (1), Bate, and "others" (2). "Barn Dance program" and other features (about four hours).

27: UJT (1), O. L. Wright's barn dance orchestra, Bate (1).

March

6: UJT (1), A. J. Brady and barn dance team of Adairville, Ky., Bate.

13: UJT (1), Henry L. Bandy, Petroleum, Ky., Carthage fiddlers (Robert King [f], Jerry Gardenhire [Fh], T. K. Fort [g], J. F. Reed [g]), Bate.

20: UJT (1), Harry Baily's Southern Serenaders, Bate.

27: UJT (1), J. R. Trout's barn dance orch from Gallatin, J. W. Deason's barn dance orch, Bate (1).

April

3: Carthage fiddlers under direction of Jerry Gardenshire, Macie Todd's string trio from Murfreesboro, Marshall Clayburn (f) with E. D. Haines (?), Bate (1). (UJT in Missouri for fiddling contest.)

10: UJT (1), Winchester String Band, Harry Bailey's Southern Serenaders, Wild Cat Tom's Fiddlers, Bate (1).

17: UJT (1), Henry Bandy (f), Marshall Clayburn (1), UDM (1).

23: UJT, Marshall Clayburn (f), Henry Bandy (1), UDM.

May

1: UJT, UDM, Carthage fiddlers, Henry Bandy (f), Bate.

8: UJT, Bate, <u>Obed Pickard</u>. Show to "include barn dance features."

15: UJT (1), Bate ($\frac{1}{2}$), UDM (1).

22: Jack Keefe (v), OP (f, g, Fh), Smith County String trio of Chestnut Mound, Tennessee, Henry Bandy (f), Chester Zahn ("ukelele artist"), Bate, UDM.

29: (Classical music until 10:30.), Bate ($\frac{1}{2}$), William Miller (haw. g., $\frac{1}{2}$), UDM ("banjoist and character singer," $\frac{3}{4}$).

June

5: UDM, Bate's Hawaiian band, Smith County string trio, OP, Keefe.

12: ("Saturday night program will include many variety acts"): Keefe, OP, Bate's Haw. Orch., Cliff Curtis and John Brittain, harm. players, Blue Grass Serenaders.

19: UDM ($\frac{1}{2}$), Carthage Quartet ($\frac{1}{2}$), Bate ($\frac{1}{2}$), <u>DeFord Bailey</u> ($\frac{1}{2}$), J.J. Lovel (bj) and Perry DeMoss (f) ($\frac{1}{2}$), Keefe ($\frac{1}{2}$).

26: UDM ($\frac{3}{4}$), Bate ($\frac{1}{2}$), Keefe ($\frac{1}{2}$), Curtis and Brittain (fh), Henry Bandy (f), Marshall Polk (v), DfB ($\frac{1}{2}$).

July

3: UJT, UDM, Bate, DfB, Keefe.

10: UJT, UDM, OP, Carthage Quartet (spirituals), Henry Bandy, J. B. Carver (f) with Elmer Coffey (bj), DfB.

17: UDM, UJT, Bate, J. Frank Reed (f) with A.C. Duke (g) of Donnelson, Tenn., Polk (v), DfB, Keefe.

24: UJT, DfB, OP, <u>Crook Brothers</u>, Neelds Joy Boys, Polk (v), Fulton Mitchell and his Old Hickory orchestra.

31: Keefe, Bate, DfB, OP ("with Mrs. Pickard at the piano"), UJT, Silver String Hawaiiana, J. Frank Reed (f) with A. C. Dukes (g).

August

7: Old Hickory orchestra, DfB ($\frac{1}{2}$), Crook Bros. ($\frac{1}{2}$), Keefe, UDM with Sid Harkreader ($\frac{1}{2}$).

14: Not available.

21: Not available.

28: Not available.

September

4: "Popular and barn dance program"—no details available.

11: Not available.

18: Not available.

25 (Special remote broadcast from Nashville State Fair grounds): Bate, Sid Harkreader (f) with Hick Burnett (g), UJT, DfB, OP, Silver String Hawaiians.

October

2: Not available.

5: (Special Tuesday-night one year anniversary program, with many artists including the following old-time performers): OP, UJT, Bate, Silver String Hawaiians.

9: Not available.

16: Not available.

23: Henry Bandy (f), UDM, Bill Barret (f) with Walter Ligget (g), OP, Happy Jack Haines.

30: ("many new features which have not yet been broadcast"): Mazy Todd's string trio of Readyville [Tennessee], <u>Theron Hale and daughters Elizabeth and Mamie Ruth</u>, Evening Star Quartet, W. G. Hardison (f) with W. R. Hardison (bj), Bate, DfB, OP, Charlie the French harp king.

November

6: Special Shrine minstrels, Smith County String trio, Little Jack Little, Municipal Five.

13: ("a few additional features"): Will Barret (f) with Walter Legget (bj), Theron Hale, Binkley Bros., Fields and Martin (haw. g's).

20: Regular program with "several new artists"; no details available.

27: UJT, others unknown.

December

4: UJT, OP, Crook Bros., Binkley Bros., DfB.

On December 5, WSM ceased broadcasting for the year to install a new 5000 watt transmitter.

But once we get beyond the "impurities" of the program's form, what about the old-time content of the first year's programs? Such content seems to have been significant and substantial, though often coming from artists who are obscure and even unknown to conventional historians of the show. It is true that performers like Thompson, Macon, Pickard, Bailey, and Bate were mainstays of the Barn Dance. All these artists have been recognized as key Opry pioneers (although Obed Pickard's role has not been fully appreciated); but who recalls Henry Bandy, Wild Cat Tom, the Smith County String Trio, Marshall Claiborne, or the Carthage Fiddlers? All of these played several times on the show in 1926. In fact, of the well-known Opry hoedown bands, only the Crook Brothers, the Binkley Brothers, and Theron Hale and his daughters joined the show before 1927. Artists appearing on more than three of the thirty-nine regular logged Barn Dance programs of 1926 included Dr. Humphrey Bate (twenty-nine times), Uncle Jimmy Thompson (twenty-seven), Uncle Dave Macon (fourteen), Obed Pickard (thirteen), DeFord Bailey (eleven), Jack Keefe, as a performer (nine) Henry Bandy (six), and Wild Cat Tom (Ridings)'s Fiddlers (four). These figures indicate not only the relative popularity of these headliners; the frequency of their appearances also gives some indication of their overall popularity with the program's early audience.

George Hay wrote that "during the first two or three months of the year 1926 we acquired about twenty-five people on the Opry," which has led to speculations that there was some sort of original charter Opry roster. If so, these radio schedules do not bear that out. At least thirty-three different old-time *acts* (as opposed to *people*) appeared during 1926 and over twenty popular acts. Although there were certainly regulars in 1926, including favorites who frequently repeated, the idea of a well-defined Opry roster probably did not take root until 1928, when the station began paying performers.

Even though the popularity of many of the performers and of the show itself was substantial, it was not evenly spread. In Nashville itself, the show stimulated more than a little controversy in 1926. At one point the management of WSM came close to giving up on it. In the summer, when radio reception was poorer anyway, the Nashville papers announced: "WSM will continue the barn dances through the month of May, but beginning June 1 will probably discontinue the old-time music for the summer, unless the public indicates its desire to have them continued throughout the hot weather. An announcement will be made Saturday night putting the matter up to the radio listeners, and the majority will determine the policy on that subject" (*Tennessean*, May 9, 1926). One reason for the threat was that many Nashville residents were becoming more and more vocal about their discontent with the spectre of hillbilly music emanating from "the Athens of the South." An overwhelming response in favor of the program would give the station the mandate it needed to defy these demands. And it came. Barely a week later, on May 16, the same paper reported:

> Recently an announcement was made putting the question of barn dance programs up to the radio public. So far the replies have been very much in favor of continuance of these barn dance programs throughout the summer. The contest will close June 1. While some of the Nashville listeners seem to prefer the so-called popular tunes of the day instead of the old-time music, they have not indicated their wishes in the mail at any extent. However, the studio program, during which are presented the compositions of the masters continue to please, according to the barometer which is brought every morning by Uncle Sam.

The Barn Dance stayed on during the summer, but this incident reflected the gulf between WSM's "two audiences": urban Nashville listeners and those in rural areas. The tension between the groups was to affect the Opry in subtle ways throughout most of its history. But it is noteworthy that the station's first-year anniversary show, on October 5, 1926, had at least a few strains of old-time music: a "barn dance feature" was included in the "Frolic" portion of the show and aired about midnight.

Consolidation

The next two years saw the Opry move from this rather confused, locally aimed, and informally structured radio presentation to a format retained for over four decades. Yet even this development was not sudden or deliberate but rather the effect of a number of changes occurring both on the stage and behind the scenes.

In the spring of 1927 the NBC national radio network was formed, and WSM as an affiliate subscribed to many of the network's programs. This meant that the station could carry the same network shows heard all over the country, though it could not yet feed shows up to the network. (This would begin in the mid-1930s.) The alluring Saturday night network fare brought new pressures against the locally produced Barn Dance show, and for a time in the fall of 1927 WSM, to accommodate network programming, cut the Barn Dance back to as little as ninety minutes. When the popular Philco show came on at 8:00 on Saturday nights, the Barn Dance was moved up to 9:00, leaving time for only five or six acts to perform. In the fall of 1927, Dad Pickard usually opened the Barn Dance, and other regulars included Paul Warmack and his band (not yet dubbed "the Gully Jumpers"), Dr. Humphrey Bate, Theron Hale, and harmonica-players Clarence and Grady Gill, as well as DeFord Bailey. Uncle Jimmy Thompson was not playing so much now, nor was Uncle Dave Macon. Yet the show flourished, drawing written responses from a broadening audience. A typical show in October "received over 200 messages from 32 states" (*Tennessean*, October 24, 1927), though newspapers commented that the appeal of the show "seems a mystery to a number of people" (*Tennessean*, September 18, 1927).

At about this time the show's name changed from simply "the Barn Dance" to "the Grand Ole Opry." Judge Hay's account of how this came about is well known. Hay and the Opry cast were waiting for a network show to end, the NBC *Music Appreciation Hour* with noted conductor Walter Damrosch, so they could come on with the locally produced show. As he concluded, Damrosch lamented that there was little or "no place in the classics for realism" and conducted a short classical piece depicting a train ride. Hay, coming on seconds later, proclaimed: ". . . from here on out for the next three hours we will present nothing but realism. It will be down to earth for the 'earthy'." He then introduced DeFord Bailey, who did *his* depiction of a train ride, "Pan American Blues." Afterwards, Hay said, "For the past hour we have been listening to the music taken largely from the Grand Opera, but from now on we will present the Grand Ole Opry."

Newspaper documentation cannot verify Hay's version of the story, though it does not seriously challenge it. In the fall of 1927 the new NBC broadcasts of grand opera on Wednesday night were a subject of wide discussion, and the term *grand opera* was in the air, even if Hay misapplied it, wittingly or not, to Damrosch's *Music Appreciation Hour*. The first reference in print to the show as the "Grand Ole Opry" was published in the December 11, 1927, Sunday *Tennessean*. The name caught on quickly, though for the next six months the show was alternately called by both names, Barn Dance and Grand Ole Opry.

During this time important changes were taking place at WSM and at National Life that were to profoundly affect the Opry. At the start of 1927 the station's power was increased five-fold to five thousand watts. Even though radio stations were now cropping up all over the country, this much power still gave WSM a listening area that enveloped half the nation. At first, WSM had been assigned a wavelength of 336.4 meters, at 890 kilocycles. This setting was shared only by KNX in Los Angeles. Then, on November 11, 1928, as part of a nationwide reallocation of power and signals, the new Federal Radio Commission assigned WSM a clear-channel status of 461.3 meters and 650 kilocycles—its radio band location even today.

WSM also began to shift the format of the Opry from a purely radio show toward a stage show performed before a live audience. The earlier Opry programs originated from Studio A on the fifth floor of the National Life Building. This was a room about 15 by 20 feet, draped with heavy curtains, with one wall glassed so people could watch a show from the hall. Crowds soon filled this hall, so the show was moved to another studio that could accommodate an audience of fifty or sixty in addition to the hall observers. Finally, the station built the auditorium studio, Studio C, which had a portable stage and could seat five hundred. The overflow audiences still continued to crowd the hall (no charge was made for attending the show), until one night when two National Life executives tried to get into the building to do some late work. They found the building jammed with Opry fans who refused to move aside, and the angry executives finally ordered the audience removed. For a time the show broadcast without any audience, and Hay feared that the whole thing would be discontinued. He argued that "a visible audience was part of our shindig," and finally the show moved to the Hillsboro Theater near Vanderbilt University on the west side of downtown Nashville. There was still no charge for tickets, though National Life agents were allowed to give them away. At the Hillsboro Theater the stage presentation of the Opry became strong enough to influence the radio aspect for the first time. Because of the rather small size of the theater, each show played to two audiences, and many performers found themselves on radio for two fifteen-minute segments instead of one half-hour segment. This platoon system of the Opry has continued to the present.

After the Hillsboro Theater, the Opry moved to the Dixie Tabernacle in east Nashville in 1936, and stayed there for a couple of years. By 1939, it moved to the downtown War Memorial Auditorium (seating capacity 2200), near the National Life Building. Here for the first time tickets were sold. Finally, in 1943, the show moved to the Ryman Auditorium, the "Grand Ole Opry House," and thence to Opryland in 1974.

In 1928 National Life itself was becoming increasingly interested in the Opry for more pragmatic reasons than "public service." At about this time the company developed a strategy to sell life insurance through monthly premiums, rather than only through annual or semiannual premiums. Field agents would collect any monthly premium less than $10 and forward it to the main office. This new installment system opened up a new market for insurance: working-class and the rural middle and lower-middle-class customers previously unable or unwilling to purchase insurance with large lump-sum payments. National Life found that it had a ready-made entree to this market in the Opry. It was not coincidence that agents were given Opry tickets to distribute in the early 1930s, or that at this time Hay began his campaign to emphasize the rustic, hillbilly aspects of the show. A popular pamphlet soon appeared, *Fiddles and Life Insurance*, published by National Life. This was essentially a picture book of the early Opry. Hay's orphan show was proving to have very lucrative connections indeed.

Other changes soon followed in the show itself. By 1928 the other Nashville stations, wanting a piece of the hillbilly action, had started rival barn dance programs, often using the same musicians as WSM (see next chapter). Partly because of this, WSM decided in 1928 to start paying their performers. The pay was low, only $5 per show, but the supplementary income appealed to many performers and assured WSM of a stable roster of talent. In addition, maintaining a payment schedule also meant an even tighter structuring of the show, and to this end Hay hired Harry Stone, who eventually took over the duties of the general manager. The program began to assume a higher and more complex profile by the early 1930s: the station appointed Stone as a general announcer, hired his brother David to help relieve Hay of announcing the Opry, and named Vito Pellettieri (who had been leading a jazz band at the station) music librarian. About 1933 the Artists Service Bureau was also formed, headed by David Stone, to help WSM acts get personal appearance bookings. Such bookings were necessary if the station was going to attract any full-time professional talent.

By 1928 the typical Opry show was running from three and a half to four hours, and had seven to eight "slots" averaging fifteen or thirty minutes each. Most of the string bands were still allowed thirty minutes; the soloists, like DeFord Bailey or Dad Pickard, were given fifteen minutes. For this year, by a fortunate circumstance, the official WSM log book has been preserved and offers the most accurate insight yet into the show's makeup. Dr. Humphrey Bate usually opened the show, and often Ed McConnell closed the program with "songs and stories," which were more in the tradition of vaudeville than old-time music. In between, a variety of acts remained, including a small but distinct percentage without hillbilly flavor. Acts appearing on more than ten of the year's shows included:

DeFord Bailey (49)
Arthur & Homer Smith (29)
Paul Warmack and His Gully Jumpers (28)
Dr. Bate and His Possum Hunters (25)
Binkley Brothers (22)
Crook Brothers (22)
Bert Hutcherson (in separate appearances from his stints
    with Bate or Warmack) (22)
Obed Pickard (20)
Theron Hale (16)
Mrs. G. R. Cline (dulcimer, 14)
Ed McConnell (Uncle Wash) (12)
Whit Gayden (trick fiddler, 12)

The Fruit Jar Drinkers, the Ed Poplin band, Uncle Joe Mangrum and Fred Shriver, Uncle Dave Macon, and Henry Bandy appeared less often. Special guests appearing only once included Uncles Bunt Stephens and Jimmy Thompson, Columbia recording star Tom Darby, the Young Brothers Tennessee Band (from the Chattanooga area and who recorded for Columbia), popular singer Nick Lucas, and Henry Bone, later manager and harp player with the Perry County Music Makers.

The informal 1928 roster of regulars was to remain remarkably constant until 1935. The sample program logs for each year show that though the format of the program shifted somewhat, the basic performers did not. The only evident changes came in the form of additions: the Vagabonds, the Sizemores, the Delmore Brothers, Smilin' Jack and his Mountaineers, and the Dixieliners. This caused the slots—the individual program segments allotted to a certain act—to jump from seven or eight in 1928–1929 to ten or eleven in 1931–1932, sixteen to eighteen in 1933, and twenty-four or twenty-five in 1934–1935. (Because of the increasing practice of platooning artists and repeating slots, however, the number of different acts on a mid-1930s show seldom exceeded fifteen or sixteen.) The slots shrunk in size from thirty minutes down to ten–fifteen minutes in late 1934. Also, as we shall later see, the musicians themselves began to become more professional and more aware of the business side of music.

By 1935 the program had lost much of its innocence and spontaneity. It was becoming increasingly professional and structured. Though most of the content was the same—the hoedown bands and cornerstones like Uncle Dave and Dr. Bate remained—the time was past when musicians could leisurely answer requests, or when an outsider could casually drop in for a song or two. The music was still reasonably close to what most Southerners themselves defined as "old-time" or "folk" music. But the increasing professionalization of the show forecast important changes to come. In a few years performers like Roy Acuff and Pee Wee King were to shift the show away from the old-time mold toward modern country music.

To assess this content more accurately, we need to turn to the individual musicians themselves—the men who made the Opry and sustained it during these important first ten years. But before we can understand the musicians, we must know something of the environment that nourished them—the Nashville of the 1920s.

Nashville in the 1920s

If you want to get a drink in Nashville,
If you want to get a drink in Nashville,
If you want to get a drink,
Give a Democrat a wink,
And you'll get it 'fore you think,
In Nashville.

—Uncle Dave Macon, "Uncle Dave's Travels," part 3

I N 1926, THE FIRST FULL YEAR OF THE OPRY, Nashville had a population of about 125,000. It was not a large city, not even by Southern standards; Memphis, Birmingham, Atlanta, Dallas, Louisville, and Richmond all boasted larger populations, some (such as Atlanta and Louisville) boasting figures double those of Nashville. National statistics ranked Nashville among the country's top one hundred in population but cited it alongside cities the size of Albany, New York; Des Moines, Iowa; and Lowell, Massachusetts. In contrast to the general urban expansion of the 1920s, Nashville had grown rather slowly—sedately, its residents would have said—and as late as 1924 Nashville was not listed by *The World Almanac* as one of the nation's leading manufacturing cities. It was a city that made its money through insurance, banking, and, because of the presence of several national church publishing offices, the printing industry.

Nashville was an odd mixture of the old and new South. The short story writer O. Henry described its atmosphere as a mixture of "London fog, 30 parts; gas leaks, 20 parts; dew drops gathered in a brick yard at sunrise, 25 parts; odor of honeysuckle, 15 parts." It was "not so fragrant as a mothball, nor as thick as pea soup." The description was not altogether fanciful. For instance, the Nashville Gas Company generated its product by burning coal, causing tar to accumulate in gas mains. The odor was something visitors did not forget. And the train yards at Union Station, in a shallow valley that bisected the downtown area, were murky with smoke from the soft coal used to fire the engines.

Down along the Cumberland River, an aging fleet of commercial steamboats unloaded their cargoes into a long row of red brick warehouses and presided over the close of an era. At the foot of Broadway, the main street that ran down to the river, the City Wharf, once the thriving dock for many of the cargo boats, had become a gathering place for preachers and musicians—a sort of Tennessee Hyde Park. A contemporary witness wrote:

> Anyone, Negro or white, man or woman, fundamentalist or atheist, is free to have his say. . . . Often ten to twenty preachers stand on the curb, on packing cases, and in truck beds, all preaching at the same time. . . . Some lure listeners by mouthing French harps or strumming banjoes. Others whoop until a group collects. There is a constant crossfire of heckling between preachers and listeners. . . . The preaching continues until about 9 o'clock at night, when the people, satiated and subdued, begin to leave. By 10 o'clock the corner is deserted.

Downtown street cars trundled through the Transfer station at Fourth and Deaderick. Church Street, the main shopping center, was clogged with black Model T Fords, Duco-finished Chevrolets, and an assortment of lesser models such as Oaklands, Bearcats, Bulldogs, and Hudsons. The west end of town, though, was more sedate. Here the sprawling college campuses of Vanderbilt, Peabody, and Ward Belmont set a less commercial tone. Workmen were completing a permanent concrete full-scale model of the Parthenon. Originally constructed in 1897, it was a part of the exposition marking the centennial of Tennessee statehood. Nashville, with its sizable Greek community, had decided the structure would make a perfect symbol for the sobriquet the old Nashville society liked to apply to its city: "The Athens of the South." Farther out the west end, beyond the huge mansions of Old Nashville's monied classes, were the parks and steeplechases where organizations like the Harpeth Hills Hunt Club and National Foxhunters Association tried their best to emulate the genteel life of the English country house. Downtown a half dozen legitimate theaters kept vaudeville alive, though they were increasingly pairing vaudeville with the new feature-length motion pictures coming out of Hollywood. Similarly, every Sunday the newspapers carried a full page or two of pictures and stories about the current vaudeville stars in town and an increasing number of "canned" wire-service publicity releases on the latest motion pictures.

Radio was still so much a novelty in 1926 that the *Tennessean* allotted both of Nashville's two major stations, WSM and WLAC, a column each to describe the highlights of the forthcoming week. But the biggest theater in town was not a theater at all but a huge edifice that had been designed as a church—Ryman Auditorium, located on Fifth Avenue, just up the hill from the riverfront and just off Broadway, the city's main east-west thoroughfare. An imposing Victorian pile of red brick and white-trimmed gable windows, it was originally known as the Union Gospel Tabernacle and was built through contributions from a notorious riverboat man, Captain Tom Ryman. In 1891, Ryman had wandered into a tent revival being held near Fifth by a famed evangelist named Sam Jones; before the night was out he saw the error of his ways. He immediately began to cast about for some way to repent for his many past sins. The idea of a big, new public house of worship seemed to be the answer. It would benefit Nashville and would assure that preachers like Sam Jones would not have to rely on tents to preach their message. For some years, the city used the building for exactly this purpose, with worshippers coming to hear out-of-town preachers, crowding some three thousand strong into the circular main auditorium, and sitting for long sermons on the church-like wooden pews of the new Tabernacle. Then, in 1905, the building was renamed Ryman Auditorium, and the structure began to take on a different role. By 1926, it was being used for all kinds of events that would draw big crowds: from operas staged by Ward-Belmont College to dramatic appearances by famous actors or magicians, from gatherings of church choirs to fiddling contests. Though it would not become home to the Grand Ole Opry for some fifteen years, the Ryman was already a fixture on the Nashville entertainment scene, and a number of early Barn Dance performers had already played its stage.

Portions of Nashville provided the stark physical terms of the contrast O. Henry described. Just across lower Broadway, just a few blocks south of Ryman Auditorium, was the "Black Bottom," a neighborhood of tarpaper shacks, decaying tenements, and rough speakeasies. From here west to the railroad gulch lived many of Nashville's Blacks, and it was in the speakeasies and dance halls of this section that the city's blues and jazz scene flourished. Nashville's blues singers were never to have the kind of fame that came to similar singers in Memphis, Atlanta, Birmingham, or even Knoxville—probably because Nashville was initially oriented much more toward radio than toward records, and radio was much harder for Blacks to gain access to in early days. However, the tiny amount of research that has been done on the early Nashville blues scene reveals that the city once hosted a fairly rich culture. In the 1920s fully one fourth of the Nashville population was black, most of it centered in Black Bottom or in neighborhoods like Salem Town, Mount Nebo, Trimble Bottom, Rock Town, and Bush Bottom. Segregation ruled; of the seventeen motion picture theaters, three were earmarked for Blacks; of the eleven hotels, four accepted people of color.

It was a culture that apparently did have some ties to early Opry musicians and to the larger world of commercial blues. Reports persist that the legendary Texas blues singer Blind Lemon Jefferson lived for a time in Black Bottom, and by 1921 the country's largest Black theatrical booking chain, TOBA (Theater Owner's Book Agency), was being partially operated out of Nashville by its co-owner Milton Starr. Files from old Nashville printing shops (such as Hatch Show Print) contain all kinds of advertising posters for black musicians like Bessie Smith and Cow Cow Davenport. Starr's Nashville theater, the Bijou, was added to the TOBA chain, thus offering a venue for the leading blues singers and Black vaudeville acts to come to Nashville.

There was also a healthy scene of black musicians who played on street corners and in front of hotels. Many of these came from the surrounding countryside to find work in factories or as yardmen, and they brought with them a rich and unstudied tradition of black old-time music. Nathan Frazier, a remarkable banjoist, was a common fixture in the downtown area. He later got to record some of his tunes for the Library of Congress, stunning later generations with his virtuosity. The Nashville Washboard Band, headed by James Kelly, played rags and jazz on their mandolin and guitar in front of the Capitol steps. In the 1920s countryside, numerous black fiddle players could still be heard. Kirk McGee, one of the legendary Opry instrumentalists, asserted as late as 1979 that he could take a guest to visit at least twelve black fiddlers in the Franklin area alone. Black guitarists like Coley Streeter, from Shelbyville, apparently actually played on Opry tour shows, and senior members of the black community recall hearing a number of black musicians on the Opry itself. Since the show did include black artists like DeFord Bailey and the Fisk singers, it seems likely that others performed as well.

Equally striking were the contrasts up the hill from the river neighborhoods. North and up a steep grade from the business district stood the state Capitol building, a pre–Civil War edifice that dominated the city in all directions. Here the State of Tennessee conducted its business, kept its records, and wrote its formal history. Yet a few blocks to the west was Gay Street and the section known to locals as the "Combat Zone." This was the town's red-light district, a rough-and-tumble neighborhood deceptively quiet by day but notoriously active at night. It was Gay Street that helped boost Nashville's homicide rate to 30 per 100,000 by the mid-1920s, one of the highest in the nation, surpassing even the rate of decadent New York or mob-controlled Chicago, in fact surpassing every city except for Memphis and Pueblo, Colorado.

And it was literally in the shadow of this same Capitol that the Opry was born. Just a block to the south of the Capitol grounds was the War Memorial Building, where the Opry would move from 1939–1943. Another block south and a block or so west, still more or less on the Capitol hill, was the new National Life Building. This was a huge, five-story structure, and its design echoed the Parthenon and "Athens of the South" theme: across its front marched six fluted Ionic columns, each with its scroll at the top and three stories high. Brass door handles emblazoned with the shield (not of Achilles, but for the symbol of the insurance company whose motto was "We Shield Millions") greeted the visitor, and inside plush carpets and crystal chandeliers decorated offices, including those of WSM up on the fifth floor. Here the Opry held forth until 1934, and here the early Opry fans stood in line in the stairwells waiting for their turn to see the broadcast through a large picture window. The Opry was so close to the Capitol that some fans who drove their Model Ts up to watch the show occasionally had to find parking on the Capitol grounds itself—after hours, of course.

In the countryside of Middle Tennessee, almost everyone spoke of going "down to Nashville." This had nothing to do with north-south direction, but with the fact that the city is located at the north end of a broad, shallow basin ringed on three sides by hills. To the north and west these foothills, part of a geological formation known as the Highland Rim, actually crowded into the town's boundaries; to the south and east, a county or so separated the boundaries from the hill country. When Opry singers celebrated "the hills of Tennessee," therefore, they were not necessarily referring to the Smokies, some two hundred miles to the east, but to a region much closer to home. Though not as spectacular or as sustained as the East Tennessee mountains, the hills of Middle Tennessee were, in the 1920s, about as remote and isolated. In the 1930s, when a new road opened up an area near Ashland City, barely thirty miles from Nashville, a local writer named James Aswell described in a letter what he found there:

Here, where Paradise Ridge rots away into a series of high limestone knobs cut by creeks and ravines, is a pocket of land and people which might have been lifted directly out of our east Tennessee
hills. Sagging moss-grown cabins, cascades and small waterfalls,
barefooted washed-out women and gaunt, hard faced men, stills,
rutted winding hilltraces. Until the highway cut through, these folk
were quite as isolated as the people of the Smokies, though
Nashville was less than thirty miles away. They are illiterate, speak
a dialect much like that of east Tennessee, tell the old stories of
witchcraft, clan vendettas, and so on, and sing the old songs.

Though many early Opry performers wound up living and working in
Nashville, many of them originally came from these remote areas, and
many were genuinely products of the folk cultures of such communities.
For example, the Ashland City area described above was the home base for
Obed "Dad" Pickard, the show's first singing star. Furthermore, by 1926
decent highways, most of them paved, connected Nashville to these outly-
ing areas. This made it possible for musicians to commute on Saturday
nights from places like Gallatin (Dr. Humphrey Bate), Lebanon (Sid
Harkreader, Jack Jackson), Murfreesboro (Uncle Dave Macon), Lewisburg
(Ed Poplin, Bunt Stephens), Westmoreland (Mr. and Mrs. Edgar Cline),
Dickson (Arthur and Homer Smith), Franklin (Sam and Kirk McGee,
Robert Lunn), LaGuardo (Uncle Jimmy Thompson), Ashland City (the
Pickard Family), and Petroleum, Kentucky (Henry Bandy). For many
entertainers, the trip meant leaving as early as noon on the Saturday they
were to play, getting to Nashville, unloading and tuning their instruments,
playing on the radio, and then beginning the long drive home in the wee
hours of the morning. The connection was difficult, but it was certainly
possible, and it certainly assured the early Opry a pipeline to the rural folk
culture that it claimed to celebrate.

This, then, was the general setting that served as the context for the
birth of the Opry: a rural area rich in folk culture and steeped in tradition
surrounding a relatively small Southern city—with a rather pretentious
self-image, a high homicide rate, and a population severely segregated
along both class and racial lines—trying very hard to become modern and
sophisticated. Yet there were more specific contexts in Nashville that were
to reflect, and eventually impact, its attitude toward country music. One
of these was radio.

Radio came to Nashville rather late in the game. By 1925 radio stations had already been in place for three years at sister cities like Memphis,

Atlanta, and Dallas; even the small city of Lawrenceburg, some eighty miles south of Nashville near the Alabama line, could boast of station WOAN. This was the station owned by gospel music publisher James D. Vaughan. It had gone on the air in January 1923 and boasted the first radio license application in the State of Tennessee. And by a curious coincidence this station had a lot to do with radio coming to Nashville.

Located at 164 Eighth Avenue North in Nashville, not far from the National Life Building, was Dad's Radio Supply Store. It was owned by L. N. Smith and managed by a radio enthusiast named Fred "Pop" Exum, referred to in their advertising as "Radio Dad." Exum had persuaded Smith to replace his auto accessory store with a radio supply store, sensing that radio was the coming thing and that most listeners would need equipment and replacement parts to build and maintain their own little crystal sets. Nashvillians in early 1925 were struggling to pick up distant signals from stations as far away as Chicago and St. Louis, and the frustration this sometimes caused was not good for the radio parts business. One solution would be to have a small local station, even if it did not carry far, to strengthen the signal and to aid with advertising and publicity. The opportunity came in the late summer of 1925, when WOAN in Lawrenceburg decided to upgrade its equipment and increase its signal. It had been broadcasting on 150 watts of power, and was now jumping to 500 watts. Exum learned of this and that WOAN's old equipment was up for sale, at a very attractive price. He talked Smith into buying the equipment and hauling it to Nashville to start a small station. A WOAN engineer came along to set it up on the floor over Dad's, and on about September 13, 1925, Nashville's first radio station took to the air.

Though it was broadcasting at only 150 watts, WDAD's range was impressive. Two weeks after its first broadcast, the station owners were claiming a transmitting radius of two thousand miles and were receiving mail from New York, Philadelphia, Des Moines, Atlanta, and Dayton, Ohio, about their musical programming. According to a story in the September 27 issue of the *Tennessean*, "There is no want of talent, officials of the station said, and so many artists have volunteered that sufficient room could not be found by [sic] them." Among these musicians were several that would later become regulars on the Opry: Dr. Humphrey Bate, Herman Crook, Sid Harkreader, and DeFord Bailey. The program schedules printed in local newspapers for WDAD during these first weeks were vague and irregular, perhaps reflecting the casual nature of the station's scheduling; many newspaper entries read simply "Musical programs." In the weeks just prior to WSM's going on the air, then, Nashville was hearing old-time country music on radio, and it was proving popular.

WDAD did not have the Nashville market to itself for very long; three weeks after it went on the air, WSM started up at 7:00 P.M. on the night of October 5, 1925. At first, WDAD met its competition with a spirit of cooperation. Dad's took out newspaper advertisements, using the presence of WSM as a pretext to urge customers to buy more radio equipment. A week after WSM went on the air, WDAD announced a change in program schedules so it would not conflict with WSM's programming. The two stations agreed for a time to alternate night programs. They even shared performers. Dr. Humphrey Bate, with his "string quartet of old-time musicians from Castalian Springs," appeared in both WDAD and WSM schedules throughout October 1925, the first country musician to be so documented in Nashville radio schedules. By the end of November, Dr. Bate had become a regular Saturday night feature of WDAD, and the station had announced that "we are going to put on special frolics from time to time." The same week that Uncle Jimmy Thompson made his famous first appearance on WSM, WDAD held a French harp contest on the air. (It was won by one J. T. Bland, who played "Lost John," with second place going to DeFord Bailey, who played "It Ain't Gonna Rain No Mo'.")

By early December, both stations were broadcasting old-time music, and a sense of competition was developing. Uncle Jimmy Thompson was offering a program of "old-fashioned tunes" on Saturdays over WSM, while WDAD staged an old-time fiddlers' contest on the air on December 12. Listeners voted for their favorites by telephone. The contest was a success, and WDAD made a point of noting, in the newspapers, that "even though other local stations were on the air, 360 telephone calls were taken over Dad's two telephones in two hours' time, which were all the calls that could be accommodated." (The other station, besides WSM, was WCBQ, owned by the First Baptist Church.) To counter this, WSM stressed the amount of mail Uncle Jimmy was receiving. Both stations were discovering the power of old-time music, and the rivalry between them was centered in this. WDAD's success with its fiddling contests and frolics was certainly a key factor in George Hay's decision to start a regular Saturday night Barn Dance show on WSM. In the early months of 1926, after the start of WSM's Barn Dance, WDAD still broadcast old-time music, including programs directly opposite the WSM show. The friendly agreement to alternate night broadcasting was short-lived. Clearly, however, WSM soon began to dominate, and though WDAD apparently continued to broadcast until late 1927, its later schedules reveal little or no old-time music. It became the first of several local stations to compete unsuccessfully with the Opry.

Two other such competing stations were WLAC, which went on the air November 28, 1926, and WBAW, which took to the air almost two years later, on November 2, 1928. From 1926 until 1930 (when it began to broadcast CBS network shows), WLAC continuously flirted with old-time music and tried to establish some sort of competition for the increasingly successful Barn Dance. By March 1927, four months after it went on the air, WLAC was making tentative gestures toward an old-time music program on Saturday nights. A few groups, such as the Gaddis String Band of Murfreesboro, which also appeared on the Barn Dance, appeared for short programs; but unlike the Barn Dance, the WLAC programs were relatively simple, without the great variety of string performers that characterized the more successful program. But in early 1928 WLAC got serious in its attempt to corral some of the old-time music audience. It started a regular Friday night show that featured performers like Dr. Bate and the Crook Brothers, established favorites who had appeared, and continued to appear, on the WSM Opry (so called since the end of 1927). This must have worked well, for in June 1928 WLAC initiated direct Saturday night competition with the Opry, abandoning its Friday show and starting up "The Sorghum Symphony." Its cast included the Binkley Brothers and Jack Jackson, fiddler John Parnell, and six or seven other string bands.

This venture was not particularly successful, possibly because it put a strain on the available number of good musicians in the area. Radio schedules reveal that many of the same bands and singers appeared on both shows, on alternating Saturday nights. One week a performer would be on WLAC, the next on WSM. The pay on either show was probably so small that neither program director could insist on exclusivity from the bands. By September 1928 WLAC had dropped "The Sorghum Symphony" and was back to a Friday night show, sending it up against the new NBC network lineup that WSM was carrying on Fridays.

The situation got even more complex in November 1928, when Nashville's third commercial station, WBAW, began operations. Almost at once, the new station announced that it, too, would have an old-time music show, this one on Thursday nights. Both WBAW and WLAC were obviously seeing the commercial potential for old-time music and were anxious to follow WSM's lead in exploiting it. Thus, for a time in late 1928, Nashville radio listeners heard country music on three successive nights each week: Thursday (WBAW), Friday (WLAC), and Saturday (WSM). Once again, the same names began appearing in the newspaper listings for all stations: artists like the Fruit Jar Drinkers, the Crook Brothers, Arthur and Homer Smith, and Dr. Bate. Since none of these acts were actually professional yet, and since all had day jobs to attend to, this new hectic schedule must have put a strain on the personal lives of these busy musicians. Perhaps this was one reason why WBAW, by the end of 1928, shifted their show to Friday nights, competing directly with WLAC. They apparently felt that they could increase the availability of musicians, even competing with WLAC, and that it was hopeless to go head-to-head with the Opry.

The new WBAW Friday night show was called "Capitol Theater Owl Club," the title locating its downtown theater broadcast origin; later, after a change of venue, it was called the "Strand Theater Owl Club." It was a late evening program that devoted much of its time to the "old-time barn dance" and was apparently successful enough that it got much of WLAC's Friday night audience, so much so that WLAC was forced to switch its program again to Saturday night, opposite the Opry. Encouraged by the success of the Owl Club format, WBAW even made some attempts to program live old-time music on Saturdays too, but this was short-lived.

In the end, however, both of these rivals to the Opry lost out. By the middle of 1930, WBAW did not even appear in the radio listings, leaving only WSM and WLAC. By then the national networks had developed, and both of the larger stations were running network fare on Thursday and Friday nights. On Saturdays, WLAC carried the CBS network shows opposite the Grand Ole Opry. Radio stations, like other institutions, began feeling the impact of the Depression, and economic concerns were certainly part of the motivation for individual stations to dismantle the fascinating, heterogeneous local programming that had marked the first ten years of radio culture. This may be one of the reasons why the rivals to the Opry failed. The head start WSM enjoyed on its rivals and the chance to build audience listening habits may be another reason. But these alone cannot explain why the other shows, often even using the same performers as the Opry, could not attract enough listeners. One factor bearing on the regional popularity of WSM was its assignment, in November 1928, of a new wavelength, which put it into a national radio class and permitted it to be heard regularly throughout the United States. Whatever the ultimate reasons for their failure, the Opry rivals in the late 1920s proved, by their very existence, that WSM's success was real and enviable and highly successful commercially.

While Nashville in the late 1920s was cosmopolitan enough to support jazz bands and amateur opera companies, and while the initial programs of WSM seemed oriented to jazz, orchestral dance music, and light classical music, the station as well as its rivals shifted to old-time music as they began to perceive the dimensions and tastes of their audience. Letters, one of the most important barometers of programming success in the days before scientific ratings, were always more impressive if they came from distances outside the city limits. WSM soon understood that they had a clientele beyond the city limits of Nashville, beyond "the Athens of the South," and that this clientele preferred fiddle and banjo music.

The Nashville of this era, though obviously rich in the kind of early country music that could support numerous radio shows, had nothing of the recording industry that would later come to characterize it. Unlike Atlanta, where the radio stations had a rather cozy relationship with the major record companies, Nashville was slow to appreciate the importance of records to old-time music. Judge Hay apparently had good contacts with the record industry, probably from his days in Chicago, and he almost certainly set up some of the recordings made by early Opry performers. In a press release he wrote for the *Tennessean* on April 17, 1927, he noted that a number of WSM's "players" were making records:

> WSM artists are meeting with unusual success in the field of musical records as a result of their broadcasting from the National Life and Accident Insurance Company's station. Several performers have made records and others have recently con- tracted to do so.
>
> The demand for old-time music is very large. The Columbia Phonograph Company recorded four numbers by Uncle Jimmy Thompson and his niece, Eva Thompson Jones, a few months ago. The latest acquisitions on Columbia records are Obed Pickard, known as the "One-Man Orchestra," a star of the Barn Dance programs, and the Golden Echo quartet, . . . who sing negro spir- ituals.
>
> In addition to those who have recorded for Columbia, con- tracts have been signed with the Brunswick people to record the efforts of DeFord Bailey, the harmonica wizard, and Dr. Humphrey Bate and his old-time band. Uncle Dave Macon, the banjo picker and singer of old-time songs, has been making Brunswick and Vocalion records for some time. Outside of New York, it is easy to see that WSM is holding its own as regards rep- resentatives on the big records. The cases mentioned above are as a direct result of broadcasting. . . .

In spite of the impressive roster, the release obviously saw record making as an adjunct to radio success and emphasized twice that record contracts were won because of broadcasting. Some of the Columbia records, in fact, carried under the performer's name the legend "Of Station WSM, Nashville, Tenn" (see chapter 10), suggesting that the fame of the performer was created by his broadcasting rather than any intrinsic merit.

In contrast to later years, during the 1920s record companies saw little use for radio; the connection between airplay and record sales did not exist. As Oliver Read and Walter Welch point out in their history of recording, *From Tin Foil to Stereo*, the sudden growth of radio in the 1920s nearly ruined the record industry, and for many years—throughout the 1930s—neither the record companies nor the radio stations thought much of playing records on the air. Many records bore the legend "not licensed for radio airplay," and until a federal circuit court decision in 1940, legal questions prevented development of modern radio programming policies regarding recorded music. Recordings were scorned as "canned music" and were looked on as a sort of fraudulent imitation of live broadcasts because audiences could not easily tell whether a music program was live or on records. In the 1920s and 1930s, typical radio listeners assumed they were hearing live music, a situation completely reversed in modern times.

Yet there were scattered instances of a closer cooperation between radio and records in the 1920s. By the end of the decade, scouts from record companies were routinely touring Southern radio stations looking for talent to record, a technique that had been pioneered in Atlanta with WSB. The stations occasionally asked field units to come to their towns to record, as was the case with the 1928 Victor field session that came to Nashville to make the first records there (see chapter 10). When the *Knoxville News-Sentinel* (on November 4, 1928) ran the headline "Canned Music Has Friends in Radio," it may have been drawing on evidence available in Nashville. On April 4, 1927, WLAC had announced that it would begin broadcasting a program of "the latest Victor releases" for one hour each week. The name and number of each record would be carefully announced before and after each selection. WBAW soon added a similar program featuring the latest releases from one of Victor's chief rivals, Brunswick. There is no way to tell whether these programs played any old-time music, nor is it clear whether or not they were sponsored by the record companies. But Nashville audiences were hearing at least some "canned music" over the air in the 1920s and were starting to accept records as at least a valid entertainment medium.

Many of the barometers that might have been used to measure how Nashville reacted to early country music in the 1920s simply do not exist. We have only a handful of letters that fans wrote to the radio stations about their music. We do not have any sales or demographic figures for the kinds of records that might have been popular in the town. We do not know how many Nashvillians had radios or how the population, broadly speaking, saw country music as an aspect of their city. We have no scripts or recordings of the Opry before 1939 and no indication of the sponsors that bought commercials on the show prior to 1935 or whether their customers were perceived as being in Nashville or out in the countryside. The one type of documentation we do have in abundance during these developmental years is the newspaper article. During the 1920s, Nashville had two major papers, the *Tennessean* (mornings) and the *Nashville Banner* (evenings). Of the two, the former had the reputation of being more "progressive," the latter more conservative. Generally, the *Banner* was more receptive to early country music, and the stories it carried were fuller, more detailed, and more sympathetic. The radio logs of the newspapers provide what is, in many cases, the only detailed information about personnel for the radio shows. The newspapers, however, include several other features that reflect the city's interest in and attitude toward the music. These include record reviews, record advertisements, articles about folklore, regular columns on songs and song histories, and accounts of musical events.

By the middle of 1928, the *Tennessean* was running a regular column of record reviews in which some old-time music, including records by local performers, was discussed. It appeared in Sunday's paper in a section called "The Firing Line," devoted primarily to business news. (All the other entertainment news, such as information about films, radio, and vaudeville appeared in a different section devoted to amusements; why the record reviews were so segregated is puzzling, but revealing.) The column was unsigned and was called either "Reviewing Brunswick Records" or "Latest Brunswick releases." The fact that the column addressed recordings issued by only one of the seven major companies suggests that either Brunswick was alone in sending out review copies of new records, or, more likely, that Brunswick supplied the column to the paper gratis, as a marketing strategy. Only the frequent misspellings of performers' names and an occasional hostile review provide any indication that the reviews might have been locally written and were not publicity releases.

It may be reflective of Nashville's taste in 1928 that the reviews regularly included jazz, light opera, popular singers, dance bands, and novelty numbers; the old-time records were almost invariably mentioned last in the review, and at times it seems that space limitations caused them to be omitted entirely. The October 14, 1928, review discussed, in this order, records by operatic baritone Richard Bonnelli, vaudevillian Wendall Hall, pop singer Ailen McQuahae, a dance band called the Hotsy Totsy Gang, Benny Goodman's Boys ("Jungle Blues," one of his first), the Royal Hawaiians ("direct from the Islands"), the United States Military Academy Band, Kentucky banjoist and singer Buell Kazee, the Brunswick International Orchestra, jazzman Red Nichols and His Five Pennies, the Vagabonds (a dance band, not the later Opry trio), Joe Green's Novelty Marimba Band, and "the old-time portion of this week's release," records by the Kessinger Brothers and McFarland & Gardner.

The reviews of old-time music are generally condescending at best and at times are harshly critical. For instance, a review of the duo of McFarland & Gardner, surely one of the more sedate and formal of the old-time singers to record, read:

> For those who like punch in their religion, Lester McFarland and Robert A. Gardner offer a "whoopee" version of "Sweet Hour of Prayer" and "In the Garden" (No. 4055). Brazen voices are assisted by mandolin and guitar in the first instance and full-fledged fiddle band in the second, a background which, with choppy waltz time, leaves no vestige of the prayerful or reverent. But there are probably some who like their hymns served up thus. (November 11, 1928)

Not all the old-time reviews are this hostile, and some are even laudatory, but overall the reviewer does not discuss old-time releases (which included some of the top names in early country music) in as much detail as he does "mainstream" records. In several instances, the reviewer makes absolutely no mention of the fact that Uncle Dave Macon and Humphrey Bate were local artists or on local radio, suggesting that the reviewer's point of view was at some remove from the local scene.

Like most newspapers in the South, both Nashville papers routinely carried advertisements for records, usually placed by local furniture stores who were then the main outlet for Victrolas and Victrola records. In other cities and towns around Tennessee, special ads were run to celebrate the release of records by local artists. As early as 1925, newspapers in Morristown ran special ads to announce the release of the Vocalion records by local Uncle Am Stuart; Bristol papers ran ads to list the records recorded by Victor there in 1927; Chattanooga papers ran display ads announcing the release of Columbia records by their favorite local fiddler, Jess Young. Yet the Nashville papers seemed reluctant to do this. No researcher has of yet found a single instance of similar advertising for Nashville artists or for recordings made in Nashville. Of course, just how reflective local advertising was of local taste remains unclear. Some stores may simply have listed the latest releases or "hot prospects," suggested by the companies from New York. Others may have actively chosen records they thought would have local appeal for their promotional lists.

Occasional ads in the Nashville papers actually did emphasize old-time music, though without any attempt to emphasize Nashville artists or recordings. One such was placed in early 1927 by the Banner Furniture Company. It listed "all the latest hits" on Columbia records, and listed some fifteen titles, most of which were in the 15000 "Old Time" series. Four, however, were in the 14000 "Blues and Race" series, including titles by Bessie Smith, Barbecue Bob, and the preacher J. C. Burnett. Also included were parts 1 and 2 of Moran & Mack's famous "Two Black Crows" series, an incredibly popular blackface routine. All these titles were mixed together in one big list, suggesting that the segregation of records imposed by the record company's "series" designation meant little to the dealers and customers of the Nashville area. This ad, as well as many of the others dealing with old-time music or blues, emphasized "mail orders a specialty," and even provided an order blank for C.O.D. orders. This would seem to indicate that the perceived market for the records was outside of Nashville, where mail order would be the best way to get records.

Throughout much of this time, the *Banner* ran a weekly feature called "The Banner Query Box," which printed old songs, historical notes, bits of folklore and superstition, and nearly anything else that its readers wrote in inquiring about. Most requests were for song lyrics, and the "Query Box" printed either the text (if the editor knew the song or where he could find the words), or asked the readers for help. Frequently readers did submit song texts and the editor printed these, along with the contributor's name and address. The "Query Box" is a rich and largely untapped resource for students of traditional song in Middle Tennessee, or for those interested in which pop songs were gaining favor, or even for exploration into folk tradition in that area.

Sometimes requests for songs generally associated with old-time music appear, and here the judgment of the "Box"'s editor seems confusing. The editor, for example, supplied the requested texts of "New River Train" and "Jesse James," both popular on records at the time, but refused a request for "Blue Ridge Mountain Blues," a favorite of local fiddler Sid Harkreader. The editor sniffed, "The Query Box does not print blues songs." In other cases, he rejects requests because a song is "too new." Usually, however, the requests reveal an abiding interest in old songs and in the folk culture and history of the Middle Tennessee area. That the editor frequently had to refuse requests may indicate again the split between the Nashville urban community, of which the editor was a member, and the rural community, from which so many of the letters came.

Finally, one can turn to the Nashville papers for their coverage of various local musical events that occurred in the city. Here, too, a pattern emerges, for most of this coverage was related to the Nashville Symphony or to classical recitals. George Pullen Jackson, later to become famous as the author of studies like *White Spirituals of the Southern Upland*, regularly covered music for the *Tennessean*. Though he was certainly aware of the value of folk music and of the sort of thing the Opry was doing, and while on several occasions he explained to the Nashville readers that jazz was to be taken seriously, there is no evidence that he made any similar defense for old-time music. Aside from the radio press releases, many of which Judge Hay wrote for self-serving purposes, the Nashville press carried little commentary on the old-time music that was about to put Nashville on the map.

In sum, one of the more remarkable things about Nashville in the 1920s, at least as reflected in documentable sources, was its profound lack of response to old-time music. Its attitude was less a matter of hostility than of indifference, which leads our examination of Nashville as social and cultural context for this music to several hypotheses. One is that the real audience for the Barn Dance and similar programs, as well as the music itself, was not so much within the city itself but in the outlying rural communities reached by the radio stations and newspapers. This fact, also, had interesting implications for the insurance company that owned WSM, as we shall see. A second hypothesis is that while Nashville was unwilling to embrace early country music in a cultural sense, it was certainly willing to embrace it economically, as shown by the radio rivals to the WSM Barn Dance. This, too, would be a pattern that would persist into the 1950s and 1960s. A third hypothesis is that Nashville emerged as an old-time music center in the 1920s because it did have a surprising supply of competent musicians, many of whom were the products of a rural folk community that was easily accessible in the hills and valleys around the Nashville basin. Though not especially successful as recording artists, these musicians were extremely successful as radio artists and were strongly attached to their Middle Tennessee community, seldom trying to exploit their careers beyond its boundaries.

WSM in the 1920s was by no means unique in its attempt to present country music on the radio. Other stations had done it earlier, at greater length, with stronger signals, and in much larger locations. Just why WSM caught on with its Barn Dance may be a question beyond full answering, but there are three factors that made the show unique: the cultural and physical setting of Nashville, the personality of George D. Hay, and the special characters of the performers who made up the show's cast. We have examined the first two of these factors. It is now time to turn to the cast of characters that made the Opry one of the most colorful radio shows in American history.

Goin' Uptown
Dr. Humphrey Bate,
Dean of the Opry

A NY CONSIDERATION OF THE MUSICIANS of the early
Opry—the artists who formed the cornerstone of the new edifice—must begin with Dr. Humphrey Bate. Bate, a harmonica
player whom George Hay called the "dean" of the Opry, was almost certainly the first musician to play country music over WSM and probably the
first to play such music over Nashville radio in general. His role has been
overshadowed by more colorful characters like Uncle Jimmy Thompson,
the traditional "founder" of the Opry. But had not Dr. Bate paved the way
and shown that audience interest in old-time music existed, Uncle Jimmy
might never have been allowed to play on the famous November 28 broadcast. Indisputable documentary evidence exists showing that Dr. Bate
played on WDAD a full month before WSM even started broadcasting and
that he played on WSM weeks before George Hay arrived on the scene.

Dr. Bate, described by Hay as "a very genial country physician from
Sumner County, Tennessee," was not as charismatic or as eccentric as
Uncle Jimmy, and he might not have evoked the immediate and dramatic
audience response that Uncle Jimmy did. But his role in the development
of the early Opry is actually as great as, if not greater than, that of Uncle
Jimmy. He recorded more than Uncle Jimmy, and in many ways his music
was richer and more complex than that of his white-bearded fiddling colleague. Certainly Dr. Bate was on the air more regularly than Uncle Jimmy,
especially after 1926; in fact, in terms of airtime, Dr. Bate's string band was
probably on the early Opry more than any other band. He soon was given

43

the 8:00 P.M. slot, where he opened the show with "There'll Be a Hot Time in the Old Town Tonight." He also worked closely and often with Hay to build up the show and recommended a number of acts, including harmonica player DeFord Bailey. In 1926, for instance, the good doctor appeared on 29 out of 39 logged shows, and in 1928 on 25 out of 52 logged shows. (A logged show is one for which we have at least a tentative lineup.) Often he performed for as much as an hour, often twice a night. Dr. Bate was in the first Opry tour group sent out in 1931, and he was one of the few early artists who saw the full potential of the Opry's development. He repeatedly told his daughter Alcyone, "Honey, you know we may have really started something down there."

But even if Dr. Bate had not been historically important, he would have been musically vital to the development of the show. His band had one of the most individual sounds in old-time music and reflected the characteristic Middle Tennessee string band tradition, with its emphasis on the harmonica sharing the lead with the fiddle. His music influenced many other Opry regulars, from the Crook Brothers to Uncle Dave Macon. His core repertoire, which has been preserved (see below), was one of the most extensive and, to use a term of the folklorist, "authentic" of any Opry performer. Yet it included a refreshingly eclectic variety of other numbers, from ragtime to Sousa marches. Dr. Bate's own harmonica style was clean, pure, and exact, reminding one more of a fiddle than a blues harp. His style anticipated the later Nashville work of artists like Jimmy Riddle and Charlie McCoy. But most important, perhaps, was the fact that the band was a team. They were no pickup group and had relatively few personnel changes for over fifteen years. They perfected a collective ensemble sound not unlike that of early New Orleans jazz, and there was nothing quite like it in old-time music.

Like most other performers on the early Opry, Dr. Bate did not make a living from his music. For most of his career he was a full-time practicing physician who saw music as a hobby and as a means to relax. He was born in 1875 in Sumner County, Tennessee, some forty miles northeast of Nashville and about halfway between Nashville and the Kentucky state line. His father before him had been a physician for about forty years at Castalian Springs, near Gallatin, Tennessee, and young Humphrey took over his practice at about the turn of the century. He had graduated from the Vanderbilt Medical School just prior to the Spanish-American War of 1898, during which he served in the Medical Corps. After the war young Dr. Bate reportedly turned down several offers to practice in urban centers, preferring the life of a country doctor and the rustic pleasures of hunting and fishing.

Though the Bate family, which originally came from North Carolina, had boasted no outstanding musicians in its branches, young Humphrey was interested in music from the first. He took his playing seriously and formed his first band before the turn of the century. Papers preserved in the Tennessee State Library and Archives document a fiddling contest held in Gallatin on October 20, 1899. It was sponsored by the Daughters of the Confederacy, was replete with a big parade and cash prizes, and attracted some forty-four area musicians. The competition provided for a series of fiddling contests (a different prize was awarded for the individual who could best play a particular tune), and the agenda included competitions in string band, Jew's harp, and French harp (harmonica). Among the invited entrants was a string band led by Dr. Humphrey Bate and included Ashley Hamilton, P. D. Belote, A. C. Warmack, Sewell Chenault, and J. C. Snow. An old photo of this band (which won the competition), or a similar incarnation, shows Warmack playing the fiddle, Chenault the guitar, Bate on harmonica, someone on banjo, and Belote on cello. (The inclusion of the cello in string bands in Middle Tennessee was quite common, to judge from other old photos. Dr. Bate later used a bowed string bass to replace the cello, giving his band a unique sound.)

Twenty years later, in October 1919, this basic band was still intact, and still winning contests. A Sumner County paper describes their winning a contest at nearby Lebanon: "The Castalian Springs Band, composed of Dr. Humphrey Bate, Sewall [sic] Chenault, P. D. Belote, and A. C. Womack won the string band contest and the Cotton Town band won the second prize. Dr. Humphrey Bate captured the prize in the harp contest."

As a boy Humphrey Bate would perform on the steamboats that ran excursions up and down the Cumberland River, which wound through the Middle Tennessee highlands. His daughter recalled: "At first, it was just him playing harmonica solos. Later I'm sure he may have carried others, but at first it was just him and his harmonica. It worried my grandmother because he would go to the river." But an even more important influence on him than the riverboat experience was an old ex-slave who had worked for the Bate family for years. Alcyone Bate Beasley remembered:

> I have heard him say that most of the tunes he learned, he learned from this old Negro who was an old man when he [Humphrey] was a little boy. I don't know whether this old Negro sang these songs to him, whether he played them on an instrument, or what. But looking over Daddy's list of tunes that he played confirms that . . . for so many of the tunes on Daddy's list nobody else ever played.

A couple of the tunes that might well have come to Dr. Bate from black tradition are the funky sounding "Old Joe" and "Take Your Foot Out of the Mud and Put It in the Sand," which seems related to the familiar "Casey Jones" melody line.

But while Dr. Bate eagerly embraced traditional material, he was no dogmatic purist in what he listened to or in what he played. "We were exposed to all types of music," his daughter recalled, "classical, popular, folk. . . . We always had a Victrola and we always had good records to listen to. But it's funny, I can't remember him ever having a country type record in the house. But we had lots of band music, and light opera, classical singers." Dr. Bate himself was very fond of John Philip Sousa's band and would take his family to Nashville to see it whenever it toured the area. And though he could not read music himself, he would listen to light classical numbers on the Victrola or played on the piano, and adapt them for harmonica. He could play a little on any instrument, though he usually played French harp, guitar, or piano.

In the years after World War I, when Alcyone was a little girl of four or five, she began to sing with her father's various bands and occasionally to travel with them. The band played at schoolhouse concerts, for steamboat excursions, for picnics, and for a time as an intermission feature in a silent movie house in nearby Gallatin. Oddly enough, for a band that supposedly specialized in "barn dance" music and flavored its breakdowns with dance calls, it did not play many dances. However, it apparently played a variety of music, from Italian waltzes to marches. And by 1925, when the two Nashville radio stations came on the air, the band had enough of a regional reputation to attract offers from both.

Apparently Dr. Bate was acquainted with a Bill Craig, a cousin to the Craigs who owned National Life. Some months before WSM went on the air, when it became evident that the station would be started, Craig asked Dr. Bate and his band to perform regularly on the air. But before WSM began broadcasting, WDAD opened, and their management also asked him to perform. Mindful of his commitment to Craig, Dr. Bate hesitated until he could clear it with National Life. When there was no objection, he agreed to start performing for WDAD. In fact, for some months he continued to play on both stations, often appearing on WDAD early in the evening and then walking up the hill to WSM.

Correspondence preserved by Alcyone Bate Beasley supplements the sketchy radio logs of this early period, and two letters especially prove that Dr. Bate did in fact appear on WDAD prior to WSM's opening, almost certainly indicating that he was the first artist to play country music over radio in Nashville. The letters also give us an insider's glimpse of this crucial month of 1925, when WDAD was the only station in Nashville. The first is a letter to Dr. Bate from L. N. Smith, owner of Dad's Auto Accessories and Radio Supplies at 164 Eighth Avenue North in downtown Nashville. It is dated September 19 (a Saturday) and refers to the broadcast of Friday, September 18, a date Bate later confirms as his first radio appearance on the station, or anywhere, for that matter. The letter reads:

> We certainly want to compliment you and your artists on the way they went over on our program, as we consider it one of the best line ups that we have had. I told you last night I would send you a list of the applause which you got, but I find that it is so much that I am going to send you the original copies and will give you the privilege of keeping these copies as we have already used them and gotten our records from them. We are looking forward to having you and your band with us again next Friday night and wish you to make up a program of about sixteen numbers to make about four fast opening numbers two groups of four each Hawaiian music—fast closing numbers. We have had a number of compliments from different people dropping in the store this morning which I know you would appreciate if you could hear.

It is a little unclear just what Smith means when he refers to the "list of applause," whether it is a log of phone calls or a collection of telegrams or notes, but it is obvious that the listener response was considerable, foreshadowing by some weeks the similar response that greeted Uncle Jimmy Thompson. Also noteworthy here is the length of time the band was asked to play the following Friday: sixteen numbers probably constituted an hour of solid music. The reference to "two groups of four" Hawaiian tunes, about half the program, further testifies to the popularity in Nashville of ersatz Hawaiian music.

The second letter is from Dr. Bate himself and is even more revealing. It was written to Mrs. Ada Armstrong at Earlington, Kentucky, near Madisonville, about one hundred miles north of Nashville. Ada Armstrong's father was Colonel W. A. Toombs, an old friend of Dr. Bate's and "the Colonel" referred to in the letter. Other personal references include "Ethel," Dr. Bate's wife, and "Buster," his son, who often played with the band in the 1930s.

Castalian Springs, Tenn.
Sept. 28th 1925
To the whole Toombs Tribe
Dear Friends:

How are you: and what has become of you? It seems that
you all have dissolved into complete oblivion since the day you
left here as not a word has been heard from you since, but since
"no news is good news" I guess you are allright—Ethel has had
a "round" with her heart since you left, caused I guess by too
much "Cafe Noir"—CocoCola, etc. but is better now—Buster
returned home from Bans Infirmary at Nashville last Friday and
is convalescing from an operation for appendicitis which he
stood fine—His attack came like a bolt out of the blue and was a
bad one and I had to get him away in a hurry. But so far I have
never seen anyone do nicer and if we can keep him quiet for a
few days I think he will be O.K. Tell the Colonel that old man
Bill Sanders had a severe Paralytic stroke last night and I very
much fear that it will wind him up.

My crowd is now playing for Radio Station WDAD (Dads)
at Nashville. It is a rather weak station broadcasting on a wave
length of 226 meters but should be easily gotten on any good
night from your place. We are let to them temporarily by Station
W.S.M. the big new station of the National Life Ins. Co. of
Nashville who will open on the night of Oct. 5th next. It
broadcasts on a wave length of 280 meters and can be easily
heard at Earlington in the daytime as well as night. We make our
initial appearance there on the night of Saturday Oct. 24th next,
playing from 10 to 11 pm. If we come in good I want to hear
from you sure and will be looking for a message that night.

We have made a big hit at WDAD and have gotten hundreds
of messages from Nashville and nearby towns and a few from
Ohio, Penn., Ill, and Indiana.

Some of them are highly complimentary. One fellow wanted
to know my dimensions. Others refuse to believe that I am
playing a Harmonica and say it is a violin. Some a sax and some
a clarinet. I am asked to play everything from Dvorak's
Humoresque to "Yankee Doodle." I can't comply with one
twentieth of these requests but play all that time allows. I
sometimes by special request play a solo or two on the Harp but
most of the time I play along with two Guitars—2nd Violin with

Miss Alcyone at the Chickering Grand (at the new station she
will be at the Steinway Grand.) Then we double up in a
Hawaiian Quartette and Miss Brigger plays the "Uke."
Occasionally she obliges with a Piano solo which may be
something like "Tour la Cheval" whatever that may be, but more
often "Yessir thats my Baby" or "Don't Bring Lulu" or
"Yearning" or something on that order which always gets more
applause from the "Rabble" than the Classical piece does. For
the Colonels special edification please inform him that "the old
Master's" shall not perish from the earth for awhile anyway as I
have been asked by the new station (WSM) to specialize on some
old time Fiddlin tunes and will proceed on the night of the 24th
to render to the best of my ability a few of his old favorites and I
hope that he will hear me and that if the music meets his
approbation that he will let me hear from him—We have all
about gotten over our stage fright as we have already played 3 or
4 tunes from Dads and have passed our test and been accepted at
W.S.M. and as it will be running smoothly by then I think if we
are lucky enough to catch a night with little or no static that we
will go over O.K. I am enclosing letter from Mr. Smith
announcer at Dads written after our first appearance there. You
will see how many pieces he called for. Well we played all that
and as many request minutes and then had to play on for over
half an hour longer, over an hour and a half.

We are playing there every Friday night or rather have been
and will be there again next Friday night from 8 till 9 or 9:30 but
I may change our playing date with them after Friday night. Am
not sure but may do so. Excuse all this about Radio but we are
tickled over getting on and are trying hard to make good. Hope
you all are well. Let us hear from you. Love to you all from The
Bates.

by H. B. (m.d.)

This letter confirms that even a small station like WDAD was being
heard as far away as Ohio, Pennsylvania, Illinois, and Indiana, an impressive if oddly directional signal strength that once again testifies to the surprising carrying power of early radio in those days of uncluttered airwaves.
The band for these early broadcasts apparently included Bate's harmonica,
two guitars, two "violins," and a piano, and the repertoire was surprisingly eclectic, ranging from light classical pieces to 1920s pop jazz songs

like "Don't Bring Lulu" and "Yes Sir, That's My Baby." The good doctor's comment about pleasing the "rabble" reminds us again of his musical cultivation and social standing, but his willingness to "specialize in some old time fiddling tunes" suggests he shared some of Henry Ford's views on American music: popular and jazz music were decadent and possibly subversive, but genuine old-time fiddle tunes were noble and patriotic.

The fact that WSM had specifically asked his band to work up some fiddle tunes is likewise revealing. George D. Hay was weeks away from assuming control of the station, and yet someone at WSM was already trying to craft an image focusing on at least some old-time music. (This too could have been a response to the fiddling fervor generated that fall by Ford's series of fiddling contests.) Though Dr. Bate says his group was scheduled to debut on WSM on October 24, he appeared in the WSM schedule in the *Tennessean* for October 18, where a "studio program featuring Dr. Humphrey Bate and his string quartet of old-time musicians" is announced from 10:00 to 11:00 P.M. And by January 3, 1926, a radio column in the same paper reports that Dr. Bate and his band had been on WDAD over twenty times since the station began operating in September. This would mean that the band had appeared there almost every Saturday night, even after WSM had begun broadcasting. In fact, a similar record of appearances is probably true for WSM. On December 20, 1925, the *Tennessean* ran a photo of Bate's band with the caption, "Players of old time favorites for WSM." It was the first photo of any Opry performer to appear in print.

On Thursday, November 5—a week before George Hay arrived and three weeks before the famous Uncle Jimmy Thompson broadcast—WSM got several of its radio artists together to broadcast from the Ryman Auditorium for the policemen's benefit. Two old-time groups were included, Dr. Bate's band and Uncle Dave Macon with Sid Harkreader. The two groups vied with each other for the more applause. The *Tennessean* described the Bate band's role in the show: "Dr. Bate directed his old-time orchestra, using himself the harmonica. His daughter, Miss Alcyone Bate, presided at the piano, Walter Liggett and Hugh Pesy played the banjo, and O. R. Blanton and Bert Hutchinson [*sic*] played guitar. They rendered several numbers of old-time and popular music, and the audience never got enough."

By this time Alcyone, now thirteen, was playing ukulele and piano with her father's band and occasionally singing numbers like "Peggy O'Neal" and "Silver Threads Among the Gold." As the band continued to perform, it began to attract its share of the fan mail. One letter, dated January 4, 1926, from Richmond, Ontario, read: "Dr. Humphrey Bate's orchestra was so plain we had a pleasant quadrille to it. It was such a pleasant change from the jazz music and the announcer's words were so plain we enjoyed hearing the Southern drawl."

Though the mail was not as great as that received by Uncle Jimmy Thompson, it was impressive, and by March of that year WSM publicity was saying that "the doctor has one of the fastest barn dance teams on the air today." As early as January 1926 Dr. Bate was a regular on the barn dance program, usually opening the show with "There'll Be a Hot Time in the Old Town Tonight." At first he shared the hour with Uncle Jimmy, but as Thompson's appearances dropped off, the Bate band soon became the flagship band for the new show.

Though the personnel of Dr. Bate's group varied slightly from month to month, seven members formed the core of the band. Dr. Bate himself usually played harmonica, Alcyone usually played piano, and five excellent local musicians finished out the band. The lead fiddler was Oscar Stone, a Nashville native who worked days as a hardwood floor layer for a leading Nashville department store. Oscar reportedly joined the Bate band on October 25, 1925, shortly after WSM started. Though a native of Obion County, Tennessee, he had moved to Sumner County as a boy and there met Dr. Bate. He was only six years younger than Bate and acted as a sort of coleader of the band. On occasion, when Dr. Bate would lead a contingent of his band that he called the "Hawaiian orchestra," Stone would lead the old-time section. When Dr. Bate died in 1936, Oscar took over the Possum Hunters and kept them going until 1949, when he himself died. Stone is given credit for composing two well-known songs associated with Bate. "Goin' Uptown," which Bate and Stone recorded in 1928, was published by Flick Music in Nashville in 1931. It is one of the few pieces of sheet music published featuring an old-time band from the 1920s on the cover. Stone also wrote "Stone's Rag," which was featured but never recorded by Bate and Stone; however, another Nashville band, Paul Warmack's, recorded it on Victor (V40009) in 1928, with Stone's friend Charlie Arrington doing the fiddling. Under various other names, the tune got into circulation among numerous fiddlers of the time. Western swing star Bob Wills called it "Lone Star Rag" when he recorded it in 1940.

Walter Liggett was Bate's banjo player for years. He was a native of Cottontown (a few miles west of Castalian Springs) and worked during the day as a truck farmer. He was the group's comedian and would "crow like a rooster" when the band left the stage after performing. He liked to wear a thatched red wig, much like the "Toby" clowns wore in medicine shows of the day.

Oscar Albright usually played the bass fiddle, or "doghouse bass" as it was called then. He was from Sideview, Tennessee, and was a farmer also. Judge Hay recalled proudly that Oscar's brother had been a U.S. "minister" to Finland but neglected to mention the more pertinent fact that Oscar was probably the first person to play a string bass on the Opry. Very few of the string bands of the '20s used one, usually preferring to let the guitarist make what bass runs he could manage on the lower strings. Certainly none of the other Opry string bands before 1930 used a string bass. But Bate did not consider the use of the bass an innovation. Alcyone recalled that "my Daddy had used a bass from the time he first had a string band." Even more intriguing is the fact that Oscar never plucked the bass, as most modern players do, but always bowed it. Alcyone recalled that "I never heard him play it any other way except to bow it. On fast numbers Oscar was a busy guy." Oscar apparently bowed the bass in short strokes, playing on the beat rather than with the melody. The effect, which can be heard on the Brunswick recordings, was much like that of a tuba in early jazz bands. It was a steady, if not sprightly, beat and gave the band a remarkably full harmonic range. It must have been much more effective in person than on the air or on records. Whatever the case, Oscar Albright must be given credit for creating much of the Bate band's distinctive sound.

The good doctor usually used two guitarists, both apparently playing rhythm. In the early WSM days these slots were filled by Staley Walton and Bert Hutcherson. Walton was a farmer from Castalian Springs who began playing with Dr. Bate's band when he was thirteen years old. He stayed with them through Dr. Bate's death, through Oscar Stone's tenure until 1949, and after that with versions of the Possum Hunters headed by Alcyone and himself into the 1950s. He thereafter played with the Crook Brothers until his death in the early 1970s. His beautiful 1933 model Nick Lucas Gibson Special added a distinctive sound to many of the band's performances. The other guitarist was Bert Hutcherson, who played on the Opry until the '80s. He played with Dr. Bate until about 1928, when he left to join Paul Warmack's Gully Jumpers. He and Warmack had a successful early morning radio show on WSM in the late '20s and early '30s.

Other musicians played with the band from time to time. Dr. Bate's son, Humphrey Bate Jr., called Buster, began playing in 1931 and quickly gained a reputation as a fine player on Jew's harp, as well as a competent guitar and harp player. He also played the tipple on occasion. Fiddler Bill Barret sometimes substituted for Oscar Stone, and Jimmy Hart played guitar for a time in the early '30s. Lou Hesson, Alcyone's aunt, helped out singing and dancing on stage shows. And Alcyone herself, billed as "the little girl with the big voice," also played piano and ukulele.

In addition to his main old-time barn dance band, Dr. Bate created several contingent groups, made up of musicians from the large band but catering to specialized musical tastes. There was, as we have seen, "Dr. Bate and His Hawaiian Orchestra," formed in response to the growing demand in the '20s for Hawaiian-style music. This band usually included Audrey Hesson, Alcyone's uncle, on steel guitar; Dr. Bate and Staley Walton on standard guitars; and Alcyone on ukulele. One of the first references to Dr. Bate playing over Nashville radio is a notice on October 25, 1925, announcing a program by "Dr. Humphrey Bate and His Hawaiian Orchestra." In addition to the Hawaiian band, there was the "Bate Trio," composed of Alcyone on piano, Dr. Bate on harp, and a rhythm guitarist. "We usually used the trio to do slower, pretty pieces," recalled Alcyone.

A number of facets of Dr. Bate's career remind one of the career of Paul Whiteman. Like the famous band leader, Bate utilized a large orchestra that featured individual soloists of great distinction (such as Stone or Hutcherson); like Whiteman he formed smaller groups out of larger ones; and like Whiteman, Bate had an appreciation for all kinds of music and was responsible for getting other "hot" artists exposure. For instance, he introduced DeFord Bailey to Hay and WSM. But Bate also differed from Whiteman: his band was less progressive than Whiteman's, and deliberately so. He seems to have consciously preserved an older string band style in the face of newer, modern sounds. Bate's Brunswick recordings are probably a fairly close approximation of turn-of-the-century rural Tennessee dance music. And, of course, unlike Whiteman, Bate never became a full-time professional musician. He continued to practice medicine, until the end, as a full-time physician. He was always careful, however, to arrange his schedule to have Saturday nights free.

Dr. Bate was no rural hayseed, then, but an intelligent, well-educated, and sophisticated man who enjoyed music of all kinds, even regularly vacationing in Florida in the winter to fish. One can only wonder, then, how he must have reacted to the "hillbilly" image Hay thrust upon him and his band. It is interesting to trace the development of this image, for it shows a lot about the overall image the Opry was trying to build for itself. In the first place, it was Hay who decided to call the band the Possum Hunters; before that, it was simply called "Dr. Bate's band," or "Dr. Humphrey Bate's Augmented String Orchestra." The two earliest photos of the band show the members in conservative, well-tailored business suits, but by 1930 Opry publicity was sending out photos of them that showed them dressed in sloppy felt hats, overalls, and suspenders. Also, a change occurs in the band's description in WSM press releases. Originally they were described as "a string quartet of old-time musicians" (*Tennessean*,

October 18, 1925). Only four years later the *Knoxville News-Sentinel* carried a WSM press release that described Dr. Bate's music as "unique entertainment that only Tennessee Mountaineers can afford" and pointed out that "every one of the 'talent' is from the back country." Two of the earliest news stories stress the fact that Bate was a physician and a distinguished graduate of Vanderbilt Medical School (see the *Tennessean*, December 20, 1925; January 3, 1926). By 1930 the following story on the band in *Mastertone*, the Gibson magazine, made no mention of this fact whatsoever but carried the rustic image to even greater extremes (June 13, 1930).

KEEPING A SOUTHERN CUSTOM UP-TO-DATE

The curtain goes up on Act One, and the audience gets a picture of a faithful old hound, baying beneath a persimmon tree. It is a sound picture. The persistent hoarse barking of the dog rings through the still black night. From a little clearing in the thicket a mile away comes floating to your ears the voices of several men, pitched high in a single blending yodel.

Very faint at first; so faint in fact that you strain your ears to catch the sound again, not knowing whether it was only a part of the night, and the woods. The yodeling voices, for now you have recognized them as such, become more distinct, as their owners draw closer. Now they ring out above even the baying dog's bark.

A loud crash, like men running through pine needles, and crackling brush; a lusty shout from the hound's master, urging the animal to "talk to him boy"; a thunder of feet on the bare earth of a little salt lick, and half a dozen panting, joyous men burst into the open, and you see them for the first time.

The 'possum hunters.

To a native of the South, the scene is familiar. It suggests 'possum and sweet potatoes. It has become more familiar in the last year or two, since the inauguration of the "Grand Ol' Opry" from Radio Station WSM, Nashville, Tennessee. For the traditional Saturday night 'possum hunt is enacted over that broadcasting station once a week.

Dr. Humphrey Bate hits the trail in the wake of the old "Pot licker" hound, with his "Possum Hunters." It is a real old fashioned 'possum hunt on which Dr. Bate and his "hill billies" take you. They are the modern version of the 'possum hunters your dad knew. Yes suh.

The "Grand Ol' Opry" is the way the WSM barn dance has been dignified. Dr. Bate and His Possum Hunters headline the show as act one. There is nothing dignified about the Possum Hunters; not if you define dignity as being stiff and reserved. Just as the old-time 'possum hunts through the flats where the persimmon trees grew were eagerly looked forward to every Saturday night, so Dr. Humphrey Bate and His Possum Hunters are awaited with equal eagerness by literally thousands of listeners tuned in on the National Life and Accident Company's radio station at Nashville.

To make their enactment of the great Southern sport authentic, Dr. Bate and his Hunters don the characteristic garb of a 'possum hunter of yore, and start whooping things up just as darkness falls, which is 8 o'clock, Central Standard Time, every Saturday night. The "Solemn Old Judge" of WSM, who in private life is George D. Hay, starts the Possum Hunters on the trail of their persimmon eating quarry.

In a little less than five years, Dr. Bate's band had regressed from a string quartet to a pack of pot-liquor-swilling hunters who could out-bay their own dogs. Though the doctor did indeed love to hunt, this sort of image mongering must at times have put his well-known geniality to the test.

In April 1928 the Bate band journeyed to Atlanta to record what would be its only commercial recordings, for the Brunswick Company. Alcyone remembered how the trip came about. "It seems to me that a man came up to the village where we lived to talk to my father about it. They set up a date. I remember they went down on the train, and stayed two or three days. Just the band went; I stayed at home for some reason." The band that made the recordings was smaller than the usual Possum Hunters unit: Stone played fiddle, Liggett banjo, Walton guitar, Albright bass, and Bate harmonica. Also on the trip was fiddler W. J. (Bill) Barret, whom Bate often alternated with Stone. Barret played lead on two of the numbers, "Eighth of January" and "Throw the Old Cow Over the Fence," for which Dr. Bate later paid him fifty dollars.

Most of the records were probably released during mid or late 1928, but there is no way to tell how well they sold. Like most artists of the day, Dr. Bate recorded for a flat fee and got no royalties. The following list provides the titles and catalog numbers for the entire Brunswick session in Atlanta that fall:

Billy in the Low Ground (calls by Bate)	Brunswick 239
Eighth of January (Barret on f)	Br 239
How Many Biscuits Can You Eat?	Br 232
Ham Beats All Meat	Vocalion 5238
Goin' Up-Town (Stone, f; Bate, calls)	Br 232
Throw the Old Cow	
over the Fence (Barret on f)	Voc 5238
Green Back Dollar Bill (Stone on f)	Br 275
My Wife Died Saturday Night (Bate vocal)	Br 271
Dill Pickle Rag (Stone on f)	Br 243
Take Your Foot Out of the Mud and	
Put it in the Sand	Br 243
Old Joe	Br 271
Run, Nigger, Run	Br 275

Some of Dr. Bate's records were mentioned in the *Tennessean*'s regular column "Reviewing Brunswick Records," and while they were praised, no attempt was made to note that the artist was local. The anonymous reviewer wrote of Brunswick 275: "Dance music of a diverting type is offered by Dr. Humphrey Bate and His Possum Hunters, who must be ranked as aristocrats among fiddlers. 'Green Back Dollar Bill' and 'Run, Nigger, Run' (No. 275) are faststepping quadrilles with plenty of swing, and the Doctor and His hunters know what its [*sic*] all about. In fact, here is one of the best trained bands of its kind this reviewer has had the pleasure of hearing."

Some of the numbers recorded were traditional fiddle tunes well known by everyone. But others of the Possum Hunters' twelve recorded sides are interesting and unusual, with roots running deep into mid-South musical culture. Apparently one of the most popular of the recordings was "How Many Biscuits Can You Eat?":

How many biscuits can you eat? This morning? This morning?
How many biscuits can you eat? This morning? This morning?
How many biscuits can you eat?
Forty-four biscuits and a ham of meat,
This morning, for breakfast, so soon.

Oh, when you see me looking straight, this morning,
     this morning.
Oh, when you see me looking straight. this morning,
     this morning,

Oh when you see me looking straight,
Come and get this biscuit plate,
This morning, for breakfast, so soon

Oh, when you see me looking mean, this morning, this morning,
Oh when you see me looking mean, this morning, this morning,
Oh, when you see me looking mean,
Bacon and eggs had better be lean,
This morning, for breakfast, so soon.
(transcribed from Br 232)

The melody structure, with its call-and-response pattern, is almost surely borrowed from black music—possibly from the Bate family's ex-slave mentioned earlier—and is also related to the folk revival favorite "This Morning, This Evening, So Soon." The song became so popular that at least one local newspaper columnist devoted a four-hundred-word essay to ascertain whether it was indeed physically possible to eat that many biscuits and a whole ham.

In fact, Dr. Bate must have loved ham, for he celebrated it in another splendid recording, "Ham Beats All Meat." In this spirited paean to pork, the good doctor makes an acute observation about folk food values:

White folks go to the butcher shop,
To buy that old cow meat,
Darkies go to the smokehouse,
To grab that ham that's sweet.
    Ham beats all meat (always good and sweet),
    Ham beats all meat (always ready to eat).
    Ham beats all meat (always good and sweet),
    Ham beats all meat (always ready to eat).
White folks in the dining room,
Eating on the mutton and lamb,
Darkies in the kitchen,
Going for the good sweet ham.
    [repeat chorus]

Here, too, one suspects a black origin for the song. A version of it shows up in a collection that black folklorist Thomas Talley assembled in the midstate area around the turn of the century (*Negro Folk Rhymes*). The song was also a favorite of Dr. Bate's good friend Uncle Dave Macon, who thought so much of it that he included it in one of his songbooks. In Bate's recording of the song, he sings the verses by himself and is joined by a vocal quartet on the chorus. He also liked to sing another comic song, "Waltz Me Around Again, Willie," which he never recorded. Composed by Will Cobb and Ren Shields about 1906, "Waltz Me Around" was recorded by early country comedian Chris Bouchillon in 1927.

A couple of the instrumentals, "Take Your Foot Out of the Mud and Put It in the Sand" and "Throw the Old Cow Over the Fence," are not widely known. Dr. Bate did many of the calls on "Throw the Old Cow," but Walton and Stone helped on occasion. It is unclear whether the calls were actually functional and could direct dances or were by this time simply ornamentation for the music. "Eighth of January," Bill Barret's fiddle masterpiece, is not the familiar fiddle tune made popular by later singer Johnny Horton, but something far older and more rare. "Old Joe," one of the strangest tunes in the old-time repertoire, came from a black source; in fact, it was recorded for the Library of Congress in the 1940s by the black string band of Nathan Frazier and Frank Patterson, and by the Nashville Washboard Band (cf. below). "Green-Backed Dollar Bill" is, however, the familiar "Greenback Dollar" song recorded and sung throughout the South.

Dr. Bate's music had a major impact on the Opry and in the Middle Tennessee area in general, and his harmonica style was widely admired. Of course, he did not use a chromatic harmonica on his earlier shows, though he bought one when they came out on the mass market later in the 1930s. He loved to play in the keys of C and D, though he also carried harps tuned to F and G as well. (He had no "harp apron," used by many modern players, but simply carried the instruments in his pocket.) According to Alcyone: "Daddy had a style of harmonica playing that I have never seen before or since. He played, especially on his slower tunes, tunes that were not altogether country, pretty things—he played them in octaves. He blocked out the eight notes between the octaves and played the two tones in unison an octave apart. It was a great sound."

Also unlike modern harp players, Dr. Bate disliked switching harps in the middle of a tune:

> He played a medley of waltzes in which he managed to play in three keys on one harp. He did it by figuring out that one of the songs was in F and that F has one flat, B flat. But it so happened that this tune—I think it was "Shade of the Old Apple Tree"—had an accidental that allowed him to play B natural. People always commented on how he could play in those three keys.

What did he think of the blues style of his colleague DeFord Bailey?

"Oh, he loved DeFord's playing, and always listened to it, but he saw it as a totally different style. Daddy, for instance, would never choke a harmonica."

Unlike many of the harp-fiddle bands of the time, and of today, the Possum Hunters seldom played harp and fiddle together in lead; one would usually lead, then they would trade off. (This, at least, is the practice followed on the Brunswick records.)

In 1931 Dr. Bate took part in another Opry first. Along with Uncle Dave Macon, Dorris Macon, Sam and Kirk McGee, Alcyone and Lou Hesson, and his son Buster, he made the first tour sent out from the Opry. Judge Hay recalled that "the good doctor was experienced and kept his boys and girls in the middle of the road, so that all of them returned whole." But Alcyone remembered more details about the tour, which apparently took place before the WSM Artists Service Bureau had been set up.

> WSM called up my daddy and told him of the idea. They had gotten together some way with Mr. Harry Beeker, who was the manager of the Princess Theater in Nashville—that was the RKO outlet here—and they picked out who they thought they wanted to send out in the act. They got Jack King to coordinate the act, and Mr. King went along with us.

Alcyone did not feel that the touring show emphasized its WSM or even its Opry affiliation but thought that "it was billed with Uncle Dave Macon as the headliner." This would have made sense, since Uncle Dave was a veteran trouper of many years' vaudeville experience. "We went to places like Madison, Wisconsin, Des Moines, Cedar Rapids, Iowa—it didn't last too long, a few weeks. We all traveled by train."

What did the people think of the music?

"Oh me, they went wild over it. We stopped the show every time—it never failed. The act was real simple. My aunt and I wore little country dresses, not elaborate costumes. Uncle Dave was in his regular getup, and it seems father wore work pants and suspenders. We kept it simple."

The tour left everyone satisfied financially, though no one got rich; but the Opry was still paying very meager wages and by Depression-era standards the tour was a financial success.

By the mid-1930s the doctor was seeing some rather dramatic changes in the Opry. The complex, sophisticated harmony of the Vagabonds and the Delmore Brothers were quite a change from the rough-and-ready informal singing of the early days. Yet Dr. Bate took it all in good spirit, and his band continued to be the flagship band of the show. Alcyone, meanwhile, was developing a career of her own and as early as 1930 had her own radio show over WSM. Later during the 1930s she sang with Jack Shook and his band, Smilin' Jack and His Missouri Mountaineers, and worked with a vocal group, Betty and the Dixie Dons. But early in 1936 Dr. Bate began to experience heart trouble. He told George Hay, "It is my wish to die in harness." The trouble continued, and Dr. Bate passed away on June 12, the night before the Opry moved into its new quarters on Fatherland Street.

For years afterward Alcyone and Staley Walton struggled to keep the Possum Hunters together, but they gave this up and in the mid '60s merged with the Crook Brothers' band. When Staley died in the early '70s, Alcyone went into semi-retirement. After some forty-odd years of making some of the finest dance music in the nation, the Possum Hunters were no more.

We cannot leave the story of Dr. Bate without examining why it was not he but Uncle Jimmy Thompson who caught the public's fancy and gained wide acceptance as the Opry's "founder." There was no overt plot against Dr. Bate. If anything, Hay thought more of him personally than he did of Uncle Jimmy. In fact, it was only after Dr. Bate's death that Uncle Jimmy began to be widely described as the first musician on the Opry; Thompson's own 1931 obituary notices make no mention of his "founding" the Opry.

A number of very real reasons explain why Uncle Jimmy attracted more contemporary publicity than Dr. Bate. One was Henry Ford. By early 1925 Ford, through his vast resources, had generated a widespread fad for old-time fiddling. Uncle Jimmy arrived in the midst of this fad, and, being an excellent fiddler, took advantage of it. Uncle Jimmy also fitted the stereotype Ford was building of the old-time fiddler; in fact, on the cover of Ford's widely circulated magazine *The Dearborn Independent* for January 16, 1926 (the week Ford staged regional fiddling contests across the country), appears an old, bald, white-bearded fiddler who in many ways resembles Uncle Jimmy. Dr. Bate, by contrast, did not fit this stereotype. In fact, the second reason for the interest in Uncle Jimmy was the way he fit with the deliberate attempt to promote the barn dance music as rustic and primitive. We have seen how Hay rusticated the image of Dr. Bate's band during the first few years of the Opry. With Uncle Jimmy, there was little need to rusticate. Whereas Bate was a genial, sophisticated, well-educated physician, Uncle Jimmy was cantankerous, eccentric, and a genuine man of the hills. And finally there is the fact that Uncle Jimmy was Hay's own discovery, whereas Dr. Bate had attained wide popularity in the station's broadcasts even before Hay arrived on the scene.

The mystery of how the Opry image developed is too involved to go into here, but a full investigation of it might reveal why Dr. Bate's role has been generally overlooked. The fact that the legend persists today, even in spite of increasing recognition of Humphrey Bate, is also a story in itself.

Dr. Bate's Repertoire

In the case of many of the early Opry performers, we have only hints of the kind of music they played: a song folio, a few records, some memories of favorite tunes. But with Dr. Bate's band we are fortunate to have uncovered a list, in the doctor's own hand, of his extensive repertoire. This document, one of the rare cases of a "golden age" string band listing virtually all of its repertoire, is reproduced here.

The list was prepared by Dr. Bate, apparently for Vito Pellettieri, WSM music librarian before 1935 (when he attained his more famous position as stage manager). It is unclear whether the list was prepared before or after Pellettieri became stage manager, but it would seem more logical that Vito would have sought the list in his capacity of librarian, to build up the music library and to check for possible copyright clearances. The list includes some annotations, possibly in Vito's hand, indicating that some of the songs had been published and were in copyright. (As early as 1932, according to Alton Delmore, the Opry was concerned with song clearances.) It was Pellettieri who preserved the list and eventually gave it to Alcyone Bate, who gave permission to reproduce it here. Alcyone also had a second list, which her father made as a sort of rough draft of the one presented here, but the songs are almost identical.

Numbers Played by "Possum Hunters" W.S.M.
1. Alabammy Bound
2. Arkansas Traveller
3. Bashful Susan
4. Bringing Home the Bacon
5. Comin' 'Round the Mountain
6. The Cunning Coon
7. The Old Racoon
8. Willie, Goin' to Tell Your Pappy
9. My Wife Died Saturday Night

10. Georgia Camp Meeting
11. Eighth of January
12. Throw the Old Cow Over the Fence
13. Goin' Uptown
14. Biscuits (How Many Biscuits Can You Eat)
15. Take Your Foot Out of the Mud
16. Black Bottom
17. Billy in the Low Ground
18. Dill Pickle Rag
19. Red Rose Rag
20. Old Joe
21. Old Hen Cackled
22. Run Boy Run
23. Goodbye Liza Jane
24. Ham Beats All Meat
25. Goodbye My Honey
26. Tom and Jerry
27. Old Bill Cheatham
28. Hop Light Ladies (McCleod's Reel)
29. Forked Deer
30. College Hornpipe
31. Sailor's Hornpipe
32. Fisher's Hornpipe
33. Lamplighter's Hornpipe
34. Rickett's Hornpipe
35. Hiawatha
36. Red Wing
37. Rainbow
38. Over the Waves
39. Dixie
40. Kiss Yourself Goodbye
41. Tennessee Waggoner
42. Stone's Rag
43. Dusty Miller
44. Stoney Point
45. Chicken Reel
46. Old Joe Clark
47. Don't You Want to Go to Heaven Uncle Joe?
48. Pull Off Your Overcoat
49. Black Your Boots
50. Give Me Back My Fifteen Cents

51. Rabbit in the Pea Patch
52. Under the Double Eagle
53. El Capitan
54. My Creole Belle
55. Hot Time in the Old Town Tonight
56. Jay Bird Died with the Whooping Cough
57. Goodbye Mary Ann
58. The Old Hoot Owl
59. Old Sally Gooden
60. Walking in My Sleep
61. Off for Charleston
62. Miss Sally
63. Andrew Thompson's Reel
64. Irish Washerwoman
65. Simpson County (Ky.)
66. The Old Rat
67. Maggie
68. Old Kentucky Home
69. Suwannee River
70. Silver Threads among the Gold
71. Peggy O' Neal
72. My Old Iowa Home
73. When Mother Played the Organ
74. That Silver-haired Daddy of Mine
75. Spring Time in the Rockies
76. St. Louis Blues
77. That Lonesome Road
78. My Man
79. Gone Crazy My Honey
80. Yes, Sir, That's My Baby
81. Don't Get Weary
82. Little Annie Rooney
83. Steam Boat Bill
84. Turkey in the Straw
85. Old Time Waltz Medley (In the Good Old Summer Time, In the Shade of the Old Apple Tree, I'd Like to Live in Dreamland with a Girl Like You)
86. Pull Out Your Bottle and Give Us a Dram
87. Flying Cloud
88. Give the Fiddler a Dram
89. Jordan McGlowain's Reel

90. Durang's Hornpipe
91. Hell Broke Loose in Georgia
92. Hell Among the Yearlings
93. Fare Well Pretty Girls
94. Nobody's Business
95. Mississippi Sawyer
96. The Bob Tailed Dog
97. Fry a Little Meat and Make a Little Gravy
98. Grand Mammy Look at Uncle Sam
99. Meet High Dad in the Morning
100. Pony Boy
101. Haste to the Wedding
102. A Life on the Ocean Wave
103. Greenwood
104. Green Back Dollar Bill
105. The Old Sage Field
106. Chinese Breakdown
107. Buffalo Gals
108. Oh Susann [*sic*]
109. Ta Ra Ra Boom de Ray
110. By Baby Loves Shortenin' Bread
111. Who Broke the Lock on the Hen House Door?
112. Missouri Waltz
113. He's a Good Man to Have Around
114. Illinois Whiskey
115. Champaign Charlie
116. Jordan Is a Hard Road to Travel
117. Kingdom's a Coming
118. Carnival of Venice
119. You've Got to See Momma Every Night
120. Golden Slippers
121. Cumberland Gap
122. Are You from Dixie?
123. Casey Jones
(124). Silver Bells
(125). Cotillions
(126). Tripoli
(127). Race Horse Two Step
(128). Italian Waltz
(129). In the Shade of the Old Apple Tree
(130). Sweet Bunch of Daisies

A cursory survey of the list reveals some enlightening patterns in the makeup of Dr. Bate's repertoire. Of the 130 songs listed, 22 titles were not recognized by this writer. Of the recognized tunes, one can categorize them into the following types:

traditional fiddle tunes: 37
popular songs, 1880–1890 era: 23
popular songs, 1920s: 12
originals (?): 6
other traditional tunes: 8
marches: 2
hornpipes: 5
vaudeville, minstrel: 13
ragtime: 6

To condense categories, one can summarize by saying that 47 of the 103 tunes were traditional fiddle tunes (including hornpipes), 13 were from minstrel tradition, and 37 were published pieces, including pop songs, marches, and rags. These percentages suggest that the Bate repertoire was actually much more traditional than some have suspected. Though an artificial rustic image was imposed on the band, their music did in fact have genuine folk roots. Well over 50 percent of the songs listed here are traditional by any definition of the term, and some of the unknown titles might well prove to be traditional, boosting this percentage even higher. If the repertoires of the other early Opry bands were anything like this one, the show was in fact succeeding very well in its stated aim of preserving old mountain melodies.

Appendix

A Tribute to Dr. Humphrey Bate
by George D. Hay
"THE SOLEMN OL' JUDGE"

WSM lost the dean of its Grand Ole Opry when Dr. Humphrey Bate, a kindly, intelligent, country physician, felt his own pulse at about nine o'clock last Friday night and told his son-in-law that he was leaving this world. His death occurred a moment later.

For nearly eleven years Dr. Bate and His Possum Hunters have opened the program which started out in a very small way in WSM's first studio, and is now housed in a tabernacle which seats four thousand people.

Dr. Bate was graduated from the Vanderbilt University Medical School just before the Spanish-American War, and served as an officer in the Medical Corps during and shortly after the war of 1898. His father before him, Dr. Humphrey Bate, Sr., practiced medicine for about forty years at Castalian Springs, eight miles beyond Gallatin. Dr. Bate turned down several offers as a young man to move to the city. He thought them over carefully, but decided that he could render more service in his own community, which needed him so badly. A man of simple tastes, he enjoyed nature to the utmost. The streams and woods found him during his off hours, and his one emotional outlet was playing the old-time tunes which he loved so dearly.

Several months ago Dr. Bate was stricken with heart trouble. He told the writer about it, and asked only one thing that he be allowed to continue on the Grand Old Opry until the end came. He was a physician, and knew the uncertainty of such a malady. He was told that his place would be here as long as he wanted it, but that he must take care of his health, whereupon he replied, "It is my wish to die in harness," which he did. It was almost prophetic in that the good Doctor passed away the night before the Grand Ole Opry moved into its new quarters on Fatherland Street, which seats several thousand people. He was among the very first on the program, which started in the fall of 1925. As a matter of fact, he played on the station before the barn dance started, along about the first of December, 1925.

His sterling character was appreciated by all who knew him, and especially the boys and girls who were associated with him on the program. He greeted everybody with a slap on the back, a smile, and some new story he had picked up around the country. He was beloved as a husband and father and a friend.

At his funeral services in the front yard outside his home at Castalian Springs hundreds of his neighbors gathered to pay tribute to the man who held service above self. To his widow, Mrs. Bate; his daughter, Mrs. Alcyone Bate Beasley; and his son, Buster, we extend our heartfelt sympathy. A fine man has passed beyond our ken, and with him goes our love and affection.

Uncle Jimmy Thompson

THE NEXT CHAPTER OF GRAND OLE OPRY legendry begins in the green rolling hills of Middle Tennessee, only a few miles west of Dr. Bate's Castalian Springs. There, on modern state Highway 109, about halfway between Lebanon and Gallatin, lies the sleepy village of Laguardo. Today it is a resort area, adjoining the popular Old Hickory Lake, and is full of access ramps, boat docks, and bait stores. The old community of Laguardo, though, is up on a hill overlooking the new highway and consists of a number of small frame houses and old sheds surrounding an old cemetery. Some of the senior residents can remember what it was like there in the 1920s, when the village could boast a population of one hundred, and when Old Hickory Lake was still the Cumberland River. It was a major trip to Nashville—forty miles—for those who wanted to go. Most pilgrims went south to the venerable US 70, Tennessee's main east-west route, and on into Nashville.

Back in 1925, one of the residents of Laguardo who did want to make the trip was a stately, white-bearded gentleman who drove the road in an old Ford truck with a little wooden house built onto the bed and who played the fiddle. His name was James Donald Thompson—most of his friends called him "Uncle Jimmy"—and for a few years in the mid-1920s he put Laguardo on the map. He also put WSM radio on the map, doing something he had been doing since the Civil War: playing old fiddle tunes. It was his appearance at the station on one cold November evening that so dramatized to listeners and station management the rich potential for old-time music on the new-time medium of radio.

The ultimate source for Uncle Jimmy's dramatic debut is George D. Hay himself, who between 1945 and 1953 wrote three versions of a book he called *A Story of the Grand Ole Opry*. His discussion of Uncle Jimmy is consistent in all three. As the keystone to "official" Opry history—and as an account that has been promulgated in countless press releases, magazine articles, and books—it deserves reprinting here as a starting point for examining the fiddler's life and career.

In his first edition of *A Story of the Grand Ole Opry,* Hay writes:

> Realizing the wealth of music material and performers in the Tennessee Hills, he [Hay himself] welcomed the appearance of Uncle Jimmy Thompson and his blue ribbon fiddle who went on the air at eight o'clock, Saturday night, November 28, 1925. Uncle Jimmy told us that he had a thousand tunes. Past eighty years of age, he was given a comfortable chair in front of an old carbon microphone. While his niece, Mrs. Eva Thompson Jones, played the piano accompaniment your reporter presented Uncle Jimmy and announced that he would be glad to answer requests for old-time tunes. Immediately telegrams started to pour into WSM.
>
> One hour later at nine o'clock we asked Uncle Jimmy if he hadn't done enough fiddling, to which he replied, "Why shucks, a man don't get warmed up in an hour. I just won an eight-day fiddling contest down at Dallas, Texas, and here's my blue ribbon to prove it." Uncle Jimmy Thompson, Mrs. Jones, and The Solemn Old Judge carried on for several weeks for an hour each Saturday night. Telegrams poured into the station.

In a later account written for his paper *Pickin' and Singin' News,* Hay added a few details to this account. When Uncle Jimmy first sat down, he announced over the air, "Tell the neighbors to send in their requests and I'll play 'em if it takes me all night!" Hay continued: "He was ready, willing, and able, but the telegrams came in so fast by the hundreds that we would have been there yet, if what little business judgement I had at the time didn't tell me to stop him one hour later [i.e., after two hours] when he was cutting wood by the cord on that old fiddle."

The first thing that is noteworthy about Hay's memories is how accurate they really are. Hay missed Uncle Jimmy's age by a few years (he was actually only seventy-seven), but most of the other details have been confirmed—even the eight-day fiddle contest in Texas. The November 28 date is confirmed by newspaper listings, as is the reference to the three participants "carrying on" by themselves for "several weeks." The very next Saturday, December 5, Uncle Jimmy played again, this time sharing his program with three WSM canaries named Faith, Hope, and Charity.

Letters continued to arrive, and some from surprising distances. One came in from Marble, Arkansas, shortly after the December 5 show:

> We live away back in the rustic regions and rural districts of the Ozark mountains, surrounded by the most wonderful landscape of beautiful scenery and pebbly brooks with their green and mossy banks. . . . We have the only radio in town, and as a matter of course we have plenty of company during the fall and winter evenings, which we most assuredly appreciate. We enjoyed your radio program Saturday evening, Dec. 5, immensely, which came in fine. Because both my son and I are fiddlers and consider Uncle Jimmy Thompson an exceptional fiddler. Because our canary bird (Bobbie), whose cage was hanging just above the speaker, heard the canaries Faith, Hope, and Charity singing and joined in on the chorus . . . which pleased the many children who were visiting us.

Equally fascinating was a letter from a listener in Pembroke, Ontario, Canada, marveling at how clear the WSM signal came through that same Saturday night. Other letters suggest that the crisp, clean, uncluttered air of late fall was carrying the WSM signal far beyond what its owners had envisioned. Was part of Uncle Jimmy's success in the timing, in the fact that he began performing during a time when the atmosphere was especially conducive to radio signals?

The next Saturday night, Uncle Jimmy did not appear. WDAD staged an over-the-air contest that evening, and he might have been involved in that. The WSM schedule that night featured Francis Craig and His Orchestra, a dance band, broadcasting live from the Hermitage Hotel; a "story hour"; and at 10:00 a concert by the gospel singing Golden Echo Quartet. On the day after Christmas, Uncle Jimmy, his niece, and Judge Hay appeared again, following a program by Craig. At 8:00 the schedule announced: "Uncle Jimmy Thompson, the South's champion barn dance fiddler, and Eva Thompson Jones, contralto, will present program of old-fashioned tunes." Here the program is allotted a two hour time slot, and we get a hint that Eva Thompson Jones was doing more than playing piano backup. She is billed as a "contralto," suggesting that she also sang. (In later years, her music studio stationery announced that she gave voice lessons.)

It was the Sunday after this show—December 27—that the *Tennessean* printed the announcement that the Saturday night affair would become a regular feature. Hay's press release bears examination:

WSM TO FEATURE OLD-TIME TUNES
"Uncles" Dave Macon and Jimmie Thompson Will Play

Old tunes like old lovers are the best, at least judging from the applause which the new Saturday night feature at Station WSM receives from its listeners in all parts of the country. Jazz has not completely turned the tables on such tunes as "Pop Goes the Weasel" and "Turkey in the Straw."

America may not be swinging its partners at a neighbors barn dance but it seems to have the habit of clamping on its ear phones and patting its feet as gaily as it ever did when old-time fiddlers got to going.

Because of this recent revival in the popularity of the old familiar tunes, WSM has arranged to have an hour or two of them every Saturday night, starting Saturday, December 26. "Uncle" Dave Macon, the oldest banjo picker in Dixie, and who comes from Readyville, Tenn., and "Uncle" Jimmie Thompson of Martha, Tenn., will answer any requests for old-time melodies.

Uncle Jimmy Thompson has been fiddlin' for more than 60 years, and the people of the South recently nominated him by almost a unanimous vote taken in Texas, as the greatest barn dance fiddler of his time. Uncle Jimmy is 82 years old, and he says by the time he is 90 he will be a young man. Not only does he play 375 different numbers, but he dances each one of 'em while he plays. He is one of the most attractive features on the program of WSM.

Uncle Jimmy made his first appearance a month ago and telegrams were received from all parts of the United States, encouraging him in his task of furnishing barn dance music for a million homes. He puts his heart and soul into his work and is one of the quaintest characters radio has yet discovered. There is a twinkle in his eye, which is, of course, not an unusual characteristic in view of the fact that there are a number of people in this world with twinkles in their eyes, but Uncle Jimmy's twinkles mean that he is happy and making everybody else happy. He is usually accompanied by his niece, whom he refers to constantly as "Sweetmeats."

Uncle Jimmy is old-fashioned and is proud of it. For that reason, when he had his picture taken with his niece, he insisted that she let her hair down. "I don't like these new fangled styles women wear," says Uncle Jimmy. He has been a farmer for many years in Tennessee, his home being near Martha in Wilson county. He was crowned America's champion barn dance fiddler in a contest which lasted eight days in Dallas, Tex., a few years ago. He had 86 opponents. Although Uncle Jimmy is a farmer with simple tastes, he has traveled all over the United States with his fiddle.

By this time, WSM had commissioned a series of photos of their new star, including the one mentioned here, a haunting pre-Raphaelite pose with Eva sitting on the arm of a chair while her uncle, fiddle in hand, gazes up at her. Another shot showed Judge Hay standing in front of the WSM microphone, script in hand, while Uncle Jimmy sat in his "comfortable chair" holding his fiddle. Soon these shots were being sent out to newspapers around the South—a powerful visual component of the legend. Also, by this time the number of tunes the fiddler knew had dropped from the unrealistic one thousand to a more believable "375 different numbers" (a phrase which did not necessarily imply that all were fiddle tunes).

Thus the core myth of the Grand Ole Opry. Without doubt, Uncle Jimmy was one of the first traditional musicians grounded in the pre–mass-media days of the nineteenth century to take his art into the modern age, on radio and records. (Uncle Dave Macon, his partner on the initial Barn Dance show, was another.) Thompson was also one of the first to gain nationwide fame: within a few months his reputation grew from locally known contest winner and square dance fiddler to master musician whose merits were debated as far away as Boston and Canada. Yet the myth of him is curiously one-dimensional and strangely circumscribed. The press was suddenly full of him for a few months, and then his mention drops off, almost as if he did not exist prior to November 1925 nor after March 26, 1926. But he obviously did and in his own mind probably saw the Barn Dance as only a part of a full and long life that moved from the Civil War to the Texas frontier. There was indeed a man behind the myth, and in some ways his story was more fascinating that anything the WSM publicists could dream up.

Decades after Uncle Jimmy's heyday, there are still people in Middle Tennessee who remember him vividly. Champion fiddler Frazier Moss actually competed in a fiddle contest with him in the late 1920s. Frazier was only ten and somewhat angered Uncle Jimmy by playing a gospel song in the contest: "You shouldn't play religious songs on the fiddle," he told Moss. Then he sat down with the boy on the curb at the old courthouse in Carthage and taught him to play "Grey Eagle"—a tune which remained in Frazier's repertoire. Johnnie Wright, part of the Grand Ole Opry team of Johnnie and Jack, and husband of Kitty Wells, grew up around Mt. Juliet, just south of Laguardo. As a child, he would join family and friends listening to WSM on a community radio at Benton Lowe's general store. "We'd lie there on those feed sacks and listened 'til the music stopped," he recalled. When Uncle Jimmy became a regular on the radio, he often would stop in at the store on his way into Nashville and give impromptu concerts. "Uncle Jimmy fiddled for all he was worth," he remembered, often as local people buck danced. Around Laguardo, many long-time residents still remember Uncle Jimmy, not only as a famous person but as a local character. They heard him tell jokes, shared a jug with him, worked beside him, and even sat on his lap. To them he is very much a real person: an independent, self-reliant, outspoken, hard-living, rough-talking nineteenth century man of the land.

Uncle Jimmy was born James Donald Thompson in 1848 near Baxter, in Putnam County, a few miles west of Cookeville, on the edge of the Cumberland Plateau, and about halfway between Nashville and Knoxville. He had at least two brothers, neither musically gifted. However, one of them, Lee, who eventually settled around Cookeville, fathered Eva Thompson Jones, Uncle Jimmy's well-known niece who played behind him on WSM. Little is known about the history of the Thompson family itself, though the line probably sprang from Scots-Irish origins.

When he was a boy, Uncle Jimmy's people moved to Texas, shortly before the Civil War. The family must have been fond of the plains, for both of Uncle Jimmy's brothers stayed there after the war, and Uncle Jimmy himself returned there several times. Jimmy was too young to serve in the Civil War, but by the time he was twelve, in 1860, he had begun mastering fiddle tunes like "Flying Clouds," a piece that would remain one of his favorites. The young man continued to learn tunes, some from men who had fought in the Civil War, others from fiddlers whose repertoires might well have stretched back to Revolutionary America. Uncle Jimmy recalled later that on August 4, 1866, he learned a "fine quadrille," the old minstrel-show number "Lynchburg" (also known as "Lynchburg Town").

Though he primarily farmed for a living, young Jimmy traveled widely and eventually returned to his native Putnam County, Tennessee. There, in the 1880s, he married Mahalia Elizabeth Montgomery of Smith County. The union resulted in two sons and two daughters: Jess (born 1886), Willie

Lee (born 1896), Sally (who eventually married and moved to Montana), and Fanny, who died in infancy. About 1902 Uncle Jimmy took his family back to Texas and settled around the Bonham area, northeast of Dallas and close to the Oklahoma line. He continued to farm but was beginning to play his fiddle more and more in public.

In 1907 Uncle Jimmy participated in the famous eight-day marathon contest he so vividly described to Judge Hay the night of his first broadcast. The contest was held in Dallas, and Uncle Jimmy won "the nation's championship in his class against nearly 100 contestants" (*Tennessean*, June 13, 1925; the actual figure given by Uncle Jimmy later was eighty-six). Information is lacking about who was in this contest, but the fact that Jimmy won indicates that he had absorbed a good deal of the Texas "long bow" style during his various stays there. His style, which has been described as "fancy," is in distinct contrast to the older, heavier styles of traditional Southeastern fiddlers, like Fiddlin' John Carson or Gid Tanner. It has much more in common with the Southwestern stylings of Eck Robertson.

By 1912, Uncle Jimmy was sixty-four, and most of his children had grown. His wife was dying of cancer, and perhaps she wanted to be back in her native state before she died. They once again returned to Tennessee and bought a farm near Hendersonville, north and east of Nashville. Soon after they returned, Mrs. Thompson did indeed pass and was buried in Smith County. By this time Eva Thompson, Uncle Jimmy's niece, was starting to teach music in rural Tennessee schools. As a young girl, Eva became, quite naturally, enamored of classical music and of Victorian parlor music considered semi-classical. She liked to accompany her father into Nashville so she could watch the touring shows playing the Nashville theaters while her father did business at the stockyards. Later she studied at Ward-Belmont College, then as now a widely respected center of musical study, and later recalled going by horse and buggy to give music lessons. In 1915 Eva was teaching in Sumner County and was indirectly responsible for introducing Uncle Jimmy to his future daughter-in-law, Katherine Womack.

Many years later, Katherine could still vividly remember the night she met him and, subsequently, Willie Lee Thompson, her future husband:

> It was at a school entertainment up here at [the town of] Number One in Sumner County—that's the way I met my husband. Eva was teaching music there, and she knew I played a banjo, so they sent home and got my banjo, and he come down to play for us, Uncle Jimmy did, and I played with him. And he was just tickled

to death to find a woman playing a banjo. So we really had a big time down there at the school. He went home and told his son about it, and that's how I met my husband.

After Willie Lee, Jimmy's youngest child, and Katherine were married, both played with Uncle Jimmy in public. Willie Lee played guitar, Katherine banjo; on one or two later occasions they joined their father on the radio. Uncle Jimmy was especially fond of Katherine and liked to listen to her sing and play the banjo on some of his favorite numbers like "Red Wing," "The Preacher and the Bear," and "Rainbow."

About 1916, when he was sixty-eight years old, Uncle Jimmy decided to remarry. He chose Ella Manners, from nearby Wilson County, Tennessee, an older woman who soon became known as Aunt Ella. After living for a time at Martha, the pair moved down to Wilson County, near Laguardo, and bought a house formerly occupied by an old physician. Both he and Aunt Ella were to live at Laguardo for the rest of their lives and to become local legends in their own right. From all accounts Aunt Ella was just as high-spirited as Uncle Jimmy. She loved to buck dance, and she loved her dram of white lightning as much as her husband. Neighbors in Laguardo recall often visiting the pair and watching Aunt Ella buck dance in a long white dress while Uncle Jimmy played the fiddle. Occasionally Ella and Jimmy would travel around the Middle Tennessee area playing for fairs and outings—pulling up in their truck, unrolling a special rug for Ella to dance on, and performing an impromptu show. They would then pass the hat and collect quarters and dollars from the audience. One neighbor recalls a fiddling session at Uncle Jimmy's house when both Uncle Jimmy and Aunt Ella had a little too much bootleg. "Aunt Ella finally fell flat on her face, and Uncle Jimmy, fiddling all the time, glanced down at her and remarked, 'Watch it now, Ella, you done gone and spoiled it thar.'" Another neighbor tells stories about Uncle Jimmy and Aunt Ella chasing each other around their old house, each with a loaded gun, firing playfully into the air.

Like many musicians in this pre–mass-media age, Uncle Jimmy spent part of his time traveling around the countryside "busking" on courthouse lawns and putting on his own little private shows. It seems obvious that he enjoyed at least a regional reputation as a fiddler before his radio days, and some friends think that he traveled quite widely from 1916 to 1925, both with Eva Thompson Jones and Aunt Ella. Former neighbor Jim Thompson (no relation) recalled that Uncle Jimmy began performing for a living when he got too old to farm.

Before he played on the Opry, he was mainly a farmer, till his age got the best of him. And while he was a farmer he had fiddled, so he just quit trying to work on account of his age and went to playin' the fiddle. And he'd get right smart o' donations when he'd go around to these different places playing. That's how they lived. They'd put on these little shows.

Uncle Jimmy had a rather distinctive means of transportation for getting around to those shows. He had taken a one-ton Model T Ford truck and built a little house on the back. It was a rough prototype of the modern camper—and this was sometime about 1922. It caused quite a stir in those days. Katherine recalled: "He had furnished it. . . . Had a floor-covering in there of matting, and had the inside all fixed up and had a cot in there. Had a water bucket, a dipper, washpan, towel, even a little wood store, so he could spend the night traveling if he wanted."

He wanted. On one occasion in the fall of 1923, he took off for Texas, on a trip that took him a month. He later told a *Tennessean* reporter: "When I got tired, I'd jest drive it in the first open place I found by the road and ask if I could stay all night. 'Yep,' they'd say, and I'd drive it in, fix my bed, and get out my fiddle." He was very proud of the little truck, and all of his friends had their favorite stories about the way he cared for it. Grandson Fred Thompson remembered that Uncle Jimmy always wiped the truck off with motor oil and refused to let anybody touch the truck body. "He was afraid that the salt in your hand, the sweat, would rust it. 'Don't touch that, boy!' he'd say, and he made 'em back up—he had a big old walking cane."

That Dallas contest in 1923 seemed to have been a turning point for the fiddler's career. He won the contest and its prize of a gold watch engraved on the back. He also won a taste for wider fame. "When he got back," said Katherine Thompson, "that contest was all he would talk about. He was keyed up to try to do something about his music. He felt like he had something and he wanted the world to know about it."

By coincidence, that same year, 1923, saw the release of the first Southern-made fiddling records, by Georgia's Fiddlin' John Carson (for Okeh) and by Eck Robertson, who had come to his recording sessions directly from the Texas contest that Uncle Jimmy had won. It was a time that also marked the start of old-time music on radio stations like Atlanta's WSB. The next year saw an old-time music boom in both media, radio and records, and Uncle Jimmy watched it with increasing interest and anticipation. His daughter-in-law remembered:

When the record market got so big and people got so interested in making records and radio and all, it really made him more anxious. He would just sit and daydream all the time after he had heard radio and records—why, he thought it would be wonderful to make records of his music, or to play it on the air. "I want to throw my music out all over the Americee," he used to say. (He wouldn't say "America," but "the Americee.") He really wanted to record and to go on the air. He wanted to get his music "caught," was the way he said it.

Recording fever finally got the best of Uncle Jimmy and in the summer or early fall of 1925 he decided to take matters into his own hands. He had learned of a little shop on Church Street in downtown Nashville that would make custom disc recordings for a fee. Most of the business was derived from doting parents who wanted to preserve their baby's early speech or a grandfather's words of advice. But those machines could, in theory, record music as well, and off he went, taking Katherine with him to play backup.

Somebody had a little recording outfit up there, and they were going to make him a little record for, I don't know, a dollar or so. He wanted to have some records made real bad. He was supposed to pay for these, and that's what embarrassed me so. We got in there and made this record; I think it was "Flying Clouds" with me playin' the banjo back of him. And this man played it back to him and it made Uncle Jimmy mad. He said, "Why, hell, thar, that don't sound like my fiddle. That don't sound a bit like me a-playin' my fiddle. There's just something wrong with your machine, or you don't understand catchin' it, one!" I felt like going through the floor, and that man, he didn't know what to say. He tried to be nice, said Uncle Jimmy could take the record for half price. But Uncle Jimmy said, "Why, I ain't a-gonna give you no half dollar. I ain't a-payin' you nothin' for that. You can just break that un right now!" Out he stormed. He put his fiddle in his case and wouldn't make no more records. And it was a little aluminum record, about the size of a saucer, and it didn't have much volume to it, and it did sound tinny. That started him, though; he was wantin' to get his music caught so it could be thronged out across the Americee. So it wasn't long after that that Eva took him up to the broadcasting station.

There are differing legends about how Uncle Jimmy actually got to the WSM studios for the first time. We have already seen the "official" account penned by Judge Hay. Relatives have somewhat different accounts. According to relatives of Aunt Ella, it all started when a member of the Manners family first took Uncle Jimmy up to WSM so he could simply tour the station and see how it worked. While there, someone mentioned that Uncle Jimmy was a fiddler, and he was asked to play a little. Unknown to Uncle Jimmy, the engineers turned on the transmitter and broadcast his playing. A similar version is given in the 1969 official Opry picture and history book, where it is alleged that Uncle Jimmy came up to tour the station on a Thursday night. His guide happened to be the Program Manager (George Hay) and when Uncle Jimmy mentioned his fiddling, Hay asked him to return the next night (Friday) to broadcast.

According to Eva Thompson Jones, however, the event occurred with less serendipity. Eva had been performing on WSM as singer of light classical music and as pianist. She later told historian Don Cummings that Hay had not been satisfied with the direction of the station's shows and asked her for suggestions. She suggested her uncle and invited Hay to meet him for an informal audition at her Nashville home on Friday night, November 27. Hay did, was impressed, and invited Uncle Jimmy to appear the next night. Katherine Thompson, for the record, agreed that it was Eva who actually got Uncle Jimmy on the show. Whatever the case, he did broadcast on Saturday, November 28. His first tune was supposedly "Tennessee Waggoner," and it was carried across the country by the 1,000-watt transmitter. Within the hour, Percy Craig entered the studio with an armful of telegrams and announced that they had heard from every single state in the union.

Almost at once, the local newspapers became fascinated with Uncle Jimmy and his colorful life and throughout January and February 1926 constantly published stories about him, including photographs. But the most astounding aspect of it all was just how fast radio made him famous. Within a month of his first broadcast, he was known "across the Americee." This became obvious when, during the first days of January, he received a challenge from fiddler Mellie Dunham of Maine. Dunham had recently been crowned World's Champion Fiddler by Henry Ford and was attaining widespread popularity in the North, owing to Ford's campaign to resurrect old-time fiddling through a series of contests. Dunham had become a favorite of Ford's and had even played at his house. On January 2, 1926, a Boston newspaper carried an article on Dunham, in which the Northern fiddler supposedly issued a challenge to his Southern rival, Uncle

Jimmy. "He may have defeated 86 opponents in the Dallas contest," Dunham said, "but they were all southerners and they don't know as much about barn dance fiddling in that section as they do 'down in Maine.'" Dunham—or somebody using his name—then sent a telegram to Thompson at WSM asking for a showdown. Without consulting Uncle Jimmy, Judge Hay quickly fired back an acceptance, suggesting the contest take place over WSM "any Saturday night in the near future." When he heard about it, Uncle Jimmy did rise to the occasion. "If Mellie Dunham will come down here to this WSM station, I'll lay with him like a bulldog."

This contest never happened and may have been nothing more than a publicity stunt to start with. But other contests did, and through 1926 Uncle Jimmy was a familiar figure at them. Some of them were older, established community contests, but many were part of the old-time fiddling craze that swept the nation, spurred on by the enthusiasm of Henry Ford. During the second week of January the Ford dealers in Tennessee, Kentucky, and Indiana sponsored a series of local fiddling competitions. Although the apparent main purpose was to foster fiddling, the marketing strategy was to draw people into the Ford showrooms to look at the new Model Ts (and hear about plans for the newer Model A). This free publicity and advertising worked well. Several Tennessee contests averaged between one and two thousand in attendance—in the dead of winter. The winners of these local contests did not win much cash, but they advanced to the regional contest. The State of Tennessee contest was held in Nashville, and from there six winners would go on to compete in the "Champion of Dixie" contest in Louisville. Winners there would go to meet Mr. Ford himself.

Uncle Jimmy won the local contest (held at nearby Lebanon) with ease and participated in the regional contest at Nashville. Because of the Mellie Dunham incident, enthusiasm was running high; "On to Detroit!" became the battle cry of the contest. According to contemporary newspaper accounts, the twenty-five winners who played in Nashville on January 19–20, 1926, had collectively played to between 30,000 and 35,000 people in eliminations. According to newspaper accounts of contest day, "groups from various sections of the whole hill country of Tennessee came to the city . . . to boost their respective contestants." "Coming from some localities in groups of 200 or more, the clans of the hills of Middle Tennessee swarmed into the city. . . ." Ironically, the state finals were held at the Ryman Auditorium, whose 3,600 seats were soon filled to overflowing. Though some reporters noted that the crowd was "boisterous" and "bore earmarks of rurality," they were impressed. A Reverend Roberts, who opened the contest with a short talk, declared that "the real significance of the meeting lay in the fact that this section, by this contest, was paying tributes to the homes of the pioneers, where such music abounded long ago." Undoubtedly some of the reporters and participating civic leaders like Reverend Roberts were caught up in Henry Ford's romanticized notion of what American fiddling meant. Once the fiddling craze died down, many Nashville citizens were quick enough to repudiate this same heritage as it manifested itself on the Barn Dance. But in general, Ford and the South agreed in their love for fiddling, though probably for different reasons. Ford saw fiddling as a dying tradition to be resurrected; most Southerners saw it as a vibrant and living tradition to be developed, celebrated, and spread across the land.

Uncle Jimmy's competition included a number of bowmen who would later appear on the Barn Dance: Lynchburg's Uncle Bunt Stephens, Kittrell's Mazy Todd, Lewisburg's W. E. Poplin, and Hartsville's Marshall Claiborne. But Uncle Jimmy was a winner, playing "Fisher's Hornpipe" and "The Mocking Bird." Claiborne placed second, and Stephens third. All three journeyed the next weekend to Louisville for the tri-state championship. Their competition there included "Blind Joe" Mangrum of Paducah, Kentucky, a fiddler who was later to play often on the Opry. But to the disappointment of Tennesseans the first place was won by an Indiana fiddler, W. H. Elmore; Bunt Stephens won second, and Marshall Claiborne third. To everyone's surprise Uncle Jimmy did not place. A Thompson family story, which family members are unsure about accepting, holds that certain parties knew about Uncle Jimmy's love of moonshine and plied him with drink just before the contest. Supposedly, when his time came to play, he was barely able to make it onto the stage. Uncle Jimmy some years later tried to visit Henry Ford in Detroit, perhaps wishing to redeem himself, but was unable to get an appointment.

The Louisville debacle hardly slowed the Thompson career, though. He continued to headline the Barn Dance program almost weekly throughout 1926. He and Eva usually started the program at 8:00 P.M. for an hour, though on occasion he was scheduled for as much as two hours. In April he was selected by Tennessee Governor Austin Peay to represent Tennessee in a radio fiddling contest staged at station WOS, Jefferson City, Missouri, which had challenged fiddlers from all states bordering on Missouri. Since the contest was judged by the "amount of applause in messages" received at the station, Missouri fiddlers obviously had the edge and won the competition. A broken arm took Uncle Jimmy out of the scene in May 1926, but he was back on the air on July 3—a remarkable recovery time for a man his age. And in November, he finally got his wish to make records. Judge Hay set up a session with the Columbia Phonograph Company, and Uncle Jimmy and Eva took the train to Atlanta. There, on November 1, he cut four sides: "Mississippi Sawyer," "High Born Lady," "Karo," and "Billy Wilson." Only the latter two were actually released by the company (Columbia 15118) on January 20, 1927. The record only managed to sell slightly over 9,000 copies—though the artist, like most old-time performers, probably had to settle for a flat fee of $25 or $50 a side. But the sales were not impressive relative to other old-time records that were selling eight or nine times that many. This presents something of a puzzle. Other early stars (like Bradley Kincaid or Uncle Dave Macon) saw their record sales shoot up as they appeared regularly on radio. In spite of Uncle Jimmy's radio fame, his did not. It was no surprise that Columbia did not release the other two sides or that they did not call Uncle Jimmy to come back for further recordings.

After 1926, Uncle Jimmy's career on the Opry was effectively over. We can document only four appearances in 1927 (most in February) and only one in 1928 (the anniversary show). When the cast of the show began to grow substantially, Uncle Jimmy's time allotment was cut back. As early as the fall of 1926 he was playing for only a half-hour at a time, as opposed to his marathon two-hour stints of barely a year before. Since recordings he made in 1930 show him still to be an excellent fiddler, questions about his departure naturally arise.

A number of reasons suggest themselves. One might be simply age: he was seventy-seven when he first played on WSM, and shortly after that he had a stroke that left him blind in one eye. It certainly became more difficult for him to get around, and the forty-mile trip from Laguardo to Nashville was not an easy one in those days. But a more basic problem was that the Opry was becoming much more formal and structured, and Uncle Jimmy was more attuned to the leisurely nineteenth century manner of performing, rather than to the precise, clock-watching style of radio broadcasts. Laguardo resident Bert Norther recalled one significant night toward the end of Uncle Jimmy's broadcasting career:

> I remember one night when Bill Bates, had the store here, we went down there one Saturday night to listen to Uncle Jimmy on the radio. Bill Bates called down there and told George Hay to get Jimmy to play "When You and I Were Young, Maggie." He cut loose on it and he never did quit. Finally they had to stop him, got him out of the way. He'd just had one drink too many.

And the drinking itself was another problem, albeit one that would plague the Opry for generations of performers to come. A free spirit like Uncle Jimmy associated fiddling with drinking, dancing, and having a good time. It seemed perfectly normal to him to take along a bottle when he played on the radio. Neighbor Sam Kirkpatrick remembered:

> I'll never forget the last night Uncle Jimmy played. He kinda liked his bottle pretty well. He was playin', and before he finished his piece there was this stopping, and we didn't hear nothing for a minute. Then George Hay come on and said Uncle Jimmy was sick tonight or something. Come to find out later he had just keeled over and passed out.

Such drinking on the air soon caused bad blood between WSM and Uncle Jimmy and was probably the most immediate reason why he stopped broadcasting. "They would have to watch him," recalled neighbor Jim Thompson. "In fact they told him they didn't want him to come down there drinking. His business down there just finally played out on that account."

After he left the Opry, he continued to tour a little, farm a little, and play for his friends. Touring was more lucrative than playing the Opry anyway. Katherine Thompson recalled that WSM originally paid Uncle Jimmy $5 a show for fiddling, and he could make four times that amount by passing the hat at local fairs. He was still able to do some farming; even in his eighties he was strong enough to carry a bushel of corn on his back to a mill several miles away.

In April 1930 he went to Knoxville to record again, this time for Brunswick-Vocalion, who had set up a temporary studio in a local hotel. He did "Lynchburg" and a medley of "Flying Clouds" and "Leather Britches" and recorded some revealing dialogue with recording supervisor Bill Brown.

Brown: How old are you, Uncle Jimmy?

UJT: 82—and I've got grown grandchildren, and great big great-grandchildren; runnin' cars and trucks yet, and a-playin' the fiddle yet. And I love to look at a pretty woman just as much as I ever did.

Brown: Say, Uncle Jimmy, were the girls as pretty back in 1866 as they are now?

UJT: They prettier—they healthier. Stout. Fat, and plump.

Brown: What kind of clothes did they wear?

UJT: They just wore nice, good clothes—plenty width in the skirts, and they was long enough to come down to the shoes. ("Lynchburg" /Vocalion 5456)

Brown: That "Flying Clouds" is as peppy as a drink of good whiskey, isn't it?

UJT: Yes, it's all right. All it lacks is a good set to dance after it.

Brown: Uncle Jimmy, did you use to get good whiskey when you were a young man?

UJT: Sure, get good whiskey, fine as could be. It was whiskey that jest made you love everybody. Make a fellow love his poor old grand-mother.

Brown: What'd you have to pay for it?

UJT: Twenty-five cents a gallon. Right to the still and get it. Go to the stillhouse, didn't have very far to go. It made you love everybody instead of wanting to fight.

Brown: Say, I've got a fellow here` that plays guitar. Want you to listen to him, see what you think of him.

Guitar solo.

UJT: Well, a guitar's pretty, but they ain't near as pretty as a violin. They're the finest musical we've got in America. . . . I call fiddle, some call 'em violins, but fiddle just as good as violin, people know what they mean. ("Uncle Jimmy's Favorite Fiddle Pieces," Vocalion 5456)

With such dialogue, the Vocalion records almost seemed designed as miniature radio shows. They would likely have sold well, but by the time they were issued the Depression was in full force, and few of them got out. (Sears & Roebuck, though, later reissued the sides on their Hilltop LP label.) And though he was no longer making headlines in the local papers, he was creating new legends of his own. Friends told about how he got into an old buckboard and raced into town full speed, scattering anybody in his way; about how he would chew a whole package of gum at a time, and then save it in a vasoline jar he kept in his pocket—reminding people that he had "biled" the jar out before using it; about how he would tell where and how he learned each fiddle tune he played; and about how he got mad at his niece Eva when she had his pants pressed before one of his Opry shows: "Hey, thar," he shouted. "Who owned them damned wrinkles in these britches? I like my britches smooth and round. Fits my kneecap."

His own history was bound up with his fiddle, "Old Betsy." It was probably made in Scotland, and he cherished it greatly. "He kept rattlesnake rattles in it," said Katherine Thompson, "and in his case a piece of red flannel. And he'd spread it over Old Betsy's breast every night—he'd 'put her to bed,' he'd call it."

Less than ten months after he recorded in Knoxville, Uncle Jimmy was dead. He died of pneumonia at his home in Laguardo, about 3:00 P.M. on Tuesday, February 17, 1931. Even his death is shrouded in legend. At least five different versions of how he died compete for belief: some stories hold that he passed out one night and froze to death; others say he caught pneumonia trying to repair his car in a snowstorm. The Thompson family says that he caught pneumonia one night when his house caught fire. Dressed only in his long underwear, Uncle Jimmy managed to put out the fire by drawing buckets of water from his well, but while doing so soaked his long johns. The underwear froze on him, and he fell ill the next day. The newspaper account from Nashville (see illustrations) mentions only that he had been sick since Sunday. The day of his funeral was cold and icy, and Eva Thompson Jones was the only member of the Opry to attend.

Uncle Jimmy's Repertoire

The list reproduced below was drawn up by Eva Thompson Jones and purports to list what are presumably the favorite "old fashion" tunes of her uncle. The date on the list is uncertain. A copy of it is on file in the Country Music Foundation archives, Nashville. The list contains seventy-six songs, but one might question how accurately they reflect Uncle Jimmy's repertoire. Most of them are popular songs from the 1890s commonly found in songbooks of that era. Missing are many of the fiddle breakdowns we know Uncle Jimmy loved to play; for instance, the list includes only two of his seven recorded tunes, "Flying Clouds" and "Leather Britches." Also missing are tunes like "Nubbin Ridge" and "Old Hen Cackle," with which he won a 1926 Clarksville, Tennessee, contest. Although of historical interest, the list is clearly less than definitive. Eva once reportedly said that many of the old fiddle breakdowns sounded alike to her, and while Uncle Jimmy undoubtedly played these listed tunes, they were probably more Eva's favorites than his.

Eva Thompson Jones Studio

School of Music Dancing and Allied Arts
123 Fifth Avenue, North
Nashville 3, Tennessee

Old Fashion Tunes
Jimmie Lind Polka
Virginia Reel
Kiss Waltz
Oh Susanna
Mocking Bird
Mountain Belle Schottish
Haste to the Wedding Jig
Rueben Rueben
The Girl I Left Behind
Leather Britches
McLeods Reel
Rosy O'More Jig
Sally Goodwin
Yankee Doodle
Home Sweet Home
Turkey in the Straw
Skip to My Lou
Liza Jane
Moonlight & Roses
Red Wing
The Yellow Rose of Texas
Maudy Lee
Ida Sweet As Apple Cider
Dear Old Girl
Good-bye My Darling Good-bye
Camptown Races
The Band Played On
Beautiful Blue Danube
Big Rock Candy Mountain
Hot Time in the Old Town Tonight
Merry Widow Waltz
When You and I Were Young, Maggie
Put On Your Old Grey Bonnet
Jeannie with Her Light Brown Hair

Clog Dance
Birmingham Jail
Wagner
Pop Goes the Weasel
Sally in Our Alley
Arkansas Traveller
Irish Washerwoman
Paddy Wack
Irish Jig
Sailors Hornpipe
Old Zip Coon
Devils Dream
Fisher Horn Pipe
The Last Rose of Summer
Darling Nellie Gray
Strauss Waltz
Dixie
Bicycle Built for Two
Maggie
Buffalo Gals
I Wish I Was Single Again
Annie Laurie
In the Shade of an Old Apple Tree
Down by the River Side
My Gal Sal
Fascination
Bill Bailey
After the Ball
Little Brown Jug
Oh Dem Golden Slippers
Beautiful Dreamer
Beautiful Heaven
Home on the Range
Two Little Girls in Blue
Old Grey Mare
Silver Threads
Flying Clouds
Old Dan Tucker
Over the Waves

"Sail Away, Ladies!"
Classic Opry Fiddlers

INE FIDDLING HAS ALWAYS BEEN a hallmark of the Opry, from the very first night that Uncle Jimmy Thompson played. As we have seen, the show's earliest days were forged during the mid-1920s craze for old-time fiddling contests, and certainly the program's initial popularity owed much to Henry Ford's efforts to promote old-time fiddling. During the 1930s, the Opry became home to the three most influential radio fiddlers of that decade, Arthur Smith, Clayton McMichen, and Curly Fox. The various hoedown bands, with their driving dance music, spotlighted men like George Wilkerson (the Fruit Jar Drinkers), Gale Binkley (the Dixie Clodhoppers), Charlie Arrington (the Gully Jumpers), Floyd Ethridge (the Crook Brothers), Oscar Stone and Bill Barret (the Possum Hunters), Theron Hale, Ed Poplin, and Mazy Todd. The last, best known for his recordings with Uncle Dave Macon and the McGee Brothers, occasionally led his own string band on the show as well. These fiddlers spread hundreds of tunes and a variety of styles across the country, even though they did not always receive on-air credit for their work.

In addition, though, the Opry in its first five years also boasted of an interesting cadre of virtuoso fiddlers who seldom played in bands, who often performed solo or with one accompanist, and whose music was not designed for dancing or for a vocalist's backup. Theirs was a fancy show-off music, music designed to display fiddle techniques and effects. It was the kind of performance that won contests, delighted audiences, and reeked of nineteenth century vaudeville and medicine shows. It ranged from the dense variations of Uncle Bunt Stephens to the chicken imitations of Whit Gayden, and from the ornate Italian waltzes of Uncle Joe Mangrum to the rowdy gyrations of Henry Bandy. While many of the fiddlers in the hoedown bands were young Turks, the display fiddlers were mostly veterans, some with birth dates reaching back before the Civil War. Though much of their appeal was visual, these musicians soon learned to translate their acts to radio and to earn the highest compliment an old-timer could give their performance: "It was a regular monkey show."

Although Middle Tennessee could not boast of one major annual fiddling contest like the ones in Dallas, White Top, Virginia, or (later) Galax, Virginia, regional contests abounded in the 1920s and 1930s. Even before Henry Ford's sponsorship of contests in 1926, Middle Tennesseans staged indigenous contests that were less publicized but equally important. Documentation exists for an 1899 "Fiddlers' Carnival" in Gallatin, where guest musicians from out of town were put up free in the local hotels, and where prizes were awarded in specific tune categories, for instance, who could best play "Turkey in the Straw" or "Natchez under the Hill." (Several members of Dr. Humphrey Bate's band appeared at this competition.) A contest in Clarksville in 1926 was described as the official state championship contest and attracted Uncle Jimmy Thompson as a guest artist. A 1927 contest in Tullahoma, which was won by the Tomberlain Brothers string band, an early Opry group, offered as first prize a suitcase filled with gifts donated by local merchants. "When our band won," recalled Ernest Tomberlain, "we took the suitcase home and divided it out. One of us got a cheese, one a belt, one a can of tobacco, and so on." An important series of contests occurred in Knoxville, and an equally important one at Chattanooga. An early "commercialized" contest, one staged by promoters as opposed to local residents, occurred in Nashville in May 1927, when Clayton McMichen and the famed recording band the Skillet Lickers, came to Ryman Auditorium to stage the "all southern fiddling contest for the championship of Dixie." Some forty-eight musicians participated in the two-day affair, including most of the early Opry fiddlers. The assembled group opened the program by playing in unison "Alabama Gal" and "Turkey in the Straw," then went down into the audience and paraded around looking for "the best-looking girl" present. (She was chosen, brought up on stage, and awarded a new hat.) Though many of the fiddlers did tunes they were famous for, there was an abundance of showmanship and trick fiddling as well: Charles Loch, the Georgian who seemed to be promoting the event, played "Liberty," "Turkey in the Straw," and "Pop Goes the Weasel" in what the newspaper described as "forty-seven different positions." Fate Norris, normally a banjoist with the Skillet Lickers, brought along his well-known one-man band, in which he played "two guitars, bells, bass fiddle, fiddle, and mouth harps. He devoted seventeen years to the mastery of his art," the *Nashville Banner* noted dryly. Not surprisingly, first and third places were taken by members of the Skillet Lickers, but Gale Binkley of the Dixie Clodhoppers did win second place by playing his specialty, "Forked Deer." The contest overall drew only about five hundred people and was not repeated in later years; but it gave Middle Tennessee fiddlers a taste of the direction fiddling contests were starting to take and confirmed that showmanship was becoming a greater part of the fiddling tradition than many of them probably wanted to admit.

About two dozen fiddlers appeared on the Opry from 1926 through 1929, some of them only appearing one time, many of them only faded names in the old Opry logs. Virtually nothing is known about Fulton Mitchell, who appeared several times in 1926, or about Perry DeMoss, Frank Presley, Emory Luther, Jimmy and Mac Maxwell, Ben Carmack, Dr. N. P. Collins, or Mac Thurman. For other fiddlers, we know only their home town, noted in Opry logs or found in the lists of area fiddling contests. These include William Baker (Nashville), J. B. Carver (Hermitage), Frank Reed (Donelson), and Robert King (from Chestnut Mound in Smith County). We know little of one Doc Carlton, who appeared about every four months playing his "musical saw." M. G. Smith, no relation to Arthur, was a regular on the program in 1926 and 1927 and apparently came from Nashville. Marshall Claiborne, a well-known one-armed fiddler from Hartsville (30 miles east of Nashville) played "with his bow between his knees and his fiddle in his left arm, which fingers and slides the strings in their tuneful pursuit up and down the rosin." Claiborne's signature tune was "Sleepy Lou," a popular local piece later recorded by Uncle Dave Macon and His Fruit Jar Drinkers. He always managed to place high in local fiddling contests and appeared sporadically on the Opry in 1926, 1927, and 1928.

Eventually, though, four fiddlers emerged from the pack as the most popular of these display fiddlers: three veterans and one youngster who learned from a veteran. These were Uncle Joe Mangrum, Henry Bandy, Uncle Bunt Stephens, and the youngster, Sid Harkreader. The remainder of this chapter will focus on these four outstanding fiddlers.

Uncle Joe Mangrum was the senior member of this quartet, having been born in 1853. Earlier research indicated that he was a native of

Paducah, Kentucky, but more recent findings reveal that he was born and reared in the West Tennessee hamlet of Dresden, in Weakley County, only a few miles from the Kentucky line. He apparently did spend much of his later life in Paducah, however, and was living there in 1926 when he played in Henry Ford's regional contest in Louisville. Paducah, after all, is only two counties north of Dresden. In 1928 he moved to Nashville, where he and his wife, Aunt Mary, lived on Sixth Avenue South.

Blind from birth, Uncle Joe, while still a boy, took up what he always called "the violin" after someone gave him an instrument. He later told an interviewer that he "knew there was music in his heart almost from birth." Growing up during the Civil War in West Tennessee, he managed to learn a repertoire of fiddle tunes, a selection of light classical numbers from Wagner and Schubert, and cross section of popular pieces of the day. He quite naturally had to commit to memory even the pieces of "the old masters,'" and soon his fame spread. When in his twenties, around 1873, he was invited to appear before the group that later became known as the Chicago Civic Opera Company. Though scheduled for a forty-five minute concert, he captivated the classical musicians for over an hour and a half, a story that he never tired of telling. For a time he took to the vaudeville stage, touring through the North and East, much in the manner of Norwegian great Ole Bull.

In 1886 Mangrum worked with Tennessee Governor Bob Taylor in the well-known "War of the Roses," when Bob ran against his own brother Alf. Though both the Taylors fiddled on the campaign trail, Bob would often bring along Uncle Joe and have him fiddle after the political speech had been delivered. Later, after he had moved to Paducah, he became friends with the Kentucky humorist Irvin S. Cobb.

By the time he started playing on the Opry, Mangrum told interviewers that he had committed an incredible five thousand pieces to memory. Many of these were classical or light classical pieces, and before his Opry days, this kind of performance usually drew the greatest praise from fans and music critics. He had also composed several tunes, including "A Lullaby" and a march that became so popular it was adopted by a national fraternal order. At some point in the 1920s he began playing with pianist and accordion player Fred Shriver. Soon the pair began using the accordion almost exclusively, since it was portable and versatile. This gave them a sound unique in the annals of old-time music. The accordion, coupled with Mangrum's wonderfully precise execution and pristinely clear tones, made the team an early favorite on the Opry. The only problem was that Uncle

Joe defined "old-time music" in much broader terms than did Judge Hay. Hay later recalled that Uncle Joe's "heart would be almost broken each week because we would not permit him to play selections from the classics and light classics, which he did very well. . . ." Hay also admitted that when Mangrum came to the Opry he "was known throughout the mid-South as one of the greatest old-time fiddlers."

Uncle Joe first appeared on the show on June 30, 1928, and after several guest appearances during that year became a regular in 1929. That year and on through 1931 he and Shriver appeared every other week. Given Mangrum's huge repertoire and Shriver's versatility, the old fiddler and young accordion player rarely rehearsed. "Each Saturday night Uncle Joe and Fred would hold a jam session right on the air," recalled Hay. "All of the members of our company were delighted when the old man and the young man teamed up to give out their best." A few hints suggest the nature of Mangrum's vast repertoire. Hay spoke of his playing "Barbara Allen," surely an unusual tune for a fiddler, and Alcyone Bate Beasley remembered best his waltzes: "He played Italian things, some of those things, you could almost see the gondolas." The five songs the duo recorded for Victor include two well-known breakdowns—"Bill Cheatham" and a version of "Katy Hill" called "Bacon and Cabbage"—and three waltzes. Only the breakdowns were issued, and they sold just a little over four thousand copies, not very impressive sales. They remain, however, one of the most distinctive of old-time records and represent one of the very earliest fiddle styles preserved on disc. Victor chose not to issue the waltzes, in spite of the fact that waltzes were Mangrum's specialties, and for years it was assumed the masters were lost. Then, in 1980, researcher Bob Pinson found two of the masters in the Victor vaults: "Mammoth Cave Waltz" and "The Rose Waltz." Both are breathtaking examples of Victorian parlor music. "Mammoth Cave" is a three-part piece that sounds like a reworked version of a Victorian sheet music composition. "The Rose Waltz" features some dazzling double-time obbligato. Neither sounds like the kind of country waltz featured on old-time hit records such as "Wednesday Night Waltz" or "Over the Waves," and the Victor executives might have felt they were too archaic for 1929.

By 1929 Uncle Joe had proven to be one of the most popular Opry performers, and he and Aunt Mary moved to Nashville to be near the show. As 1932 began, Harry Stone scheduled him to begin a weekly, instead of biweekly, appearance on the show, but on January 12 he suffered a heart attack at his home, and on the following day he died. Though his funeral was held in Nashville, he was returned to Dresden for burial. Among the pallbearers were Dr. Bate, Theron Hale, and Oscar Stone. It was one of the first such losses the tightly knit Opry cast had suffered, and the following Saturday night the program was interrupted for a tribute to Uncle Joe. A contemporary account in *Broadcast News* described the event:

> Halting the festivities at 9:30 o'clock, the time Uncle Joe was to have gone on the air, Mr. Stone asked Dr. Humphrey Bate, Uncle Dave Macon, Fred Shriver, who accompanied Uncle Joe during his broadcasts, Paul Warmack, perhaps his closest friend, and Tiny Stowe, co-announcer of the Barn Dance, to say a word. The Vagabonds sang The Old Rugged Cross, and Fred Shriver played one of Uncle Joe's compositions. Hundreds of telegrams, long distance calls and letters poured into the station, expressing heartfelt sorrow of the Grand Ol' Opry audience.

Among the listeners that evening was an inmate of the Tennessee State Penitentiary, a sixteen-year veteran of Cell Number 30. He was a faithful listener to the "best program on any man's air," as he described it, and was so moved that he mailed in a poem in tribute to Uncle Joe. It read, in part:

> Lying on my cot, with 'phones on my head,
> I heard it announced that Uncle Joe was dead.
> Like many sad hearts, from men up in years,
> It seems so heavy, my eyes filled with tears.
> Herald, Dean, and Curt, and Dave, Harry, and Paul,
> Dr. Bates and Tiny, could not express it all,
> For we prisoners regret, and officials do care,
> We all share in, extending our prayer.

After paying homage to Aunt Mary, the poet concluded:

> Sixteen long years, behind prison walls of gray,
> The Grand Ol' Op'ry keeps us young and gay.

Next to Uncle Jimmy Thompson, who actually appeared on the broadcast fewer times than did the blind violinist, Uncle Joe Mangrum represented the Opry's deepest roots in nineteenth century music.

Another early fiddle soloist who was associated with Kentucky but who was actually born in Tennessee was Henry Bandy. He was a regular on the program throughout 1926, dropped off in 1927, and made only a handful of appearances in 1928 before vanishing from the logs. Judge Hay does not mention Bandy in any of his memoirs, but Alcyone Bate Beasley recalled him vividly.

> He was one of the most colorful men I've ever seen on the Opry. He was from Petroleum, Kentucky, and was, I suppose, a farmer. And he always came down immaculately dressed: usually a dark suit, and white shirt with high stiff collar, I think the collar was separate from the shirt, a celluloid collar. And a tie. Always a tie. He was a brunette also, black hair, and a big, huge handlebar mustache. He played solo fiddle, but I do remember some guitarist who was there to do a second for him. And he held the fiddle down in the crook of his arm, not up under his chin like modern fiddlers. And he used a bow not filled with horsehair, like any other bow I had ever seen, but it was filled with a number 60 thread.

Though billed as from Petroleum, Kentucky, Bandy was in fact born December 17, 1876, in Macon County, Tennessee, about fifty miles northeast of Nashville. He moved to Kentucky between 1910 and 1918, long before he started appearing on the Opry. Bandy's father was a farmer and a blacksmith but not a musician himself. He did appreciate music, though, and bought his son a fiddle and encouraged one of his tenant farmers, Ed Harland, to teach the boy some fiddle tunes; the first was "Sail Away, Ladies," which would remain a favorite of Bandy's. Young Bandy learned quickly and was soon playing with Harland at dances at the nearby Lick Branch school. The young fiddler was also developing as a solo entertainer. Family members tell of his trying to play while dancing around the house, while telling jokes, and working at making up songs. He also became fascinated with trick fiddling and worked at playing the instrument over his head, behind his shoulder, and even off his hip. After his father died in 1898, Henry Bandy started traveling around the country, going as far as Alabama and Texas before he returned to Macon County to get married and settle down. His father had taught him blacksmithing and bequeathed him his blacksmithing tools, so Bandy was soon setting up his own shop. By the time he moved to Kentucky, he had an enviable reputation as a blacksmith and enhanced this when he came to Nashville to study ways of tempering steel with oil. He also served as a deputy sheriff and revenue officer for his county. By the time he auditioned for the Opry in 1926, he had also established a reputation as "The Old Time Fiddler," plying his art not on the vaudeville stages of Mangrum or Macon but at civic functions and schoolhouse entertainments.

Bandy's family recalls some of the tunes of his repertoire, but most of them are standard pieces in any fiddle repertory, like "Old Joe Clark," "Liza Jane," "Soldier's Joy," "Devil's Dream," "Cripple Creek," and "Chicken Reel." A few, such as "Going Across the Sea," "Sail Away, Ladies," "Sugar in my Coffee," and "Natchez under the Hill," have local affiliations with the central Tennessee–southern Kentucky area. Bandy was a stylist, though, and much of his appeal came from the way he performed these songs. This is borne out in a series of records Bandy made for the Gennett Company in 1928, recently discovered by researchers Bruce Greene and Gus Meade. For some reason, the records were never issued, but the test pressings, preserved by the family, show Bandy to be an exuberant showman in the manner of Uncle Dave Macon. He fiddles, jokes, laughs, and sings his way through four numbers, including "Sail Away Ladies," "Going Across the Sea," "Five Up," and "Monkey Show." "Five Up" appears to be an archaic version of the well-known "Roving Gambler," while "Monkey Show" is a heavily stylized version of the pre–Civil War "Going Down Town."

Bandy died in 1943, and even though he had not appeared on the Opry in years, the show dedicated the next Saturday's broadcast to him. Like Uncle Joe Mangrum, Bandy was a direct link to the nineteenth century display fiddler, and he certainly filled this role in Hay's vision of the early Opry. Like Mangrum, too, he was more important to the show than his slender recorded legacy indicates. Like Mangrum, he came to the radio show in the waning years of a rich career and left before the show became professionalized. Like Mangrum, he made a strong impression on those who heard him, but left little tangible evidence of his work. His was a potent tradition but one with too few practitioners.

Though fiddling contests were not their prime milieu, both Mangrum and Bandy did appear in some of Henry Ford's events. The third great Opry fiddler, however, found a home and won his fame at them. He was yet another "uncle," Uncle Bunt Stephens, the man WSM modestly billed as "the world's greatest old-time fiddler," and the man Uncle Jimmy Thompson classified as his keenest rival. He was a five-foot, hundred-pound farmer from Moore County, seventy miles southeast of Nashville on the old Dixie Line (N.C.&St.L). John L. Stephens was actually born and reared in Bedford County and bought his first fiddle from a tramp for twenty-five dollars in 1890, when Stephens was only eleven years old. He

grew up fiddling for dances in the rolling hills of southern Tennessee, and
did so for over thirty years before friends talked him into entering Ford's
local contest. He went on to best Uncle Jimmy at the regional Louisville
competition and eventually to win first prize at Ford's national finals. He
was a good deal younger than Uncle Jimmy, being only forty-seven when
he began to play in contests. Like Uncle Jimmy, Uncle Bunt had been married twice, and like Uncle Jimmy, he was a genuine rustic, an eccentric and
colorful character.

A visitor to Uncle Bunt's house in the 1920s described it as a "shotgun" house (constructed with rooms one behind the other, so that a shot
fired in the front would go through all the rooms in the house) about a mile
from Lynchburg, Tennessee. The front room, a bedroom with a crude fireplace, was on the ground level, and the kitchen, directly behind it, was two
steps lower. The front room was small, just enough room for the double
bed, a wash stand, one rocking chair, one straight chair, and a large country fireplace, through which the wind whistled on that winter day. The
walls were rather bare, except for two decorations: a double-barreled shotgun and Uncle Bunt's fiddle.

When Judge Hay asked Uncle Bunt to describe his trip to Detroit, the
old fiddler said:

> Mr. Ford was very nice to me. He asked me where I wanted to
> stop an' I told him I didn't care much as long as it wasn't in the
> middle o' town, so he told a big colored fellow to take me out to
> the country club. . . . After I played about a week for him I told
> him I would have to go home 'cause Lizzie didn't have no gro-
> ceries or cord wood in the house. Mr. Ford told me to stay and
> he'd have his man in Lawrenceburg send her a whole wagonload.
> An' sure enough, he done it.

Uncle Bunt's wife made her weekly visit into Tullahoma during this time
and reported that Mr. Ford had presented her husband with a new Lincoln
car, $1,000 in money, and a broadcloth suit of clothes; paid for having his
teeth repaired; and entertained him as a guest for a week (reported in the
Nashville Banner, February 15, 1926). Later Uncle Bunt talked Ford into
giving him cash instead of the Lincoln, whereupon he purchased a Ford car
and pocketed the difference. A Lincoln was nice, but a Ford, after all, was
a Ford.

Uncle Bunt never played on the Opry regularly, only for occasional
guest slots. His first appearance was on February 28, 1926, only a week or

so after he was crowned World Champion Fiddler by Henry Ford himself. WSM scheduled him for a special broadcast on Monday at 7:00 P.M.: "The radio public is cordially invited . . . to hear the world's greatest old-time fiddler," proclaimed the announcement in the *Tennessean*. Uncle Bunt played solo fiddle for a half-hour and won the applause of everyone. Hay recalled that the staff went out of their way to make Uncle Bunt feel at home, but something occurred that they had not counted on: the professional jealousy of Uncle Jimmy Thompson. As Hay has recorded it: "Uncle Jimmy Thompson was burned to a crisp, as better men than he have been when a rival takes the edge away. But, he stuck to the ship and for many months we nursed two elderly male prima donnas who couldn't see each other for the dust in their eyes."

Winning Ford's contest complicated Uncle Bunt's life considerably. In addition to his WSM appearance, he made various trips to the East and Midwest, broadcasting from Chicago in March 1926. Aunt Lizzie developed a country clog dance using a lot of petticoats, and she and Uncle Bunt eventually went on the vaudeville circuit. They spent some time at this effort, but, Hay reports, "their new life did not make them happy." They soon retired back to their old house near Lynchburg. There they lived in comfortable obscurity until Bunt's death in 1951, at the age of 72.

Uncle Bunt reportedly won Ford's contest by playing his complex version of "Sail Away, Ladies" and "Old Hen Cackle," and in March 1926 he traveled to New York to record these and others for Columbia records. Four numbers, all unaccompanied fiddle solos, were eventually released: "Sail Away, Ladies" and "Louisburg Blues" on Columbia 15071, and "Candy Girl" with "Left in the Dark Blues" on Columbia 15085. They were featured in the Columbia catalogue with an account of Uncle Bunt that noted that the fiddler's "heart is as light as the bright mountain dance music he plays," and that his victory in the Ford contest represented a besting of 1,865 fiddlers. The records were released in the Columbia 15000 (Old Familiar Tunes) series, where they jostled for sales with the new hot string band records by the Skillet Lickers and Charlie Poole; they were, in fact, the only solo fiddle records released in that distinguished series. In spite of the fact that they must have seemed archaic in light of the newer performances, the couplings sold fairly well, 15071 doing some 11,500 copies, and 15085 doing 6,700.

Next to Texas fiddler Eck Robertson's classic solos of "Leather Britches" and "Sallie Gooden," dating from 1922 and 1923, Bunt Stephens's efforts are probably the finest examples of traditional American solo fiddling recorded. Students of fiddle music have described Uncle

Bunt's masterpiece, "Sail Away, Ladies," as "probably similar to much American dance music in the period between the Revolutionary and Civil Wars," and ethnomusicologist Linda C. Burman-Hall, in a well-known study entitled "The Technique of Variation in an American Fiddle Tune," spends over twenty pages transcribing and analyzing the complex musical patterns of the piece. Uncle Bunt, whose neighbors described him as "that nice little feller that never amounted to much," would have been quietly amused.

The fourth fiddler on the early Opry was also the youngest. He was born in 1898, a full generation after Bunt Stephens and Henry Bandy, and two generations after Joe Mangrum or Uncle Jimmy Thompson. He was also, ironically, best known for years as the guitarist and vocalist who accompanied Uncle Dave Macon in his early years. But Sidney J. Harkreader was first and foremost a fiddler—who came out of a strong, well-defined regional tradition and who often appeared as a star in his own right on the Opry. Unlike the other early fiddlers, Sid lived on well into the modern era, often appearing at old-timer reunions and fiddling contests and becoming, before his death in 1988, one of the Opry's most visible and voluble links to its past.

Harkreader was born and reared in one of the most distinctive areas of Middle Tennessee, the huge cedar glades area between Murfreesboro and Lebanon. Today much of the area is enclosed by Cedars of Lebanon State Park, and in the 1940s it was a training area for General George Patton's armored troops. At the turn of the century, though, when Harkreader was born, it was filled with small farms and boasted a large black population of sharecroppers and field hands for the larger farms and who lived in small cabins scattered among the thickets.

Both whites and blacks shared a common tradition of fiddle and banjo music, and by 1926 some of the white bands from the region were carrying their music to the WSM Barn Dance. One was the Tomberlain Family, consisting of fiddler George, his son Ernest (on tenor banjo), and his nephews Waymon (banjo) and Robert (guitar). After appearing on the radio show several times in 1926, the band was offered a steady job on the Barn Dance for $20 a week. They turned it down because it was too much trouble and expense to fight the muddy dirt roads every week to drive into Nashville. Some of the Tomberlain music was influenced by two local black musicians: fiddler Clay Smith and banjoist-fiddler Frank Patterson. Patterson, born about 1880 in the Walter Hill community, developed into the leading square dance fiddler in the area south of Nashville and one of the more influential black musicians in that part of the state. According to interviews done in the early 1940s by Fisk University folklorist John Work,

1. Church Street, in the heart of downtown Nashville, ca. 1930.

2. Ryman Auditorium exterior, in the early years of the twentieth century.

3. The National Life Building in the late 1920s.

4. The lobby of the National Life Building. The WSM studio was on the fifth floor.

5. The original WSM studio, complete with drum set, piano, music stands, and even a xylophone (reminders that the station also broadcasted a lot of pop music). Observation windows are to the left.

6. The young George Hay, soon after he arrived in Nashville in 1925.

THE NATIONAL LIFE & ACCIDENT INSURANCE CO

NASHVILLE, TENN.

June 15, 1926.

Uncle Jimmy Thompson,
2016 Charlotte Avenue,
Nashville, Tennessee.

Dear Uncle Jimmy:

      We are glad to learn through your niece, Mrs. Jones, that you have recovered from your illness.

      We are booking you to appear on Saturday night at 8 o'clock July 3rd. We hope you will be able to get here. Kindly let us know as soon as possible whether or not you will be able to play.

      With kindest regards, I remain

          Yours very truly,

GDH/J.

          George D. Hay,
          Director.

"NASHVILLE PRODUCES 4 MILLION POUNDS BUTTER ANNUALLY."

7. Uncle Jimmy did, in fact, make it back to the show on July 3.

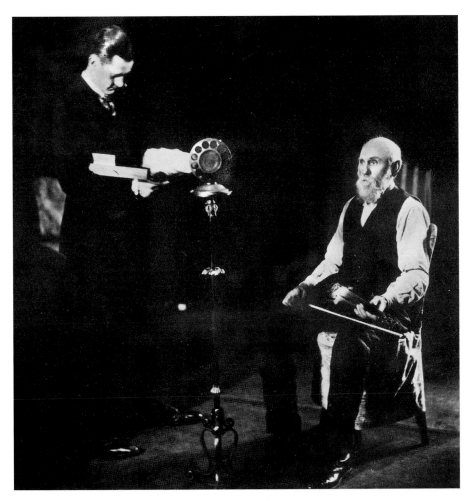

8. Uncle Jimmy Thompson and Judge Hay in a celebrated publicity photo recreating the famous November 1925 broadcast that launched the Barn Dance. The Judge holds the train whistle in his hand.

9. Uncle Jimmy Thompson and his niece Eva Thompson Jones are romanticized in this studio portrait WSM had made in 1926. This was the image that Barn Dance fans had of the fiddler.

10. A more down-to-earth picture of Uncle Jimmy and his wife Aunt Ella in front of their homemade camper, ca. 1928. This was the Uncle Jimmy his friends and neighbors knew. (Photo: CKW)

11. The famed WSM broadcasting tower, built in the countryside near Brentwood, south of downtown Nashville. For years it was promoted as the world's tallest radio tower. Engineers would often take hoses and wet down the ground around it to improve signal strength.

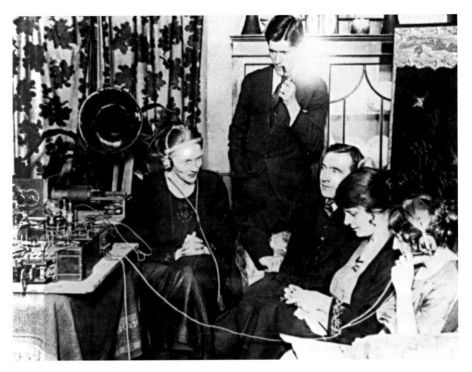

12. When the Barn Dance started in 1925, most people had to listen to radio through crystal sets and headphones.

13. Opry manager and architect Harry Stone.

14. Edwin W. Craig, founder of WSM and son of National Life cofounder Edward Craig, *left*, with Eldon Stevenson Jr.

15. Announcer David Stone.

16. This version of Dr. Bate's Possum Hunters, probably dating from 1926, spotlights Oscar Albright's bowed bass. Others include *(left to right)*: Dr. Bate, Oscar Stone, Walter Liggett, Staley Walton, and Paris Pond (an occasional substitute for Bert Hutcherson).

17. Dr. Bate and the Possum Hunters in the pose that graced the first piece of Opry-related sheet music, Oscar Stone's "Going Uptown" (1928), published by the Flick Music Publishing Company in Nashville. *Left to right*: Dr. Bate, Staley Walton, Oscar Stone, Jimmy Hart, Walter Liggett, and Oscar Albright.

18. DeFord Bailey, the "Harmonica Wizard," in a 1926 pose with his megaphone (to amplify his harmonica) and the rack he used to create train effects when he played his signature piece, "Pan American."

19. Uncle Joe Mangrum in a studio shot, 1926.

20. Mrs. Cline (from Westmoreland, Tennessee) and her "zither," as fans and historians identified the instrument for years. In fact, it was a hammered dulcimer, on which the strings were hit with little mallets. The instrument has been popular in Middle Tennessee folk music since the 1880s.

21. Two young Turks of the early Opry, Sid Harkreader and Jimmy Hart.

22. Ed Poplin's band, or the Poplin-Woods Tennessee String Band. Jack Woods is on guitar, his daughter Frances—standing next to him—on guitar, Ed Poplin (fiddle), with his daughter Louise (mandolin), and Ed Jr. (piano).

23. An art deco style frames the Vagabonds in a publicity shot made shortly before they arrived at the Opry.

24. One of the first publicity shots of the Fruit Jar Drinkers, probably in 1928. *From left:* George Wilkerson (fiddle), Claude Lampley (banjo), Tom Leffew (mandolin), and Howard Ragsdale (guitar).

25. In 1928 the new Opry cast posed for its first group photo, in the National Life Building studio, in front of the curtained windows through which the first audiences watched. The image-making had not yet set in, and everyone was wearing their Sunday best. *Standing, left to right:* Obed Pickard (bow tie), Roy Hardison, Obed Pickard Jr., Charles Arrington, Bill Etter (Crook Brothers), Clarence Minton (light suit, Crook Brothers), Bert Hutcherson, Julian Sharp (Poplin Band), Bill Batts, Matthew Crook (bow tie), Pete Batts (Poplin Band), Fred Shriver (dark glasses), Claude Lampley, Tom Givens, Staley Walton, Homer Smith, Oscar Albright, Walter Liggett, Howard Ragsdale, Oscar Stone, Jimmy Hart, Harry Stone, Judge Hay (with whistle). *Seated, left to right:* Mom Pickard, Mamie Ruth Hale, Theron Hale (light suit), Paul Warmack, Ed Poplin, Dr. Humphrey Bate, Herman Crook, Ruth Pickard (on floor), Arthur Smith, George Wilkerson, Elizabeth Hale (in chair). Notably missing are Uncle Dave Macon and Uncle Jimmy Thompson. National Life made up hundreds of copies of this photo on business cards to be distributed by their agents.

Patterson learned his distinctive repertoire around 1900 from an older black fiddler from the area. About 1916 he moved to the Rencrow community nearer Nashville and continued to sharecrop by day and work house dances at night. In March 1942 Patterson's music was recorded by Work on a series of recordings later deposited in the Library of Congress. Apparently Patterson himself never appeared on the early Opry, though several members of his string bands reportedly did as the "Tennessee Guitar Trio" in 1927.

Harkreader himself had as a mentor another local black fiddler, a "hired hand" on his father's farm named Robert Knox. In 1913, when he was fifteen years old, Harkreader had made enough money by selling hides to order a $3.95 mail-order fiddle from Sears. Knox happened by the Harkreader farmhouse one noontime and saw the newly arrived fiddle, with its pasteboard case, instruction book, and fingerboard chart. "It so happened that he was a fairly good old-time fiddle player," wrote Harkreader in his autobiography, "so he took my fiddle and tuned it like it was supposed to be tuned. Then he played several numbers like 'Cotton-Eyed Joe,' which I remember in particular. Well, after he left to go back to work, I said to myself, 'If I could just play like him, I would be the happiest boy in the world.'. . . I remember that I was always afraid that if I broke a string, I wouldn't be able to tune my fiddle again." (Harkreader need not have worried; he apparently was blessed with almost perfect pitch, and his ability to tune four or five instruments by himself at one time is part of his legendry.)

Another of Harkreader's teachers was Julius H. Robinson, an older man who led an early Opry band called the Gladeville Trio. Though the group broke up in the early 1930s following Robinson's death, and though they never made any records, the band performed on WSM frequently in 1927 and 1928. As a young man, Harkreader sought Robinson out, walking three miles to visit him. The pair hit it off and wound up playing fiddles together all night. Robinson taught Harkreader a number of "Cedar Glades" tunes, including "Old Joe," a song known to most of the black fiddlers in Middle Tennessee (Frank Patterson even recorded it). "Old Joe" quickly became a favorite at local contests where Harkreader and Robinson went and later became one of Harkreader's signature pieces, a favorite on the Opry. He eventually recorded it for Paramount Records. The bond between Robinson and the younger fiddler was so strong that after Sid moved away, he would often call the older man, and the two would exchange fiddle tunes over long-distance phone lines.

Harkreader's passion to become a musician fired his work at playing harmonica, guitar, and banjo in addition to the fiddle. Neighbors recall that his early efforts on the fiddle were so painful that his family drove him out of the house and made him practice in the cornfields. Neighbors could hear him out there, in the wee hours of the morning, squeaking out tunes and learning to sing as he fiddled. But the practice took, and soon people throughout the Glades were asking him to come and play for wintertime square dances and house parties. He would sometimes make as much as ten or twenty dollars for an evening's work. He also began playing and placing in the money at the local fiddling contests that were dotting the landscape. He soon determined to become a professional musician, a rare and daring decision in the early 1920s.

In 1923 he teamed with Uncle Dave Macon, and this began a series of tours and recordings with him as well as a variety of groups that spanned the next seven years. He became one of the first fiddlers to play over WSM, appearing with Macon as early as the first week in November 1925. He may not have been one of the first fiddlers on the Opry as such (that is, the regular Saturday night Barn Dance program), but he was certainly one of the first on WSM and one of the first to inspire the idea for the Opry. Even as he played with Uncle Dave, Sid would book other engagements and head up his own band. He had to work steadily to make ends meet and expanded his efforts in vaudeville, where he and Macon had already enjoyed success. In 1926 he was asked by a Loew's theater manager in Memphis to put together a touring group of Charleston dancers. He did so and toured with the group through Alabama and Tennessee for several months. The following year he teamed with Nashville guitar maker and teacher Grady Moore. Moore himself had spots on WSM and WLAC, where he featured himself on Hawaiian guitar. Also in 1927 Sid was contacted by agents of Paramount Records and asked to come to Chicago to record. Sid agreed and took Grady Moore along to help out. The company paid him $1,000 plus expenses for twenty-four selections.

Sid was impressed with this arrangement until he discovered that Paramount was also releasing his sides on the more popular Broadway label under the false names of Harkins & Moran. Sid took the matter to a lawyer and won a settlement from Paramount, probably becoming the first old-time musician to assert his rights in the face of the highhanded practices of recording companies in the '20s. In spite of this, Paramount asked Sid to record again in 1928. (This also indicates how popular those "bootlegged" Broadway sides were; the Harkins & Moran sides still show up today with much greater frequency than the original Paramounts.) The second time, Sid took along Blythe Poteet, a cousin of Sam and Kirk McGee, and the duo recorded twelve numbers.

Many of the Harkreader-Moore sides were sentimental songs of the McFarland & Gardner variety, such as "The Gambler's Dying Words," "Little Rosewood Casket," and "Picture from Life's Other Side." Others were traditional hymns and gospel pieces like "The Old Rugged Cross" and "In the Sweet Bye and Bye." Others were traditional fiddle pieces. "Old Joe," the Gladeville Trio piece, was well known, while "Kitty Wells" was probably learned from fellow Opry star Dad Pickard. Uncle Dave's influence can be found in the monologue "A Trip to Town," as well as "I Don't Reckon It'll Happen Again for Months and Months" and "Bully of the Town." Sid added a number of his own specialities to the session, including "Mocking Bird Breakdown" (which soon became his big crowd-pleaser) and "Drink Her Down." One of the most beautiful numbers from the session, "I Love the Hills of Tennessee," had been written by Grady Moore. Harkreader next teamed up with Jimmy Hart, former guitar player for Dr. Humphrey Bate, and the duo rejoined the Opry in 1931 as a regular act. A 1931 description of them, probably penned by David Stone, describes something of their performing style:

> Fiddlin' Sid Harkreader and Jimmy Hart! There is a team for you. Sid is a long tall boy whose love for starched collars causes him never to be without one. And they are high ones, too. Sid literally dances around the microphone when he comes to bat, but he knows how to play breakdowns. Jimmy Hart with his guitar has appeared with many of the old-time bands and makes an admirable partner for Sid Harkreader.

Sid left the show in September, moving around to other Nashville and Kentucky stations, as well as doing vaudeville. Health problems plagued him during these years and eventually led to deterioration in his longtime relationship with Uncle Dave. He continued to spotlight his fancy fiddling and even won a trip to a national exhibition in Chicago, but he also began to sense the shift in direction on the Opry away from fiddle soloists to string bands. By 1929 only Uncle Joe Mangrum was still on the show as a fiddle soloist on a regular basis, and even Arthur Smith had been absorbed into a string band, the Dixieliners. During eight weeks in the summer of 1928, Hay had experimented with Whit Gayden, a trick fiddler from West Tennessee who eventually made a lone Victor record in 1930, but he soon left the show as well.

Harkreader responded by forming his own larger string band in 1935, and in July reappeared as a regular weekly act on the Opry. Sid Harkreader and His Company, as the group was usually billed, included, at various times, Emory Martin, the one-armed banjo player; Nonnie and Bulow Smith, a zither-and-guitar combo that earlier had recorded as the Perry County Music Makers; and Clarence "Mack" McGar, an excellent mandolin player and fiddler who later joined Jack Shook's band and then became the fiddler for the Opry stage band. Sid broadcasted weekly with a five-piece band and booked out almost nightly, drawing up contracts that promised "a program of entertainment of: JOKES, MUSIC, and OLD TIME HILARITY" for 70 percent of the gross receipts, based on an adult admission price of 25¢. Sid also continued to enhance his appeal as a show fiddler, especially with his "Mocking Bird Breakdown." In May 1936, for example, he was offered $500 to come to the Cincinnati Music Hall to play this specialty against a similar version by Natchee the Indian, the leading trick fiddler of the age. Sid refused the offer.

Sid dropped off the Opry again in January 1937 to try his hand at full-time touring. Soon after that he organized his Round-Up Gang, an attempt to cash in on the cowboy music craze of the time, but this was only moderately successful. By 1940 he had decided to get out of the music business altogether and open a restaurant in downtown Nashville. Later he would return to the show to head up the Gully Jumpers and to appear in other string bands, but his glory days were clearly over.

The era of the display fiddler was a brief one on the Opry stage. In many ways, it ended in the fall of 1931, when Harkreader and Jimmy Hart left the air. Yet display fiddling was one of the show's most colorful ties to the past and a celebration of a tradition that belonged more to the nineteenth century than the twentieth. Certainly some of the Opry's dedication to the tradition was born out of the wild enthusiasm for the Henry Ford contests that helped give the show its first lease on life. But that dedication was also a product of Hay's recognition that this kind of fiddling was a genuine part of the old-time music complex that he sought to celebrate. The image of a lone fiddler standing out on a stage and attempting to entertain a crowd with nothing more than his fiddle and his skill was a potent symbol for all that the Opry stood for, and Hay sensed this. He had found in Uncle Jimmy Thompson an ideal figure to fill this role as the Opry got started. When Uncle Jimmy soon dropped off the program, Hay tried to find replacements, and for a time succeeded. But the pool of veteran fiddlers honed in this archaic tradition was shrinking rapidly, and, with few exceptions, the younger generations played a different type of fiddle music. By the mid-1930s Hay could not have aired such fiddlers even if he had been able to find more; their day was over.

"Take It Away, Uncle Dave!"

"I REMEMBER ONE SATURDAY NIGHT, in 1926, when Uncle Dave made his debut on WSM. We had read about it in the paper, but we didn't mention it about Lascassas. We had one of the two radio sets in the community, and we were afraid that everybody in that end of the county would swarm into our house to hear Uncle Dave and trample us. Nevertheless the word got around and just about everybody did swarm unto our house, except for a few local sages who didn't believe in radio."

Thus did Tennessee journalist Rufus Jarman describe the local impact of the meeting of the two most potent Tennessee influences on old-time music, Uncle Dave Macon and the Grand Ole Opry. Of all the members of the early Opry, Macon is certainly the most famous. He is the only one of the "original 25" to have been elected to the Country Music Hall of Fame, and he is the only old-timer most of the current generations of Opry goers are familiar with. Around Middle Tennessee, Uncle Dave has become a genuine folk hero, and the tales told about him number in the hundreds. He recorded far more than anyone else on the early Opry, and the recordings have remained in print longer than those of anyone else, well into the age of the LP and CD. At one point in 1975 there were no less than seven LPs devoted to Macon's original recordings. (One of them, "Laugh Your Blues Away," even won a Grammy nomination for the Best Traditional Recording of 1982.) Folklorists have said of Uncle Dave: "With the exception of the Carter Family, Uncle Dave preserved more valuable American folklore through his recordings than any other folk or country music performer." Country music historians have referred to him as "the first featured star of the Grand Ole Opry." The popular press referred to him as "the king of the hillbillies" or "the Dixie Dewdrop." Judge Hay used to introduce him by saying, "Here's the one who wears no man's collar but his own." Yet Uncle Dave described himself merely as "banjoist and songster, liking religion and meetings, farming and thanking God for all his bountiful gifts in this beautiful world he has bestowed upon us."

But if Uncle Dave has come to symbolize the spirit of the early Opry, he was in many ways quite different from the average early Opry performer. To begin with, he was perhaps the only member of the early Opry cast that did not need the Opry as much as it needed him. He came to the Opry already established as a star in vaudeville and through phonograph records. He was by no means the only early performer who had had professional experience prior to playing on the Opry (as some commentators have suggested), but he was the only artist who enjoyed a national reputation prior to working for WSM. Second, Macon made little effort to adapt his older vaudeville style (born from years of doing live shows) to the new radio medium, as did most other singers. He never really learned to be comfortable around a microphone. As Judge Hay recalled: "When Uncle Dave came on we moved him back so that he would have plenty of room to kick as he played. He has always been an actor who thought the microphone was just a nuisance."

Finally, Uncle Dave's rather intimidating zest for life allowed him to get away with a great deal more on the Opry shows than anyone else could. Uncle Dave's humor was unpredictable and at times a little rough. National Life was very mindful of the family image of the Opry and always watchful for the suggestive or the implicit innuendo. Nights when Uncle Dave had been into "the grip" (a little black satchel wherein he carried his Jack Daniel's Tennessee sippin' whiskey) gave the Opry managers no little concern. "There was no telling what he might sing then," one of them confided. "Some nights he would do songs backstage that were funny as could be, but they never, *never* could go out on the air." Yet Uncle Dave could switch from the innuendo of "I'll Tickle Nancy" to the pieties of "Rock of Ages" in an instant, and with no sense of hypocrisy. He was a genuinely good man who genuinely loved life, and this obviously sincere zeal for life endeared him to Judge Hay as well as to millions of fans. He and Judge Hay became the best of friends in later years. But some of the antics that might well have gotten a lesser artist or a lesser man kicked off the show were for Uncle Dave written off as mere eccentricities. Legends, after all, are not born of conformists.

The legends about Uncle Dave are delightful and certainly meaningful, but they are occasionally mistaken for history. His early relationship with the Opry is a good case in point. Some accounts assert that Uncle Dave was regularly performing on the Opry in its very earliest days and that he was the Opry's first featured vocal star. Neither of these stories is completely accurate, but to understand why, we need to review Uncle Dave's early career.

Uncle Dave was born David Harrison Macon, the son of a former Confederate army officer, in 1870 near McMinnville, Tennessee, about sixty miles southeast of Nashville. As a teenager he lived for a few years in Nashville, where his parents operated the old Broadway Hotel. The hotel catered to vaudeville and circus performers, and by his middle teens Uncle Dave had grown to love music and the performing traditions of the nineteenth century American stage. In 1885, when he was fifteen, he got his first banjo. In his own words (and referring to himself in the third person), it was Joel Davidson, "a noted comedian and banjoist . . . that inspired Uncle Dave to make his wishes known to his dear aged mother and she gave him the money to purchase his first banjo." A photo made a year later shows the young Macon proudly holding this instrument. But long before Macon had seen Joel Davidson in Sam McFlynn'a circus, and had begun absorbing nineteenth century vaudeville traditions, he had been exposed to another powerful influence, rural black folk music. A 1926 account of Uncle Dave reports that "born on a farm in Warren County, Tennessee, he learned the tunes of the darkies." In the few instances we have of Uncle Dave talking specifically about his songs, he does not hesitate to acknowledge this debt (see his account of "Rock About My Saro Jane" below). Indeed, he seemed to take the interplay between white and black music for granted. In 1922, when black folklorist Thomas Talley published a collection of African American secular songs collected in Middle Tennessee from 1900–1920, a great many of the texts were similar to songs or fragments in Uncle Dave's repertoire—suggesting that Uncle Dave was right and that a sizable song repertoire was at one time shared in common among whites and blacks. The blues particularly seems to have influenced his vocal stylings. On one of his very first records, "Bile Them Cabbage Down" (Vocalion 14849, made in 1924), he includes a striking parody of country blues singing.

When he was nineteen Uncle Dave married and began farming in the small community of Kittrell, near Murfreesboro, Tennessee. He played and sang informally, for both himself and his friends, and casually developed a repertoire of songs from both oral and written sources. Before long, he formed the Macon Midway Mule and Wagon Transportation Company, hauling freight and produce with mule teams. Many old-timers in the area still recalled Macon singing as he drove his team along. The daughter of a grocer on the Murfreesboro public square recalled that when Uncle Dave delivered produce and goods to her father's store, he would make up impromptu songs about what he had—much in the vein of a street caller. This phase of his life he celebrated in the song "From Earth to Heaven" (Brunswick 3297.) In 1920 Uncle Dave became a victim of technological unemployment: a truck line started in competition with Macon Midway, and Uncle Dave simply chose not to compete. At the age of fifty, he began thinking of starting a new career in music.

It was at about this same time that he visited relatives in Arkansas and was encouraged to begin making formal public appearances. The next year saw Uncle Dave's first public performance, a charity event in Morrison, Tennessee. Macon recalled: "The Methodist church there needed a new door. I gave a show, then passed the hat and collected the money, $17." Two years later a talent scout for the Loew's vaudeville circuit heard him at a Shriners' benefit in Nashville and offered him "several hundred" dollars a week to do a stand in Birmingham. The engagement was wildly successful—a two-week stint was extended to five weeks, and the theater managers were cited by the fire department for overcrowding. Uncle Dave was now a professional musician. He next found himself booked in the Loew's theater chain around the country.

Uncle Dave enjoyed the touring (banjo-playing comedians were very popular in vaudeville then and had been since the 1890s) but soon realized that he needed a full-time backup man in the act. In 1923 he was playing informally in Charlie Melton's barbershop in Nashville when the young Sid Harkreader happened to walk in with his fiddle under his arm. The two began playing and Macon was impressed with Harkreader's ready wit, musicianship, and versatility. (Sid could sing and second on guitar as well as play fiddle.) Macon engaged Sid for some bookings, and soon the pair was burning up the Loew's circuit in the South. They worked together throughout 1924, and by early 1925 Macon had added a third member to his team, a buck dancer named "Dancing Bob" Bradford.

Uncle Dave became incredibly popular in the mid-South area solely on the basis of his stage appearances. He was so popular that the regional distributor for Vocalion Records, the Sterchi Brothers furniture company, became convinced that he should make records. Thus in the autumn of 1924, just a little over a year after Fiddlin' John Carson had made the first commercial record of old-time music in the South, Uncle Dave and Sid Harkreader found themselves in New York to record. Uncle Dave's first released number was "Chewing Gum," and it was to remain one of his most popular standards. Another was "Keep My Skillet Good and

Greasy," allegedly the first tune he played on the Opry. The records were so successful they are still found in antique stores around the South today, and they launched Macon on a recording career that was to encompass some 175 commercially released selections. By the time he first sat before the WSM microphones, Uncle Dave had recorded over thirty songs and toured thousands of miles as a vaudeville headliner.

In the spring of 1925 Uncle Dave met another musical magician who was to become his traveling companion and pupil, Sam McGee (see chapter 12). Macon first met Sam when he and Harkreader did a show near Sam's hometown of Franklin, Tennessee. Sam had been playing the guitar for some time but was then working as a blacksmith in a rural village. He recalled in later years: "I never will forget what they had on their instrument cases. Uncle Dave's, it read: 'Uncle Dave Macon, World's Greatest Banjo Player,' and Sid had on his 'Sid Harkreader World's Greatest Violinist.' And I was just a little old one-gallon country boy and that really impressed me. You know, a violinist, that was something." After hearing Sam pick the then-new piece "Missouri Waltz" on his little Martin, Uncle Dave said, "Would you like to come with me if I could book us a few dates?" Sam needed no convincing, and soon he was Uncle Dave's regular companion, alternating with Harkreader.

They traveled in an old touring car with curtains for windows. Sam drove. One of Uncle Dave's eccentricities was to have Sam stop at each railroad crossing while the older man would laboriously climb out of the car, walk up to the tracks and peer carefully down each side to make sure the way was clear. Uncle Dave booked his own shows through a voluminous correspondence and believed the best form of advertising was old-fashioned word of mouth. According to Sam, they would go into a town, put on a sample show, and let the grapevine do the rest. They arranged their schedules so they could farm on the side and were always home in time for planting and harvesting. Uncle Dave was always a good farmer throughout his long career, even after achieving worldwide fame. He plowed with a mule up until his death, and each year he butchered enough hogs to provide each of his children with two sides of pork, salted and cured.

Sid and Sam were interesting contrasts as musical companions and as personalities. On the one hand, Sid Harkreader was a thin, angular, almost ascetic-looking man, thoroughly professional and rather intense about his music. He was an interpreter rather than a creator, and as at home with the fiddle as with the guitar. He also fancied himself somewhat of a crooner. Sam McGee, on the other hand, was lively and impetuous, always ready for a joke, and one of the most creative guitarists in country music history. At times Uncle Dave felt uneasy with both men. Sid was sometimes a little too serious for him, and Sam's guitar and banjo virtuosity sometimes threatened to overshadow his own talents. (Uncle Dave never learned how to "change gears" on the banjo, and carried three instruments with him, each tuned to a different key.)

With Sam being such a natural comedian and Uncle Dave having a wealth of experience with vaudeville and burlesque jokes, their in-person shows must have been something to behold. The fragments of the repartee that they preserved on occasional records show their style bristling with classic one-liners and impertinent rejoinders:

Macon: Well, Buddy, how you feel?
McGee: Feeling right.
Macon: Well, if you ain't right, get right, and let your conscience be your guide, because I'm gonna play with more heterogeneous constapolicy double flavor 'n' unknown quality than you do.
McGee: Make it light on yourself.
("Comin' 'Round the Mountain" Brunswick 263)

It was with such experience that Macon, in the fall of 1925, settled in for the winter and began to spend some time in Nashville. The old-time fiddling craze was sweeping the nation, two new radio stations were starting, and Uncle Dave was the right man in the right place at the right time. His relationship with WSM in the station's earliest days has hitherto never been clearly defined, and because of its importance it is perhaps appropriate to examine it at length.

Historians have generally accepted a chronology running thus: on November 6, 1925, Uncle Dave and Sid Harkreader perform in a special live show at the Ryman Auditorium and "set hundreds to stomping their feet." On November 28, George Hay lets Uncle Jimmy Thompson play and thus starts the Barn Dance. On December 26, Macon joins Uncle Jimmy for "an hour or two" of "old familiar tunes." The common story holds, then, that Uncle Dave appeared on WSM's Barn Dance program shortly after Thompson's debut. Hay himself has written that Uncle Dave was one of those who formally joined the Barn Dance roster "during the first two or three months of the year 1926." But a close scrutiny of newspaper files for those months reveals a vastly different story.

In the first place, the famous Macon-Harkreader concert of November 6 was not merely a concert—it was also a WSM broadcast. The occasion was the annual Policeman's Benefit show and included acts other than Macon and Harkreader. And researchers have overlooked the vital fact that the show was advertised as "An Evening with WSM" (see chapter appendix 2). The audience was urged to see "these artists and musicians in person that you listen to over your radio *every evening*" (emphasis added). It is this latter phrase that is so important, for the list of performers printed includes Uncle Dave and Sid, as well as Dr. Bate's band. Though it has been widely known that Bate was playing on Nashville radio prior to the November 28 broadcast, here we have evidence that Macon and/or Harkreader had also done so. Furthermore, it was announced only during that same week of the November 6 concert that George Hay had been hired by the station—and he was not to assume his duties until November 9. Thus Uncle Dave Macon, as well as Dr. Bate and Sid Harkreader, had appeared on WSM at least three weeks before Uncle Jimmy made his famous broadcast—and a week before Hay arrived on the scene.

The Ryman broadcast was historic in another sense: it was the first country music broadcast from the building that was later to become the shrine of the Grand Ole Opry. (For another interesting Macon-Ryman connection, see the discussion on "Cap'n Tom Ryman" at the end of this chapter.) The newspaper account (see chapter appendix 1) was very sympathetic to old-time music on the show and gave a detailed account of Uncle Dave's performance. Curiously, it also refers to his playing guitar as well as banjo. Sam McGee has said that Uncle Dave could "second only a little" on guitar, and Sid Harkreader pointed out that Uncle Dave played guitar behind his fiddling on their Vocalion record of "The Girl I Left Behind Me."

By December Uncle Dave seems to have been appearing regularly on WSM; his next documented appearance is December 19. On that night he played on the station for a while and then, accompanied by station announcer Jack Keefe, attended a local Chamber of Commerce banquet where he performed again. "It ain't what you got, it's what you can put out," he told the businessmen. "And boys, I can deliver." Uncle Dave, like Uncle Jimmy, attracted a good deal of mail, and the next week WSM announced that starting Saturday, December 26, both Macon and Uncle Jimmy would answer requests. One old-timer who recalled this show told me: "Uncle Jimmy and Dave Macon would do a show together, but they wouldn't actually be playing together at the same time. Uncle Dave, he'd play for a while, and then Uncle Jimmy'd take it for a while." Thus, Uncle Dave likely had more to do with establishing the Barn Dance than he is generally given credit for.

After the December 26 show, however, Macon did not appear on the program for a time. In fact, during the "first two or three months of 1926" that Hay talks about, when Macon, supposedly, actually joined the Barn Dance cast, he made not a single appearance that can be documented. He seems to have formally "joined" on April 17, 1926. Newspaper accounts of that week play up Uncle Dave and report that because he has been such a hit "this past winter" on the station, he will now appear twice per Barn Dance show, "early and late." For the next four months, from April through July, Uncle Dave is one of the three mainstays of the program, along with Dr. Bate and Uncle Jimmy Thompson. He begins to appear less frequently as late summer turns into fall. On one particular night he is scheduled to go on at 11:45, which suggests he might have been dropping by the station on his way home from a road trip or from a nearby concert. All told, in 1926 he appeared on about half the number of Barn Dance shows as Bate or Thompson—still enough to maintain a high profile with the audience.

But if Uncle Dave was in on the Barn Dance during its first months, he was hardly a sterling regular for the next three or four years. He continued to prefer "personals"—live concert tours and recording—over radio work. One obvious reason was money: WSM was not paying at all at first, and even when pay began, Uncle Dave could spend his time much more profitably in other media. When on the road, one of his favorite stunts was to pass the hat after a concert and ceremoniously examine the offering. If it was not enough, he would frown and start a heartrending spiel that began, "Folks, I've got seven little children that are home and barefoot. . . ." The hat was passed again, and people dug a little deeper. Uncle Dave collected the money, thanked the folks, and then explained, "And my children thank you, too. And lest you misunderstand, they are at home and barefoot because they are in bed and asleep." So Macon would spend much of summer and spring touring and appear on the radio mostly in the winter months when roads were bad and a bitter wind swept through the curtains of his touring car. In 1928, for example, he appeared on the Opry only four times in the year.

Most of Uncle Dave's early Opry shows were done alone, with Sam McGee or with Sid Harkreader. But in 1927, at the behest of a Vocalion A&R man, he formed a larger string band. He got Sam's younger brother Kirk, who played mandolin and fiddle, and a superb local fiddler named Mazy Todd. Todd was from Middle Tennessee—he actually ran a sawmill just a few hundred yards from Macon's home in Kittrell—and came from a family of fine musicians. When not playing with Uncle Dave, he often appeared with his own string trio on the Barn Dance. The main lineup was Macon, banjo and cheerleader, Sam on guitar, and usually Kirk and Mazy on fiddles. The band seems to have been organized primarily for recordings (the twin fiddle lead suggests that Vocalion might have been looking for competition for Columbia's very popular Skillet Lickers, who also used a two- or three-fiddle lead). Also, Macon dubbed the group the Fruit Jar Drinkers, even though at that time George Wilkerson headed an entirely different band on the Opry that had the same name (see chapter 8). This fact in itself suggests that Macon did not plan to use the group locally very much, and they made relatively few appearances on the Barn Dance as such. However, Uncle Dave would use Mazy on personal appearances, alternating him with Kirk McGee, Sam, and Sid.

No matter why he organized the band, with it Macon created one of the most exciting of old-time string bands. Propelled by his driving banjo, the group steamed through classic numbers like "Bake Dat Chicken Pie," "Tom and Jerry," "Hop Light Ladies," and "Rock About My Saro Jane." Macon's years of experience in playing for and calling square dances, one of his overlooked talents, is reflected in his calls on the records. "Backs to the wall and bottom shoe all!" he bellows. "Shout if yo' happy!" It was an inspired band, and one the Skillet Lickers themselves would have had trouble beating.

As the Depression continued to deepen in the early '30s, Uncle Dave pontificated on the state of things by arguing that music and morale go together and that hard times were caused by a decline in both music and morals. He told a reporter: "A man who can't enjoy music has no heart and very little soul. People today are drifting away from the old tunes, the real music, and at the same time they are drifting away from morals—one is the cause of the other." Nonetheless, the Depression hit Uncle Dave's musical profession hard. Both touring and recording were drying up. Uncle Dave did his last Brunswick session in Knoxville in March 1930. It was a special occasion for him, for it marked the recording debut of his son Dorris. He was therefore considerably angered when Brunswick failed to release a single one of the sides. Sid Harkreader recalled that he thought some sort of technical flaw in the records prevented release, but Uncle Dave would not hear of this and severed his long recording relationship with Brunswick. (He had recorded exclusively for them and their sister company Vocalion since his recording debut in 1924.) At once he set up a session with the rival company Okeh and with Sam McGee did a memorable series for them in December 1930. This date, in Jackson, Mississippi, produced at least two masterpieces, "Tennessee Red Fox Chase" and the topical "Wreck of the Tennessee Gravy Train." But most of this session, like the last Brunswick one, was not issued. Recovered test pressings from the Okeh date show that the music was fine, as usual. Okeh's failure to issue was because no one had the money to buy records. Uncle Dave was not to record for another three years, and the 1934 date, for Gennett, would come about because Kirk McGee initiated it. Altogether in 1930 Macon recorded some eighteen sides but, sadly, saw only six released.

It is thus in 1930, when other media began to fail him, that Uncle Dave first begins to appear regularly on the Opry. He appears in the radio logs with regular slots on almost every Saturday program, usually accompanied only by his son Dorris. (The McGee brothers had teamed up with Arthur Smith to form the Dixieliners, and Sid Harkreader had formed a band of his own.) His audience was waiting for him when he took his place among the WSM regulars, and he quickly became the most popular attraction on the show. Popularity in those days, before the WSM Artists Bureau had mastered the art of setting up successful tours, was measured by the amount of fan mail a performer received, and Uncle Dave customarily received more mail than anyone else, with the occasional exception of the Delmore Brothers. Indeed, the fan mail count led Uncle Dave to approach the Delmores and suggest that they team up on tours and personals. The Delmores had joined the Opry in 1933, and their close-harmony singing and amiability appealed very much to Uncle Dave. And the Delmores could keep time with him, a rather difficult feat since the older man, used to playing alone for many years, tended to vary his tempo as a song progressed. As with his other younger partners, Uncle Dave became a sort of father figure to the Delmores, sharing his considerable show-business experience with them and helping them negotiate the increasingly complex world of contracts and bookings. The Delmores, like the McGees, did most of the driving and chores required in touring. Alton Delmore recalled that Uncle Dave was a scrupulous bookkeeper: "He didn't want a penny that wasn't his, and he didn't want you to have a penny that belonged to him. For instance, when we checked up, that is counted the money, sometimes there would be an odd penny. We split three ways and of course you can't divide a penny into three parts. But Uncle Dave would put it down in his little book and remembered every time who the odd penny belonged to." Uncle Dave became close friends with the Delmores and by the mid-'30s was often staying with them at their house in Nashville.

It was also with the Delmores that Uncle Dave resumed his recording career. By 1935 the Depression was easing somewhat, and Victor Records two years earlier had initiated their budget-priced Bluebird label, sold for about half the usual record price to accommodate the record market to the hard times. To facilitate this, Victor reissued many older recordings in the early Bluebird series. But in 1934 Victor executives embarked on a determined drive to corner the old-time music market and began recording many of the best-selling groups of the '20s, like the Skillet Lickers, the Jenkins Family, and Fiddlin' John Carson. They were therefore very much interested in picking up Uncle Dave, and in 1935 he began a series of records for them.

Uncle Dave's first session for Bluebird was in New Orleans in 1935, and an incident there is representative of his attitude toward record making and his music making in general. Waiting to record after Arthur Smith, Uncle Dave was entertaining a black gospel quartet with jokes. The foursome, the Southern University Quartet, was waiting to record after Uncle Dave. The humor had gotten to the point where the black group would crack up merely if Uncle Dave looked at them. Then it came time for Uncle Dave himself to record. With the Delmores backing him, he launched into "Over the Mountain." Alton Delmore recalls what happened next:

> Uncle Dave had been looking back at the Negro quartet when he was playing and that didn't hurt anything, but when he was singing he never looked back at them till we got about halfway through. Then, right in the middle of a verse, he turned round and looked at them and the buzzer sounded. We couldn't see the technicians and Mr. Oberstein because there was a wall between us, and they were in another room. [Eli Oberstein had replaced Ralph Peer as Victor's main field-recording supervisor and talent scout for old-time and blues music.] But if something went wrong, they would buzz us and the record was no good. When the buzzer sounded we all quit playing, and in a moment Mr. Oberstein came walking in real slow like. He was not looking at anybody, but I could tell he was not pleased. He had seen Uncle Dave having fun with the quartet and he knew exactly what had happened.
>
> "Now, Uncle Dave, you are not here to sing for those boys back there, so come on now and let's get something going." He was right, but he didn't know Uncle Dave. The record would have been just as good if he had kept on the mike. That's the way he had always made records, from the beginning. "Now Cap," Uncle Dave said, "I can sing anyway I want to and still be heard. I've got a lot of git up and go." (He meant volume.) "And I've got a smoke-house full of country hams and all kinds of meat to eat up there in Readyville. I've got plenty of wood hauled up, and I don't have to be bossed around by some New York sharpshooter just to

make a few records 'cause I've done my part on the record making anyway."

Eventually, Uncle Dave calmed down and recorded six classic sides.

Uncle Dave continued to tour with Opry groups and to build his audience. Thus in 1939, when Hollywood decided to make a film about the Opry, Uncle Dave was a natural choice to appear in a major role. Although he eventually warmed to the idea, he was initially unimpressed with film, as he had been with records. When first notified of the film opportunity, his immediate reaction was to ask "How much money up front?" George Hay recalled bringing the Hollywood advance man to Uncle Dave's house prior to the filming:

> Uncle Dave was delighted. He asked the cook to prepare a real, sho' 'nuf Tennessee dinner with all of the trimmings and we drove down from Nashville on a beautiful day. . . . Uncle Dave asked the blessing and we were served a dinner which is not on sale anywhere in these United States, more is the pity. We were forced to be satisfied with rich country ham, fried chicken, six or seven vegetables done to a Tennessee turn, jelly preserves, pickles, hot corn bread and white bread. Then came the cake. . . . After dinner Uncle Dave invited us to be seated under a large tree in his front yard, where we discussed the possibility of a Grand Ole Opry picture. As the producer and your reporter drove back to Nashville, that experienced executive said, "I have never met a more natural man in my life. He prays at the right time and he cusses at the right time and his jokes are as cute as the dickens."

Uncle Dave appeared in the picture not only as a musician but also as an actor. He played the constable of a small rural town and had ample opportunity to demonstrate his classic vaudeville humor. In one scene he is umpiring a baseball game in which an Opry group plays a girls' softball team. As an Opry member tries to bat against a leggy red-haired pitcher, Uncle Dave cracks, "You're looking at the wrong curves, boy." In another scene he forces a reluctant prisoner into his cell by firing a shotgun into the floor inches from his feet. As a musician he appears in a string band led by Roy Acuff: he calls a square dance set and plays a driving banjo in a lengthy version of "Soldier's Joy." He also plays with Acuff's group in a spirited version of "Down in Union County" (the film's theme song), rendered while bouncing down a hill in an old open touring car. Finally he and son Dorris do a version of "Take Me Back to My Old Carolina Home," in which Uncle Dave sings, picks, mugs, fires his banjo like a gun, fans it, twirls it, passes it between his legs, and dances with it. It is his only film appearance, and it makes one realize just how much of his art could not be captured by phonograph records.

Uncle Dave's career on the Opry extended far beyond the period covered in this sketch, but that is another story for another time. He was the mainstay of the Opry during the '30s and one of the few old-timers that the average fan today knows anything about. While his music was vibrant and important and deserving of complete study in and by itself, it is his personality that impressed people so much. Kirk McGee, who emerged as one of the best raconteurs about the early Opry, loved to talk about Uncle Dave; and perhaps a selection from Kirk's stories makes a fitting conclusion to a profile of "The Dixie Dewdrop."

I loved travelling with Uncle Dave. He was good to get along with, you know. He was always peaceful. And he was a showman—he sold what he had. Most of his songs were just three-chord numbers, mostly in A and G, and keys didn't matter too much to him, but he was a showman. You knew you were going to have a crowd with Uncle Dave, cause he'd been in the business so long. His dress and everything was just different from everything else.

He meant for us to be just like it should be, strictly business with him in the music. But he was a show, all day, every way. He was always ready to go. He wasn't finicky about his food, where he'd stay. He just wanted to rest, and when that time of the day come, why, he was going to bed somewhere. I remember once we were at a little place called Ooltewah, outside Chattanooga; there was a school and a hosiery mill there. He went to his cousin that lived there, a first cousin, and was going to spend the night there. Of course, they wanted to talk, they hadn't seen him in a long time, and they asked him all about the family and all. So when this lady went in the other room, he said, "Now if she don't fix me a bed, I'm going to leave here." He didn't want to talk to her, he wanted that nap.

And then there was that trip to New York in 1927 to record the famous Fruit Jar Drinkers records. Well, it was the greatest thing that ever had happened to me at the time to get to go up there. Of course, Uncle Dave didn't want to get out and see anything. All he wanted to do was stay in the hotel. He was afraid something would happen and we wouldn't get back and be able to do the session. That was the main thing. And he said, "Now, boys, there are all kinds of people in New York, they'll knock your head off." I wanted to see the town. But he didn't want us to get away from him. The battle fleet was in the harbor down there, all those ships, and I wanted to go down and see that, and he said, "Oh, it's nothing but a bunch of old boats, wouldn't be nothing to it." He wouldn't go anyplace but the recording studio. And the people doing the recording, they had a time handling Uncle Dave, because he wouldn't stay put. He kept getting closer and closer to the mike. He was an old stage man, you know, a vaudeville man, and he wanted to do it just like he was doing for an audience. And the recording man said, "Uncle Dave, you're not before an audience now. We're putting this on the wax." And they had a lot of trouble with Uncle Dave stomping his foot; they finally had to get him a pillow to put his foot on. It was a wood floor, and he'd get to reeling and rocking and stomping and he'd shake the floor and vibrate that stylus and we couldn't record. So they went and got this pillow to put his foot on. Well, he didn't like that. He said, "I don't like that, 'cause I can't hear my foot; that'll ruin my rhythm."

There was once a family that had had their boy killed on a cycle of some sort. That family had never laughed until one night when Uncle Dave spent the night with them. They told me later, "It done us more good than anything that could ever happen to us." Uncle Dave, he was a man for every occasion, I don't care what it was. He could make a nice talk in a church; he was well educated. He could just hold an audience in his hand anyplace he was.

I still think about him. There's hardly a day pass that I don't think about something he told me. Even if I go up around Woodbury [just east of Macon's home at Kittrell], I remember things Uncle Dave told me about the people there. He was a great man, but the people didn't know it at the time. Around Woodbury, he was just an old banjo player. I did realize it myself as I travelled with him. I thought he was the greatest, and still do. It was a pity a man like him had to die, for he was so much pleasure to everybody.

UNCLE DAVE MACON DIES AT
RUTHERFORD HOSPITAL

Murfreesboro, Tenn., March 22 (Special)—Uncle Dave Macon, known to millions of radio listeners as the "Dixie Dewdrop" of WSM's Grand Ole Opry, died at Rutherford Hospital here this morning at 6:25 o'clock after an illness of several weeks.

He was 81 years old last Oct. 7.

Funeral services will be held Sunday afternoon at 2:30 o'clock at the First Methodist Church here conducted by Charlie Taylor, minister of the North Maple Street Church of Christ, and the Rev. Vernon Bradley. Burial will be in Coleman Cemetery on Woodbury Road with Moore Funeral Home in charge.

Uncle Dave, whose home was on a farm at nearby Kittrell, had been called "king of hillbillies." He was one of the small group of entertainers who a quarter of a century ago joined George Hay in the Grand Ole Opry, creating a new interest in folk and hillbilly music which today has grown nationwide, making Nashville known as the folk music capital of the country.

His last appearance on the Grand Ole Opry was Saturday March 1. He became sick the next day and was operated on in the hospital here several days later. He traveled with the Grand Ole Opry's road troupes until 1950. He had made many phonograph records. In 1940 he went to Hollywood and played in a movie based on the Grand Ole Opry. He was the author of numerous songs, among the best known being "Never Make Love No More," "Give Me Back My Five Dollars," "You Can't Do Wrong and Get By," "She Was Always Chewing Gum," "All I've Got Is Gone," "The Nashville Gal," "Keep My Skillet Good and Greasy All the Time," and "Country Ham and Red Gravy."

Son of Captain John Macon and Martha Macon, he was born at Viola and lived there until he was 20 when the family moved to Nashville, where his father operated the Broadway Hotel. In 1898 he moved to Readyville and a year later married Miss Mary Richardson. He moved to Kittrell where he had resided since. His wife died in 1939. From 1901 to 1920 he operated a freight wagon line between Woodbury and Murfreesboro.

Surviving are seven sons, Archie and John of Murfreesboro, Harry of Nashville, Glenn of Kittrell, Dorris of Woodbury, Esten of Chattanooga, and Paul, now in the Army. The two weeks that he has been in the hospital here cards from well-wishers over the country arrived at the rate of around 200 a day.

Appendix 1

"Cap'n Tom Ryman"

In a further instance of historical irony, Uncle Dave liked to sing a song about the builder of the Ryman Auditorium, riverboat man Tom Ryman. The song, entitled "Cap'n Tom Ryman," was collected from Macon by folklorist George Boswell in 1950. Boswell transcribed both words and music for his then-unpublished collection of Tennessee folk songs. Uncle Dave never commercially recorded it, though he did record a related version as the widely known "Rock About My Saro Jane." Boswell's text reads as follows:

Cap'n Tom Ryman was a steamboat man,
But Sam Jones sent him to the heavenly land,
Oh, sail away.
Oh, there's nothing to do but to sit down and sing,
Oh rockabout my Saro Jane, oh rockabout my Saro Jane,
Oh rockabout my Saro Jane.
Oh rockabout my Saro Jane,
Oh rockabout my Saro Jane,
Oh there's nothing to do but to sit down and sing,
Oh rockabout my Saro Jane.

Engine give a scratch and the whistle gave a squall,
The engineer going to a hole in the wall,
Oh Saro Jane.
There's nothing to do but to sit down and sing,
Oh rockabout my Saro Jane.

Uncle Dave, when asked about the song, gave this history to Boswell:

Now that tabernacle what was built down there where we play, Rev'rend Sam Jones converted Cap'n Tom Ryman. He had six steamboats on the Cumberland River and you ought to have seen that wharf just lined with horses and mules and wagons hauling freight to those boats and bringing it back. And Sam Jones preached the low country to him so straight he took them niggers all down there Monday morning and bought all that whiskey and poured it in the river. Took them card tables and built a bonfire and burned 'em up. Clean up. Niggers started this song.

The song would make an interesting case study in Uncle Dave's use of traditional material in his music. As with many of his pieces, the "core" of the song seems borrowed from black tradition, as he always acknowledged. The chorus of "Saro Jane" might well have referred to a steamboat originally, and the piece could have been a form of work song. Yet the couplet at the beginning of each stanza seems to have been interchangeable, like a blues stanza. On Macon's 1927 recording of "Rock About My Saro Jane" (Vocation 5152) he sings words identical to those above except that he does not include the "Cap'n Tom Ryman" stanza and does include several other stanzas that seem to have little in common with one another. Although Uncle Dave probably did sing the "Tom Ryman" couplet earlier than 1950, when Boswell collected it, he probably used it simply as a random stanza in "Rock About My Saro Jane." But after he saw the Ryman Auditorium become the home of the Opry, he might well have shifted the emphasis of the song to the more topical subject of Tom Ryman. Macon was notorious for mixing parts of different songs and "recomposing" them to suit himself, and some day some poor folklorist is going to ruin his liver trying to track all of them down.

Appendix 2

An Evening with WSM
(November 6, 1925)

6,000 APPLAUD POLICE BENEFIT
Many Others Unable to Crowd In; Every Act Voted "Best"

Six thousand people crowded the Ryman Auditorium last night, listened for three hours and cheered for encores as the annual program pronounced by critics as perhaps the best and most entertaining yet offered by the Nashville Policemen's Benefit Association was executed. By the time the 6,000 were hearing the first number, perhaps a third of that number were on their way back home for lack of standing room.

It was a miscellaneous program of music, instrumental, song and comedy, presenting a range from the finest touches in the classic to the old-time "breakdown," and most "scientific jazz." Not only did the audience of 6,000 hear the program of scarcely excelled local talent but through the courtesy of Station WSM of the National Life & Accident Company, the program was broadcast with the result that scores of telegrams from various parts of the United States, indicating the popularity of Nashville talent for entertainment, were received. Jack Keefe was the announcer.

HOWSE MAKES ADDRESS
Harry Lester was chairman of the committee on arrangements, assisted by Enoch Shelton and Jack Dowd. At the outset, Mayor Howse

delivered a brief address as to the purpose of the entertainment and the organization presenting it, and presented Johnnie Stiner with a badge for sale of the largest number of tickets.

The program opened with a soprano solo by Miss Neil [sic] Moran, with Jack Keefe as accompanist, after which the Beasley Smith's Andrew Jackson Hotel Orchestra was heard. "Indian Love Call," a number by Miss Moran, was particularly well received.

Then came a series of violin solos by C. Roland Flick, with Mrs. Flick at the piano, which held the audience spellbound.

JOE COMBS IN SOLOS

A turn to the less serious side of life came with the introduction of Joe Combs in two or three light, fantastic solos. In one he appeared as the Adam of Creation in the song "I Want My Rib." Eric Nissen presided at the piano in his "New Stuff" as offered by himself and Mr. Combs. They presented "Tea For Two," and "Save Your Sorrow for Tomorrow."

Thereafter, it was tit for tat and whichever was last was always best in bringing down the house, as Dr. Humphrey Bate and His Hawaiian orchestra of Castallian Springs vied with Sidney Harkreader, introduced as the "fiddling fiddler" of Mt. Juliet and with "Uncle Dave" Macon, of Readyville, introduced as the "struttingest strutter that ever strutted a strut," either with his banjo, guitar or laryngeal equipment.

MISSES HIS FIREPLACE

"Uncle Dave" confessed to some embarrassment in being transplanted from a home far back in the country to the stage without a big wood fireplace in which to expectorate and throw things. Some of the numbers presented jointly by himself and Mr. Harkreader were: "Turkey in the Straw," "Sugar Walks down the Street," "Ain't Goin' to Rain No Mo'," "Don't Reckon T'will Happen Again," and "Go Way Mule." Both Harkreader and Uncle Dave kept the audience in an uproar.

Dr. Bate directed his old-time orchestra, using himself the harmonica. His daughter, Miss Alcyone Bate, presided at the piano, Walter Liggett and Hugh Peay played banjo and O. R. Blanton and Bert Hutchinson [sic] played guitars. They rendered several numbers of old-time and popular music and the audience never got enough.

DeFord Bailey

T HE FOLK ROOTS OF THE EARLY OPRY'S music are
nowhere more clearly demonstrated than in the career of DeFord
Bailey. Bailey was one of the single most popular performers on
the pre-1930 Opry; in 1928, for instance, he made twice as many appearances (forty-nine in fifty-two weeks) as any other Opry regular. It was not
at all uncommon for DeFord to appear for two or even three sets in a single Saturday night show, usually playing harmonica solos. He did this by
himself, while still young and inexperienced, even though he had endured
a crippling illness. And he did all this in spite of the fact that he was
black.

Students of country music history have struggled for years to assess
just what DeFord's presence on the early Opry meant in terms of the inter-
relationship of black and white folk music traditions. DeFord's emergence
as a star in the music preceded Charley Pride's by some forty years; yet
how important was DeFord's role on the Opry? Was his presence there an
instance of tokenism? Paternalism? Authentic musical bi-raciality? The full
story would be the product of a complex study in itself and cannot be
developed here. But the whole problem is complicated by the fact that
details of DeFord's life have heretofore been vague and sketchy and often
drawn from secondhand sources. Only toward the end of his life did Bailey himself start to emerge from the isolation of his self-exile and to talk to
fans and admirers. Only recently, therefore, has reliable information and
authentic opinion come from him. This information, much of which was
made public in a biography that David Morton and I wrote in 1991, sheds
a great deal of light on his unusual role in early Opry history.

DeFord was born in 1899 at Bellwood, in Smith County, Tennessee, but some of his family originally came from New York. As a youth he moved nearer to Nashville and spent several years as a child around a couple of hamlets called Newsom's Station and Thompson's Station. As their names imply, both communities were oriented toward the railroad, and this had an immense effect on the young DeFord. He had to pass under a trestle on his way to school, and he recalls that often he would deliberately wait until the train went over it. "I would get up under it, put my hands over my eyes, listen to the sound, and then play that sound on my harp all the way to school." This sound, of course, later became the strains around which he built one of his most famous harmonica solos, "Pan American Blues."

When he was three, DeFord contracted infantile paralysis and his doctors did not expect him to live. He survived only after a long and painful struggle. In later years he always credited his and his family's religious faith in getting him through the ordeal. But the illness forced him to remain flat on his back in bed for a year, moving only his head and hands. During this time somebody gave him a harmonica to amuse himself with, and he quickly mastered the instrument. As he rested in bed, he imitated the sounds he heard on the rural Smith County farm: the dogs running foxes at night, the chickens, the livestock, even the distant trains. He also learned the old fiddle tunes and folk tunes his family played and sang. Though he survived the illness—a rare thing in rural turn-of-the-century Tennessee— it stunted his growth and slightly deformed his back; even as a grown man, he stood only four feet, ten inches. This disability was partially responsible for forcing him into a musical career, much as blindness forced many other old-time musicians into music.

Curiously, much of the music DeFord was exposed to during his formative years was not blues as such but, to use his own phrase, "black hillbilly music." DeFord was quick to acknowledge that in his youth he knew many blacks playing forms of old-time music. His grandfather Lewis Bailey was a champion fiddler in the region, and his uncle was the best black banjo player he ever knew. DeFord himself also became quite proficient on the guitar and banjo, as well as on the harmonica. He even played the fiddle somewhat, mostly hoedowns, but it was by no means his favorite instrument: "I just fool around a little with it." As a child, he and his cousins often played on homemade instruments. He remembered making fiddles out of corn stalks and using a "washtub" bass. Occasionally they would get simple pots and pans from his aunt's kitchen: "You know, skillets and frying pans make good music too."

World War I found DeFord working for a white merchant at Thompson's Station, a man named Gus Watson. Watson liked DeFord's harmonica music and paid him to work in his store and around his house. DeFord's playing in the store attracted a good many extra customers, and Watson in turn gave DeFord a place to live. He also kept him supplied with Hohner Marine Band harmonicas. DeFord used this type of harp throughout his later career and swore by them. He reported to his friend David Morton: "I've had all kinds of harps. I've had them roller harps and all, but ain't nothing beat this harp."

When Watson moved into Nashville about 1918, DeFord joined him, and worked at various odd jobs around Nashville, often as a "houseboy" for wealthy old-line Nashville families on Franklin Road. He continued to play his harmonica, and by 1925 he had a job as an elevator operator at the National Life and Accident Insurance Company. When WDAD started in Nashville in September 1925, several passengers told him he should go on the radio. Like many other early Opry performers, DeFord recalled playing earlier on WDAD. Perhaps his earliest documented radio performance was on the night of December 6, 1925, when he appeared on a radio French harp contest broadcast by WDAD. The *Tennessean* reported that "the first prize in the French Harp contest staged recently was won by J. T. Bland, who played 'Lost John.' The second prize was won by DeFord Bailey, a Negro boy, who played 'It Ain't Gonna Rain No Mo'.'" Actually, some evidence exists suggesting that DeFord in fact outplayed all his opponents and that the station management was reluctant to award first place to a black man. They concluded that each player, DeFord and Bland, were "the best of each race."

It was Dr. Humphrey Bate who was responsible for introducing DeFord to Judge Hay and WSM. Bate, as we have seen, for a time played on both WDAD and WSM, and one night he and his daughter, Alcyone, met DeFord as they left WDAD to walk up the hill to WSM to perform. Dr. Bate persuaded DeFord to go with them. DeFord was hesitant. "I was ashamed with my little cheap harp and them with all those fine, expensive guitars, fiddles and banjos up there, but I went anyway." When they arrived, Dr. Bate persuaded Hay to let DeFord perform on the air without an audition and reportedly said, "Judge, I will stake my reputation on the ability of this boy." Bate, of course, was an extraordinary harmonica player himself and was uniquely qualified to judge DeFord's talent. DeFord played several numbers, and Hay was so surprised and delighted that he threw his steamboat whistle in the air. He immediately asked DeFord to return, and soon thereafter labeled him "The Harmonica Wizard." From then on, DeFord's name seldom appeared without this tag. Apparently nobody at the time thought anything of Bailey's color, though a few years later condescending publicity was to refer to him as the Opry's "mascot."

In fact, the early Opry had a strong tradition of blackface comedy during the height of DeFord's popularity. By 1929 Judge Hay himself was participating in a very popular series of skits with Ed McConnell that were scheduled immediately prior to the Opry on Saturday nights. These skits had McConnell dramatizing the "trials and tribulations of Uncle Wash" while Hay played himself, the "solemn old judge." Some of the skits were undoubtedly based on the newspaper columns Hay had written while a reporter in Memphis (see chapter 1). Later, by the 1930s, duos like Lasses & Honey (Lasses White and Honey Wilds) came to the Opry after many years' experience as blackfaced comedians in vaudeville. It may seem curious that a radio audience that did not recognize DeFord's blackness would be expected to recognize the stereotypes of blackface comedy, but DeFord seldom spoke on the air and confined his act largely to playing music. Whether Hay attempted consciously to conceal Bailey's race from his Southern audience at first is not at all clear. It became obvious only later, when DeFord joined Opry tours.

"The Harmonica Wizard" quickly became one of the most popular performers on the show. His harmonica solo style was uniquely suited to the new electronic medium of radio, and he soon learned how to use the microphone for best effect. In his early days he had used an old-fashioned megaphone, the kind that the popular crooners of the day like Rudy Vallee used, to amplify his harp. Radio solved that problem, but he had to stand on a Coca-Cola crate to reach the WSM microphone. His "Pan American Blues," with its train effects, became so popular that once an engineer from a regular train that often passed through Nashville came up to the WSM studios to correct DeFord on the exact whistle pattern for crossings. DeFord listened and incorporated the correct pattern into his tune. He recalled receiving a lot of fan mail, but when asked whether he appealed more to the black or the white community, he just smiled and said, "I couldn't tell whether the writers were black or white."

By spring of 1927 George D. Hay was convinced that DeFord had a big future ahead of him. "You're nothing but a gold mine walking around on earth," Hay told him, and set about to promote the Bailey name and career. Drawing on his earlier contacts with Columbia records in Chicago, he brokered a deal for three of his WSM acts to record for the company. He paid the expenses for three acts—Obed "Dad" Pickard, DeFord, and the Golden Echo Quartet—to take the train to Atlanta to record. The understanding was that each record label would list the artist's name, followed by the legend "Of Radio Station WSM, Nashville, Tennessee." Each act but Bailey recorded several numbers (which were duly released); for some reason, the company only let him record two songs, "Pan American Blues" and "Hesitation Blues," both cut on April 1, 1927. Judge Hay was not pleased at this cavalier treatment of his new star. According to DeFord: "Judge wasn't pleased with it. He thought they should have recorded some of my other tunes too, so he decided to cancel the deal and send me to New York instead."

The Judge had contacts with another major label, Brunswick, and set up a replacement session with them just fourteen days later. (The Columbia sides, written off by everyone, were never issued in any form.) To do this, though, DeFord had to travel to New York. Hay set up the trip: DeFord took a train from Nashville to Knoxville, was met by a Brunswick rep who drove them by car to Roanoke, Virginia, where they caught the train for New York. They arrived on Easter Sunday and spent the day in a hotel. On Monday, they walked down Seventh Avenue to the studio—the same one where everyone from Duke Ellington to Uncle Dave Macon recorded—and DeFord waxed eight solos, most on one take. "I was getting fifty dollars a side and I decided to give 'em their money's worth. I tried to play my best tunes." And, indeed, he did: "Pan American Blues," "Dixie Flyer Blues," "Muscle Shoals Blues," "Evening Prayer Blues," "Up Country Blues," "Old Hen Cackle," "Alcoholic Blues," and his "Fox Chase." The first of the records—"Evening Prayer" backed with "Alcoholic Blues"—was issued in August 1927, and the other three later that fall. Each certainly sold well enough to justify their reissue by Brunswick, and, significantly, all were released in the old-time series ("Songs from Dixie"), not the blues series. Brunswick, apparently, felt that Bailey's biggest appeal would be to a white audience.

Though he was excited about recording, DeFord did not enjoy his first trip to the big city. He stayed in the McAlpin Hotel at 33rd and Broadway, and spent most of his time there. He did try the subway once but got totally lost and had to be directed back to the hotel. Nor did he get all the money that was promised him. "They were supposed to give me $400 cash money for my eight sides," he recalled, "plus royalties. But I didn't get that much. Judge Hay got 25 percent of the $400 for what he done in arranging for the sessions. Instead of giving me the rest outright, they gave me my share in $10 payments over a period of several months." Later he did get by mail some of his royalty payments—two percent of each record that retailed for 75 cents each. "As for the royalty checks, I got three of 'em.

The first one was for $80, the second was for $40, and the third was for $8. . . . The records sold 15,589 copies in less than six months."

Over a year later, on October 2, 1928, DeFord made what would be his last commercial recordings. This was the famous Victor Nashville session described in a later chapter. He recorded another eight sides, duplicating none of the Brunswick titles. Victor released only three of these, but one coupling, "Ice Water Blues"/"Davidson County Blues," was so popular that it was reissued at least three times. Ironically, Victor's sides were issued in their blues/jazz series aimed at black markets. It has been generally assumed that all DeFord's unissued sides were harp solos, but one of the numbers, "Kansas City Blues," has been known for years as a piece that featured his singing and guitar playing, one of his best vocal-guitar numbers.

These eleven sides constitute DeFord's complete discography, an astounding and shameful fact for an artist of his popularity. Numerous informal recordings were made of Bailey's playing in the 1960s and 1970s, but repeated rumors of an authorized studio album have never been verified.

However, it was probably DeFord's radio popularity that sold the records, and not vice versa. Through the 1930s his popularity continued to rise, and it was his train imitations that inspired Hay, as we have seen, to rename the Barn Dance the Grand Ole Opry. When Opry groups began touring in the early '30s, DeFord was a popular addition to any show hitting the road and, at least in one respect, got special treatment. Hay insisted that any time DeFord made an appearance, the black star was to receive a $5 flat fee, regardless of whether that particular show made any money. Most of the other Opry acts got a percentage of the gate on these shows. If the show did not attract enough audience, there was no pay. But DeFord's pay was constant, regardless; Judge Hay saw to that. This arrangement gave the harmonica virtuoso a sense of security, to be sure, but it also caused him to lose out on some lucrative gate receipts when the shows did well.

DeFord toured with a wide variety of Opry performers: Dr. Humphrey Bate, Uncle Dave Macon, the Delmore Brothers, Sarie and Sallie, Sam and Kirk McGee, the Gully Jumpers, the Fruit Jar Drinkers, Curt Poulton and the Vagabonds, Lasses and Honey, and, in later years, Roy Acuff and Bill Monroe. Some became his close friends. The Delmores won his respect when they showed him how some performers were cheating him out of his share of the gate; he also liked their music: "They was good guitar pickers, and they could sing, too." And their music, he said, reflected "that they knew about the blues." Another close friend was Uncle Dave Macon. "I slept in the room with him, rode with him, ate with him, held up his pants while he put them on. I'd talk with Uncle Dave about my problems."

Many members of the audience on these tours had never seen DeFord and had never realized he was black, but he never met with any hostility. Touring in the South in the 1930s was difficult, however. Often he encountered the same kind of problems that so many jazz artists met while touring in those days: he was almost never allowed to eat in restaurants (except sometimes in the kitchen), and many hotels—including the ones where the rest of the Opry tour were staying—refused to admit him. In such cases, DeFord would try to find lodging with a local black family, but even that offered serious problems: his size made him an easy target for criminals. Mindful of his plight, several fellow performers who toured with him went out of their way to help him. For instance, DeFord remembered with fondness how Uncle Dave Macon would get him into his hotel room by insisting that he was his valet and would refuse to stay in a hotel that would not let him take DeFord into his room with him. (DeFord also respected Macon's music: "He was the best white banjo player I ever heard.")

But as the Opry grew, DeFord's time slots became shorter and shorter. From slots of twenty to twenty-five minutes in the late 1920s his allotted airtime shrank to ten-minute slots in 1934 and to five-minute slots in 1935. And the number of slots per program shrank from three to two to one. By the late 1930s, DeFord recalls, he was going down to the station, hanging around for three to four hours, and playing one number if time permitted. The final break came in May 1941, when he was formally fired from the Opry. Exactly what happened has been one of the great controversies of Nashville music.

Everybody familiar with the situation has offered a different reason why DeFord was, in his own words, "turned loose to root hog or die." The traditional, "official," Opry explanation, for many years echoed the explanation Judge Hay wrote in his book in 1945:

> Like some members of his race and other races, DeFord was lazy. He knew about a dozen numbers, which he put on the air and recorded for a major company, but he refused to learn more, even though his reward was great. He was our mascot and is still loved by the entire company. We gave him a whole year's notice to learn some more tunes, but he would not. When we were forced to give him his final notice, DeFord said, without malice: "I knowed it wuz comin', Judge, I knowed it was comin'."

This isn't quite the way DeFord himself remembered it, though he expressed no real bitterness toward Hay. He felt that Hay himself was under pressure. "Judge Hay did all he could. . . . At that time a white man couldn't do too much for a black person. If they did, they wouldn't get any help. It was nationwide." Regarding his repertoire, DeFord recalls the situation was just the opposite, that he wanted to play new tunes, different tunes, but that Hay and the audience insisted he perform the same tunes, such as "Fox Chase" and "Pan American Blues," over and over. Certainly, any loss of musical skill was not a reason for DeFord ending his career in 1941. He was only forty-two years old, in the prime of life, and air-checks from the period suggest he was still at the peak of his skills.

Changing tastes, however, probably did contribute. DeFord once told historian Dick Hulan that by 1941 he would come down to the Opry and wait around backstage all evening just to get to play one short solo—and that he was getting tired of it. The harmonica solo, though a popular sound of old-time music and blues in the 1920s, was not in step with the increasingly elaborate bands of the 1940s. Still, when audiences found out that DeFord was no longer on the show, they responded with a substantial outcry, so much so that for several weeks the management would pay him to just come down to the show and hang around to make himself visible (they paid him three dollars a night for this.) He soon tired of this charade though, and by the summer of 1941 he had dropped off the show for good. He left with a good deal of bitterness toward WSM and the commercial music business in general—a bitterness that remained with him for years.

Opry veteran Kirk McGee, who had known DeFord from the first and who was still present at the end, offered what is probably the most accurate reason for the firing. In 1941 a major battle was raging between two huge performance rights organizations, ASCAP (American Society of Composers, Authors, and Publishers) and an upstart rival called BMI (Broadcast Music, Incorporated). Both organizations represented professional songwriters and publishers in licensing their songs when performed in public for profit. ASCAP was engaged in a boycott of radio stations that prevented the stations from playing any ASCAP songs. To get around this, the stations—including WSM, a major player in this controversy—were creating their own organization (BMI) and urging publishers and artists to affiliate with it. When he made his records in the '20s, some of DeFord's standards had been routinely copyrighted by a publisher affiliated with ASCAP. Therefore, they were banned from the air for most of 1941—even though some of them were traditional numbers the harmonica player had adapted to his style. Thus, he could not play his signature pieces like "Fox Chase."

Confused, frustrated, and slighted by all this, DeFord moved into voluntary musical exile for almost the rest of his life. For years he operated a shoeshine stand in downtown Nashville, where he always kept a harp and would occasionally play for friends and for other harp players, like Sonny Terry, who would drop by when in town. In the 1960s he made a memorable appearance on Nashville's famous syndicated blues TV show "Night Train," one of the few times that the local black community recognized his art. Then he refused offers to cut an album with Pete Seeger, to be a guest at the Newport Folk Festival, to record solo albums, and to be in a Hollywood film starring Burt Reynolds. But gradually, through the offices of a cadre of young white friends like Dick Hulan, James Talley, and David Morton, he began to play an occasional party or coffeehouse date, and in 1974 he actually returned to the Opry stage for an Old-Timers Reunion. Unknown to most people at the time, he agreed to let Morton start taping some of his vast repertoire on a good tape machine. When he died, in 1982, he had preserved a lot of his music and memories for Morton.

Though many think of him only in terms of the harp, DeFord also frequently performed vocals, accompanying himself on banjo or guitar. He played both instruments left-handed and therefore "upsidedown." His banjo style was totally unique, with a complex picking style that went deep into the nineteenth century wellsprings of black music. Often he used no picks but instead used his fingernails, grown long to form natural picks. One of his favorite banjo-vocal numbers was "Lost John," in a very archaic version that incorporated parts of the nineteenth century minstrel song "Old John Boker." His guitar specialty was "Kansas City Blues," which he assembled from the different versions of it recorded in the late 1920s by vaudeville bluesman Jim Jackson:

Well, I got me a bulldog, two grey hounds,
One high yeller, one black and brown,
Gonna move to Kansas City (move to Kansas City),
Move to Kansas City (move to Kansas City),
Gonna move to Kansas City,
Honey where they don't let you.

Well, I got me a wife and a bulldog too,
My wife don't love me, but my bulldog do,
Gonna move to Kansas City. . . .

DeFord recalled that he played and sang occasionally on the air as well as on concert tours. Sadly, this facet of his talent was never well documented on commercial recordings because all of his early records were harp solos.

A full analysis of DeFord's music would be a lengthy and complex undertaking, since he seems to represent a tradition of black hillbilly music that is all but extinct. His solos of the 1920s seem to have drawn on old-time rather than blues sources. His famous "Fox Chase" had been recorded by white hillbilly artist Henry Whitter as early as 1923, and it became a staple for all harp players. (Versions of it, however, have been traced to nineteenth century Ireland.) "Old Hen Cackle" seems derived from the well-known fiddle piece, and "Lost John" was also recorded by white artists before DeFord's recording. It may well be, however, that this latter piece originated among black people and that it entered white tradition in the early twentieth century; DeFord might well have learned it from either source. A similar statement could be made for his other two railroad pieces, "Casey Jones" and "John Henry." Yet he also borrowed from a rather distinct blues-jazz tradition in some numbers. A case in point is his famous Victor recording of "Davidson County Blues." (Nashville is in Davidson County, Tennessee.) As Tony Russell has noted, this tune is basically the same as blues pianist Cow Cow Davenport's "Cow Cow Blues" (originally recorded in January 1927), the Mississippi Sheiks' "Jackson Stomp," and bluesman Charlie McCoy's "That Lonesome Train Took My Baby Away." As a young man in Nashville, DeFord often attended the Bijou theater, where he heard traveling blues greats like Bessie Smith and Ma Raney. He thus seems to have borrowed from both white and black traditions, though it is noteworthy that both McCoy and the Sheiks were noted for their hillbilly overtones.

Given the immense number of people that have heard DeFord or know of him, it is odd that his influence has not been more apparent. Sonny Terry, perhaps the leading country blues harp-player today, remembered seeing DeFord in North Carolina years ago and picked up his version of "Alcoholic Blues." Several black musicians in the Johnson City area recall being much impressed with DeFord's visits there in the 1930s. And the later comeback shows sparked a couple of contemporary Nashville records that echo his style. But DeFord's music has in some sense existed in a vacuum. Perhaps this can be attributed to his lack of recording or to the fact that his music represented a complex and demanding synthesis of two distinct musical forms, hillbilly and blues, and that as these two forms became increasingly segregated in the 1930s and 1940s, he could not find a real home in either.

When he summed up his career for David Morton, DeFord said: "I don't get tired playing. I make them songs go as I breathe. It's just like a fish in water, and water runs through its gills." Throughout his career DeFord Bailey was a "pro" in the best sense of the word, and he was not bragging when he looked back over that career and said simply, "I was a humdinger."

The Hoedown Bands

ONE OF THE OLDEST TRADITIONS of the Opry has been the fiddle band or string band, what Judge Hay called "the hoedown band." After World War II, these bands served as little more than window dressing for an expanding parade of singers, often playing short, fast breakdowns, generally for a group of square dancers on stage. But in earlier years, the bands were much more important, appearing in almost all the early publicity pictures and often having entire fifteen- to twenty-minute segments of the program to themselves. They developed a substantial listener following, and in his 1945 book, Hay admitted that the hoedown bands "form the backbone and lend a rural flavor to the entire Grand Ole Opry." He was always careful to schedule the bands at regular intervals throughout the show, just in case some of the other acts got a little too "uptown" or a little too western. The classic fiddle tunes the old bands played were, in his words, "definite punctuation marks in our program," and the bands themselves "get us back to earth the minute they plunk the first note."

The hoedown bands were paragons of continuity on the show. No other acts lasted as long or experienced fewer changes in personnel. Hay identified four groups as "basic" hoedown bands: the Fruit Jar Drinkers, the Crook Brothers, the Gully Jumpers, and the Possum Hunters. Not until the 1950s did these groups undergo any changes in their basic personnel, and then only because of death and illness. Throughout the years, the bands weathered the various fads and innovations of country music that swept across the Opry stage, playing in their wonderfully archaic string band style with uncompromising zeal and drive. Like the old New Orleans jazz bands, the hoedown bands favored a collective ensemble sound. Though blessed with a variety of excellent instrumentalists, they seldom featured any one musician as a soloist on a regular basis, as did more modern bands like the Dixieliners or the Golden West Cowboys. The fiddler was generally the keystone of the group (except for the Crook Brothers, who started off with a twin harmonica lead), and fiddle repertoire dominated their music. Even by the standards of the 1930s, none of the hoedown bands was especially innovative or outstanding; few approached the excitement of the Skillet Lickers, the versatility of the Hill Billies, or the precision of Charlie Poole. Yet they were true to the rural dance music of turn-of-the-century Tennessee and relatively unspoiled or uncontaminated by the increasing commercialization of the show, and radio music in general.

Though Hay singled out four basic bands, three others were part of the rotation in these early days: Theron Hale and His Daughters, the Binkley Brothers Dixie Clodhoppers, and Ed Poplin's Barn Dance Orchestra. These three bands joined the show between 1926 and 1928, just as the others did. These latter three, however, dropped off the show by the late 1930s, after contributing their share to the hoedown tradition. (See chapter 3 for a detailed discussion of the most famous of these three bands, the Possum Hunters.)

The bands shared a number of characteristics. In almost every case their members lived and worked in Nashville and were thus able to commute easily to the show on short notice. All had regular day jobs, usually not related to the music scene, and they kept these jobs even after many other Opry acts turned professional. Since the hoedown bands did not have to rely on records, touring through the Artists Service Bureau, or making a living wage with their music, they were less demanding about their pay scale. They retained a lot of the good-natured informality that had been the hallmark of the Opry's earliest days—as well as a quasi-amateur status. This feature endeared them to Hay: even after the Opry had become a smooth, nationally known organization, the hoedown bands reminded him of the folk roots of his show.

This peculiar status also had an effect on the music of the bands. Few of them could boast original tunes, and most were content to play again and again the familiar standards like "Tennessee Waggoner," "Turkey in the Straw," "Whoa Mule," and "Katy Hill." Vocals were included but not emphasized as with other groups. The appeal of their music, apparently, was not in its repertoire (such as with, say, the Vagabonds) but in the playing style. The handful of extant recordings done prior to 1940—some commercially, some privately in home recordings—are exciting examples of classic Middle Tennessee fiddle band style that have an appeal far beyond their repertoire. Unfortunately, this very quality—lack of original material—mitigated against the bands' recording more commercially. As early as the late 1920s and 1930s recording companies were demanding more and more original songs. Many of the bands also added square dance calls to their performances, suggesting not so much that they were actually directing dancers on the Opry stage as directing dancers at home listening to their radio.

In a typical 1938 press release, Hay wrote of the Opry performers: "During the week, most of these performers are farmers and hunters, men of the soil. When Saturday night comes, they take down their fiddles, banjoes, jugs, washboards, mouth harps and the like and come to the jamboree." As we shall see, this simply was not true, especially with the hoedown bands. Virtually none of their members were farmers, and almost all worked at a variety of jobs in Nashville's urban environment: auto mechanic (Paul Warmack), barber (Howard Ragsdale), cigar maker (Herman Crook), policeman (Matthew Crook), jeweler (Amos and Gale Binkley), as well as factory workers or lumberyard men. Yet the contradiction is more complex than it may at first appear. Recent research into the biographies of the individual members of the hoedown bands reveals that, while most lived in Nashville, very few actually were born or grew up there. Most were born in outlying rural communities and moved to Nashville as teenagers, apparently to find work in the city's industries. Virtually none of them moved to town for musical reasons or because of the Barn Dance. Indeed, most of them made the migration during the period 1905 to 1915, long before WSM ever opened its doors. Herman Crook, for example, moved to town in 1909, as did fiddler George Wilkerson. Claude Lampley, a mainstay of the Fruit Jar Drinkers, came in 1911; Paul Warmack, leader of the Gully Jumpers, about 1913; and Theron Hale in 1915. This movement occurred within a larger growth picture: Nashville itself grew from a population of 80,000 in 1900 to 110,300 in 1910—a jump of 36 percent. Such a growth percentage is well in line with the growth shown by other Tennessee cities. But exactly how to explain beyond this the migrations of these specific musicians is a bit of a mystery.

While many of these men had vague musical ties to their rural roots, they actually perfected their musical styles after they moved to Nashville. By the time the Barn Dance started in 1925, most of these artists were well established in non-musical jobs, had already formed their styles and repertoires, and had started families. They were by no means "old-timers"; in

1926, the first full year of the Barn Dance, Herman Crook was twenty-eight, Lewis Crook seventeen, George Wilkerson thirty-three, Paul Warmack thirty-six, Ed Poplin forty-five, and Theron Hale forty-three. Many had honed their skills at house parties and community dances in the blue-collar neighborhoods of West and East Nashville. Romantics like Hay were fond of insisting that traditional music could only be learned in rural homes and mountain farmsteads. Even in later years, when Nashville had become considerably more urban than it was in 1926, the careers of influential fiddlers like Tommy Jackson and Tommy Vaden proved the possibility of absorbing a folk music tradition in the Nashville urban setting. To be sure, however, the history of the Opry hoedown bands does seem different from the pattern associated with barn dance shows in other cities. In the cases of Atlanta (WSB) and Chicago (WLS), the old-time music stars did in fact learn their skills "down home" in rural settings and then brought them already intact to their urban environments. The careers of Bradley Kincaid, as well as Karl and Harty (in Chicago) and of the Skillet Lickers and John Carson (in Atlanta) are cases in point. This did not happen among the Nashville hoedown band players—possibly because it was still a much smaller city than either of the other two.

Shortly before he left the Opry, in 1956, Judge Hay called the surviving members of the hoedown bands to a special meeting in his office. There he praised them and thanked them for their many years' work. "Nashville is about to become a million-dollar industry," he said. "And you are the ones who truly founded it."

The Fruit Jar Drinkers

In his sprawling autobiographical novel *Cradle of Copperheads*, Kentucky novelist Jesse Stuart described living in Nashville in December 1932 and attending regularly the performances of the Opry at the National Life Building. Among the groups and individuals he describes is one of the most colorful of the hoedown bands, the Fruit Jar Drinkers. "They deserved the name," he comments. "They were really Tennessee hill men, tall, lean, gangly, and they drank moonshine from fruit jars." George Wilkerson, the leader of the Fruit Jar Drinkers, would have been more than a little amused at this description. Lean and gangly though they might have been, all the band members were in fact industrious family men who had for years been residents of Nashville. All lived within a few blocks of each other, all worked at local businesses during the day, and all enjoyed moonlighting on the Opry to help make ends meet during the

Depression. Stuart's description was testimony to the power of George Hay's image-making ability. The image was also reflected in the publicity photos of the band in overalls, standing in a *Hee Haw*-like cornfield, drinking their brew out of old Mason quart jars. Little wonder that Stuart, who came from an authentic folk music background in Kentucky, and who should have known better, was taken in. The name, and the image, of the Fruit Jar Drinkers was one of the most successful instances of rusticating the Opry, and was one of the most tenacious images to peel away.

The Fruit Jar Drinkers stand out among the other hoedown bands for several reasons. Both Hay and Harry Stone have singled them out in their various reminiscences of the show's early days, and the band seemed for them to typify the essence of the hoedown style. By the early 1930s, the band was closing out the Opry Saturday night broadcasts at 11:30 or 11:45, and probably for this reason the band was also selected to try some very early touring. In 1933 they went out to the Midwest with Curt Poulton, Uncle Dave Macon, and Sam McGee. Veterans who remember the early Opry recall the band as the hottest of the house bands, with fiddler Wilkerson often singled out for his driving, propulsive style. Yet of all the old Opry hoedown bands, only the Fruit Jar Drinkers never made any commercial recordings whatsoever (Macon's Fruit Jar Drinkers was a different group altogether). Thus the Fruit Jar Drinker music is hardest to explain or discuss—it deserves the name "legendary."

Wilkerson (1893–1954) was actually a native of Stevenson, Alabama, a hamlet located in the northeastern corner of the state near Scottsboro. Little is known about his early years, but his father did not play music, though two brothers, Charlie and Brownie, did. About 1909, when Wilkerson was only sixteen, the family moved up to Nashville. During the following decade, Wilkerson married, honed his skills as a dance fiddler, and began working in West Nashville at Whitsun's Lumber Yard. (He never was a mechanic, as Hay described him on several occasions.) West Nashville in those early years was a center for young men and young families moving in from the countryside and was the scene of regular square dances, house parties, and music gatherings of all sorts. "In West Nashville in those days," recalled Lucy Gray, daughter of Fruit Jar Drinker Claude Lampley, "you either worked with lumber or with fertilizer in some way— that was the only industry there was, except for a cotton mill."

By 1918 Wilkerson had started his family and was winning a reputation as a good fiddler, often performing with his brother Charlie, a mandolin player. Shortly after the Barn Dance started, he got interested in it and, though there is no newspaper documentation proving it, his family recalls clearly that he began on the show in 1926. Certainly by January 1927 he appears in the radio logs, as a fiddler backed by guitarist Jack Sadler. Shortly after that he met Tommy Leffew, a mandolin player who had enjoyed his own solo spot on the station from time to time. Leffew (1905–1971) was a native of Adairsville, Tennessee, who had moved to Nashville to take a job at the Nashville Hardwood Flooring Company, one of West Nashville's lumber industries. By 1927 Wilkerson and Leffew had teamed up with guitarist Howard Farmer to form a string trio, which was still unnamed. Next, a co-worker of Leffew's at the flooring company, banjo player Claude Lampley, was added to the band. Lampley (1896–1975) came from Craigfield, Tennessee, in Hickman County, near what would later be called Grinder's Switch, about fifty miles southwest of Nashville. He had come to Nashville when he was fifteen, lived with an uncle, and began a lifetime job in the flooring company. There was an old organ in the Lampley family, and Lampley's father was a banjo player—possibly an adherent of the distinctive West Tennessee two-finger style that was later reflected in musicians like Alvin Conder and Omer Forster. As a young man, Lampley also took lessons from a Professor Sheets in Nashville, making him the only one in the later band who could read music. Another Hickman County native, Howard Ragsdale, soon replaced Farmer on guitar. He was about the same age as Lampley and worked in West Nashville at Hanna's "handle mill," making handles for picks and shovels. Ragsdale also became an in-law of Wilkerson's, having married Clara Ragsdale some years before. With these men in place, Wilkerson had intact the basic line-up that would become the Fruit Jar Drinkers—a line-up that would endure for the next twenty years. In late 1927, the radio logs were showing "G. W. Wilkerson and band" as regulars on the show, and by December 1927 they were referring to the group as "Fruit Jar Drinkers." By 1929 they were in the regular rotation on the show, playing every other week and by 1931 appearing every single week.

Since all the band members lived in West Nashville within a six-block area, they would often gather on Friday nights at Lampley's house to practice. This often turned into a mammoth jam session, as other bands and performers would hear about it and drop by. Uncle Dave Macon, especially, liked to sleep over at the Lampley house after returning from a week on the road, which beat driving an additional fifty miles to his home in Kittrell, then returning to Nashville Saturday night for the broadcast. It was at one of these sessions that the band got its name. One spring evening in 1927 Arthur Smith, the fiddler, had drifted in, and everyone was sitting out on the lawn, drinking ice water out of a big tub and playing some music.

There were so many drinkers that Mom Lampley ran out of glasses, and when Ragsdale asked for a glass, she barked, "Well, Rag, there aren't any more glasses!" He replied, "Get it in an old fruit jar. I don't mind being a fruit jar drinker." The name stuck, and soon the band was calling itself the new name.

Almost at once, however, a problem arose. In May of that spring of 1927 Uncle Dave was scheduled for a marathon recording session in New York, and he took along the McGee Brothers and a veteran Opry fiddler named Mazy Todd. Though he did not usually work with a full string band, the Brunswick-Vocalion company had asked Macon to form one for recording purposes. For reasons that are not at all clear, Macon decided to call his new unit "Uncle Dave Macon and His Fruit Jar Drinkers." He had never used the term before, and would never use it again, but throughout 1927 and 1928 the legend began appearing on a series of records issued from the session. According to family members from Wilkerson's band, Judge Hay was furious that Macon had "stolen" the name. He called Macon into his office and royally dressed him down for using the term without anyone's permission. Hay was planning on using the name to help promote his Opry acts, and he felt so strongly about it that he wrote the Vocalion company and asked them to stop the release of any records bearing the Fruit Jar Drinkers' name. But it was too late, and the seeds of confusion were sown. To complicate things further, some of the records became good sellers, inspiring yet more imitators, such as the Fruit Jar Guzzlers for Paramount. And the assumption that the Fruit Jar Drinkers had already recorded with Macon probably dissuaded the directors of the famous 1928 Victor session in Nashville (see chapter 10 for a full discussion) from recording Wilkerson's band.

It was at about this time that Judge Hay took the band on a promotional tour up North, concentrating in Pennsylvania. This was one of those times when Nashville public opinion was again rising against the Opry, and well-heeled friends of National Life's executives were putting on pressure to drop the unruly "hillbilly" show. To prove that the Opry had a wider audience appeal, and to recruit new talent for the show, Hay took Wilkerson's band on a "good will" tour lasting several weeks. It was successful on both counts. Letters poured into WSM praising the sound of the Opry and new acts, such as the Hawaiian guitar team of Tom Fields and Bob Martin. The increasing popularity of the Opry also allowed the band to "play out" at dances and concerts throughout the Middle Tennessee area. By the mid-1930s, Judge Hay gave Wilkerson his nickname "Grandpappy," bestowed not so much because Wilkerson was indeed the first grandpappy on the show, but because he could not refrain from bragging about it. Also early in 1936, following the lead of several other early Opry bands, the Fruit Jar Drinkers added a bass player, Truman Claiborne.

If the Fruit Jar Drinkers had a reputation for playing at breakneck tempos, it might have been because they were relatively young men. In 1927, Wilkerson himself was thirty-four, but Lampley was thirty-one, and Leffew and Ragsdale were in their early twenties. In contrast to the veterans like Uncle Dave Macon, Blind Joe Mangrum, Uncle Jimmy Thompson, or Dr. Humphrey Bate, the Fruit Jar Drinkers were the Young Turks of the Barn Dance. They took the traditional string band fare and supercharged it. Although the band never made a commercial record, even in later years, a hint of its style is preserved in a series of home recordings owned by the family of banjoist Lampley. The songs on these are mostly standards: "Rubber Dolly," the fiddle tune popularized by the Georgia Yellow Hammers in 1927; "Tennessee Waggoner" and "Soldier's Joy," familiar fiddle tunes; "Sweet Bunch of Daisies," the nineteenth century waltz that also attracted fiddlers; "Free a Little Bird," the band piece so popular in East Tennessee; "Three Nights Experience," the raunchy Child ballad widely recorded by old-time bands; and "Lightning Express," sometimes known as "Please, Mister Conductor," and sung by generations of duet acts. But the style of these performances is quite remarkable for 1936. Wilkerson plays a heavy-bowed, straightforward fiddle, using a number of rhythmic slides and odd double stops. There are few of the long, cascading runs that one hears in Arthur Smith, none of the violinist's tone so characteristic of Joe Mangrum or Gale Binkley. Wilkerson propels the whole band with his drive and timing and reminds modern listeners a great deal of Tommy Jackson, the fine Nashville session fiddler of the 1950s who grew up in Nashville and reportedly learned from Wilkerson. Adding to the band's special sound is a strong string bass, set off against Lampley's banjo, strummed and not picked. On slower numbers, like "Three Nights Experience," Lampley plays in a wonderful loose, loping, frailing style. In many ways, the performances on these fragile, old 1936 discs are quite archaic when compared to the new hot bands that were then making their way onto the Opry, such as McMichen's Georgia Wildcats. But the zest and spirit of the band overcomes both the venerable material and the archaic arrangements, and this, no doubt, is exactly what George Hay wanted. The hoedown bands were to keep alive this "original sound" of the Opry, and to do it with grace and panache.

Wilkerson became ill in 1953 and had to retire from the band. He died the following March, at age sixty. The band, with varying changes, kept going until the mid-1970s, often playing for square dancers on the show's stage, politely applauded by an audience who often knew little or nothing about their colorful history.

The Crook Brothers

As far as can be determined, the first regular hoedown band to join the Barn Dance after Dr. Bate's Possum Hunters was an unusual ensemble headed by Herman and Matthew Crook. Whereas most other bands featured the fiddle as the lead instrument, the Crooks spotlighted the harmonica. For the first five years as a band, the Crooks had no fiddle in their band at all but featured the brothers playing a twin harmonica lead. Their band was a natural culmination of a very strong harmonica tradition in Middle Tennessee and one that was responsible for an amazing variety of harp players on the early Barn Dance. The Crooks simply parlayed this regional fondness for the harmonica into a string band format. The result was a distinctive sound that endured on the Opry for over sixty years.

Unlike the names of the several other hoedown bands, "Crook Brothers" was not one of the hayseed names Hay came up with. ("I couldn't top your real names, anyway" he once told Herman.) Matthew Crook was born in 1896, Herman in 1898, in a Davidson County community called Scottsboro, about fifteen miles from Nashville. There were six children in the family, several of whom made music. Herman's father died when Herman was only three, and his mother moved the family into Nashville, where she herself died some eight years later, about 1909. Herman was reared by older brothers and sisters, and Herman and Matthew began playing the harmonica as boys, watching and learning from an older brother. They also had an uncle in DeKalb County who was an important influence. "He was one of the best buck and wing dancers you ever saw," recalled Herman, "and he could sing. Man, he had a voice. It could sound so lonesome, kind of a mournful sound. He sang all these old songs, some would go back a hundred years. One was 'Put My Little Shoes Away.' And he had a cylinder [record] player, one with a big horn, and we listened to the records, and learned some off them. But a lot of these old numbers I had heard back as far as I could remember."

As a young man, Herman Crook worked at a variety of jobs in Nashville. Soon he was married, and his wife joined him in music making. She could play the piano and guitar and backed Herman at local union halls and house dances in East Nashville. Like other musicians, the Crooks were drawn to WDAD before WSM opened and played there weeks before the Barn Dance program started. After a time, Matthew joined Herman, and the brothers organized a band that included their twin harmonicas, two guitars, and a banjo. It was this band that attracted the attention of Judge Hay in the summer of 1926 and made its debut on July 24 that year on the Barn Dance. This gave the Crooks seniority over all the other bands except Dr. Bate's. The Crooks only played occasionally on the broadcast throughout 1926 and 1927 but began to appear more frequently in 1928, soon doing weekly slots. During these early years, the Crooks also appeared on rival Nashville stations. Herman recalled playing for a time on WBAW ("Harry Stone was the announcer there then, and we were located over the O. K. Houck Piano Store") and on WLAC ("We helped put on an hour program there"). During 1928, the Crooks managed to appear as often as any other group on WSM and still be regulars on the WLAC competing barn dance. One reason for this, according to Herman, is that when WSM began paying its artists in 1928, they found so many musicians wanting to play that the station had to devise a platoon system, with most bands playing every other week. On alternate weeks, the Crooks, along with Paul Warmack, the Binkley Brothers, Theron Hale, and others had no hesitation about appearing on WLAC.

In 1927 an unusual coincidence occurred that was to have a lasting and major impact on the band. At a fiddler's contest in Walterhill, Tennessee, Herman ran into his old friend and mentor Dr. Humphrey Bate. The good doctor had with him a young man from his hometown in Trousdale County, a banjo player and guitarist who was named, coincidentally, Lewis Crook. He was no relation whatsoever to Herman and Matthew, but they were attracted to him and to his two-finger banjo style. This was a thumb-and-index style that Lewis had learned from his father, and Dr. Bate had wanted the young man for his own band. But the Possum Hunters already had an established banjoist. Herman also had a veteran banjoist, Tom Givans, but was less than committed to him. In the fall of 1929 Herman drove out to Lewis's home and formally asked him to become a member of the Crook Brothers Barn Dance Orchestra. By now the lineup included Bill Etter on piano, Clarence Minton on guitar, and three men named Crook.

Lewis Crook was a tall, gangly youth who had been born into a family of sharecroppers in Trousdale County in 1909. Among other things, his father ran a local sorghum mill powered by mules, and young Lewis had quit school after the eighth grade to help work for the family. A neighbor and friend of the family in these early years (ca. 1915–1920) was Dr. Humphrey Bate; in fact, Lewis's younger brother was named after the doctor. Dr. Bate made weekly visits to the home of Lewis's aunt, stopping in every Monday for one of her famous homemade custards. Bate would occasionally play the banjo, teach Lewis a song or two, and encourage him in his music. In early spring, when the Cumberland River flooded, Lewis and his family would often find themselves cut off on small temporary islands, isolated and left with little to do except barbecue rabbits, play cards, and make music. But by 1929 the hard times forced the Crook Family to move to Nashville, where Lewis found work at the Carter Shoe Company for $1.50 a day. He also started playing with various pick-up bands, including one with Sid Harkreader.

About a year after Lewis Crook joined Herman's band, Matthew Crook quit to work full-time on the Nashville police force. This made Herman full leader of the group and changed the complexion of the band. Unable to find a satisfactory second harmonica player, Herman added a fiddle player and began developing a style built around the odd tonal texture of the harp and fiddle playing lead together. The result was an unusual, but effective, string band sound. For a time, Kirk McGee was the fiddler, and when he quit to join the Dixieliners, he was replaced by Floyd Ethridge, who remained with the group through the 1930s. He was a native of McEwen, Tennessee (born 1908), and came from the same West Tennessee–Dickson County area that spawned Arthur Smith and Howdy Forrester. Ethridge, in fact, had performed with a young Arthur Smith at local square dances and fiddling contests in Dickson and in Humphreys County. He had a fondness for playing in a fast, high style, relying, as did Smith, on quick fingering of the E string, complemented by Herman's equally deft, smooth harmonica playing. On old breakdowns like "Soldier's Joy," "Sally Gooden," and "Fire on the Mountain," the new band was hard to beat. To round out his crew, Herman hired guitarist Blythe Poteet, Kirk McGee's cousin, born in Franklin in 1909. Blythe had absorbed much of the McGees' music and had even recorded with Kirk and Sid Harkreader in separate sessions in 1928. He had been performing on the Opry since 1932, when he was only twenty-three, playing for a time with Uncle Dave Macon. Blythe brought all this experience to the Crook band, and this gave Herman protégés from three of the Opry's most famous stars: Dr. Bate (Lewis), Arthur Smith (Floyd), and the McGees (Blythe).

As with most hoedown bands, the Crook Brothers had little original material in their repertoire, in spite of their unusual instrumentation. Their four recordings in the 1928 Victor session, all done with the pre–Lewis Crook ensemble, were all instrumentals featuring a twin harmonica lead. One was "My Wife Died on Friday Night," learned from Dr. Bate, who did it as "My Wife Died on Saturday Night." Herman explained the change by noting that, at the time of the recording, the Crooks were also appearing on WLAC's Friday night show, while Dr. Bate played on the Saturday night Opry. "Going across the Sea" was a familiar banjo-fiddle specialty and had already been recorded by Opry regulars Uncle Dave Macon and Henry Bandy. The Crook version, though, was stylistically miles away from anything that had been done with the tune before. "Love Somebody," a regional favorite that had also been previously recorded by Sid Harkreader and Uncle Dave Macon, was related to another local square dance tune called "Lexington." The fourth title was issued by Victor under the curious title "Jobbin' Gettin' There," which was a corruption of the real name Herman gave it, "Job in Gettin' There," from an old proverb Herman had known as a child, "He's a Job in Getting There," referring to unaccountable slowness. The Crooks' Victors sold reasonably well and were later reissued on the Montgomery Ward catalogs label. All of them also featured square dance calls by George Miles, a feature that Herman did not like but that the Victor people had insisted on.

In the early 1930s, Lewis Crook got up enough courage to start singing on the air, and this helped expand the band's repertoire. For such songs, Lewis put down his banjo and switched to guitar, singing as many as two or three songs in each Crook Brothers Opry segment. He featured Jimmie Rodgers hits like "Blue Yodel No. 1" and "Any Old Time," Carson Robison favorites like "Wreck of the No. 9" and "Golden Slippers," and even Charlie Poole's "May I Sleep in Your Barn Tonight, Mister?" By the 1940s, various air-checks were revealing yet another shift in the Crook sound. By then the band had added Basil Gentry, as well as Neal Matthews Sr. and Neal Matthews Jr. (who would later win fame with the Jordanaires). These three often formed a smooth, Sons-of-the-Pioneers–like vocal trio and did numbers like "As Long As I Live," "Sitting on Top of the World," and "Will the Circle Be Unbroken." These warm, evocative vocals were often framed with Herman's bluesy harmonica, which seemed to get more complex and versatile as the years went by. In the early days, Herman recalled, he and Matthew loved to play the slower numbers like "Sweet Bunch of Daisies," experimenting with the kind of harmonies possible with a non-chromatic instrument. Later Herman would also do an occasional specialty, like "Lost Train Blues" or "Lost John."

Throughout the 1950s the Crook Brothers continued to hold forth on the show, often playing for square dancers, but winning new friends and new respect during the 1960s folk revival. During this time they made a Starday LP with the McGee Brothers, using Hank Williams's old fiddler

Jerry Rivers, and won offers to play at a number of folk festivals. Herman, however, still continued to see his music as a hobby, always secondary to his "day job" of rolling cigars at a Nashville factory. Even in the 1930s he had not let the band tour with other Opry groups (though individuals like Blythe and Lewis were free to work on their own), and he saw no sense in playing the festival circuit in the 1960s. Time took its toll, finally, and eventually the remnants of his band were combined with the remnants of the Possum Hunters, and this band survived on the Opry until Herman's death in 1988. In many ways, the Crooks were the first hoedown band on the show, and, as it turned out, the last.

The Binkley Brothers

During most of its tenure on the Opry, the Binkley Brothers Dixie Clodhoppers was basically a string trio consisting of two brothers, Amos and Gale Binkley, and their long-time friend Tom Andrews. Gale Binkley played the fiddle, brother Amos played banjo, and Tom Andrews was the left-handed guitar player. Gale was known as a careful, precise fiddler who was meticulous in his noting and execution—a style that befitted his occupation as a watch repairman and jeweler. Tom Andrews was apparently from Franklin, Tennessee, and a friend of Sam and Kirk McGee. Though overlooked by Judge Hay in his various histories of the Opry, and generally ignored by other popular accounts, the Binkley band was an important fixture on Nashville radio in general in the 1920s and 1930s. It was also one of the few hoedown bands to record a significant part of its repertoire.

The Binkley Brothers Barn Dance Orchestra first appeared on the Opry on October 10, 1926, though guitarist Tom Andrews had appeared with numerous pick-up bands before then. During 1927 and 1928 the band, which Hay now rechristened the Dixie Clodhoppers, appeared about once a month on WSM and were regulars on the WLAC rival shows from 1929–1931. They began as full-time regulars on the Opry in 1932, joining the rotation and playing alternate weeks. This continued until August 1939, when they suddenly dropped out of the radio listings. Their slot was taken by a young Bill Monroe.

About 1935 the brothers opened a watch repair business in the barbershop of L. D. Bowman in the 5000 block of Charlotte Avenue, in a shopping district in extreme West Nashville. The shop was still in place in 1940, and by 1960 they had expanded and were billing themselves as "Binkley

Brothers Jewellers," located a block down the street. Aside from this, not much is known about the personal history of the Binkleys. Gale was known for his version of "Forky Deer" and was well known at area fiddling contests. In 1929 or 1930 the band participated in a marathon three-day fiddling contest in Chattanooga and walked away with second place.

The Binkleys for a time used as their vocalist a Lebanon, Tennessee, native named Jack Jackson. Billed as "the Strolling Yodeller," Jackson too had been appearing both on WSM and WLAC. With his boyish good looks, his styled pompadour hairdo, and his clear, well-trained voice, he attracted a considerable following. A newspaper of the time referred to him as "perhaps the most popular radio entertainer in the South," and he was one of the first Nashville performers to publish his own songbook, to appear on sheet music covers, and to try to make a full-time living with his music. A specialist in yodeling, Jackson had learned his technique not from Jimmie Rodgers, as had most of his contemporaries, but from a man in nearby Murfreesboro, Tennessee, who had picked it up in Switzerland during World War I. By the late 1920s, Jackson left Nashville and the Binkleys to work for a time at WFIW in Hopkinsville, Kentucky, but he returned to WSM in 1932 to head up a cowboy group called Jack Jackson and His Bronco Busters. When he retired from music a couple of years later, the band was taken over by Zeke Clements.

In 1928 the Binkleys and Jackson joined forces for a series of Victor recordings and stage appearances (see chapter 10). Six sides were released, all featuring Jackson's vocals and giving him equal billing on the record label. Their version of "I'll Rise When the Rooster Crows" backed with "Give Me Back My Fifteen Cents" was the biggest hit of the entire Nashville session, and thus the first country hit to come out of Nashville. "Rooster" especially has remained popular through reissues and has become a standard in modern old-time music. Jackson thought he had learned the song from Uncle Dave Macon and, indeed, owned a copy of Macon's 1925 Vocalion recording of it. There are, however, significant differences in text between the Macon and Jackson versions, which suggests at least one second source. The song itself may be related to an 1881 song by one Harry Davis called "Dem Golden Shoes." Whatever the source, Jackson's voice was a perfect match for Gale Binkley's fiddling, and their Victor recording remains as one of the masterpieces of early country music.

Unfortunately, the partnership between the Binkleys and Jack Jackson did not last long. By 1929 Jackson was out on his own again, recording four titles for Columbia (including an effective "Flat Tire Blues") and moving restlessly from station to station. He continued to attract bushels of fan mail from all over the upland South, revealing how the audience's taste in country music was shifting more and more to singers. The Binkleys went on as a trio, content to play part-time on the show and tend to their watch repair business.

Theron Hale and His Band

The band headed by Theron Hale was also different from any of the other hoedown bands. To be sure, it was a family unit, consisting of fiddler Hale and his two daughters, Mamie Ruth (mandolin and fiddle) and Elizabeth (piano). But it had a lighter, more delicate sound than most of the others, and contained more than a touch of nineteenth century parlor music. It had a genteel aura, more in line with the spirit of Uncle Joe Mangrum than Uncle Dave Macon. This was in part due to the fact that the Hale daughters both had formal musical training. Ruth studied violin with a number of teachers and later taught at Vanderbilt; Elizabeth was a college graduate who taught in the Nashville city schools.

Theron Hale himself was in his forties when he began working on the Barn Dance, making him a generation older than many of the other hoedown band players. He was born in 1883 in Pikeville, Tennessee, about one hundred miles southeast of Nashville in the rugged and isolated Sequatchie Valley. He came from a musical family: his father and uncles were both leaders in the Baptist church and taught shape-note singing in the area. His nephew was Homer Davenport, a legendary old-time banjo player who moved to the Chattanooga area, where he recorded and performed with the Jess Young band in the 1920s. Davenport's unusual three-finger style attracted considerable attention at the time and anticipated by some twenty years some of the methods used by Earl Scruggs. Hale's family recalls that much of Davenport's style came from Theron Hale (though Theron preferred fiddle to banjo and seldom played banjo on the air). Hale's daughter Elizabeth recalled of his banjo work: "He played in the old style, without picks, and I think he taught Homer that same way."

Hale himself was educated at the old People's College in Pikeville, Tennessee, and at Carson-Newman College, a church-related school in Johnson City, in East Tennessee, not far from Knoxville. He continued to play music during his college years, but saw it only as a hobby. In 1905 he married a Pikeville woman, Laura Vaughn, and soon started a family. In 1912 he moved his group to Altoona, Iowa, where he farmed for three years. By 1915 he decided to try his luck in Nashville and for a time ran a Middle

Tennessee dairy farm; but by the mid-1920s he was working as a sewing machine salesman, traveling widely, and making a good living for his family. In later years he owned a used piano business in Nashville.

As his two daughters were growing up, Hale would play music with them around the house. In 1926, shortly after the anniversary of WSM, according to Elizabeth, "Some one told the Solemn Old Judge about us. He was wanting to find old-fashioned music at the time, and asked us to come up and have an interview with him." On October 20, the Hales began performing on the Barn Dance, and during the next two years they performed about once a month and in 1929 began as weekly regulars. This pattern continued for the next four and one-half years, until late May 1934. By this time Mamie Ruth had married and moved out of town. Theron and Elizabeth tried to keep the band going with replacements but found it unsatisfactory. Finally, in 1934 they quit.

One of the reasons Mamie Ruth was so hard to replace, and partially accounting for the band's distinctive sound, was that she often played fiddle with her father, doing an alto second to her father's lead. This twin-fiddle sound was like nothing that had been on the Opry before. Another distinctive part of the sound was that it did not feature a guitar, but Elizabeth's piano. Though the piano is not generally thought of as a standard instrument in old-time music, it was in fact quite popular on the early Opry. In addition to Elizabeth's work in the Hale band, pianos were heard at various times in the Possum Hunters (Alcyone Bate), the Poplin band (Ed Poplin Jr. and Louise Woods), Uncle Dave Macon's band (Jewell Fagan), the Dixieliners (Arthur's daughter Lavonne), the Crook Brothers (Bill Etter), and, for a short time, the Fruit Jar Drinkers.

Elizabeth recalled that the signature number of the band, the one everyone remembered Theron Hale for, was "Listen to the Mocking Bird": "That was our main number. Some gave us credit for launching that song in the popular sense. No one else played it like we did. On the chorus, my father would do the whistle on the violin with his finger." Other favorites included "Red Wing" and "Over the Waves." In fact, much of the Hale music was characterized by slow, two-part waltzes that featured the twin fiddle harmonies. When a faster tune was called for, Theron would usually play it by himself, though, according to Elizabeth, "he could never attain to that really fast, smooth playing." No one can recall Hale ever talking much about his formative years as a fiddler—or from whom he learned his style or whether it was formed in Pikeville or somewhere else. (One of his recorded-but-unreleased tunes, however, was "Wink the Other Eye," a Sequatchie Valley tune later popularized by Curly Fox.) He did admire the work of fellow Opry bowmen Arthur Smith and Sid Harkreader, and he called Howdy Forrester "the best ever" and never ceased to marvel at his bow technique.

The Hales were well represented at the 1928 Victor Nashville session. They wound up recording some eight tunes on twenty-one masters, four of which were issued and one of which ("Beautiful Valley Waltz") survived on a test pressing. Not surprisingly, "Listen to the Mocking Bird" and "Turkey Gobbler" made up the first release (Victor 40019), while "The Jolly Blacksmith" (a version of "Flop-Eared Mule") and "Hale's Rag" (derived from an old printed rag by Kansas City composer Charles L. Johnson) made up the second release (Victor 40046). On the latter two cuts, Mamie Ruth played mandolin to her father's fiddle. Left in the can were "Wink the Other Eye," "Kiss Waltz," and a cryptic piece called "The Old Race Horse." Elizabeth remembered: "None of us were too happy with the records. We always felt they put the piano so far away from the microphone that it lagged in the music. It was out of phase, a little behind, with the rest of the music."

The Hale band did not tour or play in public except for their radio shows. No one in the band had any great desire to try to professionalize their music, and Hale seemed to "retire" from the show in 1934. In later years, he would return occasionally to play for friends and for area square dances. In the 1940s he began to work a lot with Sam McGee (who in fact inherited Hale's banjo) and with a banjo player named Fred Colby. For a time he played for social gatherings at Vanderbilt and at the local YMCA—"places where they still wanted the old type music," as Elizabeth said. Sometime in the early 1950s Hale made a series of fiddle records for a label called Old-Time Tennessee Play Party—custom produced for the local Tennessee State Extension program to stimulate square dancing. These are quite good, and apparently feature Sam McGee on guitar and banjo. They proved to be Hale's final legacy, though; he died on January 29, 1954.

The Gully Jumpers

In many ways, Paul Warmack's band, the Gully Jumpers, was the real workhorse of the early hoedown bands. In 1928 it appeared on the Opry some twenty-eight out of fifty-two shows, more than any other string band. Its members also sometimes had their own shows or segments, attaching an "all-star" aspect to the group. It was a key participant in the 1928 Victor session, making some twenty masters. And in early 1933, when WSM put together its first advertising rate book and sent salesmen into the field to drum up commercial sponsors, the Gully Jumpers was the only real hoedown band (with the exception of Dr. Bate) thought popular enough to be listed. The band survived the deaths of several key members and remained an Opry fixture until the 1960s.

For most of the '20s and '30s, the core personnel of the Gully Jumpers included the leader, Paul Warmack, on mandolin, guitar, and vocals; Charles Arrington on fiddle, Roy Hardison on banjo, and Bert Hutcherson on guitar. Warmack (1890–1954) was a native of Goodlettsville, a small town north of Nashville, and he spent most of his life in Davidson County. He married in 1913, and in 1921 opened up his own garage, Paul Warmack's Auto Service, on North First Street in downtown Nashville, by the river. In 1936 he went to work as a mechanic for the state highway garage and continued to work there until his death. His banjo player, Roy Hardison, was also a mechanic and garage foreman. Fiddler Charlie Arrington, whom Hay described as "an Irishman with quick wit," had a farm about twenty miles from Nashville, in the Joelton community. Guitarist Bert Hutcherson was a woodworker by trade and later employed by National Life.

The Gully Jumpers seemed to coalesce rather slowly, with the various members appearing on the Opry with other groups in different configurations before and even after Warmack managed to bring them all together. Warmack himself first appeared on the air in May 1927 with fiddler Odie Collins, Hardison, and the Binkley Brothers' guitarist Tom Andrews. Hutcherson was a member of Dr. Bate's band at one time and later on appeared as a solo singer and guitarist. By July 30, 1927, the band was being billed as "Paul Warmack and His Barn Dance Orchestra," and on December 24, 1927, the name "Gully Jumpers" first appeared in the radio listings.

The band seems to have caught on fast. By 1928 Warmack and Hutcherson had branched out and were doing an early morning WSM show in addition to playing the Opry. Known as the "Early Birds," the duo came on the air at 6:00 A.M. and helped to pioneer the idea of an early morning music show—a tradition that WSM maintains to this day. They would sing duets, and Hutcherson would play some of the guitar solos he was known for, like "Dew Drop Waltz" and "House of David Blues." Soon Bert had his own Opry segment and appeared some twenty times in 1928 playing solo guitar and singing. He appeared again as a regular in 1930 with the same act. He was probably the first guitar soloist to be featured on the Opry, and he influenced a number of other musicians, including Sam and Kirk McGee. For years Bert gave guitar lessons in downtown Nashville, spreading his style even further. Unfortunately, he never recorded as a soloist and even the Opry air checks came along too late to capture his music. Just exactly what style he perfected, where he learned it, or what it sounded like, is not known.

In January 1933, when WSM created a press book and decided to sell commercial time on the shows of specific performers, the Gully Jumpers were one of the few country acts included. Their local popularity was reflected in the impressive advertising rates assigned to their segments. An advertiser buying time on the Gully Jumpers' segment was charged $40 for a single ad a week; three times a week was $85; six times was a $100. Advertising on the Early Birds' morning show was cheaper in some cases: $25, $65, and $100 for the same schedule.

This prime-time rate was one of the higher rates listed, far more than for the station's pop singers and even more than the Dixieliners were getting. For a time, at least, Hay and WSM had hopes that the Gully Jumpers might be a good candidate for turning professional, since with all their activity they were making relatively good money. Even their Victor records (see chapter 10) seemed to promise a bright future. But, for whatever reason, it never worked out, and by 1934 the Gully Jumpers had made their run at the brass ring and missed. They were content to remain a regular staff band on the show, keeping the old tunes alive, working their day jobs in Nashville.

The only dependable reflection of the Gully Jumpers' repertoire is found in the eight tunes they recorded for Victor in 1928. They include parlor songs like "Put My Little Shoes Away" and "I'm a Little Dutchman" (a variant of "Wee Dog Waltz" or "Lauderbach"), "The Little Red Caboose behind the Train" and "Tennessee Waltz" (not the Pee Wee King–Redd Stewart hit, but an earlier one). Warmack sings in two of these, in a lilting Irish tenor somewhat like Vernon Dalhart's voice. The other side of the band is reflected in a second group of recordings made later in the week at the 1928 session: "Stone Rag," "Robertson County," "Hell Broke Loose in Georgia" (unissued), and "Five Cents." "Stone Rag" was composed (but never recorded) by Oscar Stone of the Possum Hunters. It was, in fact, a rather widespread fiddle tune, surfacing even as "Lone Star Rag" by western swing star Bob Wills. "Robertson County" appears to be a regional tune, as is "Five Cents," known in Kentucky as "New Five Cents," and featured by the Gully Jumpers well into the 1950s. These two groups of tunes—the old sedate parlor songs and the fiddle breakdowns—may seem to give the band a dual-personality cast, but it would be more honest and accurate to say they merely reflect the band's versatility and help to explain its intense popularity during the transitional years of the 1930s.

Ed Poplin's Barn Dance Orchestra

Though it was not well represented on recordings and did not survive into the modern post-war era, the band led by fiddler W. E. Poplin was one of the most distinctive and most fondly remembered of the hoedown bands. Hay recalled the band with special fondness, noting that Poplin himself was a rural mail carrier and that the band played well, "specializing in folk music, although once in a while, before we could or did stop it, Uncle Ed would slip in an old popular song, such as 'When You Wore a Tulip and I Wore a Red, Red Rose.'" The band was built around Poplin's fiddling, and the vocals and guitar work of his long-time friend Jack Woods. At various points it also included members of both the Poplin and Woods families, as well as former Sid Harkreader sideman Jimmy Hart and two Woods cousins, the Batts Brothers (who would wind up running a Nashville garage).

Poplin himself first appeared on the Opry on March 31, 1928, when he played a half hour on the fiddle with piano backing from Lorene Thompson. By April 21, he had returned with his "orchestra" and began regular appearances at the rate of one a month. By 1929 the band was on regular rotation, appearing every other week. This schedule was followed for the next seven years, making the Poplin band one of the most consistent acts on the broadcast in the 1930s. Their tenure ended in the fall of 1937, when Harry Stone began adding new, more professional, acts.

The Poplin band came from Lewisburg, in Marshall County, about ninety miles south of Nashville, and it was the product of a deeply rooted string band tradition in the area. James Claud "Jack" Woods (1886–1956)—on guitar, mandolin, and vocals—was the youngest of a musical family of eleven children born to John Bedford Woods, one of the original settlers in the Marshall County area. Early newspaper clippings describe a Civil War reunion of the 32nd Tennessee Infantry held in Belfast (Marshall County) in October 1900 at which the "Woods Brothers String Band" provided the music. This band featured the older sons of John Bedford. The family lived in an 1809 dogtrot log house at the foot of Round Hill near the village of Belfast, and on summer evenings, the townspeople could enjoy their family string band music as the band sat in the dogtrot and practiced. Jack, as the youngest son, naturally picked up the songs and styles of his older brothers but learned a lot of his guitar from a nearby black family named Holt, who also maintained a string band. Jack himself married in 1912 and soon started his own family. Two of his daughters, Louise (born 1914) and Frances (born 1915), were especially apt pupils: when barely out of their teens, they began to accompany their father when he played at local square dances or the big 4th of July celebrations in Lewisburg and Belfast. Though born in the country, Jack himself preferred town life and would soon become a barber in Lewisburg and Belfast. It was in the barbershop one day that he met Ed Poplin.

Poplin (1881–1951) was a rural mail carrier who had been born near the community of Poplin's Crossroads, near Shelbyville, Tennessee. He counted among his friends the famed Uncle Bunt Stephens, who came from nearby Moore County, and whose clean, deliberate style Poplin emulated. Like so many rural mail carriers, Poplin was a genial and gregarious man, but one who was a stickler for being on time, being in tune, and keeping a steady rhythm. He had contacted the Opry staff through relatives who lived near Nashville and was quick to grasp what Hay was trying to promote in his new radio show. He soon made Jack Woods a part of his plan, creating a synthesis of two of the best musical traditions in south-central Tennessee. "They worked the children in pretty soon," recalled Louise Woods. By 1927 Woods and Poplin had been joined by three of their children: Louise Woods (bass, Hawaiian guitar), her young sister Frances (mandolin and vocals), and Ed Poplin Jr. (piano and tenor guitar). All the children were barely in their teens when they started working with the band.

Louise Woods recalled what kind of routine the band would follow on these earliest Opry nights:

> We'd go into Lewisburg from Belfast about noon, and go to Mr. Poplin's house. He was a stickler for us being on time. We'd all get in one car, with the bass fiddle case tied on top, and Mr. Poplin's oldest boy would drive us. We'd get up to the National Life Building about three o'clock, unload the instruments, take 'em up to the seventh floor. We'd go into one of the little tune-up rooms they had for us and get all tuned up. My dad used to insist we all tune to the piano, and he and Mr. Poplin would spend hours getting us all tuned up right. Then we would leave the instruments in the room and Frances and I would go down to Church Street and do a little shopping. Then we'd go back.
>
> I remember helping Sarie and Sally zip up their dresses, and it wasn't long after that that they asked us to start wearing old-time dresses, and mother made these bonnets for us. They had this little theater they used, and they always had big crowds. They had ushers to move the crowds in and out—they'd let one bunch stay in for a while, and then take them out and bring some more in. In fact, my sister met her husband, Ed Guthrie, there; he was one of

the ushers. We'd usually do two fifteen-minute shows, then get in the car and sing all the way home.

One night we got up before the mike and got ready to sing "Left My Gal in the Mountains," and Mr. Poplin was supposed to sing it. But he forgot the words and got up there and just kept singing, "Left my gal in the mountains, left my gal in the mountains," over and over. It tickled Daddy to death, and on the way home that night he kept saying, "Pop, where did you leave your girl?"

The Poplin band did more vocals than any other hoedown band, and this might explain why the Victor recording crew spent so much time with them at the 1928 session. They were allotted an entire day, more than any other act, and they generated eight sides, five of which featured vocals. (One take of the band's theme, "Are You from Dixie?" was spoiled when Jack Woods broke a string—"it sounded like a mule kicking.") The session was an accurate reflection of the band's working repertoire and included two of Poplin's famous waltzes, a then-popular song called "Honey, Honey, Honey" sung by twelve-year-old Frances, a couple of fiddle tunes, and the band's most popular piece, "Pray for the Lights to Go Out." Judge Hay remarked that this tune was one of the Poplin favorites and said, "Where he dug up this concoction, nobody seems to know at this writing." In truth, the song was a 1916 effort by two Arkansas songwriters, Renton Tunnah and Will Skidmore, and was introduced as a "new 'Ballin' the Jack' song" that same year by veteran minstrel Lasses White in Neil O'Brien's touring minstrel show. Though White was on the Opry at the same time Poplin was, Jack Woods had learned the song much earlier and brought it into the band. The Victor recording of the song by Poplin was never issued, but the song was recorded a few years later by Bob Wills. The words carry a lot of the flavor of the Poplin appeal:

Father was a deacon in a hardshell church,
Way down South where I was born.
People used to come to church from miles around
Just to hear the holy work go on.

Father grabs a sister round the neck and says,
"Sister, won't you sing this song?"
The sister tells the deacon that she didn't have time,
Felt religion comin' on.

Just then somebody got up, turn'd the lights all out,
And you ought to heard that sister shout.

Chorus:
She hollered Brother—if you want to spread joy,
Just pray for the lights to stay out.
She called on deacon for to kneel and pray,
You ought to heard that sister shout.
Throw'd up both hands and got way back,
Took two steps forward, and balled the jack.
She hollered, Brother—if you want to spread joy,
Just pray for the lights to stay out.

Father tried to quieten down his lovin' flock,
Called on all the saints above,
And that all he could hear way down there in the dark,
Was Baby, Honey, Turtle Dove.
Deacon grabs his Bible firmly in his hand,
Prayed to be showed wrong from right.
Just then, as if his prayers were answered from above,
Someone got up and turned on the light.
He feels himself slippin,' grabs the first gal near,
And she sings this sweet song in his ear.

(Chorus)

No one today recalls why only two of the Victor sides were issued. One reason might have been poor sales. Victor 40080 ("Are You from Dixie" and "Dreamy Autumn Waltz"), released in June 1929, some nine months after it was recorded, sold only 4,328 copies—low even compared to the rather meager sales of other Nashville sides in the series. It might also have seemed to Victor A&R man Ralph Peer that the Poplin-Woods repertoire was a little too heavily pop. Whatever the case, the high expectations with which Victor started recording one of the most popular Opry bands soon vanished, and no more sessions followed. For the rest of its tenure, Poplin-Woods was a radio band and a stage show band. Possibly because three of the band members were in their teens and more aware than their elders of pop tunes, the broadcasting song lists did contain a number of pop songs done in string band style, such as "Sweet Georgia Brown," and the Kate Smith hit from the 1920s, "Please Don't Talk about Me When I'm Gone." This latter song was the closing theme of the band's radio segment, always sung as a duet by Frances and Louise. As the band began to book out and do schoolhouse dates on the strength of the Opry popularity, they added even newer songs, such as Gene Austin's hit "My Blue Heaven." Louise Woods told a story of one particular schoolhouse concert where Ed Poplin announced that the band would be happy to take requests, and an older gentleman in overalls stood up in the back and asked, "Can you all play that 'My Blue Heifer?'"

Like most of the other hoedown bands, the Poplin band was lukewarm in its attempts to "professionalize." Its two founding members both had successful full-time occupations, and to make matters worse, they lived farther away from Nashville than any other band. Even most of its touring was limited to southern Middle Tennessee. But in spite of all this, its appeal was strong enough to win it a commercial sponsor on the Opry. The family recalls that one evening when Ed Poplin came home after an Opry show, he had a check in his pocket not from WSM, but directly from a sponsor. One of Poplin's few attempts to play the political game at the Opry backfired during his first year on the show. The Woods family had relatives in Michigan, and shortly after the band started broadcasting, Jack wrote them and asked them to write fan letters to WSM, stating that they had heard the Barn Dance loud and clear and that Poplin-Woods was their favorite band. The proud relatives obliged, and deluged the station with postcards and letters raving about the Poplin performance of the preceding Saturday. The problem was that the band had not performed on the show for that particular Saturday. David Stone and Judge Hay, fortunately, took it in good spirits, and afterward kidded Poplin and Woods about it.

In many ways, the Poplin-Woods band was a prototypical Southern string band of its time: it came from a rural area, it drew upon and maintained family traditions, and it had deep roots in the folk music of its native region. It was on the Opry as much as any other hoedown band and gained a wide and substantial appeal. Its predilection for newer tunes, however, suggests that the Tennessee string bands were more exposed to modern musics like jazz, Tin Pan Alley, vaudeville, and the pop dance bands that were being heard on the new network programs. This dichotomy posed an interesting aesthetic problem, but the band's solution was also rather typical: they maintained their older playing styles and instrumentation and simply imposed on it these new songs. The compromise worked for a time, but by 1937, when the show was demanding even more professionalism and more originality, the Poplin-Woods band decided to give up the struggle and retired from the scene. They left a roomful of warm memories and lilting echoes.

Family Tradition

ON JULY 4, 1934, JUDGE HAY led a procession of cars out of Nashville, heading west on Highway 70. They left early in the morning, for they had a drive of 150 miles to cover and were scheduled to be at their destination by 10:00 A.M. They were headed to an outdoor picnic ground in West Tennessee, where they had been booked to put on a series of one-hour shows throughout the day. A man named C. R. Dowland, now a Nashville businessman, had grown up in West Tennessee and had contracted with the new Opry booking agency to do a show in his neck of the woods. Though individual Opry acts, and small touring contingents, had done personal appearances for some time, this would be the first big test of WSM's Artists Service Bureau, formed the year before as the Opry was becoming more and more commercialized. If WSM wanted to attract professionals to the show—acts like the Vagabonds, the Sizemores, and the Pickards—then the station had to be able to help them find personal appearances to supplement their income. The new Bureau set about doing that, taking for its commission 15 percent of the gate.

George Hay was a little apprehensive as the caravan drove toward the Tennessee River. He had reason to be: an earlier attempt by the Artists Service Bureau had been a flop. He later wrote in an unpublished manuscript: "Our first appearance was given in a colored church a short distance from our studios. We had a large company and put on a good show but very few came to see it. We turned the money back to the church and wished them well. They seemed to appreciate our effort and we felt good about it." This time, though, he felt that they were taking the show "to a place typical of the Opry." He also knew that Dowland had been advertising the show for weeks, inviting people from the countryside to come and see in person the stars they had been hearing on their radios.

Soon the caravan approached the grove of trees where an outdoor stage had been erected. "The country roads around the grove seemed to be littered with cars, horses and buggies and mules and wagons parked alongside," Hay wrote. Even with an escort, the Opry group had trouble making its way through the traffic and crowds and barely made the stage by 10:00 A.M. Standing patiently under the big trees were hundreds of people—later Hay learned they numbered around eight thousand. Benches had been set up neatly, but even at this early hour fans had pushed their way forward and were crowded just a few feet in front of the stage. Off to the side were several long rough tables where "side meat," bread, and soft drinks were sold by the promoter.

People gathered around as the musicians unpacked their instruments and began tuning up. Soon Judge Hay was on stage, delivering his spiel and introducing his acts. The Gully Jumpers performed and then the Crook Brothers. Arthur Smith, a native of the area, brought the Dixieliners on for a set, and then it was time for the star of the show, Uncle Dave Macon. "The Dixie Dew Drop will stroll out on stage to give out," Hay wrote in his manuscript. He carried three banjos, each tuned differently, and he "whips one of those banjos until it cries."

The show went on throughout the day—an early equivalent of a modern day bluegrass festival. Dowland stood backstage with Hay, explaining that only on a holiday such as this could he expect to get these hard-working West Tennessee farmers out of their fields and to an event such as this. Hay nodded and quietly filed that insight away for future use. Finally, at the end of the day, it was time to settle up. The show had been playing "on percentage" and now Dowland brought out the receipts—hundreds of quarters that had been collected at the gate during the day. Dowland and his associates, along with Hay and members of the Gully Jumpers, began to count and divide up. Two local deputies, armed with what Hay called "48's," stood guard while the quarters were divided up into cigar boxes. As the moon rose, the weary crew made its way back to Nashville.

The Artists Service Bureau had actually been founded in 1933 but did not reach high gear until 1934. The station paid for a professional photographer to take photos of all the WSM artists interested in touring—the pop singers as well as the Opry members—and these were compiled into big press books that functioned as catalogs for potential bookers. Below each photo was a short description of the act and the asking rate. Soon acts were going out to schoolhouses, local halls, movie theaters, mining camps, civic affairs, and the kind of huge outdoor picnics like the one in West Tennessee. One up at Blacksburg, Kentucky, about fifty miles from Nashville, managed to draw twelve thousand people. Throughout the 1930s, these picnics provided a favorite venue for the Opry. The troupe would sometimes include as many as twenty acts, in a sense bringing the Opry to the people and literally recreating a typical Saturday night show.

These early attempts to merchandise the Opry were also consistent with another major addition to the show's support staff. In the fall of 1934 WSM hired a staff musician to be the station's "music librarian" and Opry stage manager. With more full-time professionals on the show, the "old-time" nineteenth century tunes and traditional folk songs no longer dominated as the only fare heard on the show. The new acts, such as the Delmores and the Vagabonds, were writing their own songs and singing newer songs from the current Tin Pan Alley folios. An ugly incident between the Vagabonds and the Delmores in 1933 had shown the need for more careful clearances and coordination. (According to Alton Delmore, Curt Poulton and the Vagabonds, with their publishing knowledge and contacts, had tried to "steal" the rights to a number of classic Delmore songs; and, indeed, copies of the Vagabonds' *Old Cabin Songs No. 3* (1934) contained an inserted sheet of music to the Delmores' "When It's Time for the Whippoorwill to Sing," with composer credits to Goodman, Upson, and Poulton.) As country music moved into an age of publishing contracts, copyrights, royalties, songbooks, performance rights, and recording sessions, the Opry and WSM found itself needing someone to handle this end of things.

The person WSM selected was Vito Pellettieri, an unlikely choice. A classically trained violinist who had played regularly with the Nashville symphony, he had agreed to lead an early WSM studio orchestra that, clad in tuxedoes, regularly broadcast from the mezzanine of the Hermitage Hotel in downtown Nashville. Pellettieri was not overly enthusiastic when asked to help with staging the Opry at the Hillsboro theater; he agreed, however, and did a good job. But then, he recalled to Jack Hurst, "I went home, took me a big drink, and told my wife there weren't enough devils in hell to ever drag me back there." But there was his boss, Harry Stone, and there was the worst Depression in history, and Vito did return. His duties soon included building up the station's library of sheet music and song folios, doing song clearances, and asking performers to give him lists of the songs they planned to do on the next show. (In fact, he also asked some of the acts to give him lists of their entire repertoire.) This took some of the spontaneity out of the show, but it did improve the organization and structure. It also prepared the show for its eventual jump to network status in 1939.

The Pickard Family

In one sense, Uncle Dave Macon was probably the first "vocal" star of the Opry, since he appeared on the very first scheduled program. But Uncle Dave's singing was inextricably bound up with his banjo playing, and people were hardly aware of him as a singer per se. On some early shows he was even billed as "banjoist and character singer." The first artist to become a vocal star in the modern sense of the term was an Ashland City, Tennessee, native named Obed ("Dad") Pickard. He first played on the Opry in May 1926, and within a few years he had become nationally known as the leader of the singing Pickard Family. The Pickards were the first group to use their Opry appearances as a springboard to a wider national career and in doing so set the pace for many Opry performers of later years. Though they were on the Opry for a relatively short time, their widespread popularity caused them to influence the whole tenor and direction of the show.

Obed Pickard was born July 22, 1874, and spent his youth learning to play a variety of instruments. His hometown had a brass band, and it was said that Obed could double for any instrument in the band except clarinet. He was also adept with the more traditional folk instruments, including fiddle, guitar, Jew's harp, mandolin, and banjo. As a young man he served in the Spanish-American War and had the privilege of entertaining Admiral Dewey himself on the flagship *Manila* after the war was over. Returning to Tennessee, he married an Ashland City girl, Leila May, whom he fondly called "little Mother." The couple had four children, Ruth, Bubb, Charlie, and Ann. From about 1900 to 1925 Obed supported them by working as a commercial traveler and at times running a sort of collection agency.

In 1926 Pickard met Judge Hay and became a regular on the Opry, but there are two different stories about how his career got started. The traditional version of his coming to the Opry seems to stem from an article about him in the October 28, 1928, *Tennessean*, which recounts how a family tragedy, "the accidental death of one of his daughters . . . brought Mr. Pickard to the studios of WSM. He came first to express his appreciation of a message which reached him while he was travelling in Virginia, notifying him of the terrible accident." WSM had apparently broadcast an appeal for Pickard to call home, and he later stopped in to thank the station manager for helping. While he was there he sat through part of the Opry, and a few weeks later returned with his instruments willing to play.

A different story is told by Pickard's sons Charlie and Bubb, who assert that their father was first asked to play on the Opry when Hay happened to walk into their uncle's bank in Nashville. Hay told this uncle that he was going to start in Nashville something like the *National Barn Dance* in Chicago. Obed happened to walk in about that time, and his brother recommended Hay audition him. Obed mentioned that he had played for Admiral Dewey, and Hay was sufficiently impressed and asked him to play regularly on the show.

Both stories probably have some truth in them, but it is interesting how Hay consciously tried to build up the first story. He repeats it in his book and no doubt fostered it during Pickard's tenure on the show. Hay seemed to sense that such little bits about his performers helped audiences identify with them. They were also responsible for generating an entire folklore about early Opry stars.

Whatever the case, Hay quickly found a nickname for Pickard—"the one-man orchestra"—though he was almost from the first accompanied by his wife on piano. The earliest announcements of his shows seem to stress his comedy as much as his music. At first Dad Pickard seems to have been considered somewhat of a novelty act. Gradually as the Pickard children reached age, they were added to the act: Ruthie on the accordion, Bubb the guitar, and then Charlie with the guitar. (The first song Charlie sang on the Opry was "Uncle Josh.") It was an old American vaudeville custom to use kids in the act, and the Pickards simply transferred this to radio. It was an instant success, and within a couple of years the Pickards were voted one of the most popular on the Opry. And it was the first all-vocal act.

About 1928, when Bubb was about twenty, he got restless and went to work in the Detroit factories. In June of that year the family decided to take a vacation and visit him. They took along letters of introduction from Hay to the managers of stations WJR in Detroit and WGAR in Buffalo. The family did some broadcasts in Detroit and earned the first money they ever made in radio, $25 for two numbers. (Dad had continued to work as a traveler while broadcasting on WSM.) Their music attracted the attention of Henry Ford, who asked them to come to his offices and sing a few numbers. Obed—probably helped out by an overzealous journalist—described the scene in a 1930 issue of *Radio Digest*:

While we were playing away there for a number of the employees, a slender quiet man slipped into the room. I noticed my wife, who was playing the piano, began to get a little nervous and then I glanced up. It was old Henry Ford himself! and he was listening with a smile on his face as wide as Lake Michigan, and (you know he's crazy about those early American songs!) his foot was tapping out the time on the floor and his head was swinging to the time of the music! Yes, sir!

I might have been scared under other conditions—playing before the richest man in America right there in his own domain. But do you know I wasn't scared a bit; it seemed the most natural thing in the world! He got so interested I thought he was going to dance, but he didn't! He just stood there, as interested a listener as the Pickards ever had. And then just as we were playing that famous old reel-tune Sourwood Mountain . . . You know how it goes—

"I got a gal on Sourwood Mountain Dum diddle di do, diddle diddle dee!"

blamed if he didn't jerk a little jews-harp out of his pocket and play with us! And he could play, too! Just as natural as could be! it's a fact, or I hope I may never!

It was worth the trip out there to Detroit just to see Henry Ford standing there in his office playing that jews-harp and keeping time to Sourwood Mountain. He came over and talked to us afterwards and said some mighty nice things about what we played.

Did we like him? Yes sir, he's simply fine—the pleasantest spoken, most modest man you'd find in ten states! I swear he reminded me of the old-time southern gentleman that I used to know down in Tennessee.

Partly as a result of this exposure, the Pickards auditioned for NBC in Buffalo. Dad's comedy songs impressed the NBC scout, and they soon signed a forty-week contract to appear in a sort of minstrel show NBC was doing, "The Cabin Door." The newspapers in Nashville wrote long, glowing accounts of their triumph, and Hay seemed especially happy at their success. The act next worked for the Interwoven Stocking Company and were called the Interwoven Entertainers. The next year found them in Chicago doing "The Farm and Home Hour" for NBC, and Obed played a dramatic role in a play about a miner and his family. But in 1931 Mrs. Pickard became ill, and the group returned to Tennessee.

They thus began a second stint on the Opry, from 1931 to 1933. With their wide experience they were the stars of the show, and now that all the family was playing, their appeal was even broader. (Bubb, however, was not playing with them; he was continuing to work on WJJD, then in Aurora, Illinois, and trying to develop a market for hillbilly music.) In 1933 Mrs. Pickard was better and Bubb had lined up new jobs for the family in Chicago, so they left again to go North. The next few years saw them broadcasting on stations in Chicago, Philadelphia, New York, and New Orleans. They built up an immense following, solely on the basis of radio. At one point in New Orleans their mail was peaking at 7,200 pieces a day. They later moved their base of operations to San Antonio, where they worked with the famous border station XERA, and then eventually to California. There in 1949 Dad Pickard became the star of one of the first TV series shows. He died five years later, though his family continued to record and perform.

Any study of the Pickard repertoire would be a vast and complex task. Though their commercial records are rather few, the songs they performed on radio transcriptions number into the thousands and have not even been cataloged. Yet their notion of traditional music seems to have been essentially formalistic. Hay recalled, "Mrs. Pickard and Ruth were accomplished musicians, who had studied the art for many years. They did not care much for the homespun tunes in those early days, but it was not long before they put their hearts into the act. . . ."

Obed himself made his first big hit with a cover version of the then-popular nineteenth-century lament "Kitty Wells." (In fact, for years later most Opry veterans still referred to the song as Dad Pickard's.) The first group of songs recorded by the family (in December 1928, after they had left WSM for the first time) included "popular" folk songs like "She'll Be Comin' Round the Mountain," "Down in Arkansas," and "Get Away from That Window." A later session yielded nineteenth century standards like "Buffalo Gals," "The Little Red Caboose behind the Train," and "In the Shade of the Old Apple Tree." Two sides showing Obed's solo virtuosity are "Sally Gooden," which reveals his ability on the Jew's harp, and "My Old Boarding House," a hilarious version of the Uncle Dave Macon–Charlie Poole favorite, "Hungry Hash House." These records, made for the Plaza Company, were extremely popular, and some of them were released on as many as eleven different labels. Dad Pickard himself told the *Radio Digest* reporter: "I am mighty glad of the opportunity to play and sing these old ballads and folksongs. I feel that we are doing something worthwhile, for we are helping to preserve something very sweet and fine which otherwise would be lost."

This sort of self-consciousness about material reminds one of Judge Hay's own romantic notion of Southern folk music but is even more a probable reflection of Henry Ford's sentiments. The Pickards, however, seemed to understand that they were functioning as popularizers of traditional material and were content with the role. And their role pointed the way for many Opry vocal groups of the future.

The following is Dad Pickard's own account of his career, written for their 1934 songbook. Note the curious absence of any mention of WSM and the early Opry.

FROM "THE HILLS OF TENNESSEE" TO THE STUDIOS OF N.B.C. I am here relating the first real story of "my little family" in the hope that it may reach the hearts of some doubting Thomas's, for I firmly believe with all of my heart if you leave your life and everything you do in HIS hands, HE will take care of you.

Our home town is Ashland [City], Tennessee, and perhaps if it weren't for radio we would never have been heard outside the confines of this little country town in the Tennessee Hills. We had a little collection business and were getting along pretty good and making some money. We worked hard, though, but I guess we were one of the few who ever made any money in it, and what money I made was spent with "the little family" so we all had a lot of fun.

Apparently we were getting along "great" so when Leila May suggested that we give up this collection business and try the radio, I thought she was insane and she carries to this day a mental picture of the expression I had on my face and the pity I had for her for making such a suggestion. I tried my best to impress upon her that our old mountain, home spun airs wouldn't be of interest to radio listeners but she insisted that God gave us all some little talent and we ought to give it to the world. Finally "the little Mother" said, "Dad, let's have a little vacation." So, we jumped in the car, drove to Louisville (my, what a town), then to Detroit, then to Buffalo and then to New York. And, Oh Boy! What a town. Our opportunity came. After a hurried audition, we were given a spot and we clicked on "The Old Cabin Door" program right off the reel and well, we got cheated out of the balance of our vacation and we haven't had it yet. The "little Mother" is responsible for our rise (or fall) to radio fame for I was never sold on it until we got our "black and white" from the N.B.C. I was only going on that glorious childlike faith that somehow He'd see us through.

You know my gang's a great gang. There's Obed, Junior, better known on the N.B.C. chain as Bubb; and Ruth Phaney, who is the "school boy" with the changing voice; and Ann, who is only four and a half years old and the only child employed regularly by the N.B.C. The truth of how folks just naturally absorb these old-time Hick and Hoe down Hill Billy Songs is evidenced by what little Ann does; she can hum and sing the melody, and keep the rhythm of every tune or song that we sing. And now we are beginning 1934 with Chuck, another member of our family. Chuck sings and picks the old banjo.

Since our first "Old Cabin Door" program, we have appeared in many different programs; such as on Lucky Strike Hour, in Socony Land Sketches, as Jolly Bill and Jane, as Gold Spot Pale, etc. We are now on the National Farm and Home Hour from N.B.C. Chicago Studios every day at noon to 12:45 P.M., except Sunday.

We are grateful to our "Great Silent Audience" for any degree of success that we may have achieved. One of our little darlings, our oldest daughter Leila, is safe on the other side and May and I really believe that our greatest inspiration comes from her to carry on, never falter, never fail. And some time we shall all be together again singing and playing the old mountain tunes on that happy golden shore with the angels to die no more. To all of our friends everywhere, this little book is dedicated and now GRAND-MOTHER, wind up the clock and POLLY you put the kettle on, and we will say "GOODNIGHT EVERYBODY."

Dad Pickard

Asher Sizemore and Little Jimmie

The Opry's shift away from a largely instrumental to a vocal format manifested itself in a variety of ways, but one of the most significant was sentimentalism. Child performers were a key part of this. Children have always been popular on the American stage, and even some of the pioneer country string bands, such as Fiddlin' Powers (from Virginia) and Da

Costa Woltz (from Galax, Virginia) sometimes included child instrumentalists. On the screen, artists like the Little Rascals, Jackie Coogan, and especially Shirley Temple captivated crowds during the 1930s. Numerous country acts sought to develop this child star tradition as well, though they sometimes ran afoul of newly passed child labor laws in some Southern states. But one of the most successful was the act that followed the Pickard Family on the early Opry, five-year-old Jimmie Sizemore and his father Asher. For many veteran Opry listeners, Asher and Little Jimmie are the best-remembered figures on the 1930s show. And, indeed, they were off and on the show throughout the whole decade: joining in September 1932, they played almost every week in 1933, about three months in 1934, and from January to April in 1935. After a stint on the NBC network, they returned for eight weeks in 1936–1937 and for four months in 1939. It is not surprising that during this time Little Jimmie became the most popular preteen in country music.

Twenty-six-year-old Asher Sizemore came from the mountains of Kentucky, a fact which he constantly exploited. Sizemore was born in Manchester, Kentucky, and began his career as a bookkeeper for a coal mining company in Pike County. (Characteristically, Judge Hay romanticized this into the statement that Asher was a coal miner.) Asher married Odessa Foley, the daughter of a minister. A few years later, in 1928, Jimmie, their first son, was born at Paintsville, on the Big Sandy River. By 1931 Asher, with his good looks, smooth voice, and snappy suits, was appearing on radio in Huntington, West Virginia, and within a year had moved on to Cincinnati (WCKY) and Louisville (WHAS). It was then that WSM's Harry Stone approached Asher and asked him to come to Nashville. They were one of the first groups the station actively sought out to hire.

A great deal of Asher's performing style seems to have been derived from fellow Kentuckian Bradley Kincaid, who had been a huge success over Chicago's WLS. Like Kincaid, Asher played on his Kentucky folk song heritage, translating old mountain songs into smooth, well-modulated radio fare. Like Kincaid, he alternated his genuine ballads with sentimental, gospel, and novelty songs. Like Kincaid, he made his way with only a simple guitar accompaniment. And like Kincaid, he supplemented his income by printing up his own songbooks to sell by direct mail.

After Asher joined WSM, he soon found he had to invent some of his own ways to augment his income. One was recording. In 1934 Asher and Jimmie journeyed to San Antonio to record for the newly formed Bluebird label. Some dozen sides resulted, not many of them particularly successful. One was "Little Jimmie's Goodbye to Jimmie Rodgers," a topical lament about the late Blue Yodeler that was in fact modeled on an earlier tribute by Dwight Butcher. Others were "Chawin' Chewing Gum," the old Carter Family song, and "How Beautiful Heaven Must Be," the gospel song that Uncle Dave had popularized on the Opry. The pair also did some tours but soon discovered that their best way of making spare change was the Kincaid way—publishing songbooks. The first of these, printed in Nashville by Parthenon Press in 1933, was entitled *Old Fashioned Hymns and Mountain Ballads*. This was something new for most Opry artists, and Judge Hay was impressed: "They got out a songbook which sold by the thousands." Asher was also impressed and throughout the 1930s he published a new songbook almost annually. The quarters rolled in, stuffed into envelopes and addressed merely to WSM, Nashville. It was something that would not be repeated until Roy Acuff's early days of a decade later.

A look at the contents of this first book offers some interesting details of the on-air repertoire. First of all, the book earmarked songs for Little Jimmie: "Little Cowboy Jim," "Now I Lay Me Down to Sleep," and folk songs like "What'll I Do with the Baby-O," "Put My Little Shoes Away," and the one most fans still remember, "My Little Rooster":

I love my rooster, my rooster loves me,
I cherish my rooster on the green bay tree,
My little rooster goes cocka do do de doodle de doodle do doodle de doe.
I love my duck, my duck loves me,
I love my duck, my duck loves me,
My little duck goes quack, quack, quack, quack quack quack quack quack
    quack.

The gospel songs, which take up fully half the book, include several from the James D. Vaughan Company, the shape-note publisher from Lawrenceburg, Tennessee, such as "I Dreamed I Searched Heaven For You" and "Gathering Buds." Secular ballads include "The Forgotten Soldier Boy," "Barbara Allen," "The Orphan Girl," and "The Dying Cowboy." One of the most lugubrious efforts, "I Miss My Dear Sweet Mother," is credited to Asher himself. The duo always closed their program with a prayer and had a noted minister write a testimonial as a preface to the songbook.

In 1933, when Little Jimmie was going on six, his father boasted that "he can sing from memory more than two hundred songs and there are numerous others that he joins in with Dad on the chorus." Asher also reported, apparently thinking it was cute, that "after each engagement Little Jimmie always asks the question, 'Dad, how much dough did we make tonight?'" Judge Hay, not used to seeing such materialism in a child so young, was concerned "for fear the emotional strain would be too much for Jimmie." The boy seemed to survive quite well, however, and by the late 1930s the Sizemore act was expanded to include his younger brother "Buddy Boy."

Hay himself recalled that much of Asher's appeal lay not in his repertoire itself, but in the fact that he was very good at talking to his audience and introducing his songs—something that few Opry performers did in these early days. Asher was certainly as aware as Judge Hay of the importance of image and sought by both personal appearances and songbooks to expand the nature of radio as a commercial medium. And in merchandising so well the family ties, he was linking the new professionalism with one of the most venerable of folk singing traditions: family performance and oral transmission.

The Original Nashville Sound
Nashville's First Recordings

THE GRAND OLE OPRY during its "classic" years of the
1940s and 1950s was rather closely related to the Nashville
recording industry, and many historians feel that the show was the
main reason the recording industry developed. Several of the key executives in the country recording industry were graduates, in one way or
another, of the Opry. But it would be wrong to assume that an active relationship has always existed between the Opry and the business of making
records. As we have seen, pre-1930 Opry members recorded a good deal
less than did other major old-time artists of the age. Even through the
1930s, as the Opry began to gain wide national acceptance, the regulars
on the show recorded far fewer sides than their counterparts on WLS's
National Barn Dance. Yet the early Opry grew without much help from
recordings, and the early development of the show suggests that a history
of country music based solely on recordings would be distorted.

However, because Nashville has since acquired the reputation of being
the world's center for country recordings, there is a certain historical significance in tracing just where and when Nashville's first recordings were
made. Nashville's modern recording industry dates from the mid-1940s,
when Decca became the first major company to record country music regularly in Nashville. At about the same time, Bullet Records became one of
the first Nashville-based companies to feature country music and western
swing. The real impact of Nashville-based recording dates from that time.
However, there were earlier, rather abortive, attempts to record in

Nashville, and their story sheds some light on the history of the early Opry. Some evidence suggests that a commercial cylinder company operated in Nashville about the turn of the century, but little is known about the company's activity. At that time, cylinder production was almost a cottage industry, and cylinders were copied only a few at a time. From a technical point of view, the first recordings actually made in Nashville were probably 7-inch aluminum discs made for customers by a Nashville music store. A number of old-timers recall going up to a music studio on Church Street in downtown Nashville and, for a fee, cutting a two-minute home recording, just as Uncle Jimmy Thompson did. The operator of the makeshift studio usually charged only a dollar or so for a custom record, and of course each disc was a unique copy. Research indicates that this studio was operated as a service of the O. K. Houck Piano Company, which occupied the second floor of the old Vendome Building on Church Street, a well-established Nashville music house that had been active since the 1880s. In the middle and late '20s this was the largest music store in Nashville. Apparently the recording service was operational as early as 1925, to judge from Katherine Thompson's account of Uncle Jimmy's experience. Also, the Perry County Music Makers (the Tennessee string band with the zither lead) probably obtained from this same studio the demo recording that they sent to Brunswick in 1929, winning a recording session the following year.

The Church Street records were about the size of the Silvertone home discs marketed by Sears in the 1930s, and contemporary accounts suggest that their sound was shrill, tinny, and unreliable. Nonetheless, they seem to have functioned well enough as audition records, and were probably often used as such. None of the records has so far been recovered from the Nashville area, and it is possible that they wore out quickly. Although no one has yet discovered the identity of the individual actually engineering the recordings, many early old-time performers from the Opry and the other early Nashville radio shows quite possibly made their way to the second-floor studios. And the anonymous technician must have the distinction of being Nashville's first recording engineer. The service definitely existed from 1925 to 1930, and might well have continued on into the '30s. Because they were custom produced, most of the records obviously had little influence beyond the immediate community.

Another important early Nashville recording series was that done by famed Fisk University folk music scholar John Work. Fisk had apparently acquired a disc-cutting machine in the mid-1930s, and Work lost no time lugging it to various sites to record various types of black folk music in the area. Most of this was religious music of one sort or another, but he did record a handful of local blues singers and two superb local black string bands. One of these bands was composed of fiddler Frank Patterson and banjoist Nathan "Ned" Frazier. Both men were in their fifties when Work recorded them, and both performed a style and repertoire that Work deemed archaic, even when he recorded them in the fall of 1941. Patterson originally came from the cedar glades region southeast of Nashville and was an influence on at least one of the early Opry string bands (see chapter 5). Patterson was a dynamic banjoist who reminded contemporaries of Uncle Dave Macon and who was usually found busking on the streets of Nashville. Work recorded about a dozen sides by Frazier-Patterson and subsequently sold the discs to the Library of Congress; they were eventually issued in LP form in 1989. The second group Work recorded, this time in June 1942, was the Nashville Washboard Band headed by mandolin player James Kelly. This group, which often played on the courthouse steps in downtown Nashville, included Kelly's mandolin, two guitars, a washboard, a bass fiddle, and a "tin can." This group played tunes like "Old Joe" (the same one done by Dr. Humphrey Bate and also by Frazier-Patterson), "Soldier's Joy," and swing era pieces like "I'll Be Glad When You're Dead, You Rascal You." Only one of the Kelly sides was ever released for commercial sale, and that not until the 1980s. Indications suggest that black musicians associated with either or both of these groups and appeared occasionally on the Opry, but their significance and influence on the development of other Opry acts has yet to be fully appreciated. Work might well have continued his recording activities in Nashville had not World War II intervened and had not Fisk made increasing demands on his time. Work was a fine judge of talent and was thinking of trying to develop several black gospel groups in Nashville into commercial stars like the Golden Gate Quartet. Had he been able to implement these plans, he might well have done further and more commercial recordings.

The honor of making the first commercial recordings in Nashville must go to the Victor Talking Machine Company (as the company was then known), whose field unit made a single visit to the city in the fall of 1928. Victor brought to Nashville their portable recording unit, recently designed by Western Electric and bearing the trade name "Orthophonic," and recorded some sixty-nine songs by local country and gospel talent. These sides or those of them that were released represent a fascinating chapter in Nashville music history. They represented the first, albeit unsuccessful, attempt to use Grand Ole Opry music as a base for a local ongoing recording program.

During the late 1920s, Nashville was becoming known across the country as the home of the Opry and as a healthy radio center, but it was by no means the major recording center for country music. That distinction went to Atlanta. As the record industry began to recognize the market for old-time music in the mid-1920s, it discovered quickly that the best way to find and record real country talent was to record "on location."

The development of electrical recording techniques in the mid-1920s made it possible to pack all of the equipment needed to record into a touring car. Mobile recording crews, usually consisting of a producer and two engineers, took to the field throughout the South in the late '20s in search of new, authentic, "downhome" talent. Atlanta quickly emerged as a fertile source for such talent, and Columbia and Okeh centered their field operations there, usually visiting in the spring and fall of each year. Many talent search-parties came to Tennessee, however: Victor recorded at Bristol and discovered the first country music superstars, Jimmie Rodgers and the Carter Family; Columbia recorded at Johnson City; Brunswick did sessions in Knoxville. By late 1927, though, Memphis had emerged as the major recording center for Tennessee; in fact, it was second only to Atlanta in popularity as a regional recording center. Victor used Memphis as its major location in the South and began to send recording crews there each spring and fall for sessions that lasted for weeks. To be sure, much of the material recorded in Memphis was blues or jazz, but a significant percentage was country music. After one of these long Memphis sessions, in late September 1928, the Victor crew, on their way back to Atlanta, stopped over in Nashville to sample the talent.

What they found in Nashville in 1928 was an abundance of talent, some of it already well experienced with recording. By the latter part of that year several Nashville stars had already journeyed to other locations to make records. Even as early as July 1924, before the WSM Barn Dance program took to the air, Uncle Dave Macon and Sid Harkreader went to New York to record for the Aeolian Vocalion company; in March 1926 champion fiddler Uncle Bunt Stephens recorded for Columbia in New York; Uncle Dave Macon and Sam McGee recorded for Vocalion in New York in April 1926; and the Macon–Fruit Jar Drinkers session was in May 1927, again for Vocalion in New York. Dr. Humphrey Bate and the Possum Hunters had gone to Atlanta in May 1928 to record for Brunswick, while Uncle Jimmy Thompson had recorded some eighteen months previously for Columbia at the same location.

In late March 1927 several WSM performers journeyed to Atlanta to record for Columbia. These included Obed Pickard (before his family joined his act), the Golden Echo Quartet (a gospel group), and DeFord Bailey. As noted earlier, the resulting releases from these sessions sometimes identified the artists as "of Station WSM, Nashville, Tenn." This may have simply meant that WSM paid for the trip, but in any event the labeling was good publicity for both station and artist. In the late 1920s, when far fewer stations crowded the airwaves, a major station's audience was by no means restricted to a city or even to a state. WSM was then easily heard throughout the eastern half of the United States, and its artists were known almost throughout the country. The call letters of WSM on a record would doubtless be recognized by many buyers.

Thus, the Victor recording crew that fall in 1928 had good reason to expect that a session in Nashville might yield interesting results. Musicians there had proven themselves on radio, and many of them were recording for rival companies. The company had discovered a blues bonanza to the west, in Memphis, with their discovery of the Memphis Jug Band and others. They had discovered a hillbilly bonanza to the east part of the state, in Bristol, with Jimmie Rodgers and the Carter Family. Why not try the center of the state as well? The local radio stations were certainly eager to cooperate. Sid Harkreader, who, later on, remembered the session but did not participate because of his Paramount contract, thought Judge Hay, or some of the station executives, actually invited the Victor people to come in. Virtually all the acts recorded were on Nashville radio, though not all on WSM; some were on rivals WLAC and WBAW.

Typical of the work of the experienced recording crew, the Nashville session was carefully planned in advance. Curiously, a good indication of the planning was that absolutely no mention was made of it in the local newspapers. A year earlier, in Bristol, the newspapers were full of stories about that session because producer Ralph Peer was trying to lure new talent for auditions. The fact that they did absolutely no publicity in Nashville suggests that the talent was already arranged and that they felt no need to search for unknown talent.

Ralph S. Peer, the director of the first Nashville session, was perhaps the most famous talent scout and producer in country music history. Not only had he discovered Jimmie Rodgers and the Carter Family the year before, but he is generally credited with recording the first blues record (by Mamie Smith, for Okeh, in 1920) and the first commercial country record (by Fiddlin' John Carson, for Okeh, in 1923). By 1928 he had perfected a technique of making recording "sweeps" through the South, traveling by car to several cities on one trip, with two engineers and "half a carload" of recording gear. They would stay out for as long as two months, regularly shipping the big wax masters back to the pressing plant in Camden, New Jersey. The fall 1928 tour started in Memphis, where they spent most of September recording some thirty-five sessions of blues artists. The tour then went to Nashville, recording some ten acts in seven working days, then to Atlanta (fifteen acts in ten working days), and finally back to Bristol on October 27 (some thirteen acts in nine working days). Peer thus spent less time, and recorded fewer acts, in Nashville than in any other city on the fall tour.

Although several participants recalled that the sessions with Victor were held in the WSM studios, the actual session sheets in the Victor files—made out on the spot by the engineers—indicate conclusively that the recordings were done in the YMCA Building. In 1928, this building was located at Seventh and Union in downtown Nashville, just two blocks east of the National Life Building, where the WSM studios were, and about two blocks south of the state Capitol building. Louise Woods, of the Poplin-Woods band, recalls that the room had blankets hanging from the wall, and a set of red and green lights indicated when to start playing. In addition to Peer, two Victor engineers were present. Though these men were the first ever to oversee a session in what would later be "Music City U.S.A.," we know them only by their initials: "S.S." and "G.A." They were almost certainly not local but members of the Victor staff in Camden, New Jersey, and doubtless they had little inkling of their role in history.

The crew recorded nine groups in all, and of these seven were regulars on the Opry: the Binkley Brothers, Paul Warmack and his Gully Jumpers, the Poplin-Woods band, the Crook Brothers, Theron Hale and his Daughters, Uncle Joe Mangrum and Fred Shriver, and DeFord Bailey. The two other groups were the Vaughan Quartet and the Gentry Family Quartet. The Vaughan group was sponsored by the James D. Vaughan Music Company of Lawrenceburg, Tennessee, and was created to travel, broadcast, and record in order to demonstrate new songs in the Vaughan songbooks. The Gentry Family Quartet, a gospel-oriented group, sang unaccompanied and appeared on WLAC. Though neither group actually appeared on the Opry, the Vaughan quartet did appear regularly over WSM.

On Friday, September 28, the first day of the sessions, two groups recorded: the Binkley Brothers with Jack Jackson (four tunes) and Warmack's Gully Jumpers (one number). But something was wrong with all of these takes. Perhaps the machinery was not working properly, but in the case of the Binkley Brothers, Peer did not like the Binkleys' singing and insisted they find a better lead singer. The next week they did: Jack Jackson. Then Peer rerecorded all the Binkleys' numbers on Tuesday, October 2.

So it was on Monday, October 1, that the first Nashville records to be released to the public were made. The artists were Paul Warmack and his Gully Jumpers, with Warmack doing the singing. Between 2:00 P.M. and

6:00 P.M. that afternoon, the band completed nine takes of four tunes: "Put My Little Shoes Away," a familiar Middle Tennessee tune that later was a favorite of bluegrass star Mac Wiseman; "I'm a Little Dutchman," a variant on the familiar "Wee Dog Waltz" or "Where Has My Little Dog Gone?"; "Tennessee Waltz," not the well-known Pee Wee King–Redd Stewart hit but an earlier original composition by Warmack and his fiddler Charlie Arrington; and "The Little Red Caboose behind the Train," a parody of the "Little Old Log Cabin in the Lane." Of these, Peer saw fit to release only the latter two titles, on Victor 40067, issued on May 17, 1929 (see the session log at the end of this chapter). It would sell 7,864 copies.

Is this, then, the first record made in Nashville? Yes and no. By a few hours it was undoubtedly the earliest commercially issued record made in Nashville. However, it was not the first record issued from the Nashville session; that honor would go to the Vaughan Quartet and the Binkley Brothers. The former's coupling of "Master of the Storm" and "What a Morning That Will Be" came out on Victor 21756, released December 2, 1928, barely two months after the session. On the same date was issued Victor 21758, "All Go Hungry Hash House" and "It'll Never Happen Again," two Binkley Brothers–Jack Jackson sides they had learned from Uncle Dave Macon. These records, though recorded five days after Warmack's, were thus, as actual commercial records, made public some five and a half months before Warmack's. To complicate matters even more, one of Warmack's unissued sides ("I'm a Little Dutchman") that preceded "Tennessee Waltz" and "The Little Red Caboose" was discovered in 1980 in the New York vaults of RCA Victor and was issued in a 1986 historical compilation entitled *Sixty Years of the Grand Ole Opry* (CPL29507). Thus a case could made for *it* being the first Nashville recording as well, even though it took Victor some fifty-eight years to release it.

All in all, out of the sixty-nine songs recorded at the Nashville session, only thirty-six were released by Victor on the standard 78 rpm format. They generally represent more instrumental music than vocal music, but this imbalance may not necessarily reflect the state of the music on the Opry as much as that some of the show's prime vocalists, such as Uncle Dave Macon and Dad Pickard, were already under contract to other labels. Most of the records were released in Victor's new 40000 series, "Old Familiar Tunes and Novelties," initiated at the start of 1929. Victor 40009, Paul Warmack's two breakdowns, came out on January 18, as did the Gentry Family's anti-evolution song "You Can't Make a Monkey Out of Me" (Victor 40013). February 8, 1929, saw the release of titles by Uncle Joe Mangrum (Victor 40018) and the Crook Brothers (40020); April 5 the release of three more discs, by Theron Hale (40019), the Vaughan Quartet (40045), and the Binkley Brothers (40048). Titles continued to come out through the spring and summer, culminating in the last Binkley Brothers coupling (40129) in October, a little over a year after the session. A couple of sides by DeFord Bailey were not issued until late 1932, both of them in the label's country series and blues series.

One of the best eyewitness accounts to the session came from Jack Jackson, the vocalist with the Binkley Brothers' Dixie Clodhoppers. He recalled, "Neither of the Binkley brothers even pretended to sing, and the Victor folks said they wanted a vocalist on the records, that they wouldn't even consider them without it, so they called me on the telephone and I went to see them, and we got together that way." Jackson had been signed to a "letter of option" with Victor for almost a year prior to the Nashville recordings. This was a fairly common practice in early field recording, whereby an advance talent scout spotted promising acts and signed them with a letter that promised to record them within a year. The artists, in turn, agreed not to record for any other record company before that time. No money was exchanged in such a signing. Jackson said that a Victor representative (whose name he did not recall, though it was quite likely Peer) came through Nashville in 1927 and signed such letters of option with several local radio performers. "They went at it the slowest way in the world. They'd get you to sign an option for twelve months and then wait eleven months before acting, and then they'd get in a big hurry. They paid us $100 a record and they wouldn't even talk about royalties with you."

Though he was one of the first performers to record, Jackson recalled that the recording gear was already in place when he arrived. Then the engineers began working with his singing style.

Well, the first thing, they tore me all to pieces. . . . They'd make samples and play 'em back to you. There were certain letters they told me before we started wouldn't come out. The s and t, like first, that st wouldn't come out, and w-i combinations. I had to sit there and practice those things. When I got through, I didn't sound like myself at all, trying to make them dig into the record. You had to hit those real hard in order for them to come out then. By the time I got through with that we might have spent the whole day just doing that, making tests. Trying to get those w's and st, anyway they had a list, they knew what wouldn't take out. They didn't have any trouble recording the instruments, they had trouble holding them back. They had to set the banjo player almost out in the yard.

Another thing that bothered him was the microphone. "It was just right in my nose; it was just two or three inches away; my nose almost touched it." Such problems were so distracting that Jackson always felt that he did not sound right on the records and thought that was one reason why some were never released.

Neither Jackson nor anyone has suggested that Nashville took any special notice when the records were released. No notice appeared in the newspapers, nor did any special advertisements by local record dealers, as had been the case in similar circumstances in Bristol and Johnson City. Though the dance band recordings of WSM's Francis Craig were announced and trumpeted in local papers, nothing was said about the country records: "They just kind of appeared," remembered Jackson, sadly.

All of this brings us back to the central mystery of the 1928 session: why were so few of the sides issued? No other Victor field session resulted in such a high percentage of unreleased sides, almost 50 percent. One possible answer might be a poor sales history of the early releases. We do have sales figures for the 40000 series, and they do reveal that none of the Nashville records became big hits, on the level of Rodgers or the Carters. The best-selling Nashville release in the 40000 series was Victor 40045, the Vaughan Quartet's "I Want to Go There, Don't You" backed with "His Charming Love." The best-selling nongospel release in the series was Victor 40048, the Binkley Brothers–Jack Jackson "I'll Rise When the Rooster Crows" backed with "Give Me Back My Fifteen Cents." The Vaughan sold 18,876 copies; the Binkley 17,778. Except for the other Vaughan releases, which sold around 10,000 copies each, most of the rest of the Opry band releases averaged 4,000 to 6,000 copies each. Such figures seem small by modern standards but were not meager in comparison with other Victor sales in the "Old Familiar Tunes" series in the first half of 1929. Hits by Rodgers and the Carters did top 100,000 copies, and Carson Robison's pop-country pieces often got to 50,000, but most of the regular field session sides only averaged from 4,000 to 10,000 copies. Thus, the Nashville sales were not that much out of line, and sales by the Binkley Brothers, the Vaughan Quartet, and the Gully Jumpers certainly should have seemed promising enough.

Another possible answer to the "failure" of the session might lie in some cryptic notations on the recording session sheets. As historians have noted for some years, Ralph Peer was interested in doing field sessions, in part, to get publishing rights: either for original songs that could be copyrighted or for old songs (such as those of A. P. Carter) that were obscure enough to be rearranged and copyrighted. Few of the Nashville recordings fall into either of these categories: many were either clearly in copyright or familiar enough not to rearrange. On many of the session sheets, therefore, we do not find the customary note to "See Mr. Peer for information," but instead the citation "No info L. L. Watson." According to longtime RCA producer Brad McCuen, L. L. Watson was the head of Victor's copyright clearance office in Camden, and the man through whom all composer credits had to be cleared. These references in the Nashville sheets to him may therefore indicate that, for various reasons, Peer was unable to get the normal number of publishing rights for the session and was, therefore, lukewarm about releasing all of the material.

For whatever reason, though, the first commercial recording session was deemed a failure, and no major recording company would return to the city for over fifteen years. Almost incidentally, the session documented our only glimpse of many first-generation Opry performers, but it had, in the end, little effect on the development of the radio show itself. The liaison between the Opry and the recording industry that would eventually give the show such an edge over other similar efforts would have to wait until a later era.

The Session

Set out below are the recording data on the Nashville session, as preserved in RCA Victor files, and collated and published in Brian Rust (*The Victor Master Book Vol. 2 (1925-36)* (Pinner, Middlesex, England, 1969). The data have been slightly rearranged to clarify the day-to-day progress of the sessions. The information comprises (from left to right) matrix number (the recording's original serial number); number of takes recorded at that session, title, and release number, if any.

Friday, September 28

Binkley Brothers' Clodhoppers

470981	2	Watermelon Hanging On De Vine
470991	2	Little Old Log Cabin In The Lane
471001	2	Give Me Back My Fifteen Cents
471011	2	All Go Hungry Hash House

Paul Warmack & His Gully Jumpers

471021	2	Tennessee Waltz

Monday, October 1

Paul Warmack & His Gully Jumpers

471023	4	Tennessee Waltz	V40067
471031	3	Put My Little Shoes Away	
471041	2	I'm A Little Dutchman	
471051	2	The Little Red Caboose	
		Behind The Train	V40067

Tuesday, October 2

Binkley Brothers' Clodhoppers

470983		Watermelon Hanging On De Vine	
470993	4	Little Old Log Cabin In The Lane	V-40129
471003	4	Give Me Back My Fifteen Cents	V-40048
471013	4	All Go Hungry Hash House	21758
471061	2	When I Had But Fifty Cents	V-40129
471071	2	It'll Never Happen Again	21758
471081	2	Rock All Our Babies To Sleep	
471091	2	I'll Rise When The Rooster Crows	V-40048

DeFord Bailey

471101	2	Lost John	
471111	2	John Henry	23336, 23831
471121	2	Ice Water Blues	V-38014
471131	2	Kansas City Blues	
471141	2	Casey Jones	
471151	2	Wood Street Blues	
471161	2	Davidson County Blues	V-38014
471171	2	Nashville Blues	

Wednesday, October 3

Theron Hale & Daughters

471181	2	Listen To The Mocking Bird	V40019
471191	2	Turkey Gobbler	V40019
471201	2	Beautiful Valley Waltz	
471211	2	Kiss Waltz	
471221	2	Jolly Blacksmith	V40046
471231	2	Wink The Other Eye	

| 471241 | 2 | Hale's Rag | V40046 |
| 471251 | 2 | The Old Race Horse | |

Gentry Family Quartet

| 471261 | 3 | You Can't Make A Monkey Out Of Me | V40013 |
| 471271 | 2 | Hop Along, Sister Mary | |

Paul Warmack & His Gully Jumpers

471281	3	Robertson County	V40009
471291	2	Stone Rag	V40009
471301	2	Hell Broke Loose In Georgia	
471311	2	Five Cents	

Thursday, October 4

Poplin-Woods Tennessee String Band

471321	2	Sally, Let Me Chaw Your Rosin Some	
471331	2	Flop-Eared Mule	
471341	2	Dreamy Autumn Waltz	V-40080
471351	2	Lovers' Call Waltz	
471361	2	Pray For The Lights To Go Out	
471371	2	Are You From Dixie?	V-40080
471381	2	Honey, Honey, Honey	
471391	2	Robert E. Lee	

Friday, October 5

Crook Brothers' String Band

471401	2	My Wife Died On Friday Night	V-40020
471411	2	Going Across The Sea	V-40099
471421	3	Job In Gettin' There	V-40020
478301	2	Love Somebody	V-40029

Vaughan Quartet

471431	3	I Want To Go There, Don't You?	V-40045
471441	2	When All Those Millions Sing	V-40071
471451	3	The Master Of The Storm	21756
471461	3	Sunlight And Shadows	V-40097
471471		My Troubles Will Be Over	V-40071

471481	2	His Charming Love	V-40045
471491	2	What A Morning That Will Be	21756
471501	2	In Steps Of Light	V-40097

Saturday, October 6

Blind Joe Mangun–Fred Shriber [*sic*]

471511	3	Mammoth Cave Waltz	
471521	3	The Rose Waltz	
471531	3	Bacon And Cabbage	V-40018
471541	3	Bill Cheetam	V-40018
478161		Cradle Song	

Gentry Family Quartet

471551	2	Jog Along, Boys	V-40013
471561	2	In the Evening Take Me Home	
471571	2	Jesus Paid It All	
471581	2	The Church In The Wild Wood	

Note: only original Victor releases are noted, but some masters were leased later to Bluebird, Sunrise, Montgomery Ward, and even the British Zonophone label.

The First Professionals
The Vagabonds

B
Y THE EARLY 1930S THE OWNERS OF WSM had realized that what some had referred to as Edwin Craig's "plaything" was in fact becoming a major influence in the cultural and economic landscape. In spite of the Depression, radio was emerging as a powerful selling tool, and by 1935 some 70 percent of American households had radios. By 1927 the NBC network had begun, providing to member stations a high quality of music and drama, and these same member stations began to seek professionalism in their own staffs. WSM, and the Opry, were no exceptions.

The "professionalization" of the Opry began, in one sense, with the hiring of Judge Hay in 1925, but the next stage began in 1928, with the hiring of Harry Stone. He was originally hired to help Hay with announcing and managing details. A native of Florida, Stone and his family (including his brother David, who later would become a key WSM and Opry announcer) had moved to Nashville by the early 1920s. Harry became interested in radio while working on a tiny station run by the First Baptist Church early in the 1920s. Unlike Hay, who was more of a creative artist—what we today would call an "idea man"—Stone was practical and more business oriented. He had the ability to take Hay's ideas and commercialize them. In later years, Stone's brother David recalled of Hay: "He was a lot of fun. But he never wanted to settle down to the details of running a big enterprise." By 1932 Stone was named general manager of WSM and was becoming a more powerful figure in Opry matters than even the Judge himself. The real move toward professionalizing the Opry cast came from him as much as anyone. Though some of the musicians on the show thought of him as a cold, pragmatic bean-counter, Stone seems to have genuinely loved the music of the Opry, probably more so than anyone on the WSM staff, with the exception of Judge Hay. He was no carpetbagger but a Southerner who wanted to find ways to spread the Opry's music across the country.

Thus the Opry began to undergo a slow but important change in the early 1930s. It still featured many of the traditional or semi-professional artists who had helped found it—performers from the upper South who worked day jobs and played music on weekends—but now began to attract musicians who were working at their craft full-time. This, too, was nothing unique. All over the country, regional stations were learning that they could produce enough income from advertising to support a full-time staff of entertainers. Both Hay and Stone saw the advantages in this, and both were pleased when the Opry added its first full-time singers who actually tailored their act to the new medium. This was a smoothly singing trio called the Vagabonds.

By the time the Vagabonds came to the Opry, they were seasoned show business veterans with a flair for publicity that rivaled that of Judge Hay. Their own tendency to modify history to suit publicity needs may account for the fact that Hay's writings about the group contain an unusual number of inaccuracies, stating, for instance, that they were the first non-Southern group on the show, even though some in the group were from the South. Curt Poulton, in fact, was born in Delaney, West Virginia, in 1907, and the other two were deliberately vague about their backgrounds. In their first songbook, they stated that "the Vagabonds are all sons of ministers. In their early youth they lived the lives of traveling preachers' boys, as their fathers were Circuit Riders among the rural and mountain people of our great land." This may have been partially true; Dean Upson's father, Ray G. Upson, was for a time the minister at the Evangelical United Brethren Church in the mountain village of Nashville, Arkansas, in the 1920s. But the formation of the group occurred far from any Southern folk roots.

In 1926, as the Opry was struggling through its first year, brothers Dean and Paul Upson began singing together at Otterbein College in Westerville, Ohio, near Columbus, in the center of the state. One of their friends was young Curt Poulton, who had grown up in high school playing ukulele, then banjo, then guitar, and the three occasionally sang together in their spare time. By 1927 the Upsons had moved to Chicago, where Paul began attending the YMCA College, doing religious work, and singing in the YMCA College Quartet. One of the other members of this quartet was "W. B." Kincaid, who would shortly himself win fame over Chicago radio as Bradley Kincaid. This quartet was no volunteer amateur group; they toured widely, appearing as far away as Louisville, and worked with a nationally known comedian named George W. Campbell. Encouraged by this, Upson, a tenor, formed his own trio in September 1927, with his brother Paul singing second tenor and a man named Robert Dugan singing baritone. For a few weeks, this trio appeared on power-house station WLS as the Three Hired Men and then, on December 4, 1927, debuted on station WBBM as the Vagabonds. Later publicity for the group would claim that these early performances made them "the first organized Male Radio Trio." Although the details of this claim might be hard to validate, the trio was, significantly, one of the first to see that radio stimulated new styles of music and that the notion of a "Radio song" was emerging as a viable new genre in pop music.

Perhaps this awareness is what soon impelled Dean Upson to replace his baritone singer with their old college chum Curt Poulton. In February 1928 he sent a wire to Poulton asking him to quit college and join them in Chicago; he quickly agreed. The Upsons soon found that in Curt they got not only an accomplished singer and comedian but a good guitar accompanist. According to Vervia Poulton, Curt's wife, the trio was soon singing pieces like "Dream Train" and "a lot of popular songs." By December 1928 they were receiving national reviews in magazines like *Radio News*, which singled out their work on Chicago stations KYW and KFKX: "They have a way about them—a novelty in their song arrangements—that gives new interest even to an old song, although new ones are their particular specialty." In August of that year they made their first recording as vocalists for band leader Charley Straight on a Brunswick record: "Waiting and Dreaming" and "Do You, Don't You, Love Me Sweetheart," both unabashedly pop songs. They also attracted attention by using one of the first electric guitars in music, using a "tone amplifier" and pick-up system invented by one H. C. Kuhrmeyer of Chicago. The device was about the size of a suitcase and was featured by the Vagabonds at the annual Chicago Radio Show on Columbus Day 1928. How long they used this device is unclear, but publicity photos taken a year later show Poulton returning to his acoustic guitar.

In February 1929, the trio moved to KMOX in St. Louis, and Herald Goodman came on board to replace Paul Upson. Goodman became their business manager. He had been working with the NBC network in Chicago and became the driving force behind their promotion. Almost as soon as they arrived in St. Louis, they organized the Vagabond Company, with their own radio production studio and office. They created their own program ideas and pitched them themselves to clients—an early form of what now is known as syndication. For a time they were on a fifty-six–station hookup with NBC and then found their own sponsors for a successful show called "The Vagabond Club;" clients ranged from the Anheuser-Busch Brewing Company to the Lewis Medicine Company. During summers, they toured with a Vagabond Revue, going as far afield as England, Paris, and Berlin. Telegrams preserved in the Poulton scrapbooks show that their repertoire favorites included largely mainstream pop fare such as "Pagan Love Song," "Marie," "I'll Get By," and "Old Pals Are the Best Pals After All." Then, for some reason, their popularity began to wane, and as the Depression deepened they found their career stalled.

At this point Harry Stone invited the trio to come to WSM, as part of his effort to professionalize the Opry. They agreed. Vervia Poulton recalled, "About this time, the music trend was becoming more 'folksy,' and the Vagabonds began to concentrate on 'Heart and Home' type songs—plus a hymn for each program." This change of direction seemed perfect for the Opry and WSM, and the group arrived in Nashville in August 1931, just in time for the fall season.

Unlike most of the Opry regulars, the Vagabonds were hired as WSM staff musicians. Alton Delmore, in his autobiography, explained the difference:

> There were two classes of entertainers at WSM. The staff members, the ones who got paid every week and knew they had a good job and security, and the other class was the Grand Ole Opry talent, who played only once a week and were paid a very token fee for each Saturday night.

Staff musicians were expected to perform on other shows on the station, and thus, while the Vagabonds were immediately given a spot on the Opry, they were also given slots on WSM's Friday evening minstrel show program staged by Lasses White; their own show called "Songs of the Old Homestead," which was soon given a Saturday night slot immediately preceding the Opry; and an early morning show on weekdays. In a 1932 souvenir songbook, they described the kind of routine this created for them.

> The Vagabonds . . . are constantly employed in their chosen profession, and at all times are busily seeking new ways of entertaining the millions who have become their regular fans.

They start their day very early, usually doing their first broadcast as early as 6:30 or 7:00 A.M. Then their next job is to get together in their office quarters and go carefully over the mail received the preceding day. Each letter must have careful attention, and where an answer is needed they take time to attend to it at once.

Usually following this morning meeting they take time to eat their second breakfast. They are well known for their Table Power. Eat! And when that word is spoken they all smile and start following their noses to where the coffee odor is strongest.

Back to the Studio for rehearsal. This morning rehearsal lasts from two to three hours. If you think singing and rehearsing for three hours is fun, and no work, try singing for three hours and then see if you can speak.

Thus the life style of the nascent country music professional. While Opry regulars like Amos Binkley were spending the day at their watch repair shop, or Paul Warmack spent his time replacing tie rods in Model Ts, or Uncle Dave Macon spent his day plowing with his favorite mule, the new professionals like the Vagabonds were polishing their art, working up new material, and building fan support by answering letters. Furthermore, the very fact that such statements like the one above even appeared in their promotional songbook is significant. It emphasized that the Vagabonds worked *full-time* at their music—they "are constantly employed in their chosen profession"—and suggested that this made them more worthy of audience respect. It also suggested that the audience was not used to such professionalism in Southern radio and that this novelty needed explanation.

George Hay's memoirs confirm Vervia Poulton's memories that only after they came to WSM did the Vagabonds really begin to emphasize folk songs and what they themselves called "heart songs." Folk songs came first. In the first edition of their songbook, the trio notes that "in this compilation of songs you will find those which have for years been sung and loved by singers in homes, churches, and theaters throughout the United States." These songs were "originated by the Pioneer Settlers in the mountains of the Southland" and passed down by oral tradition; thus, the text of each song might vary a little from what some other folks were familiar with. Included in the book were pieces of generally unquestionable authenticity—"Barbara Allen," "The Fatal Wedding," "Sourwood Mountain," "Red River Valley." By mid-1932, though, the emphasis was shifting to include heart songs: slow, sentimental pieces heavy on nostalgia and well-worn Southern images. They were often recently written, though they were often crafted to sound like old songs. And though the heart-song genre had been around since the mid-nineteenth century, radio, with its suitability for quiet, close-harmony singing, was starting to revive it.

For the Vagabonds, the song that opened the door was "When It's Lamp Lighting Time in the Valley," a lyric about a wandering boy whose mother places an old lamp in her cabin window to guide him back home— even though he can in fact never return due to some unnamed crime. With its theme of the modern world—crime, prisons, big cities—juxtaposed against the bucolic past, "Lamp Lighting Time" is a quintessential heart song. Though the Vagabonds were later to claim authorship for the piece, the original sheet music publication lists Joe Lyons and Sam C. Hart as composers; regardless, it was to become the Vagabonds' most popular song, and later Curt Poulton would claim that it sold half a million recordings by a variety of recording artists in fifteen different countries. (Oddly, the Vagabonds never recorded it except on a rare, special custom recording on the Old Cabin label.) A few months earlier the group had started using another prison song, "Ninety-Nine Years," which was quite similar to "Twenty-One Years," a major hit by New York–based songwriter Bob Miller. According to Alton Delmore, Miller brought suit against the Vagabonds, and eventually won a judgment. This doubtless taught the trio a lesson in the difference between folk and folk-like music, as well as the vagaries of copyright law, and they soon applied this lesson to other songs they wrote. They were soon adding to their songbooks and repertoire new heart-song hits like "Little Shoes," "Little Mother of the Hills," and "In the Sleepy Hills of Tennessee," balancing them with older hymns and traditional songs, and arranging them in their patented, smooth three-part harmony.

To complement their musical skills with heart songs and smooth harmony, the Vagabonds developed a number of innovative and promotional techniques. These included starting Nashville's first country music publishing company, creating the first souvenir songbooks of any Opry act, making and distributing some of the music's first promotional records, and putting together what were probably the first Opry touring groups. In January 1932, just five months after the trio arrived in Nashville, they published a booklet called *Old Cabin Songs for the Fiddle and the Bow.* Subtitled "Songs of Three Preachers' Bad Boys," it contained words and music to ten songs, all familiar folk standards except for "Ninety-Nine Years." In addition, there was an introduction by Harry Stone, an account of the Vagabonds' career, and a brief history of the Opry, with thumbnail sketches of the various performers. The Vagabonds' sketch is significant because of the way in which it seems to emphasize their links to "the mountains of Kentucky and Tennessee" and to insist that "they are proud of the memories of their boyhood days, when they played in the hills and valleys, and learned to live, from the people of the sod, who are very near to their hearts." The Opry history is significant because it marks the first time an account of the Opry had appeared in any sort of souvenir book for fans. As such, the portrait deserves a closer look.

Six acts, in addition to the Vagabonds, are pictured and described: Uncle Dave Macon, "one of the most picturesque of the Old-time Singers at WSM"; Dr. Humphrey Bate and his Possum Hunters; Paul Warmack and his Gully Jumpers; Theron Hale and his band; George Wilkerson and his Fruit Jar Drinkers; and DeFord Bailey, "a little hunchbacked colored boy" who says "he has learned how to make the harmonica Take Effect.'" This is a fairly complete list of the Opry cast as it was in early 1932, with the exception of three groups: the Crook Brothers, the Binkley Brothers, and W. E. Poplin's band. The Opry itself, according to the text, has been an "institution at WSM for more than five years" (which would seem to suggest that at this point WSM dated the Opry's history from its 1927 naming rather than its 1925 inception), and is recognized as "one of the nation's outstanding programs," having drawn messages from every state in the union, as well as Canada, Mexico, and Cuba. "It is not uncommon to see a sheaf of telegrams containing four or five hundred, in the middle of the season, come into the Studios of WSM as a result of this shindig, barn dance, and breakdown." This text echoes Judge Hay's posture of puzzlement over the show's continued popularity (though, in fact, Hay might well have helped write the account): "For some reasons which have not been altogether explained or defined, the Old-time Folk Tunes of the Tennessee Hills have caught on. . . ." It goes on to emphasize the informality of the show: "It is distinctly a human affair which may be termed a big get-together party of those who listen in. Messages are announced which have brought old friends and even members of families together after absences of many, many years." The tunes themselves are "distinctly elemental in constructions," but if a casual listener could "witness the effort and interest displayed by Opry musicians in perfecting tunes which they had not heard," he would be impressed. The account closes with an invitation to "be our guests every Saturday night," but it makes clear that this refers to listening on the radio; nowhere in the book is there any invitation to come to Nashville to attend the live show.

The Vagabonds' *Old Cabin Songs* was sold by mail and was phenomenally successful. A second printing came out in March 1932, then a third a mere ten days later. By October the book had gone through six printings and had expanded to include nineteen songs. By then the book's title page boasted that it was the product of the Old Cabin Company, "Music Publishers," located first at WSM and later at another office in downtown Nashville. Virtually all the songs added to this new edition were fresh originals by the Vagabonds and presumably published by Old Cabin. How many songs by other writers the company published is unclear. Their songbook went through six more editions in 1933, but, curiously, by 1934 the book was being published by the venerable Forster Music Company in Chicago. By then, most of the Old Cabin list had apparently been transferred to this larger company. The Vagabonds nevertheless did seek out some songs for their Old Cabin; Alton Delmore recalls getting a lot of pressure from the trio in mid-1933 to place his songs with them, a move which eventually led to much confusion and some hard feelings between the two acts (discussed further below). But by 1934 Forster did most of the publishing, and the Old Cabin Company—now located in the Hitchcock Building—was specializing in producing and booking "The Vagabonds' Traveling Unit Show 'The Grand Ole Opry.'" This package tour, which at times included the Vagabonds, Uncle Dave Macon and Sam McGee, the Fruit Jar Drinkers with George Wilkerson, and a girls' trio called the Bond Sisters, was billed as a "theatrical production" highlighting "the true personality of each of the performers" and reflecting "that originality and spontaneity which is so characteristic of the real native hill folk."

In addition to producing song books and staging tours, the Vagabonds used Old Cabin in other innovative ways. In January 1933 the group traveled to Richmond, Indiana, where they recorded five of their most popular numbers in the studios of Gennett Records. These were:

"When It's Harvest Time in Peaceful Valley"
"Little Mother of the Hills"
"Little Shoes"
"When It's Lamp Lighting Time in the Valley"
"99 Years"

These were the first non-pop recordings done by the trio, but they have long puzzled discographers because none of them was ever commercially issued on Gennett or any of its subsidiaries. Instead, they appeared on their own Old Cabin label. This in itself was nothing unusual; Gennett had been producing "custom pressings" for artists since 1925, and any singer who could afford to pay for a thousand copies of a record could have it pressed up, decked out in the artist's individual label, and shipped out to him for resale.

What the Vagabonds did that was unusual was to ship the records free of charge to radio stations as a means of promoting their songs and their act. The scheme even attracted the attention of *Variety*, which commented:

> The Vagabonds have originated an idea to co-operate with some of the smaller radio stations in the South. . . . Finding it impossible to appear in as many stations as they would like to do, and having constantly to turn down invitations, they decided to record some of their favorite numbers and distribute them. Reports received thus far indicate that the audiences of these stations are highly pleased with the production records which are distributed free of charge. They are used as sustaining features in daytime broadcasts.

Later on in the 1930s the idea of recording transcriptions for use as fillers on stations would become commonplace, but in 1933 it was novel and helped immeasurably to spread Vagabond songs and the Vagabond sound across the South.

When the trio finally got into the studios of a major record company, it was almost an anticlimax. Through Goodman's contacts in Chicago, they landed a contract with RCA Victor, and in April 1933 they traveled to Chicago to record eight songs. Here they did most of their big hits again—with the odd exception of "Lamp Lighting Time in the Valley," which RCA had already assigned to the Don Hall Trio to record some two months earlier. The Vagabond records were successful, especially when issued through the budget-priced Bluebird line and later through Montgomery Ward's in-house label. RCA called the trio back into the Chicago studios twice more in 1933, an indication of their intense popularity that year. A grand total of some thirty-two sides resulted, and a brief analysis of them shows both the strengths and weaknesses of the Vagabond repertoire.

The table below tabulates the different kinds of songs the group recorded at its three 1933 sessions for RCA/Bluebird.

	Session 1	Session 2	Session 3
New Tin Pan Alley	2	5	7 *
Sacred	2	1	0
Traditional	0	1	5
Originals	4	3	0
Older pop	0	0	1

* A Delmore Brothers song, newly composed but not yet published.

The category "new Tin Pan Alley" denotes songs by composers other than the Vagabonds that were copyrighted and published by established song publishing companies like Forster (in Chicago), Jenkins (in Kansas City), and Joe Davis, Shapiro-Bernstein, Witmark, and others, all in New York, and published about the same time of the recording. Many of these songs were ersatz country heart songs, written by skilled professionals but aimed at a rural or sentimental audience: "The Little White Church on the Hill," by Dorothy Fields and Jimmy McHugh; "That Little Boy of Mine," co-authored and popularized by big band leader Wayne King; and "In the Vine Covered Church Way Back Home," by Frank Sheldon and Jack Filler. The category "Original Songs" refers to pieces either composed or claimed by the Vagabonds themselves, and "Traditional" refers to public domain songs widely recognized as folk.

Fourteen of the thirty-two recorded songs are in the first category, new Tin Pan Alley songs—almost half. Another nine are either sacred or traditional—about 28 percent. The seven original songs—including their most popular—represent about 22 percent of the total. As the Vagabonds' popularity increased, they began to rely more and more on others' songs, on the work of professional writers and established publishers; the number of their original songs dropped off. This may help explain why they were so desperate to sign up songs by the Delmore Brothers and young WSM songwriter Fred Rose for Old Cabin, and why they were pressuring Alton Delmore so strongly to sign up with them. They sorely needed material and rightfully perceived that the Tin Pan Alley tunes they were getting from the Chicago publishers were not doing the job. They were beginning to realize a truth that many country performers would learn during the 1930s—that it was hard to sell non-country songs to a country audience and that a successful professional in the new country music business had to have a source of original material. The Delmore Brothers, who would replace the Vagabonds as the Opry's leading vocal act, had this; the Vagabonds did not.

By the overall standards of pop music in the early 1930s, the Vagabonds were not all that unusual. Radio and record studios were awash with male trios or quartets featuring slick, snappy arrangements with simple piano or guitar accompaniment. The Mills Brothers, Paul Whiteman's Rhythm Boys, and the Revellers all sought to expand the boundaries of harmony singing. But on the Opry stage, where most of the singing had been based on the nineteenth century vaudeville theatrics of Uncle Dave Macon, or the rather simple vocal parts of the Pickard Family, the Vagabonds were a sensation. They made an impression on the Opry cast. As full-time professionals with show business experience, as staff musicians in addition to Opry regulars, and as "stars" with special privileges, they even incurred a certain amount of resentment. Alton Delmore remembered, "We got the crumbs when they left. We were never recognized by our bosses like the Vagabonds were. . . ." This was obvious in the 1933 press book described above, where the following pay scale was given for the Vagabonds:

1 time per week	$75.00
3 times per week	$175.00
6 times per week	$300.00

This is about three times the rate listed for a more traditional Opry band, the Dixieliners. And as the other Opry performers sought ways to make a better living with their own music, they watched the Vagabonds, watched and learned. They were seeing the way of the future.

But trouble was coming. Vervia Poulton remembers that more and more of the act's income was coming from personal appearances and that in 1934 "we began to feel the stringent effects of this condition which hit the entire country"—the worsening Depression. All of their promotional innovations, effective and trend-setting though they were, could not overcome the fact that audiences had no money to spend on entertainment. In 1934 they split up: Herald Goodman went to Oklahoma, Dean Upson returned to Chicago, and Curt remained at WSM to work as a soloist. The other two couldn't stay away from WSM long, though. A version of the group resurfaced briefly on the Opry in 1937 and 1938, but did not last long. Herald Goodman then formed a hot western swing band, the Tennessee Valley Boys, which featured the twin fiddling of young Howdy Forrester and Arthur Smith. Later, he took a version of the band to KVOO in Tulsa and made a handful of Bluebird records. For a time, Curt Poulton led a band of West Virginia pickers and worked briefly on the Opry and on Knoxville's *Mid-Day Merry-Go-Round*. Later he worked as a single in Illinois and the Midwest. Toward the end of his life he became interested in photography and spent the rest of his time working in that area. He died in 1957. Dean Upson eventually came back to WSM in the early 1940s to work as commercials manager. In 1948 he helped start the *Louisiana Hayride* show in Shreveport. He spent later years as a hospital administrator.

The Dixieliners

I N THE SPRING OF 1932 TWO OF THE YOUNG Opry's most potent traditions reached their zenith through one memorable string band. The traditions were those of the fast-paced, dynamic hoedown bands, on the one hand, and the deep-rooted display fiddlers, on the other. The band that brought them together so successfully was the Dixieliners, composed of Arthur Smith on fiddle, Sam McGee on guitar, and Kirk McGee on banjo. Although the band only existed in its original form for five years, never made any recordings as a unit in its prime, and its members were among the most casual and easygoing on the Opry, many historians and musicians feel it might have been the best string band in country music history.

The members of the Dixieliners were not exactly young Turks on the show; each had been born before the turn of the century, and each had substantially developed his distinctive playing style before he came to the Opry. Indeed, each had served an apprenticeship with other musicians on the early Opry before the advent of the Dixieliners—Sam and Kirk McGee with Uncle Dave Macon, and Arthur Smith with his cousin Homer Smith. All three had come from venerable folk traditions, had absorbed these traditions, and had the creativity and ambition to parlay these traditions into music of great commercial appeal. In 1932, when the band was actually formed, Sam was thirty-eight years old, brother Kirk thirty-three, and Arthur Smith thirty-four. They were a full generation younger than the Macons and the Bates and the Mangrums, and perhaps less than a decade younger than the members of the staff hoedown bands. Yet the music they made sounded radically different from that of the earlier bands. This was in part due to the fact that in the McGees and Smith the Opry had its most technically proficient and versatile musicians. Sam was a superb banjo player as well as a guitarist and was quick to learn the slide guitar styles of people like Cliff Carlisle. Kirk was the best singer in the bunch but also a fine guitarist (in addition to being a banjoist) and a competent fiddler. Arthur was a distinctive singer and played a nice "clawhammer" banjo in addition to the fiddle. In most of their road shows and on many Opry spots, the Dixieliners managed to showcase their individual talents as well as their collective ones. Indeed, the talents of the three were so evenly balanced that, years later, people who knew the band have difficulty assigning a leader to it.

The story of the McGee Brothers begins in rural Williamson County, about twenty miles due south of Nashville. Here the Highland Rim starts impinging on the flat Nashville basin, creating a landscape full of rolling hills and small subsistence farms then best suited to mule plowing and tobacco growing. Though Franklin, the county seat of Williamson County, is a bedroom community of Nashville today, in the 1920s it was a thriving town with a large black population and with memories of a famous Civil War action, the Battle of Franklin. The McGee clan came from an area south of Franklin called Peytonsville, where the family homestead was a huge log house with a massive fireplace and stone hearth. Here John F. McGee, father of Sam and Kirk, presided over long fiddling sessions and music parties that often included other members of the extended family. In later years, other relatives of Sam and Kirk would make their marks on the Opry and Middle Tennessee music. Blythe Poteet, a cousin, would record with Kirk and play for many years with the Crook Brothers. Rachael Veach, another cousin, would join Roy Acuff's band as a banjo soloist in the late 1930s. E. V. Bagsby, who preserved a distinctive banjo style, was a cousin who never made the Opry but who won regional fame at fiddling contests. And John McGee himself always placed high in local fiddling contests and once shared the stage with the famed Skillet Lickers band from Georgia.

By the time Sam was born in 1894, the marathon picking sessions his father organized were already thriving. As a boy, Sam would stay up into the small hours listening to the music. "Time didn't mean so much to them as it does to so many now," he recalled. "They'd stay up 'til two or three o'clock in the morning playing country waltzes, breakdowns, two-steps. I'd be there, taking it all in 'til they made me go to bed." Kirk came along in 1899, and soon both boys were not only listening to but making music. Sam's first instrument was the banjo—"My father wanted someone to play accompaniment after him." Kirk started on mandolin and banjo, later branching out to fiddle and guitar. Their first teacher was their father, who knew, recalled Kirk, "three to four hundred old fiddle tunes." He played many of the standard fiddle tunes known today, like "Mississippi Sawyer," "Leather Britches," and "Bonaparte's Retreat," but "he seemed to play them more slowly than they do today. Every note was clear and sharp." John McGee also steeped the boys in local history and Civil War stories, and their mother sang them old ballads and Christian songs like "Wayfaring Stranger."

By the time the boys were in their early teens, they were playing for local dances, garnering 10 cents a set for square dances and watching in disbelief as thrifty Williamson County farmers managed to string out a set for fifteen or twenty minutes. Sam thought he was "really cleaning up" when he took home a whole $1.50 after playing his first dance in 1906. Though the boys' father would not play at dances for religious reasons, Sam and Kirk soon found other mentors. Sam accompanied an old fiddler named Willie Williams, while Kirk learned banjo licks from an old man named Felix Bennet. Later Kirk traveled with a local medicine show, watching with horror as the quack doctor filled his bottles with gasoline and flavored it with strawberry syrup. When their father bought a country store, both boys began to listen with interest to black workers who would spend their lunch breaks around the store, occasionally playing on guitars. At this time—1910—the guitar was a relatively rare instrument in the rural South, and both brothers were impressed, especially with two black men named Jim Sapp and Amos Johnson. Johnson was probably from Western Kentucky, but he traveled widely and was known to guitarists like Mose Rager and Merle Travis in Kentucky. Nothing is known about Sapp, but his music fascinated Sam. "His songs would just ring in my head," he recalled, and up until his last years he played a tune called "Jim Sapp Rag" in tribute to Sapp. Such musicians also taught the brothers about different guitar tunings—Sam had originally learned chords from an old instruction book—and the use of slides and bent notes. By the 1920s both McGees were playing the new instrument called the guitar.

When the McGees were later rediscovered during the folk revival of the 1960s, much was made about this black influence by folklorists eager to make connections between white and black musics. In truth, the blues was only one of a number of formative influences on the pair. Equally important were the Anglo-American ballad tradition, ragtime, nineteenth century parlor music, barbershop quartet singing, and gospel music. All these forms were readily available in pre–World War I Tennessee, and Sam and Kirk eagerly borrowed songs and styles from them. In the late 1920s, when the brothers gained access to the recording studios and preserved a sizable chunk of their repertoire, songs from all these different sources were represented.

In addition to songs, there was the matter of performing styles. With Sam, this involved learning how to use the guitar as a solo instrument as opposed to just a rhythm instrument. An old man named Tom Hood, who lived "over in the hills" south of Franklin, was both his teacher and his role model. Hood was the first white man he had ever heard playing for dances with a lead guitar, and Hood was the man who convinced him to "get away from the banjo and get me a guitar." Soon Sam could pick anything on the guitar that he had picked on the banjo, and between 1910 and 1920 he crafted a unique "flat-top" style of solo guitar playing. When Uncle Dave Macon first heard Sam play, he exclaimed that he had never heard a guitarist who could play rhythm and melody at the same time, "like there were two guitars." Like other old-time guitarists, Sam achieved this by using his right (or picking) hand to do variations on what technicians call an "alternating bass style," where the thumb provides the rhythm patterns and the index and middle finger provides the melody. As a young man, Sam would supplement this by using a capo (sometimes down as far as the fifth fret) and a variety of unorthodox techniques such as slides, pinches, brushes, pull-offs, and string bending. A news story from the early 1920s describes a fiddling contest in nearby Hickman County, where Kirk, John McGee, and Sam all competed. It was Sam's unusual guitar playing, though, that won the day. "A delightful feature of the program . . . was the clever work of Sam McGee, of near Franklin, a versatile musician and comedian whose accompaniments and interpolated song numbers kept the audience clamoring for more. Somehow, this young man produced unheard of music from the guitar. . . ."

Around 1924 Sam began to expand his career beyond the local fiddling contest and dusty square dances. He met Uncle Dave Macon, who was by then a recording star and a vaudeville veteran, usually teamed with fiddler Sid Harkreader. Sam had been running a blacksmith's shop out in the country and had come into Franklin to buy supplies; on the courthouse square, he saw Uncle Dave playing the banjo and cutting up, passing the hat for spare change. Sam was hooked and watched with utter fascination all afternoon, until the entertainer packed up for the night. When he returned home that night, Sam told his wife, "I just seen the funniest old man I ever seen in my life." A few weeks later, when Sid and Uncle Dave did a local schoolhouse show, Sam invited them home, and Macon got to hear him play the guitar. Almost at once, he asked Sam to join him in playing a few dates in the area, and before long Sam had closed up his blacksmith's shop. In January 1925, Sam joined Harkreader and Macon on the stage of the Loew's Bijou Theater in Birmingham. Billed only as "Guitarin' Sam" (his publicity read, "He climbs all over a 'wicked' guitar"), he appeared on stage in a rural costume, sat on a plaster-of-Paris tree stump, and played guitar solos while a dancer named Bob Bradford did his buck-and-wing. For one dance, Sam worked up an old guitar piece into a number that was designed for the dancer, and gave it the name "Buckdancer's Choice." It would become one of the McGee trademarks.

Thus began a twenty-year association—one hesitates to call it an apprenticeship—between the McGees and Uncle Dave Macon. Kirk began working with Sam and Uncle Dave about a year later, and the three soon found themselves traveling on a harrowing circuit that included obscure little country schoolhouses, auctions, fiddling contests, vaudeville stages, medicine shows, and circuses. Kirk remembered how the three of them traveled with one particular circus through the Midwest during this time:

> We were the only musical act along. There were jugglers, guys that did handstands, and all that, but we were the music. We did about thirty minutes on stage, sung and fiddled just like we were back in the mountains. Uncle Dave would get off what jokes there were. I remember the way the act started. Uncle Dave says, "Boys, what are we going to play for the folks?" And my line was, "Uncle Dave, let's do the number that we did at the little schoolhouse back over in the mountains the other night. Do you remember what it was?" And he'd say, "Oh yes, So-and-so," and we'd do that number. And we always wound up with a square dance; he had two or three girls traveling with the show that helped the dance. I was fiddling, did one or two numbers with the banjo, and Sam played guitar. I remember one place we played, Madison, Wisconsin, and mine was the first five-string banjo they ever saw. They couldn't figure out what this thumb string was for. They had seen a tenor banjo, seen it strummed, but they had never seen a banjo picked five-string style.

With Uncle Dave billing his act as "Uncle Dave Macon and his Sons from Billygoat Hill," with Sam dressed as a rustic clown, and with all three playing up their backwoods roots and "back in the mountains" image, it would seem that the Macon-McGee act anticipated by several years the rustic image that George Hay later imposed on the Opry. Macon seemed to feel, for whatever reason, that the highly complex string band music that he and the McGees played was best presented to the public in exaggerated hillbilly trappings. This was what Sam and Kirk both in later years would call Macon's "showmanship," and Sam especially seemed impressed by it. He spoke with great admiration about a trunk full of old jokes and songs that Uncle Dave had written down over the years, a trove of material that was apparently sold at the auction following Macon's death in 1952. He also tended to associate banjo playing with rustic comedy long after he left Macon and often showcased his own superb banjo playing with jokes and mugging. "I never did learn much about playing from him," said Sam of Macon, "but I did learn how to handle an audience."

One of Sam's favorite Uncle Dave Macon stories illustrates this; it describes a contest where he actually defeated "the Dixie Dewdrop" in a head-to-head banjo competition. "Uncle Dave was rated as one of the greatest up until the time he died. And he was the greatest entertainer, but when it came to playing, there was a lot of them who could beat him playing." One time in 1926 both Macon and Sam signed up to play in a banjo contest in Birmingham. "Going down there when the time come, Uncle Dave says, 'Sammy, I'll make a deal with you. If you'll give me half you win, I'll give you half I win.' And I said, 'That's a deal!' and we shook hands on it, because Uncle Dave was so well known, he was sure to win. Got down there and they played by numbers and played behind curtains and nobody's name was called and the audience couldn't see who was playing. I played two numbers, one right into the other, 'Old Black Joe' and 'Swanee River.' Of course, I couldn't tell much about it, but I thought I was playing pretty good. They went on, maybe thirty banjo players. Well, I got the first on that, and Uncle Dave, he didn't get anything. He says, 'Now don't tell that on me.' And I never did tell many people about it til after he was dead. I still don't know if it would be right to tell it now, but it's the low-down truth."

An enriched repertoire and a sense of entertainment style were not the only benefits the brothers got from their work with Uncle Dave. One of the most tangible and immediate was the chance to record. Macon was a veteran at this, had contacts in the record business, and was directly responsible for getting the McGees into the studios. (Their appearances on the Opry prior to recording were few and far between and probably had little to do with their record contracts.) Between 1926 and 1934 the brothers recorded, singly or together, some thirty released songs and appeared on twice that many as sidemen for Uncle Dave. This made them, next to Macon, the most recorded of the pre-1935 Opry acts.

Their recorded repertoire was eclectic, to say the least. While Sam liked rags, instrumentals, and novelty or comic songs, Kirk tended to the blues, sentimental songs, and gospel tunes. One of their most popular records was "C-H-I-C-K-E-N," a 1902 Tin Pan Alley song that the brothers learned orally from a Franklin barbershop quartet who sang it as a "comic" 1920s song. Even though the McGees later dropped it out of their repertoire because of its racial overtones, dozens of young folk revival bands picked it up in the 1960s and 1970s. From an old woman named Mrs. Will Sowell in rural Williamson County, who had a huge "ballet book" full of handwritten old songs and ballads, the brothers got "A Flower from My Angel Mother's Grave," an 1878 minstrel song. Also from Mrs. Sowell's book came "Charming Bill," often called "Silly Bill," a widely collected traditional Southern song. "Hannah, Won't You Open the Door," which Kirk learned in a medicine show, is another turn-of-the-century Tin Pan Alley song that went into oral tradition, as is "In a Cool Shady Nook," recorded by other old-time singers under the title "Somewhere Somebody's Waiting for You." Another source was James D. Vaughan's influential gospel song publishing company, located south of Franklin about forty miles, in Lawrenceburg. Vaughan's quartets often appeared in the WSM listings in the 1930s, and Kirk had attended singing schools taught by Vaughan teachers. He brought into the act a number of their songs, such as "If I Could Hear My Mother Pray Again," a 1922 gospel quartet favorite, and "Only a Step to the Grave," from a 1923 Vaughan songbook.

Comic songs were also a part of their repertoire. Many Opry veterans best remembered Sam, especially, for his comic songs rather than his guitar work. One was a version of "Kickin' Mule":

Once that little Chinaman's mule, he swallowed a yellow dog,
He kicked the feathers off a goose and pulverized a hog,
He bit a Thomas cat in two and broke an elephant's back,
Captured a Texas railroad train and kicked it off the track.

Another was a vintage nonsense song called "A Ship Without a Sail," which anticipated by three decades the later songs of Homer and Jethro:

A man without a wife,
A ship without a sail,

But the funniest thing I ever saw,
Was a shirt without a collar button.
Hi-dee-iddle dee diddle ta tum ta tum ta tum.

Old mother Hubbard, she went to the cubbard,
To get her poor daughter a dress,
And when she got there, the cubbard was bare,
And so was her daughter, I guess.

Another that Sam learned during his travels with Uncle Dave was a song he liked to call one of his "ugly songs," comic songs that employ a sort of reverse bragging: "My Family Has Been a Crooked Set," which the brothers recorded in 1927 at an Uncle Dave session.

My family has been a crooked set since 1843,
They are so really crooked that they sleep like the letter Z.
Our motto is to do them brown, and do them by the score,
Do everybody they can do till they can do no more.

Several McGee songs can in fact be traced directly to black sources, but only two of these are anything like blues in the classic sense. They are "Salty Dog Blues" and "Salt Lake City Blues," both of which Kirk got from a 1924 Paramount record by veteran bluesman Papa Charley Jackson. "Railroad Blues," one of Sam's best-known numbers, has blues features, such as guitar pulls, bent notes, choked chords, and a wordless falsetto sung in unison to a guitar break; yet in other ways, the piece is reminiscent of ragtime, with its repeated two-octave guitar breaks and tempo. "Easy Rider" has a series of free-floating stanzas that were probably taken from blues tradition, but the piece is played at breakneck speed on Sam's Gibson banjo-guitar, and sounds more like bluegrass than blues. "Knoxville Blues," another famous piece featuring Sam's solo guitar, is not a true blues either, but a combination of a local piece called "Little Texas Waltz" and a chording piece called "Poor Boy a Long Way from Home"; the same is true for the stately "Franklin Blues," part of which was an old parlor guitar piece Sam learned from a local physician, Dr. John Merritt.

Since the McGees lived only thirty miles from Nashville, and since they were becoming well known through their work with Macon, it was only natural that they be attracted to the Barn Dance. Sam had a classic one-liner to explain their involvement: "They came down here and said they wanted players who were outstanding in the field—and that's where they found us, out standing in the field." Sam apparently first appeared on the air as an accompanist for Uncle Dave; "It was like striking a match," he recalled. "Uncle Dave already had the name and the buildup, you see; and they wanted something like that." After his first Saturday night appearance on the show, in early 1926, Judge Hay wrote Sam a personal letter, encouraging him to come back. "I hope you will come back again Saturday for the show, for I'm sure it will continue if you can." Kirk soon made his first appearance on the show as well, though both often appeared with other string bands or with Macon rather than by themselves. Indeed, the actual name "McGee Brothers" does not appear in the official Opry listings prior to 1929—though Sam and Kirk each appear with other groups. Sam, for example, played for a time with George Wilkerson's Fruit Jar Drinkers, and Kirk was the fiddler for the Crook Brothers for a time. By July 1929, in one of the earliest out-of-town news accounts of the Opry (in the *Knoxville News-Sentinel*), Sam's guitar work is singled out, as "Sam Magee [*sic*] from Tennessee" who plays "a 'wicked' guitar." By now, too, Sam was getting a lot of fan mail about his guitar solos, asking about his tunings and what kind of guitar he was using (it was a little Martin, made in 1927). Both brothers were also on the first formal tour the Opry sent out, the 1931 tour of the Midwestern RKO vaudeville circuit, featuring Dr. Bate and Uncle Dave Macon.

Starting about 1930, however, Macon was starting to bring his son Dorris into his act more and more, and the McGees found themselves in demand primarily for recording sessions or special occasions by the older man. For a few months they floundered, unsure of the direction of their careers. Both had heard another young fiddler on the show they both respected as a musician, and on a whim decided to look him up. They drove over to his home in nearby Dickson, Tennessee, visited the afternoon, played some music, and soon found they had a lot in common. All three had grown up in rural surroundings and learned from fathers who were musicians; all three shared a common repertoire of Middle Tennessee tunes and songs; and all three took their music very seriously. Each was a demanding, exacting musician, a superb technician, and each had ambitions about developing his repertoire and skill. The fiddler's name was Arthur Smith.

Smith had been born Arthur Leroy Smith on April 10, 1898, in rural Humphreys County, about sixty miles west of Nashville. Bold Springs, the hamlet where he was born, was about halfway between the modern towns of Waverly and McEwen, in a sparsely populated area full of rolling wooded hills. There his father, William Calvin Smith, had a family farm, and Arthur got there what education he was to have—to about the fifth grade, not uncommon in those days. Smith's father was a fiddler of sorts, but he died when Arthur was only five. Family legend tells of Arthur as a boy of four or five trying to play the fiddle by propping it up on the floor; this interest in playing continued, and soon he was holding the instrument in a more orthodox way. As a teenager, he began learning from older fiddlers in the Humphreys-Dickson County area.

Many of the fiddlers in this area played in a distinctive style that emphasized fingering at the expense of bowing, a fondness for the E string, clean and fast noting, and a tendency to make rather daring octave jumps, even in fast tunes. This western Middle Tennessee style produced a number of influential musicians, both before and after Arthur. They all lived in an area that extended geographically from Humphreys County to the west, Perry County to the south, and Dickson and Hickman Counties to the east In later years this area would produce three more great Opry fiddlers: Floyd Ethridge, who would play many years with the Crook Brothers; Howdy Forrester, who would become Roy Acuff's fiddler in the 1950s; and Paul Warren, who would become lead fiddler for Johnnie & Jack and, later, for Flatt & Scruggs. All partook in this tradition that nourished Arthur Smith, and between these four key fiddlers, the tradition was spread nationwide.

Special influences on Smith were the Stringer brothers, Grady and Jim, local figures who never recorded or made it big but who preserved the older styles and tunes for people like Smith. Grady Stringer claimed to have sold Arthur his first fiddle—a Sears-Roebuck model costing $6.50. One of the tunes Arthur picked up from the Stringers was a song they called "Band Piece." They had learned it from an old fiddler in the area who had gotten it off an old cylinder record, where it was played by a brass band, hence the title. The Stringers picked it up, modified it, and taught it to Arthur; he modified it still more and named it "Indian Creek," in honor of the road the Stringers lived on near McEwen. It later became one of Arthur's best-known tunes and most popular recordings.

As teenagers, Arthur and Grady played local square dances together, but, as Grady put it, "Arthur kindly got ahead of me." By 1920 Arthur had the reputation, though he was only twenty-two, of being the best around. He had married in 1914; his wife Nettle was a guitarist who accompanied him on guitar at square dances and who sold chickens to buy him his first fiddle. By 1921 the pair had a growing family and had begun to realize that there was little money in farming and less in fiddling. That year they moved into Dickson, the area's largest town, and Arthur went to work cutting crossties for the N.C.&St.L. Railroad, a popular road that arced across Tennessee from Memphis through Nashville to Chattanooga. It was known locally as "the Dixie Line." Soon Arthur was promoted to linesman and a few years later moved to maintenance, where he traveled all over the system with a repair crew—"up and down the Dixie Line," as he would later put it in a song. As he traveled, he played the fiddle, met other fiddlers, and heard other regional styles. He had plenty of lonely nights to sit in his bunk car and experiment with new tunes and different ways of playing them.

By this time the Barn Dance had started up, and by 1927 Hay and his staff were actively looking for good musicians to build up their repertoire company. By happenstance, a fellow employee of the Dixie Line that year was Harry Stone, soon to be a WSM announcer and later General Manager. He had heard of the fiddling lineman and put George Hay in touch with Smith. Family members recall that Arthur appeared informally on the Barn Dance in 1926, but his name does not appear in any radio logs of the year. His first documented appearance on the show was on July 16, 1927, when he appeared accompanied by a first cousin named Homer Smith. Homer was a guitarist and singer and was also employed on the railroad. The duo was popular enough to appear three more times that year, and soon they had nailed down a regular thirty-minute slot. In 1928 the "Smith Brothers" (as they were often mistakenly billed) appeared on the radio show some twenty-nine times, more than any other act except DeFord Bailey. The Smiths usually came on just after the segment by the Gully Jumpers and just before a solo spot by guitarist Bert Hutcherson. Hutcherson's guitar work impressed Arthur, and he learned several tunes from Bert's guitar repertoire.

Throughout 1929, 1930, and 1931 the Smith cousins continued to play on the show, successfully weathering the storms and changes that winnowed out so many other part-time bands from the Opry's ranks. We have no idea today exactly what Arthur and Homer sounded like; they were somehow overlooked by the record companies in their talent hunts of the 1920s, when so many other contemporary fiddlers recorded. We can assume that Arthur was quickly developing his style, and he was certainly impressing people. Cowboy star Jimmy Wakely, who would later work with Arthur in the 1940s on a national radio show, recalled that he first heard, and clearly remembered, Arthur in 1929, and Clark Kessinger, the remarkable stylist from West Virginia, was visiting Arthur's home by this time. Sam and Kirk were listening, too, and when Homer decided to quit in early 1932, they wasted no time in hitting the road to Arthur's home in Dickson.

Though the McGees had no qualms about Arthur's fiddling, they were a little dubious about just how compatible they were with Arthur. Their former partner, Uncle Dave Macon, was an easy-going, fun-loving man who often put showmanship before musicianship; Arthur, by contrast, was a tall, intense, strong-willed man who took everything seriously, from fiddling to fishing. (He once worked out a plan to dynamite a fish hole down on the river near Waverly—then as now an act of dubious legality—and to mask the noise, he timed his explosion so it would go off just as a nearby freight train passed.) Arthur "didn't have a lot of showmanship, at least at first," recalled Kirk. "He was very solemn. He didn't have a lot of flash, I guess you'd say." Sam added: "He was sort of somber, a little stiff, you know." The high-spirited McGees were willing to give it a try, though, and had soon worked out a plan whereby the brothers would drive over and pick up Arthur at the railroad yards on Friday nights, spend the weekend playing various engagements and the Opry, and return Arthur for work Monday morning. In fact, Arthur hung onto his regular railroad day job well into the 1930s.

The band first appeared under the name Dixieliners on the Opry in May 1932, almost five years after Arthur and Homer had made their debut. Arthur played fiddle, Sam guitar, and Kirk banjo. Years later, Kirk would reflect that Arthur's style did not really change much when he joined them but that his instrumental virtuosity certainly stimulated them—and vice versa. Sam characterized the new band as a no-frills, hard-driving string band with a minimum of novelty music and a high percentage of instrumental music: fiddle standards, blues, rags, and original numbers crafted from traditional models. Arthur, recalled Kirk, "just whipped it out and played, but they sat up and listened." For a time, about the only "novelty" aspect of Arthur's music was his bit of trick fiddling on "Mocking Bird," one of his most famous numbers, and his knack of singing harmony to his fiddle on pieces like "Who's Gonna Shoe Your Pretty Little Feet?" Eventually, the McGees began to involve Arthur in a little singing, usually as the third voice in their trios, and the shy fiddler found he liked it. Kirk remembered, "It took us the longest time to get Arthur to where he would sing on stage, and then it seemed we couldn't get him to shut up."

The Dixieliners soon had two ten-minute segments on the Saturday night Opry, but they never had a chance to record together—they were at their hottest in 1932 and 1933, when the record industry was at lowest ebb from the Depression. Thus the money they made with their music, and the influence they were to have on Southern music, came from a grinding schedule of personal appearances. WSM tried to help out by making the

Dixieliners one of the few string bands to be included in its January 1933 rate book, designed to solicit commercial sponsors for WSM acts. This book announced that sponsors could buy time on the Dixieliner shows at the rate of "1 time per week" for $25, or "3 times per week" for $75. (This was about one-third the going rate of the Vagabonds.) Publicity brochures were also printed up, describing the band as "The Dixieliners . . . a sweet fiddle and two rural comedians." At other times, the Dixieliners were part of a package tour that would include fellow Opry performers like Uncle Dave Macon, the Vagabonds, the Fruit Jar Drinkers, the Delmore Brothers, DeFord Bailey, and Blythe Poteet. A favorite circuit for such tours included Virginia, North Carolina, Eastern Kentucky, and all over Tennessee. One of the first out-of-state appearances for the trio was the little mining town of Clintwood, Virginia. "Those people went wild over Arthur's fiddling," recalled Kirk. "They got a petition up and got us moved up an hour on the Opry, so a lot of the miners could listen to us between shifts. Got a petition with 1,500 names on it. They got it done." A constant problem was the need to get back to Nashville every Saturday night for the Opry—in an age of narrow, poorly designed, two-lane highways. Arthur often whiled away long drives by working up new fiddle tunes. Another problem of concern to the group was the 15 percent commission on earnings taken by WSM and another 10 to 15 percent charged by rural schoolhouses as rent for the show.

Often, the Dixieliners were joined on tours by Arthur's oldest daughter, Lavonne, who played piano. A typical road show would run to about ninety minutes, with Kirk and Arthur sharing the emcee work and Sam donning a red wig to play the familiar comic "Toby," common in so many old medicine shows. Arthur would be featured on one part of the show, the McGees on another; though Sam and Kirk usually backed up Arthur, he seldom backed them. When along, Lavonne would get a couple of piano solos like "St. Louis Blues" or "Darktown Strutters' Ball." All the troupe would be on stage for a few numbers at the opening and close of the show. There were also stunts played on the audience. Sam recalled, "We used to play little games, had a stunt where, if we were out in the crowd and had to get through, why I would go into this fit: jerking, tongue hanging out, you know. And we'd get right through that crowd. Arthur didn't know what to make of that sort of stuff."

The trio promoted their personals in a variety of new ways. The McGees had learned from Uncle Dave Macon the old tried-and-true method of going to rural schoolhouses out of the blue and striking a deal, or networking through correspondence with old contacts. The Dixieliners went a step beyond this. For a time they had an "agent" whose job it was to distribute handbills and posters around the towns they were playing. Another method was to buy "trailers"—short movie film bits that were run after the main feature at local theaters where the band was to appear. These clips—and the group had a dozen different ones that they had made for nine dollars each—showed still photos of the band, gave the time and place, and had fiddle music in the background. Ironically, this music had to be dubbed off commercial 78 records by Clark Kessinger, since the Dixieliners had not recorded any themselves. Even more ironically, Arthur learned a couple of Kessinger's tunes by listening over and over to these trailers—tunes he played at the shows and later even recorded, such as "Hell Among the Yearlings" and "Turkey in the Straw" (which Arthur dubbed "Straw Breakdown.") The band also blitzed small radio stations in the area where they were to play. During the early 1930s the schedules of smaller stations were remarkably flexible, and on some occasions a manager would even go over and open up (i.e., unlock) a station that had already shut down for the night, just for the chance to broadcast an impromptu performance by these "stars of the Grand Ole Opry."

By the time Arthur joined with the McGees, he, like them, already had a distinctive repertoire that his fans knew and expected to hear. Perhaps the tune most closely associated with him during his early years was his version of "Blackberry Blossom." Kentucky fiddlers had been playing a tune of this name since the Civil War, but though the A part of Arthur Smith's tune somewhat resembles this "Blackberry Blossom," Arthur's seems to be a distinct tune—so distinct that some modern fiddlers refer to Arthur's tune as "Blueberry Blossom" to keep them straight. Arthur worked up his tune about 1928 and began playing it over WSM. A Smith family legend tells of Arthur continuing to play the tune without naming it, and the Opry officials finally deciding to conduct a write-in contest asking listeners to choose a name for the tune. As the story goes, bushels of mail came in, and a woman in Arkansas won by suggesting the name "Blackberry Blossom." Later, when Smith got into a recording studio, this tune was one of the first he recorded, and he continued to play it throughout his life. A later generation of bluegrass banjo players, including Earl Scruggs and Bill Keith, translated the tune to the banjo repertoire.

Smith also played his version of a number of traditional fiddle tunes, including "Bonaparte's Retreat," "Katy Hill" (a West Tennessee workhorse, which Smith called "Goin' to Town"), "Flop-Eared Mule" (which Smith redubbed "Fiddler's Dream"), and "Turkey in the Straw" (redubbed "Straw Breakdown"). More interesting, though, were his various fiddle blues: "Lost Train Blues," probably learned from the Crook Brothers on the Opry; "Florida Blues," which has overtones of the jazz standard "Wang Wang Blues;" "Dickson County Blues," which sold so well on records that it generated a sequel called "Dickson County Blues No. 2"; "Fiddler's Blues" and others. These "blues" tunes do not resemble the slow, dirge-like songs of singers like Bessie Smith, nor the free-form improvisations of country blues singers like Robert Johnson. Smith made the "fiddle blues" almost a genre of its own, characterized by slides, slurs, and long, keening double stops, as well as a strong, medium-tempo, driving rhythm. The Dickson-Hickman county style that nourished Smith as a youth, with its fondness for sliding up to notes and for unorthodox harmonies, lent itself well to this kind of blues; it is probably also one of the reasons why Smith was able to create such tunes so readily.

Smith by now also had a battery of faster tunes that he called "rags," and some of these too became fiddle standards. Few of them were rags in the classic sense, with the three or four part structure and deliberate tempo of, for instance, a Scott Joplin rag. Though formal ragtime did make its way into the repertoires of old-time fiddle and string bands, the term "rag" was also used rather loosely by fiddlers for almost any kind of up-tempo tune that featured strings of unsyncopated sixteenth notes. "Red Apple Rag," the Smith rag that was probably the most popular and that was preserved by more fiddlers than any other, is a fairly straightforward three-chord piece, played in $\frac{2}{4}$ time, and featuring only two strains, a "high" and "low" part. No analogues for this have been found either in ragtime or in earlier fiddle repertoires, which suggests that it is original. The same could probably be said for "Peacock Rag," which the family says Smith "put together" about 1928. Another favorite, "Smith's Rag," is a different story, however. It features high, fast noting and an A strain that resembles the well-known "Dill Pickle Rag." The second strain, the "low" part, is suggestive of a stride piano figure. But then we hear a third strain, quite unrelated to the first two and in a different key—in other words, a classic ragtime pattern. How conscious Smith was of these structurings, of course, we shall never know, but the fact that he merged them with the fiddle tune style that he inherited helps explain his wide popularity during the 1930s, as well as his continuing influence on fiddle music since then.

Sometime in late 1934 Arthur also began to tour some with the Delmore Brothers from Alabama, who had joined the Opry in 1933. Whereas the McGees were known for their instrumental virtuosity and novelty songs, the Delmores specialized in intricate, close-harmony singing, and in original songs. In many ways, they were less "traditional" than the McGees, and this quality too was to have an effect on Arthur. Blythe Poteet, who toured with both the Delmores and the McGees, thought that the Delmores and Arthur got the idea to work together and record together by sitting around hotel rooms on tours, jamming and playing informally between shows. Arthur had always been interested in songwriting, and he found in Alton Delmore a skilled musician who could read and write music and who knew the ins and outs of song publishing. Furthermore, the Delmores had contacts with the record industry. They had started recording for Victor's Bluebird label in 1933, and their vocal style and new songs appealed to the new generation of A&R men, like Bluebird's Eli Oberstein; such men were catering to the new, vocal-oriented record market of the mid-1930s.

Oberstein had scheduled a Delmore session in New Orleans for January 1935. During the course of correspondence about setting up the session, Alton mentioned Arthur to Oberstein and asked if Arthur could come to the session for a tryout if he paid his own expenses. Oberstein agreed. Thus, in mid-January, while the Delmores (with Uncle Dave Macon) drove to New Orleans, Arthur used his free lineman's pass to travel down on the N.C.&St.L. After a short audition, in which the Delmores backed Arthur, Oberstein agreed to record the fiddler and to pay all his travel expenses. The day of the session, January 22, dawned cold and snowy, with a pervasive freezing dampness that startled even old New Orleans residents. Arthur and the Delmores finished breakfast and then reported to the recording studio. "We were in for a shock," Alton recalled. "The RCA company had rented an old, abandoned building that didn't have any heat in it, and it was just about as cold in that building as it was on the outside. Mr. Oberstein had got hold of a little old coal oil heater and it would not burn, just smoked a lot, and that was the only heat we had." The musicians would record a song, then stop to rub and warm their fingers before the next song. To complicate matters even more, the building was next to a busy alley. Recordings were repeatedly interrupted by the rumbling of delivery trucks. But, Alton remembered, Arthur "played a lot louder than we did, and with our two guitars we could compete with the trucks pretty good."

In spite of all this, Arthur's first session produced several important and influential records. He made his bellwether recordings of "Blackberry Blossom," "Red Apple Rag," "Lost Train Blues," and "Fiddler's Dream," as well as a pair of waltzes. He did his version of "Mocking Bird," which had become a standard on the Opry and which engendered the old joke among Opry fans that Arthur "played the 'Mocking Bird' so clear you could almost see the feathers." (His Bluebird recording of the tune was popular enough that it appeared in the company's Spanish-label series as "El Sinsonte" by "Arturo Muniz.") Rounding out the session was "Doing the Goofus," Smith's version of the old novelty jazz tune from the 1920s more commonly called simply "Goofus."

"Mocking Bird" and "Fiddler's Dream," on Bluebird 5843, became the first Arthur Smith record to be issued, and over the next twelve months the company released the remainder of the New Orleans session. But sales were disappointing. Toward the end of 1935, Oberstein wrote Alton saying that RCA was going to have to drop Arthur's contract. Although he personally liked Smith's fiddling, the age of the old-time fiddle record was past, and Arthur did not take up any slack by singing on the records. Alton, however, saw a possible way out. He knew that Arthur had been singing a little with the McGees and that he had been begun to dabble in songwriting. If Arthur would be willing to let Alton help him out and work up some vocal numbers, they might get Oberstein to reverse his decision. Arthur was certainly willing, and when Alton wrote Oberstein about the idea, "Mr. Oberstein liked the idea fine. He said he didn't want to let Arthur go in the first place." Arthur, recalled Alton, "had some songs about finished and I helped him finish them . . . and together we got a good batch of material for the session."

It was a good batch indeed: four more fiddle tunes but alternating with four vocals. The highlight was, undoubtedly, "There's More Pretty Girls Than One," with Arthur singing lead, backed by the Delmores. Based on various well-worn folk lyric stanzas, the song soon became one of Bluebird's biggest hits.

> I am a rambling man,
> I've rambled this world 'round,
> I've always been a rounder, boys,
> Since my gal turned me down.
>
> There's more pretty girls than one,
> There's more pretty girls than one,
> Now don't be blue, I'll tell you true,
> There's more pretty girls than one.

Surprisingly, Smith was not the first to record this song, which was to become so closely associated with him. An April 1929 recording by Kentucky fiddler Leonard Rutherford (who had learned the song by hearing Smith do it on the radio) was for sale in the Sears catalog by September of that year, but it lacked the smoothness and wistfulness of Smith's record, and did not sell as well. On the back side of "More Pretty Girls" was the other big vocal hit from the session, "Chittlin' Cookin' Time in Cheatham County." Cheatham was a rough and tumble area bisected by the Cumberland River and lying west of Nashville between Nashville and Dickson County. It boasted such communities as Dodge, Rest, and Foxbluff, as well as Ashland City. Chittlins, more properly *chitterlings*, are pig intestines that are cleaned, scraped, and deep fried during hog butchering time. The song used the old jazz tune "St. James Infirmary," fitted up with new words by a fellow named Busby, who, according to Kirk McGee, "used to hang around WSM."

With the success of these new vocal records, a pattern was set whereby the Delmores and Arthur would do sessions together for the next two years. (Arthur would never get a chance to record with the McGees until the 1950s.) In all, Arthur did some fifty-two sides with the Delmores, most of them released under the name "Arthur Smith Trio" instead of "Dixieliners"—suggesting that Arthur saw the group as a recording band that was quite separate from the regular radio and touring band with the McGees. He also backed the Delmores on a number of their own records, and some Bluebirds featured all three musicians to such an extent that the company released some issues of a side under Smith's name, and other identical issues of the same song under the Delmores' name. Many of the records were also issued on the Montgomery Ward label and sold through the company's huge catalog system. To continue to record the fiddle tunes he was so known for, Smith had to continue to sprinkle his sessions with vocals—the percentage continued to be about 50-50.

Smith's Bluebird repertoire was a rich and diverse body of work that yielded more than its share of country and bluegrass standards. Songs came from all sorts of sources. "Adieu False Heart" and "I Stood on the Bridge at Midnight" were nineteenth century parlor songs, while others came from old-time musicians Smith met on his tours: "Bound to Ride" (featuring Arthur playing a driving two-finger banjo style) came from Jimmie Rodgers sideman Oddie McWinders, while "Take Me Back to Tennessee" came from a visit with the Carter Family. "Love Letters in the Sand," later resurrected by Mac Wiseman and made into a bluegrass standard, was an old pop song from the Gene Austin era. Remodeled from various traditional and original sources were "Pig in the Pen," "My Home's Across the Blue Ridge Mountains," "Kirby Jail" (also known as "Little

Darling"), and "Walking in My Sleep"—all songs that went into string band and bluegrass tradition. For many listeners, though, the favorite Smith vocal was an innocuous song called "The Farmer's Daughter," with its refrain about "all the little chickens in the garden." Another piece, "Beautiful Brown Eyes," became one of country's first big crossover hits in 1951, when it was recorded by Rosemary Clooney and again by Jimmy Wakely.

During the later 1930s, Smith also participated in numerous stage shows billed as "fiddling contests" or "fiddling showdowns." Flamboyant promoters like Larry Sunbrock would hire Arthur to go up against other well-known fiddlers of the time, such as Clayton McMichen, Curly Fox, Clark Kessinger, and Natchee the Indian. While these were by no means contests in any real sense—they were often determined by audience applause or by local dignitaries—they helped further enhance Arthur's reputation. This was in spite of the fact that he did not go in for the kind of trick fiddling, showoff tunes, and histrionics that others used to stir up an audience. He took his fiddling seriously, with an intensity more akin to that of a modern contest fiddler. This was compromised only when Arthur had been drinking, but as the thirties wore on, this problem began to loom larger. In 1938, Arthur failed to appear at one of these "commercial" fiddling contests staged by the Opry, and it resulted in a three-month suspension from the show. One of the replacement acts brought in while Arthur was off the air was a young fiddler and singer from Knoxville named Roy Acuff (see chapter 15).

This incident certainly damaged Arthur's relationship with the Opry management and seemed even to affect his work with the McGees and the Delmores. By 1938 he was touring less with both of them. For a time he played with a slick, western-flavored Opry group named Jack Shook and His Missouri Mountaineers, featuring Nap Bastien and Dee Simmons. Later in 1938 Smith was hired by Herald Goodman, the former member of the Vagabonds, for his new band, the Tennessee Valley Boys. Howdy Forrester recalled that Goodman knew his new band needed a well-known Opry star to draw crowds; "Arthur was about the hottest act on the Opry at the time, so Goodman hired him." Arthur toured widely with this band, which was also for a time an Opry regular, and which included Forrester on fiddle, his brother Joe Forrester on bass, Billy Byrd on guitar, and Virgil Atkins on banjo. This band backed Arthur on his 1938 Bluebird recordings, which included "In the Pines" and "I've Had a Big Time Today." Young Howdy became one of Arthur's most apt pupils: "He taught me a lot," Howdy recalled, from his later position as Roy Acuff's fiddler in the

1950s through the 1980s. Goodman left the Opry in early 1939 to take the Tennessee Valley Boys to KVOO in Tulsa, and Smith went with him. The Dixieliners last performed on the show in January 14, 1939; after that the act was listed only as Sam and Kirk McGee.

Arthur Smith's career certainly did not end when he left the Opry, but it certainly destabilized. For the next decade he rambled restlessly from job to job, from coast to coast, rarely staying more than a year with any band. He showed up at his last Bluebird session, in Atlanta in 1940, without any backup band at all, and persuaded Bill Monroe, who was also there doing one of his first solo sessions, to loan him the Blue Grass Boys to back him for eight sides. For a time, then, Arthur retired from music and boarded with a family of coal miners in West Virginia, but he was soon back on the circuit. We get glimpses of him in Birmingham playing with Zeke Phillips and His 49ers; in West Virginia with the Bailes Brothers; in Detroit at the Jefferson Inn with his son Ernest; with the York Brothers in West Virginia; with cowboy singer Rex Griffin in Birmingham; with the "Saddle Mountain Round-Up" in Dallas; and, after the war, with cowboy star Jimmy Wakely in California. From 1946 to 1948 he appeared in films with Wakely and stunned high rollers at the Las Vegas hotels by playing his version of "Orange Blossom Special" (with Wakely), which he had helped popularize.

In 1951 he was once again trying to sober up, back in Nashville and out of music, working as a carpenter. He continued to jam informally, and became a source for the new young bluegrass musicians, such as Earl Scruggs, Paul Warren, and Bill Keith. He made a comeback in the 1960s, when folklorist Mike Seeger reunited him with the McGees for a series of LPs and festival gigs. It was none too soon: Arthur's health began to fail in 1969, and on February 28, 1971, he died in Louisville of cancer. He was brought back to Tennessee and buried near McEwen, just a few miles from where he had first learned to scrape out a tune on his father's fiddle.

Though few realized it at the time, Arthur Smith was probably the most influential musician on the 1930s Opry. He was no passive preserver of tradition; rather, he took traditional phrases and fragments and welded them into new, distinctive forms. He took traditional tunes and interpreted them in fresh and distinctive ways. Of his seventy-six prewar recordings, only about a third can be called "traditional" by folk music definitions. The majority of the tunes are original creations of a dynamic artist, an artist who used as his aesthetic the conventions of old-time music and old popular music. Smith knew his strengths and weaknesses, and he instinctively designed tunes to match them. Almost everyone who knew Arthur and his music explains how "personal" his style was. The articulate Jimmy Wakely recalled: "To a degree, Arthur was limited . . . but only to the degree that he was so great a fiddle player with a definite style that he didn't have to play anything else." But in a less holistic sense, while other early Opry stars like Macon and Bate and the Pickards continued to fight a rear guard action against changing musical taste, Arthur Smith and the Dixieliners were on the cutting edge of the newer musical styles that anticipated western swing, bluegrass, and "contest style" fiddling. He brought the grand Opry fiddling tradition to its peak and translated it into modern terms. The week Arthur died, Roy Acuff spoke from the stage of the Opry and eulogized him as "the king of the fiddlers." It was typical Nashville hyperbole, but in this case no one wanted to argue.

"When It's Time for the Whippoorwill to Sing" The Delmore Brothers

HE MOST POPULAR GROUP ON THE OPRY in the mid-1930s was a group that became what many consider the most potent singing duo in country music history: Alton and Rabon, the Delmore Brothers. They joined the show in the spring in 1933 and within months had won nationwide reputations. To the casual fan, the Delmores might have been just another brother duet act from an age when the music was full of such acts, such as the Callahan Brothers, the Monroe Brothers, the Bolick Brothers (Blue Sky Boys), and the Shelton Brothers. But the Delmores were far more than just another duet act; they were one of the first of these acts, and they retained their popularity longer than most of the others. They generally featured original songs, and they sang them in a soft, close-harmony style that influenced generations of country performers. Though they were a transitional group on the Opry, they were also one of the most vital transition groups in the music's history. They linked blues, country ragtime, old ballads, and shape-note gospel songs of the nineteenth century South with the polished, arranged, complicated media-oriented styles of the pop music of the time.

The Delmores were also transitional in another sense: they were among the first country acts to appeal to a wider audience. As we have seen, any Opry act trying to make a living with their music had to appeal to an audience wider than just Opry fans. Such performers had to be able to hold down weekday shows on WSM to get enough of a salary to survive. The Delmores learned to do this well and even to transmit their appeal through their phonograph records. Some of their records, like

"Beautiful Brown Eyes" and "More Pretty Girls Than One" (both recorded with Arthur Smith), were among the earliest "crossover" hits in the music, selling both to rural and urban audiences. Like the Sizemores and the Vagabonds, the Delmores were literate and sophisticated, but unlike them the Delmores had a genuine folk base for their music. They not only had style but content—not a content derived from the nineteenth century world of "heart" or sentimental songs, but from the rich, soulful traditional culture of northern Alabama. And this content was filtered through the creative imagination of one of the music's finest composers, Alton Delmore.

Though much of the Delmore success came from their own innate skill and drive, part of it also came from their being in the right place at the right time. Jazz critic Whitney Balliett has written of the importance of the hand-held mike in changing the style of American pop singers; it moved them away from the loud, booming styles of the acoustic era to the subtle nuances of the Crosbys and Sinatras. A similar argument could be made for the advancement of country singing. In the 1920s it was necessary for the Carter Family and Riley Puckett to sing at high volume for their audiences to hear them under primitive staging conditions. But by the 1930s, radio had made it possible to sing softly and still be heard, and portable sound systems had developed to the point where live concerts could achieve the same end. The first generation of country stars—Jimmie Rodgers, Uncle Dave Macon, the Carter Family, the Skillet Lickers—could not depend exclusively on radio to establish their reputations. Their artistic style was formed in an earlier, more acoustic age. But the second generation of country stars sensed the need to fit their art to the medium, and the Delmores were among the first of this generation. With radio, their carefully crafted harmonies could be appreciated and their evocative lyrics understood.

Both Delmore Brothers were born in Elkmont, Alabama, just a few miles from the Tennessee line, Alton on Christmas Day 1908, Rabon on December 3, 1916. Their parents were tenant farmers who struggled to eke out a living from the rocky red clay of the area, and the brothers saw their share of hard times early in life. But musical talent ran in the family; the boys' mother and uncle were both well-known gospel singers who could read and write music. Their uncle Will (W. A. Williams) was a music teacher who taught shape-note singing and who had published several gospel songs. Often the entire Delmore family would gather to sing at revival meetings and church homecomings. Alton's mother taught him to read the old seven-shape-note music, and he himself learned the "rudiments" by going to the rural singing schools in the area. In fact, in 1926, when Alton was only eighteen, he published his first efforts at songwriting in one of the paperback shape-note books of the time. This particular one was called *Bright Melodies*, and it included two songs with credit to Alton (music) and his mother, Mrs. C. E. Delmore. Neither song stands out much from the eighty or so other new ones in the book. One is called "We'll Praise Our Lord," the other "A Vision of Home Sweet Home" ("Jesus who loves me, my pilot will be, / As I'm crossing death's rolling foam."). The book was published by a local firm, the Athens Music Company, which had been started by songwriter and music teacher C. A. Brock, whose son Dwight would win fame as a gospel pianist. The effect on Alton of having a shape-note publishing company in his backyard is hard to overestimate. In fact, the general interest in gospel singing in this corner of Alabama, which includes part of Sand Mountain, was undoubtedly crucial in his development. The region produced an amazing number of later singers and composers, such as Jake Hess (of the Statesmen), the John Daniel Quartet, and the Louvin Brothers. Throughout his later career Alton would continue to publish gospel songs in the paperback books published by companies like R. E. Winsett, and he would eventually help form one of the most successful of all quartets, the Browns Ferry Four.

By the time Rabon was ten (about 1926), the brothers were playing and singing together and crafting the close harmony sound they were later famous for. They sang informally at community events such as fairs and fiddling contests. Alton later recalled that a major influence on their singing had been the amateur gospel quartets that flourished in the region. Rabon was also trying to learn the fiddle by this time, with Alton backing him on guitar. Soon they were winning first place on a regular basis in the singing categories of the Limestone County fiddling contests, and local newspapers began to praise them in print. Alton, who was working at this time as a printer and as a cotton gin hand, recalled: "We never tried to sing loudly. We couldn't have if we had wanted to because we both had soft voices." One of their first successful appearances was at a contest on the Elk River in western Limestone County:

> It came time for Rabon and me to play and some of the fine bands had already been on stage and made a big hit with the crowd. . . . The only thing was we could not play as loud as the others had played. . . . We picked out two of our best ones. I think the first was "That's Why I'm Jealous of You." We sang it a lot in those days and it was a good duet song. When we first began to sing, the

crowd was kind of noisy but we hadn't got through the song before there was a quietness everywhere. You could have heard a pin drop. Then we knew that we had a good chance at the prize, even if there were only two of us. When we finished there was a deafening roar of applause. If the crowd had not quieted down, there probably would never been an act called the Delmore Brothers.

Encouraged by this success, Alton began writing to radio stations and record companies asking for a tryout. At first he got polite but firm refusals. Then the brothers met the Allen Brothers, from near Chattanooga, who had recorded a string of records for Victor and Columbia, including a "mountain blues" hit called "Salty Dog." The Allens took pity on the younger singers and suggested they could get attention by using more original material. They followed this advice and in 1931 landed an audition with Columbia Records.

Later in '31 the brothers recorded their first commercial sides in Atlanta. These were "Alabama Lullaby" and "Got the Kansas City Blues" (Columbia 15724), both solid performances on a major label. But it was 1931, and no one had money to spend 75 cents for a record; the release managed to sell only 500 copies. The promised contract was not forthcoming. However, at the Columbia studios the brothers got to meet some of the famous Columbia artists that the brothers had listened to as kids: Riley Puckett, Fiddlin' John Carson, Clayton McMichen, and Blind Andy Jenkins (composer of "The Death of Floyd Collins"). These greats of an earlier age all praised the Delmores' singing, and John Carson exclaimed: "Now if you want to hear some real singing, just shut up and listen to these two boys and then I'll bet you'll be glad you did." Before they left, Alton and Rabon began jamming with the veterans, working over "Left My Gal in the Mountains." Alton recalled, "It was one of my biggest thrills of all time in show business."

About this time Alton began writing to Harry Stone at WSM. "We all knew that the Grand Ole Opry was the greatest show on the air at the time. Or at least people in the South thought so, and we were southerners." But for a year Stone repeatedly wrote back, offering little encouragement. The brothers persisted. "We were still playing schoolhouses and any other place we could book and still the old fiddlers' contests, and we brought home some money nearly every time—precious money that kept some food on the table, along with daddy's help. We were treated almost as celebrities in our home in Limestone County, Alabama, but we didn't have the money to make the thing real."

Finally, in the spring of 1933, the boys received a letter from Harry Stone asking them to come up for an audition. Though Stone did not say so, the Pickard Family was leaving WSM to go to Chicago, and he needed to replace them with another singing act. The Delmore audition got off to a bad start. It was set up for Monday, but the brothers did not drag in until Tuesday, angering Stone, who had planned to take in the opening game of the Southern League baseball schedule that day. The brothers blundered again by singing their version of "When It's Lamp Lighting Time in the Valley"—the Vagabonds' theme—with the Vagabonds present in the room. In a huff, the Vagabonds walked out, mainly because they were so sick of the song. But then Stone asked the boys how many original songs they had, and Alton guessed around twenty-five. He then asked them to play some sample "request" songs—standards and current favorites that listeners expected, like "Silver Haired Daddy of Mine." Stone then left the room, and the brothers, assuming they had failed, started down the stairs of the National Life Building. Suddenly Stone appeared over the top railing and shouted down that they had a job on the Grand Ole Opry. They made their debut on April 29, 1933, in a regular fifteen-minute segment following DeFord Bailey.

The Delmores' stay on the Opry was stormy and controversial at times, but it gave them the exposure and national audience they needed. Soon they were receiving more fan mail than anyone else on the show except Uncle Dave Macon. They actually read much of their mail—it was as yet a novel experience to get fan mail—and made up lists of numbers that were requested, and Alton even typed many answers to the letters. They soon developed an unusual rapport with their audience but were still unable to book any show dates. In December 1933, they traveled to Chicago to make their first Depression-era records for Victor on the cut-rate Bluebird label, which sold records for 35 cents, about half of the cost for a regular Victor. This was the start of a long relationship with the label.

The Delmores drove up with another Opry singing group, the Vagabonds. When they arrived, they met Eli Oberstein, who would be responsible for almost all of the Bluebird country and blues sessions. He was impressed with what he heard and scheduled the brothers for a total of seventeen sides. These included two that would become the brothers' greatest early hits, "Gonna Lay Down My Old Guitar" and the comic "Brown's Ferry Blues." Alton had composed "Brown's Ferry" when they had been bested at a contest by a group singing "comic" songs. He decided that if the public wanted comic songs, he would give them one. He named the song for an old ferry site near the Delmore home on the Tennessee

River. The duo had been singing on WSM for a year before Harry Stone heard them doing it in a jam session and insisted they include it on their broadcasts. As their records were released, both on Bluebird and on the mail order Montgomery Ward label, the Delmores became the biggest recording act on the show.

In spite of this, the brothers often had to struggle to make ends meet. Like the Vagabonds and the Sizemores, they needed to have weekday appearances on the station to make a living wage; but unlike the Vagabonds, they had not come to WSM as seasoned entertainers. Alton described their plight as being between "two classes of entertainers at WSM." Staff members, like the Vagabonds, had the security of a salaried position, whereas the "Opry talent" received a "token fee for each Saturday night. Rabon and me found ourselves in the middle of the group. We didn't get a good salary but we played three times a week on the morning shows and sometimes on other programs they had when they needed someone like us."

At first, the brothers tried to solve this problem by trying to find bookings on their own. Uncle Dave Macon, noting that by 1935 the Delmores were getting more and more mail, asked them to tour with him on the tried-and-true circuit of schoolhouses and small-town meeting halls. By now Macon had set up an impressive network of school teachers, Chamber of Commerce officers, lodge leaders, civic boosters, and local politicians who had known him from his early days. According to Alton, "If he wanted to play a week in a certain part of the country, all he had to do was to write somebody a letter and they would book him and he always made good money." This method, of course, bypassed the newly created WSM Artists Service Bureau, with its 15 percent commission; but since Macon was an established star with established ways, little was said. Alton and Rabon worked well with Uncle Dave—even to the point where the three of them sang trios on favorites like "Over the Mountain," and for a couple of years they worked as his regular touring partners. "Everybody was happy, and we began to make some pretty good money right at the beginning," recalled Alton.

By 1936, though, this arrangement was causing trouble. Judge Hay, assisting with the Artists Service Bureau, was trying to set up some package tours that would pair a hot new act with some of the older groups whose popularity had begun to wane, or with some of the newcomers who had not yet proven themselves. The Delmores were hot, and Hay saw no need for them to be paired with Macon, another of his biggest draws. For a time, therefore, he paired them with fiddler Arthur Smith—until Smith himself, on the strength of his own Bluebird records, emerged as a star in his own right. "Then," said Alton, "they took him and put him with another act and wouldn't let us use him any more." Always anxious to professionalize their work, the brothers found themselves on occasion paired with veteran Opry acts who still looked on their music as hard-drinking, informal fun. When Alton complained to them about too much drinking, or not taking their show dates seriously, one of them said: "By God, I was playing on the Grand Ole Opry when you and your brother were just plain cotton pickers, and I ain't gonna let no goddam cotton picker tell me what to do." The touring problem became an increasing point of friction between the Delmores and Opry management. On one occasion, Alton managed to work out a separate contract between them and the Sudekum theater circuit ($70 a day for the two of them), but Hay learned of it and stepped in to insist that the Sudekum take an entire Opry package tour—one that quickly went bust.

By the middle of 1937, the Delmores were being singled out in WSM press releases as the most successful performers on the show. One read: "Young farmers, these boys, aged 28 and 23 [sic], have beat out some 'new' folk songs which have given them instantaneous popularity with followers of the Grand Ole Opry." Much was made of the duo's recording career. "In every nook and corner of the land, one can hear recordings of the Delmore Brothers being played—in corner drug stores, at church festivals, in private homes, wherever the charm of the folk-tunes, or hillbilly songs, penetrates." During their stay on the Opry, the brothers managed to record some eighty sides for the Bluebird and Ward labels. For a time they even had their own separate listing column in the Ward's catalog. Their best-seller was "Brown's Ferry Blues," which by mid-1937 had racked up sales of more than 100,000 copies—an astounding figure for the Depression-wracked economy. Their average sales per record, according to the WSM press release, was 35,000, and their yearly earnings from recording and copyright royalties averaged around $4,000. Much of this largesse came from the fact that the biggest songs, "Brown's Ferry Blues," "Gonna Lay Down My Old Guitar," "Southern Moon," and "When It's Time for the Whippoorwill to Sing," were placed with an ASCAP publisher, which meant that these and other Delmore originals were being "covered" by numerous other radio and recording artists. WSM also gave the Macon-Delmore trio credit for introducing 1936's top country hit, "Maple on the Hill," as well as 1937's biggest hit, "What Would You Give in Exchange for Your Soul." Curiously the trio had never recorded either side, though they apparently featured them on the air and at personal appearances.

The exact ways in which the Delmores formed a new synthesis from older components of Southern music can be seen by examining their very first Bluebird session in 1933, mentioned earlier. The session has to rank as one of the most auspicious debuts in country music (discounting the unsuccessful Columbia experiment). It produced four songs that were to become standards: "Gonna Lay Down My Old Guitar," "Brown's Ferry Blues," "Blue Railroad Train," and "The Frozen Girl." Others became Delmore favorites and part of their core repertoire for almost two decades: "Lonesome Yodel Blues," "Big River Blues," "The Girls Don't Worry My Mind," and "I'm Leaving You." Alton had hoped to record another original, the tremendously popular "When It's Time for the Whippoorwill to Sing," but the brothers got into a wrangle with the Vagabonds about publishing rights, and the Vagabonds wound up recording the song instead of the Delmores. Things were so confused that the Delmores did not record the song until 1940, when they moved to the Decca label.

One type of synthesis the Delmores used was to take the "blue yodel" falsetto singing that had been popularized by Jimmie Rodgers a few years before and add to it a high, intricate harmony. Such a harmony yodel impressed Eli Oberstein no end, and he rushed into print, as the first Delmore issue, two numbers that featured it: "Lonesome Yodel Blues" and "Gonna Lay Down My Old Guitar." Alton's autobiography is silent about where they learned this technique, but it had been used on recordings as early as February 1932 by the team of West Tennessee singers named Reece Fleming and Respers Townsend. Their harmony yodel—a stiff, hooting sound—cannot compare with the graceful, pliable style of the Delmores. This harmony yodel became an important staple of their stylistic arsenal, and they used it with increasing dexterity as the years rolled on, eventually creating with it masterpieces such as "Hey, Hey, I'm Memphis Bound" (1935). And the Victor A&R men came to think so highly of the technique that they went out of their way to note in the session ledgers which songs had yodels and which did not.

Another Delmore innovation was the use of close harmonies and a soft, almost intimate, manner of delivery. Before the Delmores emerged, country duet singing had been casual and slapdash at best, as with the popular Darby & Tarlton ("Birmingham Jail"), or stiff and formal, as with McFarland & Gardner ("When the Roses Bloom Again"). Much of this early style used "open" harmony, where the tenor sings a fourth interval, a note higher than the nearest natural harmony, much in the manner of modern bluegrass singing. The Delmores, however, drew upon their formal musical training, with its harmonics and sense of pitch, to create a style of very close harmony, often sung just a third under the lead. Most of the time it was Alton who sang lead to Rabon's harmony, but if the range of a song dictated it, the brothers would switch back and forth, even in the same song. This same kind of close harmony soon showed up in the work of a generation of singers, including Karl and Harty, the Blue Sky Boys, the Callahan Brothers, and the Girls of the Golden West. The soft harmonies also worked, as we have seen, because the listeners could now hear them with the new carbon microphones of radio and the new public address systems used for personals. Alton himself sensed the watershed between this first and second generation of country musicians when he described (see the discussion above) the Delmores' first live public appearance at the old fiddling contest.

A third aspect of the fusion of old and new was the team's superb guitar work, which survives today in the modern work of Doc Watson and Chet Atkins. Many of the "turnarounds"—the instrumental passages between vocal verses—on the first session were played on a little tenor guitar, played on occasion by Alton, on other occasions by Rabon. Alton had taught Rabon how to play the instrument. He remembered: "I had brought it home with me from Decatur [Alabama]. I taught him the first chords on it and I played it like a tenor banjo. So that's the way he learned to play it." The Delmores were probably not the first country act to use a tenor guitar—for a time the Vagabonds even included one in their act—but they were certainly the first to use it as a lead instrument and the first to do breaks with it. In addition, Alton himself was a formidable flat-top style guitarist who once amazed the legendary Riley Puckett by outplaying him on his own specialty, "The A Rag." Though some fans have compared Alton's playing to that of east coast bluesman Blind Boy Fuller, Alton himself acknowledged other masters. In his late teens while convalescing from an illness,

> I started listening to various recording artists, Jimmie Rodgers, Carson Robison, Nick Lucas, Riley Puckett, and Eddie Lang. These are the fellows I copied mostly. I would take a little from the style of the first one and then the other til I had my own style. And besides playing some of their runs and riffs I emphasized the melody and would play the song like anyone would play it on the piano or the violin or any other lead instrument, and that is where my style is different.

Alton's mention of Nick Lucas is intriguing, since Lucas also published an influential series of instruction books and on occasion spotlighted the tenor guitar. Throughout the 1930s the Delmores would remain the only duo to feature the tenor guitar; most of the others favored the mandolin or second guitar. It helped define the Delmores' unique sound.

Finally, there are the Delmore songs themselves—perhaps their most important examples of fusing the older musics to create something new. Their second Bluebird release, Bluebird 5538, contained "The Frozen Girl" and "Bury Me Out on the Prairie." Both are steeped in tradition. The former, with its haunting "No home, no home" first line, is more commonly known as "The Orphan Girl" and had been collected by folklorists and even recorded by singers like Buell Kazee and by McFarland & Gardner before the Delmores did it. In a later King re-make of the song, Alton would announce that it was "over a hundred years old." While the song was often sung as a solo in earlier days, the Delmores brought to it their harmony and a surprisingly fast waltz tempo on their guitars. Yet it all worked. It was a hit for Bluebird and became a favorite in the Delmore repertoire. "Bury Me Out on the Prairie," under alternate titles like "I've Got No Use for the Women" and "The Gambler's Ballad," had also been collected by folklorists prior to the Delmore recording. The Delmores probably got it from the Vagabonds, who included it in their 1932 songbook. To it, the brothers brought, again, their harmony, a brisk tempo, and sparkling tenor guitar breaks. Throughout their career, the Delmores would continue to reinvent old folk songs, albeit sparingly, and only when the songs fit their style.

The real centerpiece of the Delmore repertoire—and the secret weapon that gave them the advantage over lesser groups like the Vagabonds—was the body of original songs created by Alton. Based on older lyric patterns and rhetoric from gospel songs, blues, and nineteenth century Tin Pan alley chestnuts, they nonetheless seemed fresh and new because of Alton's synthesizing abilities. Two examples appear on the Delmores' third Bluebird release (Bb 5358), "I'm Leaving You" and "I'm Going Back to Alabama." The former uses the classic blues stanza pattern in which the first line (in this case, "I'm leaving you this lonesome song") is repeated three times before the completing line ("Cause I'll be gone, long gone, some day 'fore long"). This in itself is not so unusual—Jimmie Rodgers did a lot of it—but the Delmores add to it a call-and-response echo on the first three lines, much in the manner of a gospel quartet. The mixture works, and Alton would repeat the formula on later songs like "Fifteen Miles to Birmingham." "I'm Going Back to Alabama" is derived from the South-as-nostalgia mode that citybillies like Carson Robison and Vernon Dalhart exploited in the 1920s and 1930s: after rambling around a bit, it's always great to go back home to those cotton fields and magnolia trees. This, too, would be a familiar Delmore theme, but with a difference—Alton's keen eye for specific details. Where Robison sang of a vague "blue ridge mountain home," Alton singled out specific Southern locales: states like Alabama, Georgia, Tennessee, Mississippi and cities like Memphis, Birmingham, Nashville. Others sang of "prison" in a vague generic sense, whereas Alton wrote about "Alcatraz Island Blues." This strain too might well have been borrowed from country blues singers, whose songs were often full of specific geographic details, some so clear that later historians could use the clues in the songs to track down the anonymous original singers.

Alton's keen appreciation of the Southern landscape afforded him sharp images and accurate references: night birds cry in "I'm Going Back to Alabama," and the moon in summer is so bright it lights your way as you roam. The Delmores' songs used this landscape year after year and also peopled this landscape with real people—not fainting Victorian maidens, bright-eyed Daisy Maes, or earnest suitors.

While the form and style of the older songs were appealing, the brothers knew that they would have to graft onto it a more modern view of love. Thus, while "Lonesome Yodel" features the refrain, "You're gonna be sorry for what you done," the more modern and honest "I'm Leaving You" starts off, "I'm leaving you this lonesome song." Images of separation abound in many of the songs, as do references to isolation, hurt, and anger. "There's no one to cry for me" runs a line from "Gonna Lay Down My Old Guitar," and "If I sink just let me die" reads one from "Big River Blues." At other times a biting misogyny surfaces: in "Bury Me Out on the Prairie" they sing the line "I've got no use for the women"; in another a line goes, "I don't let the girls worry my mind." A generation before honky-tonk music would supposedly reflect modern love for the first time, the Delmore songs were speaking both to the older generations, in sentimental phrasings, and to the younger ones who, like the Delmores themselves, knew and responded to expressions of the pain and confusion of turbulent emotions.

As the 1930s progressed, the Delmores added more and more hit records to the body of 1933 material. These included "Nashville Blues" (1936), "False Hearted Girl" (1937), "No Drunkard Can Enter There" (1937), "Southern Moon" (1937), "I Need the Prayers of those I Love" (1937), "Weary Lonesome Blues" (1937), "Fifteen Miles from Birmingham" (1938), and "They Say It Is Sinful to Flirt" (1937). With Arthur Smith (see chapter 12) they recorded "There's More Pretty Girls Than One" (1936), "Pig at Home in the Pen" (1937), "Walking in My Sleep"

(1937), "Beautiful Brown Eyes" (1937), and others. With Uncle Dave Macon, they even had a hit in 1935's "Over the Mountain." During this time they also published two songbooks, *Songs We Sing on the Grand Ole Opry*, ca. 1937, containing some forty-three songs drawn primarily from their recorded repertoire, and *Sweet Sentimental Songs from the Heart of the Hills*, published in 1936 with ex-Vagabond Curt Poulton and containing thirty-two songs, including most of the Delmore hits. Neither book was issued by a regular music publisher, such as M. M. Cole or Peer-Southern, but by the singers themselves. It would be 1940 before the Delmores would see a folio of their work brought out by an established music company (American Music).

In January 1938 David Stone suspended Arthur Smith from the Opry for three months because he missed an important personal appearance in West Tennessee. This began a long chain of events that would eventually result in the Delmores leaving the Opry. With Smith out of the loop, the Delmores had to find another band to tour with. David Stone came to them and said he planned to audition four different bands on four consecutive weeks as guests on the Opry. The Delmores would then choose the one they liked best, and this band would be hired as a road band to back the boys on personals and tours, but only for a six-month period. "They will never be a genuine act of the Grand Ole Opry," he told Alton. After listening to the four bands, the brothers told Stone their choice: a Knoxville group called the Crazy Tennesseans, headed by a young man named Roy Acuff. Alton recalled that Stone was surprised; he had personally considered Acuff's the worst of the four bands, but now he agreed to hire them to fill out the dates that had already been booked. When he wrote Acuff, on February 10, 1938, Stone painted a different picture, due in part to Acuff's huge amount of fan mail: "I am teaming you up with the Delmore Brothers for several personal appearances. These boys have tremendous popularity in this territory, but they cannot build or manage their own unit so I think it would be a great combination for the acts." By February 19, Acuff was sharing the morning show with the Delmores, and the following day his band backed them on their first joint show date, in Dawson Springs, Kentucky. According to the original deal Stone worked out with Acuff, the whole troupe would travel in Acuff's station wagon—five members of the band plus the two Delmores—and the gate receipts would be split 50-50: half to the Delmores, half to the Acuff band. This type of arrangement seemed to work out for a time, and Alton and Roy used to sit out in the station wagon and sing old gospel songs between shows.

Acuff's popularity soared, and soon he was able to carry a tour on his own. He and the Delmores split up, but the two groups shared mutual influences. The Delmores soon recorded from the Acuff repertoire such items as "Wabash Cannonball" (1938), "You're the Only Star in My Blue Heaven" (1938), and "Wabash Blues" (1939). Acuff, for his part, waxed versions of "Walking in My Sleep" (1940) and "Beautiful Brown Eyes" (1940).

Next, the Delmores worked with Pee Wee King and His Golden West Cowboys, but by the start of 1938 Alton and Rabon were actively scouting around for a new radio home. Their reasons were complex. Judge Hay, who had recently returned to work after a sabbatical, did not get along with the brothers at all, and he was still influential in dictating tour routes and package-show make-ups. The Opry management continued to make it difficult to supplement WSM work with independent outside bookings; for instance, the Delmores played every single Saturday night throughout 1937 and up to their departure in 1938. Their enforced estrangement from Smith, one of the few Opry regulars who were their equal in musical skill and creativity, frustrated them, and watching their "temporary" backup band (Acuff) turned into the show's new hottest act puzzled them. Added to this were personal problems. Principal among these was their feeling that some of the Opry regulars and staff disapproved of Rabon's unconventional life-style and were jealous to start with. The result was a subtle but continual tension.

Finally, the brothers became so anxious to leave that they accepted a job at WPTF in Raleigh, a job offering no regular salary, in hopes they could generate enough supplementary income through personals. In September 1938, then, they put together a band that included former Golden West Cowboy Milton Estes, bass player Joe Zinkan, and singer Smiley O'Brien. After singing the last song on their Opry segment—it was "What Would You Give in Exchange for Your Soul"—they packed their two cars and started out down highway 70 to the east. It was December and, as Alton recalled, "raining and dismal."

Before the Delmores left, Harry Stone tried to persuade them to stay. "The key is always on the outside," he said. This proved not to be the case, however. Although the Delmores did come back in 1939 and 1940 for guest appearances, they were never asked to rejoin, and by 1939 a Delmores clone, the Andrews Brothers, had been hired to replace them. The Opry was history for the Delmores, but the five and a half years they had spent there had launched them into a long and fruitful career. Ahead was a dizzying round of radio stations, a series of hit records with the Brown's

Ferry Four, a series of hits on the postwar King label, and a stint at border radio. Later hits included "Hillbilly Boogie" and "Blues Stay Away from Me." Alton would go on to write over a thousand songs in his lifetime, songs that would be recorded by everyone from Tennessee Ernie Ford to Bob Dylan. He would also write a remarkable autobiography (see endnotes). The real end of the Delmore career came as early as 1952, when Rabon died. Alton lived on, trying to keep his hand in the music, until his own death in 1964.

"Dear Lesperdeezer"
The First Comedians

Lasses & Honey

The first Opry performer that could be classified as a full-time comedian was Lee Roy "Lasses" White, a blackfaced minstrel man who came to WSM about 1932 to start a Friday night minstrel show. He arrived in Nashville with a partner named Lee Davis "Honey" Wilds, who had worked with him for a number of years, and the pair was soon known as Lasses & Honey. Hay recalled that they "took a spot on the Opry soon after they got their minstrel show going full blast at WSM. They used material which fitted the Opry and became stars of the big shindig almost immediately." They first appeared on the Opry in April 1934 and for the next three years were regulars except for summers, which they took off to tour and vacation. They were indeed popular, commanding high fees for touring, recording for a major company (Bluebird), and issuing annual song and joke books. They were probably the most successful act booked by the newly organized Artists Service Bureau, and to quote Hay again, "They had 'em hangin' on the rafters in the schoolhouses throughout the territory served immediately by our station."

A typical Lasses & Honey show would carry enough entertainers to go for two hours, and Lasses White had so much material—skits and songs—that he would often play the same towns time after time without repeating much. These trunks of old scripts and songs that White owned certainly enriched his Opry tenure, but they also represented the venerable and deep-rooted minstrel tradition that White brought to the show. Just as the Opry offered a refuge for other forms of old nineteenth century stage styles—such as the comic banjo songs of Uncle Dave Macon and the show-off fiddle tradition of Uncle Joe Mangrum and Henry Bandy—so now did it offer a new lease on life for the kind of minstrel song and humor that had died out on the big vaudeville circuits decades before.

In some respects, one of the last avatars of this tradition was Lasses White (1888–1949). Born on a farm in Texas, White became interested in theater after his family moved to Dallas. He began playing in what would today be called summer stock and soon discovered he had a quick wit and a limberness of voice that lent itself well to minstrel blackface. He appeared for a time with the Swor Brothers (one of whom would, years later, show a young Grandpa Jones how to put on his fake mustache and stage makeup for the first time) and then, about 1912, became an under-study for a minstrel show legend, William George "Honeyboy" Evans. Born in Wales in 1870, Evans was probably best known for his coauthor-ship of the song "In the Good Old Summertime," which he produced in 1902. He also headed up one of the biggest of the minstrel show troupes. According to historian David Ewen, "The company of one hundred min-strels headed by George Evans in the early twentieth century was one of the most famous minstrel show troupes of the post–Civil War period." Some historians feel that Evans's group rivaled the original Christy Min-strels shows that helped start the whole minstrel tradition. Evans had sensed changing tastes, however, and had tried adapting his act to vaude-ville, but with only limited success. By the time White joined him, he was returning to the minstrel format and trying to resurrect it. All of this came to a sudden end in February 1915, when Evans, on tour with White and the "Southern Honey Boys," died suddenly in Birmingham.

In spite of his fame, Evans died almost penniless, and young Lasses White stepped in, took over Evans's role, and completed the tour on behalf of Evans's widow. This won him much good will and drew attention to his own considerable abilities. The following year, 1916, he was a headliner with Neil O'Brien's Minstrels, where he introduced the song "Pray for the Lights to Go Out" (see discussion of that song in chapter 8). In Dallas, which he continued to use as his headquarters, he published one of the first of his own compositions, "Nigger Blues." How much of it White actually wrote and how much he redacted from older traditional sources may never be known, but the song's opening lines are among the best-known pop blues lyrics: "The blues ain't nothin', / The blues ain't nothin', / But a good man feelin' bad." White would continue to use this as one of his standards throughout the 1930s, long after the title itself became too embarrassing for record companies to use.

For a time White toured with the Al G. Field Company—the same organization that would later serve as home base for a similar blackface vocalist who would impact country music, Emmett Miller. By 1920 White had his own troupe and was recording sketches from his shows for the Columbia Phonograph Company. He finally opened his own touring show, in Memphis about 1923, and it was here that he first met George Hay, then a reporter at the local paper. Hay recalled this show vividly and seemed especially impressed that White had to give six encores to his new hit song, "Sweet Mama, Tree Top Tall." By 1924 White was publishing his own song folio, with jazz-age originals like "You Got to Strut It" and "When You Come Out of Your Two-Time Mind, Don't You Try To 'Daddy' Me." By 1928 White was straining hard to update the minstrel format for a more modern audience. The review of a January 1928 show of the All-Star Minstrels at the Orpheum in Nashville makes this clear. The show still included older acts like "Dixie Memories," set down on the "old Sewanee River" with "the old darky by his cabin" crooning those "old Southern favorites underneath the mellow moon," but it also included updated versions of Southern stereotypes like White's specialty, "The Dixie Black Bottom," and a long skit built around a trip taken by a party of city types to the dude ranch owned by a flapper in Mexico. Such shows still appealed to the small town theaters in the South, but White must have realized that he was going have to adapt even further, to a newer format, to attract wider audiences. When WSM asked him to consider adapting his minstrel show to the radio format in 1932, he jumped at the chance.

For radio, White pared down his group to twenty: ten singers and jokesters, and ten musicians, including a few from the Opry and others from the WSM staff orchestra. The show was scheduled for Friday nights. It was reasonably successful and still in place as late as 1936. No scripts or recordings of this Friday show apparently survive, and it is difficult to tell just how much of the All-Star Minstrel stage shows remained. Nor do we know exactly what Lasses & Honey did for their regular fifteen-minute Opry stints, but the annual songbooks issued by White from 1934 to 1936 offer a few clues.

First, Lasses & Honey became masters of song parody, just in the way Homer & Jethro did thirty years later. Some of the parody was directed at the sentimental old songs that were becoming staples of country radio music. One such song was the lachrymose "Trail of the Lonesome Pine," which White repeatedly lampooned with savage effectiveness. One version ran:

> In the mountains of Virginia lived some mountain goats,
> One Old Bill ate some dynamite, thinking it was Quaker Oats,

And then a nanny and Bill very soon,
Began to butt and fight,
She did not know what Billy had eat,
Till she hit that dynamite.

Through the Blue Ridge Mountains of Virginia,
Billy sailed by the Lonesome Pine,
His front legs came down in New York town,
Way down in Georgia they found his spine,
Knoxville found the whiskers of Bill,
His hind legs—they are both missing still,
They found his horns in the mountains of Virginia,
And his tail in the Lonesome Pine.

Bizarre though it is, this parody shows White's genuine songwriting skills. It echoes closely the sounds of the original words, and the refrain is structured to conclude on a "shaggy dog" pun in which "tail" is substituted for "trail" with perfect logic. White manages to puncture the sentimentality of the original while at the same time creating a surreal piece of slapstick. An even better instance of White using older minstrel techniques is his 1935 parody of the same song, where he plays on the "ugly" humor of the tradition.

In the Blue Ridge mountains of Virginia,
In a stream by the Lonesome Pine,
When I saw June in her bathing suit,
I changed my mind 'bout her being a beaut,
Oh, June, she had a big glass eye,
And her teeth were like the stars in the sky,
(Spoken: They come out at night),
She had a shape like the mountains of Virginia,
and one limb from the Lonesome Pine.

A second type of parody was political or topical. Country or western songs like "The Last Round-Up," "Casey Jones," "After the Ball," and "Frankie and Johnny" became the models for a variety of songs about Roosevelt and the New Deal. Few of these could be called "protest songs;" most were strongly in support of Roosevelt, though in some circles that was in itself controversial. The Lasses & Honey version of "Frankie and Johnny" cast Roosevelt as Frankie and Vice President John Nance Garner as Johnny:

Frankie and Johnny met the Senate,
Said, Now, men, listen here,
Our people that voted for us,
Didn't vote for men with fear;
Let's do our part—and not do them wrong.

A 1934 song called "The New Deal" pokes good-natured fun at the alphabet-soup agencies created by the new Washington bureaucracy.

My hat's off to Mr. F.D.R.
We're seeing signs again—Wanted—men for hire,
He put through a deal called the N.R.A.,
And it's going to help the U.S.A. okey,
He also formed the C.R.B.,
And then he put through the C.C.C.,
Then along came another called the C.W.A.
That is helping to shove Depression away,
There's the F.C.A. and the R.S.B.,
And the G.S.C. and the F.C.T.,
They're all going to help both me and you,
For prosperity's coming P.D.Q.

Such topicality marked a return to some of the earliest days of minstrelsy, the 1840s and 1850s, when figures like Davy Crockett and Andrew Jackson and topics like a National Bank were familiar references in minstrel songs.

A third type of Lasses & Honey parody involved simply borrowing the structure and melody of a familiar song and fitting a completely new set of words to it. The result was a song that sounded old-time enough but dealt with thoroughly modern topics. "Taxi Jim," a favorite that the team also recorded for Bluebird, used the framework of "Casey Jones" to tell the story of a "jitney bus" driver who decides to become a race car driver. "One Eyed Sam" (also recorded), "Poker Pete," and "Cowboy Joe, the Cowboy Gambler" all deal in a light-hearted way with card players and high rollers—and all are relatively free of the ethnic overtones that marked many of the earlier "coon" songs. "Jimmy Bone" is a familiar brave-engineer song with the added twist that Jimmy's wife, upon hearing of his death on the line, stabs herself, saying, "When you bury my daddy, you can bury me, too." "Honey Bee" is a ballad about Jimmie Sneed, who tries to murder his girlfriend, Honey Bee; he is captured, taken to the scaffold, and is about to pay his price when Honey Bee herself arrives in the nick of time, explaining "you only bruised up my head."

White also had an effective command of the sentimental genre, as witnessed by his Carson Robison–like "In the Cumberland Valley of Tennessee" (also recorded), "Mother of Home Sweet Home," and the popular "If You Knew What It Meant to Be Lonesome," which remained in country repertoires throughout the 1940s.

These songs, as well as most of the jokes and skits the team used, were apparently the work of Lasses White. One is struck by how well-crafted the songs are and how different in tone they are from the earlier White specialties like "Nigger Blues" and "You Got to Strut It." White was adapting his humor to the new medium of radio and to the milieu of country music, and he was superb at it. Just as the Vagabonds had adapted their earlier pop song styles to the Opry and moved toward a folk and old-time repertoire, so did White, another experienced professional, adapt his style and repertoire to the Opry image. What is remarkable in both instances is how quickly and readily the performers themselves perceived this image. It was a clear, well-defined image that Hay and Stone made of the Opry, and they didn't hesitate to impose it on their new generation of Opry acts.

In May 1936 Lasses White moved to Hollywood, where he found yet another way to adapt his minstrel skills as a character actor in cowboy films. He appeared in several with Jimmy Wakely and entertained in the USO during the war. Honey Wilds stayed at WSM to continue the blackface tradition with a series of other partners, including Tom Woods (Jamup & Honey) and Bunny Biggs (a second Jamup). In 1940 he became one of the first Opry stars to take to the road in a tent show.

Sarie & Sally

Two of the most loved Opry artists in the 1930s were a pair of self-described "old mountain women" named Sarie and Sally. Neither of them actually performed much music (often when they toured they worked with the McGee Brothers), but they created a series of dialogues that anticipated by a generation the classic routines of Rod Brasfield and Minnie Pearl and that formed a verbal counterpart to the image that Hay was crafting for the Opry music. The creative force behind Sarie & Sally was a small, dynamic woman named Edna Wilson, who played Sarie. She was born Edna Earl Umensetter on Lookout Mountain near Chattanooga in 1896. As a child, she roamed the mountain, going all the way from the top to the bottom hunting persimmons, avoiding the chain-gang prisoners who worked in the woods, and watching with curiosity as her father and uncle helped build, and then operate, the famed Incline Railway. Her father was a carpenter with enough means to send Edna to the Notre Dame Academy in Chattanooga for early high school; then, in 1912, the family moved to Nashville. There Edna met Rhey B. Wilson and soon married him. A son followed (in 1920), and for the next few years Edna Wilson played the role of a mother and homemaker.

This all changed in the late 1920s. As she explained it herself: "It was while living in High Point, North Carolina, that the idea of entertaining developed. I was invited to go with a party one night to Pilot Mountain on a fox hunt. And while sitting around the campfire eating, I happened to start conversation using the lingo of an old country woman and introduced myself as Sarie Brown. The next day I was asked to entertain for a Sunday school banquet. I secured suitable clothing for the occasion, and though I was terribly nervous I did manage to do a monologue. From that time on, I was invited to perform for many clubs, etc." Her "suitable clothing" was an old bonnet, a long dress, and some old "specs" that made Edna look much older than her thirty-odd years. It was a transformation not unlike the one Grandpa Jones made when he first started out. She coupled her costume with a device she would later refer to as "talking country," using a dialect and colorful phrases she remembered from her childhood in Chattanooga, relying on the language itself, rather than situations or stories, to create the humor. "I started talking country to people that were country," she said years later, "and they fell for the country brogue."

In 1930 the Wilsons moved to Lakeland, Florida, where Edna met a young college student named Ralph Odum, who became fascinated with her "Sarie Brown" routine and asked her to write some skits featuring him as a male partner. Edna created a script called "Sarie and Silas," in which Odum played a rural mail carrier to Edna's widow character. Soon they were broadcasting the act over station WFLA in nearby Tampa, one show a week (9:15 A.M.) for five dollars a week. After a few months of this, though, Odum decided to go to Stetson University to study law, and the act broke up.

Unwilling to see the act die so soon, and painfully aware of how scarce work was for her husband during those early Depression days, Edna engineered a return to Nashville in the fall of 1934. Edna recalled that one of her younger sisters, Margaret Faith (born in 1903), had a childhood talent for mimicry, and Edna asked her to join in a new act that would feature Sarie's cousin Sally in place of Silas. Margaret hesitated, noting, at the age of thirty-one, that she and her husband, Marshall Waters, had a family of their own and a plate full of responsibilities. She finally agreed and after days of rehearsing, the pair went to WSM. They did not try out for the Opry but for a regular slot in the mainstream schedule. Ollie Reihl, the program manager, liked what he saw and offered them a fifteen minute slot, three days a week, at a salary of $20 per week each. "Sarie & Sallie" debuted on WSM at 5:15 P.M. on November 28, 1934. The show seemed to be a success, but one of the sponsors wanted to test their real audience strength. A common technique in those days was to offer a free photo to any fans who wrote in, and one week in late 1934 Sarie announced this. "Three days later we were called to the station," Edna recalled. "When we arrived we found, to our surprise, there were mail bags filled with cards and letters all over the place . . . in all, over forty thousand pieces of mail. That was the happiest day of my life."

Judge Hay also took note of the incredible, immediate success of Sarie & Sallie and quickly created a slot for them on the Opry. As early as January 26, 1935, barely nine weeks after their WSM debut, the team made their first Opry appearance. For the next two and a half years, Sarie & Sallie did regular bits on the Opry and kept up their regular "continuity" shows, three a week, on WSM. None of their material was improvised; it was all carefully scripted by Edna Wilson. The non-Opry shows had an ongoing plot line, much like a soap opera, whereas the Opry shows were shorter five-minute "routines" that were not sequential. It was a bruising, demanding schedule: in 1935 the duo appeared on the Opry forty-one times (or weeks), forty-eight in 1936, fifty in 1937, and in 1938 they made the Opry every single Saturday night. Eventually their popularity on the Opry and on Opry tours led them to drop their continuity show.

Fans and promoters began referring to the team as "a female Lum and Abner"—so much so that by 1939 Edna was telling newspaper reporters that she refused to listen to the Lum & Abner shows on radio "because she insists upon originality for the Sarie and Sallie program." Most of the fans, though, knew something of the background of the two characters. Since Edna Wilson preserved a good many of the original scripts from these early days, it is possible to recreate this background in some detail.

In an early show, Sarie introduced herself as "Mrs. Sarie Brown, the wife of Hiram B. Brown, dead." Hiram has been killed at a local sawmill:

I was washin' when some fellers druv up from the saw Mill. They set, Air you the widow Brown? And I set, No, but I'm Mrs. Brown. When he up and set, Why you air a widow, for I've got yer old man's corpse in my buggy.

Soon Sarie's cousin, Sally White, arrives from a nearby town of Cloverdale; she is younger than Sarie, headed toward spinsterhood, and eager to help Sarie spend the insurance money Hiram has left her. She brings with her a parrot, Elmer, who causes much worry to Sarie's old cat, Tom. "I 'low at how he wuz thinking that eny thing at big at airy buzzart a flittering about the house oughter be calmed down a bit," says Sarrie. Sally snaps, "Don't you call my pedigreed parrot a buzzart." This sort of repartee forms the staple of the scripts, sprinkled with encounters with modern life (everything from the TVA to golf to beauty parlors), puns, and various folk remedies and sayings.

Home remedies and descriptions of country food abound. A cousin cures a goiter by wearing a string of amber beads, "them little stones what are the same color as tobacco juice." A weed poltice or kerosene salve is good for bunions, and ginseng liniment made from apple vinegar, turpentine, coal oil, and mutton tallow helps with the "rheumatiz." A favorite meal is cold sweet potatoes and molasses, and a local women's club in Cricket County often turns into a snuff-chewing contest. Sarie, ever untrusting of banks, hides her insurance money on the back porch "in a sack of cow-peas," while Sally has to chase "myster-flies" out of the woodpile. Folk proverbs and proverbial phrases liven the dialogue: "A man of words and not of deeds is the same as a garden full of weeds"; "He's got my hair a blossoming for the grave"; "On the other hand, she had warts"; "He was mad as a boiled owl." Sarie's exclamations grew so popular they became catch-phrases for the act: "Flutterin' flutterflies"; "Ah, the gnat's pappy!" "Creepin' caterpillers!" "Red pigs and sorghum!" and perhaps the most popular of all, "Dear Lesperdeezer." Edna Wilson thought so highly of these exclamations that she kept long lists of them for handy reference.

Subjects for the skits included predictable accounts of rural Tennessee life: housewarmings, spelling bees, breakdown dances, fishing, trouble with cows and horses, July 4th celebrations. Edna Wilson also honed to a fine point the country-rube-meets-modern-world theme that was to become so well known with later generations of country comics: the complexities of daylight saving time, the mysteries of the radio, the magic of home photography ("pictur takin' with my Kodakies"), beauty parlors, airplane travel, auto races, golf, basketball, dentists, and the big city ("Whut is Central Park, Sallie?" "Why, it's a big place whur they raise pidgeons"). Social fads of the 1930s are discussed: chain letters, the China Clipper, astrology, even knock-knock jokes. Edna's versatility allowed the team to present an impressive amount of topical material: the TVA and

WPA, Tennessee Governor Browning, upcoming fiddling contests and "Radio Jamboree" tours, the 1936 Texas Centennial—even down to specific personalities and issues geared to an annual meeting of life insurance office managers (LOMA). Bands that Sarie & Sally toured with, such as the Golden West Cowboys and the Dixieliners, as well as Opry personalities like David Stone and Judge Hay, made their way into sketches. Occasionally the sisters would sing a verse or two of "Careless Love" and would often discuss the pros and cons of buying a radio. Sarie, after all, came from a family of music lovers; "Pa had an ear for music," she noted, "but he got so old en feeble I had to hold his ears whilst he listened."

One of the scripts from 1935 focuses on the Opry and gives a fair sample of the Sarie and Sally technique, as well as a glimpse of the Opry of the time:

SARIE: Here, Sally, push over will you, so I can set here too. My, ain't there a sight ov people gathered here tonight ter see the show?

SALLY: Why shore—and Sarie jist think ov all them whuts a-listenin ter this show ov Lasses en Honey en The Grand Old Opery on the radio.

SARIE: Do ye reckon, Sally?

SALLY: Sarie, this here Satidey night show on WSM is heard en knowed from the big end ov the world ter the little end.

SARIE: Sally, thars the Possum Hunters en thars the Cully Jumpers en thars—

SALLY: Sarie, stop pintin'—you've got the house *full* ov people a gapin' at ye.

SARIE: Well, you're a settin here with your mouth a standin wide open, en ye act like yore neck mout be made ov rubber. Thars Uncle Dave Macon en his little boy.

SALLY: Whur at, Sarie?

SARIE: See that man over thar with the side whiskers en the bunch ov whiskers on his chin?

SALLY: Mercy me, did ye say little boy? Why how big do youngerns grow whur you come from? This boy is a young man, Sarie, en my sakes how he kin pick thet thar guitar.

SARIE: En sing, too, I'm here to speak, but it takes his pa Uncle Dave ter cut the di dos, why, iffen he don't split yore sides thars something wrong with yore funny bone.

SALLY: Sarie, who's the nice man whut blows the horn en wars the big hat?

SARIE: Ah low now his name has slipped my memory, as clean at airy whistle. but I heard em call him The Judge a while ago.

SALLY: Thars the Fruit Jar Drinkers, Sarie.

SARIE: Uh huh. I wisht yore Pa could be here.

SALLY: My Pa hain't nary fruit jar drinker, I'll give ye ter know.

SARIE: Fer ever more, Sally, when oh when did ye ever see sich a big fiddle?

SALLY: Never thet I kin recollect, Sarie. En did ye hear them say thet it was a bull fiddle?

SARIE: A bull fiddle? Well, I reckon thets the vary reason they got all them straps on hit, en got the fiddle buckled down besides.

The sisters' puzzlement over the bass fiddle among George Wilkerson's Fruit Jar Drinkers is revealing. The band had been one of the first on the Opry to use a bass, especially played in the slapped way (as opposed to the bowed bass). A similar fascination with instruments appears in a 1938 skit about the Dixieliners:

SALLY: Them thar McGee fellers air from Tennessee.

SARIE: Shor nuff—ye a speakin now bout Sam en Kirk?

SALLY: Why yas. En say, Sarie, whut about Sam a settin thar a playin music on air guitar made out ov steel?

SARIE: Oh dear lesperdizer, child I heard him say as how it wuz a steel gitter, too, but I hain't believin nary word ov it ter be the pure truth fer steel's too all fired heavy fer one man ter tote by his self, I'd say right flat footed.

SALLY: Ah, me too, but I will say, Sam knowed how ter pick out the sweetest music I ever laid ears to.

SARIE: (laughs) Why, yas, en say the funniest things in the world I do know. I jist set thar em felt shore I'd split my sides a whoopin and yellin.

SALLY: Well, I wisht ye'd tell whut it wus that Kirk wuz a wearin' thar on his stomach, tied with air rope round his neck.

SARIE: Why thet wuz knowed to be air banger, Sallie. En whut did he say bout a havin the compound doubel back?

SALLY: Yas, I berlieve he did speak ov air double back, but that was the name ov the tune he was playin', Sarie.

SARIE: I reckon so, fer he did git his back all ruffled up, I took notice. Oh, hit shore wuz a might fine show ter come off. I had more pleasurement that I ever bargained fer.

SALLY: Ah, happy days me too, Sarie. En do ye reckon Arthur Smith
shore nuff had air live mockin bird, whenever he wuz a playin
"Listen to the Mocking Bird?"
SARIE: Now whut about hit, what about hit? Why hit sounded so true
ter the a beind air mockin bird thet I do berlieve I seed fethers fly
whenever Arthur set his fiddle down.

(Apparently Kirk McGee's banjo tune, which Sarie called "Double
Back," was an original that was not preserved in Kirk's later
repertoire. However, it might also be what Kirk called his new
Gibson banjo with a resonator on the back.)

By 1938 Sarie and Sally were touring constantly with various Opry
bands: the Golden West Cowboys in February and March, the Dixieliners
in the fall, and even Acuff's early band. In April and May they joined up
with one of promoter Larry Sunbrock's package shows, along with Uncle
Dave, Curly Fox, Natchee the Indian, and others. The Dixieliners' tour
starting in October 1938 gives some idea of just how strenuous an Opry
tour of that time could be. Traveling by car, always having to return to
Nashville on Saturday night, the group played Cincinnati on Friday, October 7; returned to Nashville October 8; played a series of dates in Pow-
derly, Fayette, Winfield, Carbon Hill, and Alexander City in Alabama the
week of October 10–14; returned to Nashville; drove north to play at
Evansville, Indiana, on Sunday (October 16); returned to Alabama by
Tuesday, playing as far south as Roanoke on the 20th; returned to the
Opry for a show on the 22nd; then left for a week's work in Roanoke and
Bristol, Virginia, returning again to Nashville on the 29th for the Opry and
three days' rest. The first week in November saw them set out again for
Georgia, and a new cycle.

The pace of touring took its toll; on July 19, 1938, Sally (Mrs. Margaret Waters) fell ill, and Sarie worked as a solo act until October 15. This
was a harbinger of things to come. In January 1939, the team left the Opry
and formed their own touring band, the Cabin Creek Band. This group
consisted of Charles Wigginton (bass), "Smokey Joe" McGee (fiddle), and
Jimmy Widener (guitar and comic role of "Ichobod, the Country
Cousin"). Jimmy Widener, in later years, would become an important session guitar player for Jimmy Dickens and Hank Snow, among others; he
would eventually and tragically become a murder victim in 1973. But in
1939 Sarie & Sally barnstormed with a fervor, freed from the Opry restrictions of returning Saturdays to Nashville. In June and July they went to

Hollywood, where they appeared in the film *In Old Monterey* with Gene Autry and Gabby Hayes; this added even more to their touring appeal. By January 1940, they had joined forces with the Rice Brothers at KWKH in Shreveport, which led to extensive touring in the Arkansas-Louisiana-Texas area. Edna's husband, Rhey Wilson, also began doing some of the promotion during this time, creating a "Dixie Radio Jamboree" package that would bring in a few national stars and augment them with local radio favorites. They left the Rice Brothers after six months, and eventually Margaret's health weakened again. Under the circumstances, the team agreed to split up for good and played their last formal date together on March 29, 1941.

Edna worked as a solo act for WSB in Atlanta for a time, then moved to Gainesville, Florida, where she appeared on WRUF. In 1943 an advertising agency in Memphis made her an offer for radio work there, and she and Rhey journeyed north again for what would be a ten-year stay. Working over WMC, in a variety of both radio and TV formats, Edna created a new character, "Aunt Buny," perhaps less sharp-tongued and more ingratiating than Sarie but just as appealing. Brief stints on the "Ozark Jubilee" and "Louisiana Hayride" followed, but by the 1960s Edna and Rhey had retired to Nashville. Still plagued by ill health, Margaret Waters died on November 2, 1967.

Robert Lunn

The third great Opry comedian of the 1930s was a man known almost exclusively for one song and for his myriad variations on it. He was Robert Lunn, and his piece was "The Talking Blues," an odd hybrid genre that involved talking in a stylized, sing-song way over a simple guitar riff. It was an old form—certainly not original with Lunn—but a wonderfully flexible one that Lunn took to national fame and eventually to its most famous practitioner, Woody Guthrie.

Lunn was born Robert Rainey Lunn in 1912 in Franklin, Tennessee, the little town south of Nashville that had been home to the McGee Brothers. He spent his youth in vaudeville, where he used his left-handed guitar playing and average singing voice to develop a fine sense of showmanship and timing. He also developed skills as an imitator and ventriloquist. In the early 1930s he, like many other ex-vaudevillians, moved to radio, working first over WCHS (Charleston, West Virginia) and KWTO (Springfield, Missouri) before coming to Nashville. (His original Opry tenure began in March 1934 and continued through June 1938.)

By this time he had learned a version of what was then called "The Original Talking Blues." It was a series of free-floating stanzas, some from black tradition, that were casually strung together and always began:

> If you want to get to Heaven, let me tell you how to do it,
> Grease your feet with a little mutton suet,
> Fan right out of the devil's hands,
> And fly right over to the promised land.
> Go easy.
> Make it easy.
> Go greasy.

Later on, the subject invariably turned to chickens:

> Behind the henhouse on my knees,
> I thought I heard a chicken sneeze,
> It was only a rooster saying his prayers.
> And giving out hymns for the hens upstairs.
> Such preaching.
> Hens a-singing,
> Roosters praying.

As far as we know, the song in this form had originated with a South Carolina singer and comedian named Chris Bouchillon. In 1926 he and his brothers, who worked as a string band called the Bouchillon Trio, traveled to Atlanta to record some of their work for the Columbia Record Company. According to Frank Walker, the executive in charge of the session, Bouchillon tried to sing the "Blues" but had a horrible voice. Walker finally asked that his brother strum the guitar and that Chris just sort of talk the lyrics. According to the Bouchillon family and friends, Chris had already been "talking" the piece for several years before the session. Whatever the case, the Columbia record featuring it became a runaway bestseller, finally topping out at over ninety thousand copies and carrying the song and the form all over the South. (It also led to a series of other "Talking Blues" records for Bouchillon.) Chris never sought to capitalize on his fame and to try his luck as a professional musician. Rather, he spent much of his life working in an iron foundry and later running a dry cleaning shop. He probably never knew how far afield his record traveled. In 1927 the folksong collector Ethel Park Richardson found and printed a version of "Talking Blues" in her book *American Mountain Songs*. She said she had gotten this version from Gid Tanner, the leader of the Skillet Lickers. Thus, between the record and the book, it was easy to imagine the "Talking Blues" being circulated rather widely.

I have been unable to learn if Lunn ever met Bouchillon in person, but he almost certainly knew his record. When he arrived in Nashville in the early 1930s, he got a job at the plush Hermitage Hotel. This was a showplace of downtown Nashville, where most of the music and radio executives stayed and which later bore on its wall pictures of visiting dignitaries; one was a photo showing Gene Autry at the registration desk. When Lunn went to work there, the hotel had its own little low-watt radio station that piped music into the guest rooms. Lunn began performing live on this station and featuring his "Talking Blues." Someone from the Opry happened to hear him and invited him to perform on the WSM show on Saturday nights. Lunn's odd patter attracted listeners and mail, and he soon found himself billed as "The Talking Blues Man." Before long he also had a sponsored slot, courtesy of Clark's Teaberry Chewing Gum.

For several years Lunn would perform his "Talking Blues," building on Bouchillon's original verses and adding new ones—some traditional "floating" verses based on old songs and dance calls, some totally original, quite a few about current events. This reached the point where Lunn had over a hundred verses in his repertoire. The fans loved it. In 1936 Lunn was voted the most popular performer on the Opry, and—it was said—seven extra people had to be hired to take care of his fan mail. (One letter was from a young man named Roy Acuff asking for a job with Lunn.) Lunn also toured widely with various touring Opry shows. Oddly, he never got around to recording his "Talking Blues" during his heyday with the Opry. He finally did it in the early 1950s, when he cut it for Mercury. He did publish the song in a 1942 song folio devoted to Opry songs, and he filed a separate copyright on it. In 1943, while he was in the service, Lunn composed an equally popular sequel called "Military Talking Blues." Like most other talking blues stanzas, it was part satire, part social protest—in this case, against the lockstep discipline of Army barracks life. After the war, Lunn returned to the Opry, doing comedy for Roy Acuff's tours and watching his son (a good guitarist) perform with several Opry groups. He retired in 1958.

Not only did Lunn's weekly broadcasts help spread the "Talking Blues," but a number of his contemporaries did record it. Curly Fox made his version for Decca, harmonica player Lonnie Glosson for Sears'

Conqueror label, Bill Gatin for Decca, and the Prairie Ramblers (as "Go Easy Blues") for Bluebird—just to name a few. Some later performers, like Tex Williams ("Smoke! Smoke! Smoke! That Cigarette"), developed the talking blues form into a sort of country "patter" song, a la Phil Harris. As early as 1938 a young Woody Guthrie had borrowed the form for his "Talking Dust Bowl," beginning yet another track for the style, one that would lead into the folk music movement of the 1940s and 1950s. It all added up to an impressive progeny for such a modest little song.

26. Uncle Dave Macon in his first publicity photo, taken in 1925 when he was playing his first shows for the Loew's theaters. He would soon abandon the rube-like straw hat.

27. Uncle Dave Macon relaxes with the Delmore Brothers, Rabon *(left)* and Alton *(right)*.

28. The 1931 RKO tour group. *Standing from left*: Kirk McGee, Dr. Bate, Dorris Macon, Buster Bate, Alcyone Bate, and Lou Hesson. *Seated*: Sam McGee (with new banjo-guitar), and Uncle Dave Macon.

29. "Talking Blues" man Robert Lunn, ca. 1934.

30. By the time of this 1934 photograph, most of the Opry cast had donned overalls and bandannas. *Bottom row, from left:* Buster Bate (with tiple), Claude Lampley, Howard Ragsdale, Tom Leffew, George Wilkerson, Charley Arrington, Tom Andrews, and Gail and Amos Binkley. *Second row, from left:* Oscar Stone, Oscar Albright, Dr. Bate, Walter Liggett, Dorris Macon, Uncle Dave Macon, Paul Warmack, Roy Hardison,

and Bert Hutcherson. *Third row (standing), from left:* David Stone, Herman Crook, Kirk McGee, Arthur Smith, Sam McGee, Robert Lunn, Bill Etter, Staley Walton, and George D. Hay. *Fourth row, from left:* Blythe Poteet, Alton and Rabon Delmore, Lewis Crook, Dee Simmons, Nap Bastien, and DeFord Bailey.

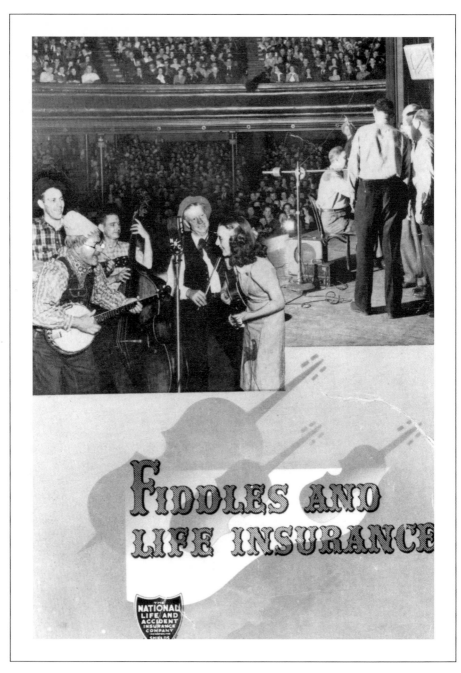

31. In late 1936, National Life issued this giveaway booklet, featuring Opry photos and insurance pitches; later editions appeared through the 1940s. Visible on the cover are the Possum Hunters, led by fiddler Oscar Stone.

32. One of the few surviving pictures of the old Dixie Tabernacle on Fatherland Street in East Nashville, ca. 1935.

33. Sarie and Sally do one of their telephone routines.

34. Lasses and Honey, from a 1933 publicity book.

35. The Binkley Brothers Dixie Clodhoppers, the first band to release a commercial record from Nashville. Amos is on banjo, Gail on fiddle, and Tom Andrews on guitar. Mandolin player Elmer Simpson filled in part-time.

36. The Gully Jumpers: *from left,* Bert Hutcherson, Roy Hardison, Charley Arrington, and Paul Warmack.

37. Crook Brothers Band, in a 1933 publicity shot from a rural Middle Tennessee mill. Herman (harmonica) and Lewis (banjo) sit on the top, with *(from left)* Blythe Poteet, Kirk McGee, and Bill Etter, *below.* An anonymous youngster in overalls watches from behind the car.

38. Theron Hale and daughters Mamie Ruth, *left,* and Elizabeth, *right.*

39. This famous 1934 pose of the Dixieliners was literally shot in a pig pen (part of the pig is visible at the far left). Fiddler Arthur Smith felt embarrassed and demeaned by the pose.

40. Little Jimmie Sizemore, in a bow tie and a shiny satin costume.

41. The Missouri Mountaineers, ca. 1938. *From left:* Fiddlin' Arthur Smith, Jack Shook, Nap Bastien, Dee Simmons, and Bobby Castleman.

42. Pee Wee King's Golden West Cowboys, 1938. *Standing from left:* Curley Rhodes, Cowboy Jack Skaggs, and Abner Sims. *Seated from left:* Pee Wee King, Texas Daisy, and Milton Estes.

43. This early photograph of the Bill Monroe band in the War Memorial Auditorium includes "Cousin Wilbur" (Bill Wesbrooks), bass, fiddler Art Wooten, Monroe, and Clyde Moody (mandolin).

44. Photograph taken from backstage at the War Memorial Auditorium, 1939. Visible are Roy Acuff, at the microphone, with Brother Oswald playing the dobro.

45. Judge Hay, about 1939, with his trusty cigar and
steamboat whistle, "Hushpuckena."

46. Bidding farewell in the *Grand Ole Opry* movie are Roy Acuff's Smoky Mountain Boys: Lonnie Wilson, Jess Easterday, Acuff, Rachel Veach, and Brother Oswald (Pete Kirby).

September Song
The Late 1930s

O N MARCH 5, 1938, GEORGE D. HAY returned to work at
his office at WSM. He had been gone some fourteen months,
since December 1936, the result of a recurrent and debilitating
nervous problem that had often left him exhausted. He had used the time
to try to relax, to visit some of his relatives in Indiana, and to sketch out
some new ideas for the Opry. Though he was only forty-three that year, he
seemed to be struggling with a mid-life crisis, with the continued growth
of his show and with the emergence of WSM into a national powerhouse.

By most accounts, Hay was a rather high-strung and creative type to
start with, and this was complicated by his health problems. He also had
a vision problem, and only a few close friends knew he had to wear special thick-lens eyeglasses. His job had been stressful from the start. His
daughter Margaret remembers growing up in Nashville and having to deal
with prejudice on the part of her classmates; "until I was in high school,
my schoolmates delighted in calling me 'Hayseed.'" As Hay tried to take
his place in the Nashville business community, he too felt this pressure.
"As a member of the local Rotary Club," she recalled, "my father would
lament after the Tuesday luncheon of chicken à la king and green peas that,
with smiles and snickers and some not-so-polite innuendoes, he was made
to feel a pariah in desperate need of a good Samaritan. . . . We were
socially neither fish nor fowl." Even the simple job of getting around
Nashville was a problem, especially on days when the Opry was broadcast.
"With no car, father left on the bus early Saturday afternoon to get the

Opry boys ready for the show. After midnight he would come home on the last bus from town, exhausted and wrung out from his four-hour stint of announcing, welcoming people who wanted to shake his hand, and comforting the Opry performers who invariably had personal problems to be solved." Small wonder that by the end of 1936 the pressure was beginning to show.

During Hay's absence, station manager Harry Stone had continued to "professionalize" the show, and now Hay was able to see up close a number of key changes that had transpired during the previous fourteen months. A 1937 press release announced that the cast of the Opry now numbered some fifty individuals, which translated into about twenty regular acts or bands. This was an impressive growth since 1930, when the show had only twelve regular acts, or even since 1935, when it had only sixteen acts. By now these acts were drawing about 325,000 letters a year, and the live shows, in spite of the fact that National Life was now charging 25 cents a head, were attracting visitors from a dozen states. In June 1936 the show had moved from the Hillsboro Theater, with its capacity of 2,400, to the Dixie Tabernacle on Fatherland Street in East Nashville.

The Tabernacle, which would remain the Opry home until it moved to the War Memorial Auditorium in July 1939, was not as classy as the Hillsboro Theater but could hold as many as four thousand fans on a good night. It resembled, as much as anything, an oversized horse barn. The floor was sawdust and the seats were long, splinter-filled slat benches. Unpainted rafters framed the roof overhead, and roughhewn support poles interrupted the line of sight at frequent intervals. On hot summer nights, the sides of the building could be "rolled up," letting in cool air and breezes but letting the boisterous crowd applause echo out across the otherwise peaceful residential neighborhood. Loudspeakers were mounted on top of the stage, and the permanent stage set itself featured a backdrop of the interior of a log cabin with a huge stylized fireplace, replete with mantle and old clock, in the center. Photos of the time show an audience comprised of both young and old, with some of them actually in the process of disembarking from flatbed cattle trucks.

Stone and Hay had very real and substantial differences in musical taste, but during the fourteen months Hay had been gone, Stone had added only a few acts to the show: the Lakeland Sisters, who joined in January 1937; Curly Fox and Texas Ruby, who became regulars in August 1937; the local duo of Leon Cole and Red Hawn in September 1937; and, the most significant of Stone's additions, Pee Wee King's Golden West Cowboys, who came to WSM in June 1937. Barely a month before Hay returned in 1938, Stone had hired the man who would dominate the show for the next decade, Roy Acuff. Hay was not especially fond of either King or Acuff. He constantly quarreled with King over his western swing style and slick presentation, and he had already turned down Acuff because he felt he simply wasn't good enough.

The problem with professionalizing, as both Hay and Stone found out, was that few of the new full-time radio entertainers stayed at a station for much more than a year. This pattern developed because such new professionals had to supplement their radio salaries with constant touring. In a time of narrow roads and uncomfortable cars, the range of such touring was limited to a radius of about a hundred miles from the station, making it easy to "play out" a territory, touring so often that fans tired of seeing the show. This was starting to become a problem for the Opry acts as well.

But within a few months of Hay's return in 1938, an unusual number of Opry acts left, including several that had been around for some time. The Vagabonds left in June, though members of the band resurfaced in other groups. The Delmore Brothers left in September, ending a five-year stint. "Talking Blues" man Robert Lunn left just weeks after Hay came back, in March; he had been one of the most regular performers of the decade. The Lakeland Sisters ended their brief stay in June, as did Leon Cole and Red Hawn. Just why this dramatic emigration took place is not clear, but Stone and Hay at once set out to fill in the ranks. In April they hired the Tennessee Valley Boys, a new "southeastern swing" band headed by Herald Goodman, formerly of the Vagabonds. Recording for Bluebird in 1938, they featured numbers like "The Great Shining Light" and "New Lamplighting Time in the Valley," and for a time included Arthur Smith on fiddle. In October the show hired the Hilltop Harmonizers, a West Virginia band now headed by another ex-Vagabond, Curt Poulton. This band, which featured smooth harmony singing and even an occasional organ accompaniment, was originally from Ashland, Kentucky, and had earlier played on the *Village Barn Dance*, over network radio in New York. Their personnel included Big Foot Keaton, Bob Shortridge, and Curley Wellman, in addition to Poulton. This band, at least the edition heard on the Opry, apparently never recorded, and by May of 1939 both the Tennessee Valley Boys and the Hilltop Harmonizers had left for KVOO in Tulsa.

To replace the popular Delmore Brothers, Hay and Stone took the advice of promoter J. L. Frank, who by now was working both with Acuff and the Golden West Cowboys, and hired the Andrews Brothers in early 1939. The brothers, James (twenty-four, born in Elkmont, Alabama) and Floyd (twenty-five, born in Milton, Tennessee), like the Delmores, had come to Nashville from Alabama. They were taught music by their mother, who played the organ and had a solid grounding in church music. "Both boys know hundreds of old-time songs, and expect to write songs while doing radio work," stated a press release of the time. (Floyd's full name was Joshua Floyd Bucy, suggesting he was in fact a half brother to James.) Their first and only recording session (they are not the same Andrews Brothers that later recorded for MGM) was for ARC in Memphis in July 1939, and the songs from that session seem to be Delmore-styled: "Filling Station Blues," "Far Away from My Old Virginia Home," "Mother's Gone from the Cabin," "West Virginia Railroad Blues," "Mother Watch O'er and Guide Me," and others. With them on the session was the fiddle player Slim Smith, who had also recently joined the show.

Hay's main duty after he returned continued to be announcing for the Opry, a job which he took very seriously and for which he often carefully scripted. And though Harry Stone continued to serve as general manager of the station and to make the ultimate decisions about the Opry, Hay's influence remained important. (By then, Stone's brother David was also serving as an announcer and running the Artists Service Bureau for the show.) But Hay also had new responsibilities as well. One was to organize and maintain the station's Audience Relations Department, which meant generating publicity and press releases and dealing with the hundreds of letters that were now coming in. He also started a show of his own called "Strictly Personal," in which he dealt with questions from fans (though, as he explained, "the more personal types will be accorded written replies.") The show was so successful that Hay was soon doing a printed column of the same name for the monthly magazine *Rural Radio*, which began in Nashville in 1938. Sometimes Hay used the column to criticize Southern radio's direction, as he saw it. In the March 1939 issue, for instance, he railed against the rise of "experts" in modern society and noted that "we have been in the newspaper and radio business for about twenty years, but we do know that our business could stand a few broadcasters and a few less experts." Did the "experts" at WSM include people like Harry Stone, who was more interested in making money than he was in celebrating Southern culture?

By the end of the 1930s, radio stations were proliferating all over the South. While few stations matched WSM's 50,000 watts of clear channel, the new Crosley operation in Cincinnati took to the air at an incredible 500,000 watts. Then there were the illegal "border stations" like XERA across the Rio Grande from Del Rio, Texas, which would brazenly shoot their unregulated 500,000-plus watts signal across the border and throughout the United States. Not surprisingly, one of the first features in *Rural Radio* was a strident piece called "Menace from Mexico!" advising listeners that "the proper treatment" for such broadcasts "is quite simple—turn the radio dial to decent programs from American stations" (March 1938, p. 8). But WSM took other measures as well. On May 16, 1938, it petitioned the FCC for permission to boost its own power to 500,000 watts. The request was apparently rejected. Nevertheless, in its self-promotions the station continued to emphasize the "world's tallest tower" at its site in Brentwood and encouraged its engineers to wet down the ground around the transmitter to improve its signal strength. Generally, it worked. When Roy Acuff joined the show, WSM's signal strength impressed him: "When I came here, I realized this was different. It was like a network show. Because of our 50,000 watt clear channel, we were covering everything from the Rocky Mountains to Maine, and from Canada into the islands off the Florida coast. We almost blanketed the country, especially late at night."

The Artists Service Bureau, the Opry's own booking agency, was now under the direction of David Stone and was expanding dramatically to meet the needs of the new professional groups. By early 1940 it had scheduled appearances by Opry members in fifteen states and more than 2,500 cities and towns; certain regions were so popular that Stone set up local representatives in them. These included North Carolina (Charlotte, Stokesdale, and Valdese), West Virginia (Williamson), Florida (Red Bay), and Arkansas (Newport). Demographic maps appearing in *Broadcasting* magazine from this time also show heavy Opry traffic in Western Kentucky, northern and extreme southern Alabama, the Appalachian corridor centering on Bluefield, West Virginia, as well as scattered pockets in Mississippi, Florida, Georgia, Pennsylvania, and New York. By now Opry tours were package deals with two or three stars, one big one like Uncle Dave or the Delmores paired with a newer one like Roy Acuff or the Andrews Brothers. The WSM bureau used its contacts to set the bookings. Often these were done in theaters, in conjunction with feature films. The bureau provided posters and even planted newspaper stories, and in some cases even made short movie trailers. Usually one of the announcers, sometimes David Stone, went along to act as a master of ceremonies. And for all this, the Opry took 15 percent of the gate receipts. It was not a bad deal by modern standards, but for artists who had been used to booking their own shows and keeping all the receipts, it could seem extravagant.

By now the Opry had no trouble finding sponsors for its radio show. By the end of 1939, it was selling the "prime time" segments of the show from 8:00 to 10:00 P.M. only in units of thirty minutes, at flat rates of $350 each. A half hour after 11:00 could be had for $150, and quarter-hour segments between 10:00 and midnight started at $100. Some of the sponsors who were regular clients of the Opry still suggested a rural complexion to the audience. Both Allis-Chalmers and International Harvester, tractor giants from the Midwest, were regulars, as were companies like Penn Tobacco Company, the R. J. Reynolds Tobacco Company (Prince Albert), and the American Snuff Company. Though Carter's Chickery apparently did not try to sell baby chicks by mail, it did offer one week on the Opry a premium of a cardboard baby chick feeder and were deluged with over 7,000 requests. More mainstream were Ludens (makers of the cough drops), *Household Magazine*, and the Akron Lamp Company. A match company offered a sheet of words to a popular new song if listeners would send in two "proofs of purchase"; as many as 4,400 wrappers came in one week. A WSM advertisers' brochure for the time put it eloquently: "The homespun voice of America speaking to the homespun heart of America, through radio."

By now WSM was starting to send regular live mainstream programs to the NBC network. Jack Stapp, a former CBS executive from New York, had arrived to take a job as second in command to Harry Stone. A native of Atlanta, he saw the chance to sell Southern pop culture to the networks through his old contacts, especially those at NBC. The big WSM studio band of veteran band leader Francis Craig was often heard over the network from WSM. Craig had appeared on the station's premier broadcast back in 1925. By 1938 he had a big band, replete with string section, and vocalists like young Dinah Shore. (He also had the station's second African American performer, in addition to DeFord Bailey. This was a diminutive teenager named Pee Wee, who dressed in a brass-button uniform and cap, played the mandolin, and danced as part of Craig's act.) A regular dramatic show that made the networks was "Adventures that Made America," featuring the veteran Broadway actor Lark Taylor, "dean of the WSM drama corps." Regular programs by the Fisk Jubilee Singers were also picked up by NBC, and by 1939 WSM had begun to experiment with live "remotes" from the field. These ranged from one of the last wild boar hunts (from Tellico Plains, Tennessee) to the Atlanta premier of *Gone with the Wind*—replete with the applause of the first audience and interviews with Clark Gable and Margaret Mitchell. WSM won national recognition and goodwill in early 1937 when, after the Ohio River flooded much of the upland South, the station turned over its facilities to sister station WHAS in Louisville to relay emergency information and warnings.

As WSM became more powerful and able to generate its own income, the relationship between it and its parent, National Life and Accident Insurance Company, Inc., started becoming more complex. As late as 1937, tickets to the Opry were still available from the local National Life "Shield Man" at no cost, a sort of ingratiating perk. But starting in 1938, when the show began to make tickets more widely available for a small charge, this began to loom less important. By now, too, surveys had shown that as many as one third of the audience was coming from "other cities and states," increasing the advantage "Shield" men had for using the Opry to sell insurance. While some agents still introduced themselves to rural customers as being from "the Grand Ole Opry Insurance Company," others were as quick to point out to urban clients that they were from National Life, "Owners and Operators of Radio Station WSM." The various WSM promotional publications from this era are also revealing. Unlike their rival WLS in Chicago, who published a handsome monthly magazine called *Stand By!* devoted to their radio personalities, WSM was content to issue a few irregular editions of a publication called *WSM Radio News*. Heavy on photos about the Opry, the *News* also gave a lot of its space to trumpeting the general activities of the station and its non-Opry personnel. Copies were distributed free through local insurance agents, and though the Opry photos were sprinkled with references like "The Grand Ole Opry, broadcast by WSM, the station of the National Life and Accident Insurance Company," the *News* offered only one page of out-and-out advertising for the insurance company. Later in the 1930s the company issued a different sort of pamphlet, *Fiddles and Life Insurance*, that was a basic picture book of the Opry, replete with plugs for the insurance company. WSM for a time did run a radio show called "The Story of the Shield," which dramatized accounts of people being saved through good insurance, but to what extent the company actually advertised on the Opry is not clear.

This, then, was the general setting George Hay found when he returned to work on March 5, 1938. WSM's cross-town rival, WLAC, the CBS affiliate, had more or less given up trying to compete with the Opry and WSM's hold on country music. While WLAC featured bands like the Arizona Ranch Riders for the early morning shows, and a Hawaiian trio called the Rhythm Boys on other occasions, their big musical stars were hooked down from the CBS network: Benny Goodman, Guy Lombardo, Paul Whiteman, Deanna Durbin. WLAC's handout books were printed on heavy, quality paper, with elaborate photos headlined "The Athens of the South." Most of their local staff musicians had formal and classical training: Charles Nagy, from New Jersey, was the station's Musical Director and was described as "definitely temperamental." Unlike WSM's Francis Craig, Nagy and the WLAC band preferred "sweet music." By 1939 WLAC seemed to be appealing to the kind of "blue-hair," old-line Nashville that WSM had originally courted.

On the night Hay returned, the Opry featured sixteen acts. The Possum Hunters, carrying on without Dr. Bate, still opened the show promptly at 8:00 with "There'll Be a Hot Time in the Old Town Tonight." Then came the new hot band, the Golden West Cowboys, followed by the Delmore Brothers, the Missouri Mountaineers, the Vagabonds, Uncle Dave Macon, the Gully Jumpers, the Lakeland Sisters, the Fruit Jar Drinkers, Sarie & Sallie, DeFord Bailey, the Crook Brothers, Robert Lunn, Sam and Kirk McGee, Leon Cole and Red Hawn, and the new singer Roy Acuff. Hay must have been gratified to realize that no fewer than eight of the acts were veterans from the earliest days of the show in the 1920s. Most of his beloved hoedown bands were still in place, as well as pioneers like Uncle Dave and DeFord Bailey. Considering the dramatic way country music had changed in the 1930s, with the advent of western swing and country crooners, this was remarkable. In fact, the only real breaks from the classic tradition were the western swing sounds of the Golden West Cowboys and the Missouri Mountaineers (they alone featured an accordion in their bands), and the eclectic repertoire of Roy Acuff.

The Missouri Mountaineers

The Missouri Mountaineers, in fact, had emerged as the show's single most popular band in the late 1930s. The group first appeared in the radio listings on February 2, 1935, and continued to appear on virtually every program through the end of 1939, a record no other group of the time could match. The founder of the band was a versatile left-handed guitar player and singer named Jack Shook. Like many of the newer musicians, he was not a Southerner, hailing from Decatur, Illinois (born September 11, 1910; died September 23, 1986). Starting in radio when he was only fifteen, he had appeared on stations KMOX and WHO, among others, before coming to WSM. He also worked for a time with popular singer Kate Smith on the Columbia network out of New York. By the time he organized the Missouri Mountaineers, he had married and was writing songs in the mold of the then-popular Sons of the Pioneers.

Alcyone Bate Beasley once described the Mountaineers as a "sort of Sons of the Pioneers group" that was built around the smooth trio singing of Shook, bass player Nap Bastien, and second guitarist Dee Simmons. Rounding out the group was an accordion player—at first Elbert McEwen, then later Bobby Castleman—and a fantastic fiddle player, Mac McGarr. McGarr was a native of the same region of southern Kentucky that had produced such masters as western swing star Cliff Gross and Prairie Ramblers mainstay Tex Atchison. He was one of the fastest, most dextrous fiddlers in radio. It was he who kicked off the famous theme of the Mountaineers, "Up Jumped Trouble," a piece that would enter the repertoires of fiddlers throughout the South. (Though McGarr would be replaced by Arthur Smith for a time in the late 1930s, he would continue to perform on the Opry throughout the 1940s, often leading the house band and generally serving as a dependable utility infielder.)

Though the Mountaineers were heard on the Opry consistently from 1935 through 1939, almost every week, very little has ever been written about them. They remain the most unsung and unappreciated band of the early years. Why? One reason is that they never recorded commercially, and even today we have little idea of how they actually sounded. On a handful of air checks made by a fan in Virginia, they do pieces like Carson Robison's "Open Up Dem Pearly Gates" and "Arkansas Traveller," as well as breakdowns like "Alabama Gal." The performances are driving and spirited, full of zest and good humor. Another reason for their underappreciation is that the band apparently did not tour much, possibly because some of them were working as regular WSM staff musicians. Shook himself worked with Nap Bastian and Dee Simmons, along with a series of female singers, as Betty and the Dixie Dons, a pop singing group that did soft, moody songs on weekdays.

In later years, Shook continued to work at WSM, often appearing with one of the early morning staff bands that worked WSM's TV shows. He also became one of the city's first studio session men, playing rhythm guitar for greats such as Chet Atkins and Hank Williams. He died September 23, 1987, in Nashville, never really receiving full credit for his Missouri Mountaineers and how they came to be.

The Golden West Cowboys

The most flamboyant and sophisticated of the new bands that had arrived during Hay's sabbatical was the one led by the accordion player Pee Wee King. In later years, they would be known as Pee Wee King and His Golden West Cowboys, but in the original Opry tenure they were called simply the Golden West Cowboys. Their story started on Easter weekend in 1937, shortly after the great floods hit the Ohio basin and WSM loaned its transmitting facilities to Louisville's WHAS. "We had been playing over WHAS in Louisville," recalled Pee Wee. "Our manager J. L. Frank said, 'Let's go to the Opry and audition.' We played a theater at Horse Cave, Kentucky, on Friday, and on Saturday we drove on down to Nashville, to WSM. At 11 o'clock that morning we auditioned for David Stone and Harry Stone and an engineer named Percy White. And they said, 'Gee, why don't you just stay over and do the Grand Ole Opry with us tonight?' So we did the Opry that Saturday night, then we went back to Louisville, knowing that in two weeks we were coming back as permanent members of the Opry." The first time the Cowboys appeared in the formal Opry radio listings was June 26, 1937.

The Golden West Cowboys that spring had six members, large for an Opry band. Pee Wee King was, of course, the leader and accordion player but did not act as master of ceremonies because his Northern accent was hard for his audience to follow. He left the emcee work to guitarist-banjoist-singer Milton Estes: "Milt had one of those heavy Georgia-Alabama country accents, and that's what we needed," Pee Wee recalled. On the fiddle was Abner Sims, from Corydon, Indiana, a typical radio fiddler with blazing speed and a taste for western swing. Doing a lot of the lead singing was "Cowboy Jack" Skaggs, from Brownsville, Kentucky, and the comedy and bass work was handled by Curley Rhodes (from Wisconsin) and his sister, Texas Daisy, who yodeled and sang cowboy songs. The band soon had regular Opry slots at 9:30 and 11:00 P.M., as well as a 6:30 A.M. morning program.

What did the Golden West Cowboys bring to the Opry? King himself insists it was organization. "Most of them on the Opry were farmers and had jobs and did this on a Saturday night only. We were trying to make a living in the music business. We knew studio work because of our radio work. There was no hesitation, no drawn-out pauses between our tunes. We knew what we were doing because we were organized. We opened up with a novelty tune, followed it with a ballad, came back with a duet, maybe a trio, then a triple yodel, then came back with an instrumental, then a sacred number—we already had our package together." Drawing on their vaudeville experience, the band showed the Opry how to use "play-on music" to introduce a performer and "chasers" to dramatize a singer leaving the stage. Common enough today both on the Opry and other variety shows, this was quite a novelty for the Opry in 1937. The Golden West Cowboys also dressed to kill. They were not the first band to dress in coordinated costumes, as some have claimed, for earlier bands like those of

Zeke Clements and the Missouri Mountaineers had wowed crowds with their costumes. Nor were they the first western act on the show, as some have claimed. As early as 1930 a group called the Oklahoma Cowboys, headed by Ken Hackley, did a short stint on the show. And in September 1934 Zeke Clements brought his western band, the Bronco Busters, to the show. A press release of the time noted: "Featured with Zeke is Texas Ruby, a lady with a bass voice, and three gentlemen who left their ponies to plunk a guitar. The Bronco Busters feature western folk songs and a few of the hillbilly tunes." In January 1937, the Lakeland Sisters joined the show for an eighteen-month run. They wore leather vests, fringed dresses, stylish cowboy hats, and seemed destined to be the Opry's answer to WLS's popular Girls of the Golden West. One of the sisters played a Hawaiian-style guitar, and one a standard. With such acts in its history, the Opry provided an established slot for a fancy-dressing western act by the time King and his crew came on board.

And the Golden West Cowboys did look sharp and sought to project what King called "a good image. Not only do you do the radio show, you pleased people in the audience, and we were conscious of it both ways: radio and visual-wise." The band also brought down two other innovations: they were among the first of the Opry cast to join the musicians' union, and they brought with them their own booking agency in the person of King's father-in-law, J. L. Frank. Frank was an innovative promoter and booker who had good contacts on the national music scene; they were, in fact, good enough that barely a year after the band joined the Opry it was in Hollywood making a film with Gene Autry. (The band and its Opry base impressed Hollywood enough that the Republic studio bosses began to think seriously about a film that would feature the Opry itself.)

Though some of the new Opry stars were now coming from the Midwest, none had come from quite as far away as had Pee Wee King. Though he would later be associated with Kentucky, he was born and reared in the middle of the rich dairy country around Abrams, Wisconsin. His given name was Frank Kuczynski, and his Polish-American father led a local polka band. Young Frank soon had his own accordion and was leading his own radio band when cowboy star Gene Autry hired him to be his backup group on WLS's *National Barn Dance*. Autry one day dubbed him "Pee Wee" and approved when Frank decided to change his last name to King (in honor of the waltz specialist Wayne King). After Autry left to make films in Hollywood, Pee Wee reformed his band, calling it the Golden West Cowboys. (He chose this name, he recalls, because he "had a crush" on the popular WLS duo the Girls of the Golden West.) For several months this new band worked over WNOX in Knoxville, WHAS in Loiusville, and then came to the Opry in June 1937.

"Our band," King recalled, "was a melding of many sounds and traditions, but I always thought of the Golden West Cowboys as basically a modern western swing band." He had been fascinated with the sophisticated string band sound that was being generated by Clayton McMichen's Georgia Wildcats, who were King's immediate predecessors on the Opry. (Some feel, in fact, that the Golden West Cowboys were hired to replace McMichen.)

King and his band also emulated Louise Massey and the Westerners, *National Barn Dance* stars, and identified with their hit "My Adobe Hacienda." Both of these bands used carefully arranged twin fiddles, smooth harmony vocals, and a swinging beat that owed more to Benny Goodman than the Skillet Lickers. "McMichen had a fine band," King remembered. "They were the Glenn Miller of the country music field." As for the Westerners: "We copied the Westerners. I figured . . . we could pattern ourselves in the western mold that way; we wouldn't have too much trouble getting bookings. Country music had things to do with events and everyday life and people's feelings. And in Western music we dealt with the atmosphere—the sky, the wind, the ground, the territory, the hills, the prairies." Ironically, though, this groundbreaking band never recorded; in fact, King was not to record commercially until 1945, when the band had become pretty bland and slick. Indeed, Art Satherley, the ARC talent scout, did audition them for a recording session, but demurred. He told King, "I believe what you have is salable, but I already have Bob Wills."

Because of this, it's a little tricky to get a clear picture of exactly what the original Golden West Cowboys sounded like. A handful of home air checks made by fans, though, reveals the band was a lot "hotter" than later incarnations. At the band's core were the driving forces of Curley Rhodes's string bass (Rhodes was by far the most dextrous bassist on the early Opry) and Abner Sims's lightning fiddle. Even Pee Wee himself took wild, exciting solos on the accordion, and sometimes the band played breakdowns for Robert Lunn's dances. They seemed to like show-off solo routines like "Mama Don't Allow It" and Bob Wills's favorites like "Take Me Back to Tulsa." Little Texas Daisy was a fine yodeler who did Jimmie Rodgers songs like "Roll Along Kentucky Moon." Pee Wee and J. L. Frank tried some original songs, such as the gospel pieces "There's a Beautiful, Beautiful Home" (1938), "Singing as I Go" (1938), and "Temple on the Hill." Other singers like Gene Autry, Bill Monroe, and Roy Acuff also recorded some of Pee Wee's original love songs, such as "Darling How Can You Forget So Soon?"

Judge Hay was more than a little alarmed at some of the things he saw happening with the Golden West Cowboys. When he first saw Pee Wee's accordion, he proclaimed, "That's not a country instrument." Pee Wee responded, "It's a Western Instrument and we play Country and Western music." When Frank decided to add a square-dance troupe to perform on stage with the band, Hay at once stopped it, announcing that it was "too modern." With the band scheduling almost nightly personal appearances, they found they had to juggle bookings to make sure they were close enough to Nashville to make the Saturday night Opry. Although the Opry paid them little, the management cut them no slack in being at the Saturday show on time.

In later years Hay and Pee Wee would continue to fuss over things like the use of electric instruments and drums, but each would come to appreciate the other's views. The Golden West Cowboys would become one of the most popular touring bands in Opry history, and Pee Wee would himself come to understand the Opry's concern with tradition. And Judge Hay would in later years admit to Pee Wee that he had been ten years ahead of his time. The Opry had to keep up with the changing face of country music, and Pee Wee helped it do that. But at the same time, Hay and Harry Stone continued to look for new performers who could reinvigorate the classic traditional sound that the show was known for. They were about to find two of the most important in a mountain singer named Roy Acuff and a mandolin player named Bill Monroe.

"The Homespun Voice of America"
Roy Acuff and Bill Monroe

W HETHER OR NOT GEORGE HAY ever actually auditioned Roy Acuff for the Opry is unclear. Acuff's band had been popular over Knoxville radio and had recorded some thirty-four sides for the American Record Company—both impressive credentials for a job on the Opry. Some members of the Acuff band, which then was still going under the name the Crazy Tennesseans, recalled having two "guest shots" on the show sometime in 1937 and Judge Hay offering them a permanent job. The problem with this scenario is that Hay was on his leave then and would not have been present. Acuff himself recalled that Hay refused even to give the band an audition in the earlier months, which nearly caused Acuff to give up hope of a position with WSM. He was planning what he called "a desperate move" to Indianapolis when J. L. Frank intervened. Acuff had met the promoter when the Golden West Cowboys had worked at Knoxville, and had watched with interest as he so readily got the Cowboys on the Opry. Now he leaned on Frank to put in a good word for the Tennesseans, and Frank did talk to David Stone about giving the band a shot. With Hay still away, Stone had free reign and set up a guest appearance for February 5, 1938.

At this time, Roy's main job in the band was as a fiddler. He was an adequate but by no means flashy instrumentalist. Much of the singing was done by Sam "Dynamite" Hatcher and Red Jones, though Acuff had developed a few specialties. That cold February night the show was still being held at the drafty Dixie Tabernacle on Fatherland Street. Acuff recalled how it went: "I was supposed to fiddle, and I did, but not too well. I was nervous. I was excited. But I sang 'The Great Speckled Bird' that night and the mail came in. . . . I went to Knoxville and in two weeks they sent my mail. It came in bushel baskets." But some of the WSM bosses were not so impressed. Hay didn't think much of Acuff's singing or his fiddling. David Cobb, one of the station's new announcers, went to Stone the day after Acuff's tryout. "I sincerely did not want to say anything to hurt Roy's reputation," he recalled. "But I said the sooner he found another way to make a living, the better it would be for him." But David Stone, ever the money man, was impressed with the baskets of mail and sent Acuff a telegram a few days later, asking if he could start work on February 19. When Acuff agreed, Stone sent a follow-up letter explaining that, due to the mail, they had arranged for the band a "commercial spot" on the Opry (for a small salary), as well as an early morning show at 7:00 on Mondays, Wednesdays, and Fridays. Many Opry veterans felt that Acuff's big break came at the expense of Arthur Smith, who was becoming notoriously undependable and who had recently been suspended for failing to show up at a big touring show. In any event, Acuff got on the show, if by the skin of his teeth, and had soon moved into a trailer park in Madison, a hamlet to the north of Nashville.

Acuff's early life has been well documented in various biographies and autobiographies, and little detail needs to be added here. He grew up in the small town of Maynardville, Tennessee, in Union County, about twenty-five miles north of Knoxville. Though he grew up in a rural community, he was not the poor "Smoky Mountain boy" some publicity later made him out to be. His father had attended nearby Carson-Newman College and worked as a part-time lawyer and minister. As a boy doing his chores, Acuff listened to the high, mountain singing of neighbors and friends, learned from his father how to play the fiddle, and attended "singing schools" taught out of the shape-note hymnals. The fiddling especially affected him: it "built something in me that I have never forgotten." He also listened to Victrola records by people like Uncle Am Stuart and the Skillet Lickers, trying to play along, becoming frustrated until he learned that the Victrola had a little screw that altered the rpm of the platter, thus affecting the pitch of the music and the key a fiddle tune was played in. By 1932 Acuff, then almost thirty, made his first professional music when he traveled with a blackface medicine-show tour with a neighbor known as "Doc" Hauer. So while artists like Pee Wee King were playing polkas and pop music from films, Acuff was getting steeped in the authentic folk music traditions of East Tennessee.

Acuff was soon working for square dances and parties with a group of friends that would make up the core of his band: Red Jones, Clell Summey, Jess Easterday, Lonnie Wilson, and Pete (Oswald) Kirby. It was this group that eventually got work over WROL and became known as the Crazy Tennesseans, a band that, in Acuff's terms, "fiddled and starved." It is little wonder that they were eager to get to WSM, and little wonder when Stone and Hay suggested they change their name to the Smoky Mountain Boys. "The name 'Crazy Tennesseans' was disrespectful, sort of like the word *hillbilly*," recalled Acuff. A more likely reason is that the adjective "crazy" was being widely used on radio in those days to denote bands that were working for Crazy Water Crystals, such as the Crazy Hillbillies. No one at the Opry wanted to leave the impression that a WSM act was working exclusively for a patent medicine laxative company and not for the station.

The song that made Acuff, and played such a key role in the Opry of the late 1930s, was "The Great Speckle [*sic*] Bird," as it appeared on Acuff's original recording. The song's popularity spread with quicksilver speed. On April 18, 1938, just two months after Acuff became a regular on the Opry, he got a memo from a WSM secretary: "Roy, will you please let us have a copy of the words to the Great Speckled Bird? Several people have written us wanting them. Please stop by my office sometime soon and give them to us." Acuff's original recording of the song, done in Chicago on October 26, 1936, sold so fast that barely five months later ARC rushed him back into the studio (this time in Birmingham) to record a follow-up or "answer" song to it. This was "Great Speckle Bird #2," cut on March 22, 1937. Rival record companies, sensing one of the hits of a generation, rushed out cover versions: the Morris Brothers did a Bluebird version in the summer of 1937, and Wade Mainer did a version entitled "She is Spreading Her Wings for a Journey" on Bluebird that fall. In 1938 versions appeared by Jack & Leslie (Decca), Roy Hall (Vocalion), and Charlie Monroe (Bluebird and MW). M. M. Cole wasted no time in copyrighting a version on March 30, 1937.

Though it was his career song, "The Great Speckle Bird" had a tangled and complex history that puzzled Acuff himself. He never claimed that he had written it, only that he had gotten it from a man named Charlie Swain, who sang with a quartet called the Black Shirts over the same Knoxville radio station Acuff had been on. He remembered paying Swain a quarter to write down all the words to the piece, and soon Acuff was singing it over the air himself. Though in later years some would claim that the composer was a singing preacher from Missouri named Guy Smith, it seems far more likely that the song originated in a controversial religious movement called the Church of God that was headquartered in Cleveland, Tennessee, about fifty miles south of Knoxville. The Black Shirts quartet were all associated with the church college. In the second stanza of Acuff's recording, he sings that the Great Speckled Bird is the Bible, "representing the great Church of God." Did this refer specifically to the Cleveland-based Church of God, which had come under some stringent criticism? Acuff worried about it and later explained that he took the phrase to mean any church of God, a generic term. But thousands of listeners might well have taken the song as some sort of dogma or propaganda. Whatever the case, it was the song that got Acuff his first recording session (in 1936) and a passport to the Opry. Years later he quipped, "The song brought Roy Acuff to the Opry. I didn't bring it, it brought me."

The band that Acuff brought to the Opry bore little resemblance to the Smoky Mountain Boys of the '40s and '50s. It included Frank "Red" Jones, singer, guitarist, musical arranger, and business manager; Jess Easterday, guitarist and mandolin player; Clell Summey, dobro player; and Roy himself, as fiddler and singer. Shortly after they started on the show, Roy also sent for a girl singer named Tiny (Imogene Sarrett), who had been with the group in their later Knoxville days. With the exception of Tiny and Dynamite Hatcher (who stayed behind in Knoxville), this was essentially the same band that had been together since 1934 and that had recorded the two sessions for the American Record Company. Though the label credits for these records clearly indicated Acuff was the leader ("Roy Acuff and His Crazy Tennesseans"), the records themselves featured different band members: Red Jones and Sam Hatcher on vocals, Clell on dobro, Hatcher on harmonica, and Roy on fiddles and vocals. Hatcher seemed to prefer blues-tinged numbers like "Steamboat Whistle Blues" and "Freight Train Blues." Jones went for the jazzier, more popular songs like "Yes Sir, That's My Baby," "My Gal Sal," "Red Lips," and the Bob Wills piece "Old Fashioned Love." Acuff tended to sing on the more traditional and sentimental pieces, such as "Lonesome Valley," "Charming Betsy," "You're the Only Star in My Blue Heaven," and "Tell Mother I'll Be There."

These early sessions have a quality of split personality to them: modern pop songs jostle next to the older country and mountain favorites. And this split apparently reflected the makeup of the band itself, with Roy and Jess being the defenders of the older style. It did not take Acuff long to figure that with Hay's constant admonition to "keep it down to earth," the Opry and its fans preferred the more traditional sound. Acuff was willing to oblige, especially since his two biggest hits ("Bird" and "Wabash Cannonball") were both traditional. This eventually led to a literal split in the band, and in January 1939 Red Jones, Clell Summey, and Tiny left to pursue their more pop styles in Knoxville. To replace them, Roy got a different group of Knoxville musicians, dobroist Pete (Oswald) Kirby, guitarist Lonnie Wilson, and bass player Jake Tindell. In June 1939 he hired Rachael Veech as a singer and banjoist. She was a cousin of Opry veteran Sam McGee and would later be passed off as Oswald Kirby's sister. In Wilson, Rachael, and Kirby, Acuff had three fine traditional musicians, but also three skilled rustic comedians.

Before he met Fred Rose and began using more new material, Acuff's early repertoire established his reputation and forged his own type of "new traditionalism." He borrowed songs from Uncle Dave Macon ("Coming from the Ball"), the Delmore Brothers ("Beautiful Brown Eyes"), Roy Hall ("Little Pal"), the Carter Family ("Will the Circle Be Unbroken," "Wabash Cannonball,") Smoky Mountain Glen Stagner ("Blue Eyed Darling"), Bill Cox ("Answer to Sparkling Blue Eyes"), Dorsey Dixon ("Wreck on the Highway"), Arthur Smith ("Walking in My Sleep"), the Coon Creek Girls ("Living on the Mountain, Baby Mine"), Jimmie Rodgers ("Mule Skinner Blues"), and Gene Autry ("Be Honest with Me"). His gospel repertoire included numerous songs published by the shape-note gospel publisher W. E. Winsett of Dayton, Tennessee. These included the Thomas Dorsey song "Shake My Mother's Hand for Me," "The Great Judgment Morning," "That Beautiful Picture," and "Precious Jewel." Other songs came from standard sources, such as Stamps-Baxter and Albert E. Brumley. There were also a handful of traditional blues, such as the well-worn bordello song "The Rising Sun" (which Acuff both recorded and put in his first songbook), "Lying Woman Blues," and "K.C. Whistle Blues." Though the bulk of his material was borrowed, about a fourth of the songs in the early recordings and songbooks were Acuff's own. Most were sentimental or gospel pieces like "My Mountain Home Sweet Home," "I'm Building a Home," and "My Radio's Dialed to Heaven On High." But by arranging the borrowed songs, by framing them with the new dobro sound and with Oswald Kirby's high tenor, by delivering them in his own high, passionate voice, Acuff succeeded marvelously in transforming the older tradition that had built the Opry. It is no wonder that bare months after he arrived, he was drawing more mail than anyone else and was attracting thousands on tours.

By October 1939, things were going into high gear at WSM. Through the William Esty advertising agency in New York, and the R. J. Reynolds Tobacco Company (makers of Prince Albert smoking tobacco), the Opry had found a thirty minute slot on the NBC network and was preparing to go nationwide. Through the spring and summer the staff had been fine-tuning the cast in preparation for national exposure. Their major problem was, of course, how to preserve the Opry's distinctive identity while making it slick enough to appeal to a general network audience who were used to Bing Crosby and Benny Goodman. To this end, in November the station signed Ford Rush, another distinctive interpreter of traditional song, whom Judge Hay had worked with at WLS Chicago in 1924 and 1925. But in August the Binkley Brothers Dixie Clodhoppers, one of the veteran hoedown bands, left the show, leaving vacant a key slot for a string band. This was solved in October when a four-piece band from Greenville, South Carolina, showed up for an audition; the leader was a nattily dressed man named Bill Monroe.

Both Hay and Stone had been aware of the spectacular success of Bill and his brother Charlie during the mid-1930s. Their records like "What Would You Give in Exchange for Your Soul" had been the only real rivals to the records by the Delmores, and their radio and touring work throughout the Carolinas had been serious competition for the Artists Service Bureau. Now the Monroes had split up, and each was leading his own band. Bill had finally settled in at WFBC in Greenville but by the middle of 1939 had played out that territory and had decided his band was ready for a run at the Opry. He was full of confidence: "He told me to go back and tell the other boys to get their toothbrushes ready," recalled his guitarist Cleo Davis. "We're going to Nashville," Monroe vowed.

Whether Monroe had been in touch with Stone and Hay, or whether he just showed up out of the blue, is not clear. But years later, Bill Monroe remembered the audition in detail: "Started there in '39, the last Saturday in October in 1939. . . . I went into Nashville on a Monday morning. I'd come from Greenville, South Carolina; I was going to move to some other radio station. I believe that they told me that Wednesday was their day to listen, but they would be back. Judge Hay and Harry Stone and David Stone was all going out to get coffee; as I got off the elevator on the fifth floor they was going out. And they come back and I played 'The Mule Skinner Blues' for them, and 'Bile That Cabbage Down,' 'John Henry,' and another one, and they said I had the music that National Life needed. Said I had more perfect music for the station than any music they'd ever heard. They said, 'If you ever leave the station, you'll have to fire yourself.'"

Bill Monroe's name first appeared in the formal radio listings on October 28, 1939, just two weeks after the show started on the NBC network. Although the Blue Grass Boys were not on the first few network half-hours, barely a month later, on November 25, they were featured as a "guest" on the network portion and were regulars on that portion thereafter. This original band was just four pieces: Monroe on mandolin, guitar, and vocals; Art Wooten on fiddle; Cleo Davis on vocals and guitar; and Amos Garen on upright string bass. Lacking any detailed documentation, determining whether the band impressed more through its instrumentals or Bill's vocals is difficult. His first performance on the show was supposedly his driving version of Jimmie Rodgers's old "Muleskinner Blues," for which he (allegedly) got three encores. In an unpublished memoir, Hay said of Monroe: "He is close-mouthed in his speech but makes up for it when he takes his mandolin in hand and whips it. His voice has a rather plaintive note in it, reminding one of the sound of wind blowing through tall trees."

But Monroe himself emphasized how different the instrumental sound was. His new band, propelled by the string bass and if necessary by two guitars, echoed the breakneck tempos of the Monroe Brothers, who played the fastest turnarounds in the business. And though the band still featured familiar string band fare like "Bile That Cabbage Down," "Katy Hill," and "Columbus Stockade Blues," they recast them in high, difficult, and unusual keys. Monroe recalled: "We pitched the music up where it would do a number some good. If you play in B-natural and sing there and your fiddle is right up there playing where you're at, and the banjo, well, it just makes a different music from where it would be played if it was just drug along in G, C, or D. We was the first outfit to ever play in B-flat or B-natural and E. . . . Fiddle men had a fit and they wouldn't hardly tackle it and they'd swear they wanted to play straight stuff. . . ." While in the Carolinas, Monroe had also been impressed with the strong a cappella black gospel quartet tradition there, and he soon added that to his repertoire. He featured pieces like "Farther Along," "Crying Holy unto the Lord," "Were You There When They Crucified My Lord," "Do You Call That Religion," "Did You Ever Go Sailing?" and "He Will Set Your Fields on Fire" (all preserved on various air checks and home recordings). "There wasn't a quartet on the Grand Ole Opry before us," Monroe felt. That is not quite accurate, but there never had been a quartet styled like the Blue Grass Boys, with fast, intricate, stacked harmony. When Monroe and his band finally got to record, for RCA Victor in October 1940, it is not surprising that the session reflected the kind of mixture described here. Nor was it surprising that by 1940 Monroe was a regular on the network portion of the Opry.

Unlike Acuff, Monroe did not start "booking out" as soon as he had joined the show. He recalled: "We worked on the Grand Ole Opry about ten weeks before they would even try to book me. Our first date was out of Nashville about twenty-five or thirty miles. I remember we taken in forty-five or sixty-five dollars. . . . But you was still getting a small admission fee. And then we started playing in Alabama. Seemed like that was the first state seemed like we could draw good in. And then it went to spreading, you know, into West Virginia and Kentucky, and of course, I held a good standard in the Carolinas." Monroe's new music, eventually to be dubbed "bluegrass" and what Alan Lomax would later call "folk music in overdrive," was another way of refurbishing the older traditions for a new generation. The WSM bosses were right: Bill Monroe did have the kind of music they needed, and though it took him a while to refine it, he eventually settled in as one of the most popular regulars.

For some years the William Esty Agency of New York had been employed by WSM to sell time on the Opry. The station itself had been providing noncountry network feeds since the mid-1930s, and good contacts between Nashville and New York were in place. During the late fall of 1938 Esty added a new sponsor to the Opry, the R. J. Reynolds Tobacco Company, whose Prince Albert smoking tobacco was widely popular through the South. The account executive, Dick Marvin, got interested in the idea of trying to sell Reynolds on sponsoring part of the show on the NBC network. Though his colleagues were skeptical, Marvin pulled it off and announced to Hay and Stone that, starting in October 1939, a limited number (twenty-six) of NBC affiliates would try taking the show. The date for the premiere was set, October 14, 1939. The "limited network" ranged from Virginia to Mexico, and a number of NBC and Esty executives were on hand for the pilot show.

For years, this first show existed only in memories, like the very first WSM opening night show back in 1925. Then, in the 1980s, someone at the Esty agency found in the basement a series of lacquer "airchecks" of the early show's in-house transcription recordings made by WSM to ship to NBC and to Esty. Among them were copies of this first show.

As the feed began, listeners heard the WSM call letters, announced as the station of the National Life and Accident Insurance Company in Nashville, Tennessee, showing that National Life still had a proprietary interest in the show. Then David Stone, who does all the commercials, announced that Prince Albert, "the South's most popular tobacco, presents the South's most popular program, 'The Grand Ole Opry.'" Next Roy Acuff and his band starts playing a theme song, "Have a Big Time Tonight," with customized lyrics to fit Prince Albert. Judge Hay is introduced, and as Acuff fiddles, he explains, "Friends, these are the same people you've been listen-

ing to for fourteen years; the only difference tonight is that they're coming
to you from the Mexican border to the mountains of Virginia. Our show
is ready to ride right down the middle of the road to our friends and neighbors throughout America." Acuff then breaks into a rollicking "shout"
tune, "Ida Red," which features a lot of his own fiddling; though nothing
is made of it, Acuff had recently recorded the piece.

Next comes the first full Prince Albert commercial, explaining how
Prince Albert had been proven to be "cool smoking;" it was recently
involved in a test where a "smoking machine" tested it against thirty other
brands and declared PA the winner. Next Hay introduces Uncle Dave
Macon: "Now here's our Senator from the Cannon County Hills, with his
chin whiskers, gold teeth, gates-ajar collar, old horse and buggy parked out
front, and his son Dorris, Uncle Dave Macon." Macon then proceeds to
sing his autobiographical song, "Cannon County Hills," in which the local
moonshine puts the "bright lights of Broadway to shame." Macon brings
some chuckles from the crowd, but the applause is only average. Now Hay
turns to George Wilkerson and his Fruit Jar Drinkers, one of the original
hoedown bands, and explains, "We're gonna cut a cord of wood right
here." Propelled by a string bass and a tenor-like banjo, the band does "Up
Jumped the Devil." Hay continues: "Now friends we introduce our little
mascot, DeFord Bailey." The harmonica wizard does a creditable job on
one of his signature songs, "Pan American Blues."

There are congratulations and telegrams to acknowledge. Prentice
Cooper, the Governor of Tennessee, is for some reason in Jacksonville,
Florida, and says: "I'm glad this Saturday night program of old fashioned
Southern music will be enjoyed by our folks of so many other states,
through the medium of the NBC network, including states from Virginia
to Texas." Cowboy star Gene Autry writes from Hollywood that he is
"looking forward with much pleasure to the members of this program
coming to Hollywood to appear with me in the Republic picture entitled
'Grand Ole Opry.'" This is curious, since Autry never appeared in the final
picture, though it was in the planning stages. Did a conflict arise? A salary
dispute? Judge Hay seems not too surprised at the announcement and
quips to Gene, "We're ready whenever you are." The most colorful
telegram of the night comes from Congressman Luther Patrick, from Birmingham: "Glory be! the Grand Ole Opry has at last found its place in the
sun and mark my words, brothers, she'll stay thar!"

Roy Acuff returns to sing what Hay calls "one of the most popular
numbers on the Opry," "The Great Speckled Bird." Again, there is only
modest applause. A second Prince Albert commercial explains that the

tobacco is "cooler smoking" because the company uses "crimp cut" and premium tobacco. Uncle Dave returns to do "Nobody's Darling," replete with trills and throat yodeling. Wilkerson's band does a quick "Old Joe Clark," and then Hay brings out DeFord Bailey again. "Come on out here, little DeFord, wake up, son." He plays a subdued "Fox Chase." Then more telegrams: from Republic pictures saying, "May the Grand Ole Opry live for years and years." W. Lee O'Daniel, the governor of Texas and one-time leader of the Light Crust Doughboys, sends regards and says, "I hope when you go to NBC you do not go high-hat but you retain the traditional dignity of the Grand Ole Opry which has so long touched the hearts of millions of us common citizens." Curiously, this proclamation brought the biggest applause of the night. "You needn't worry," Hay adds. "We're gonna keep it just like it is." "It has become a password in almost every home," cabled Tennessee war hero Sgt. Alvin York.

The final few moments of the show move quickly. Brother Oswald and Rachael (by now set up as brother and sister) race through "John Henry," Acuff fiddles his way through "Old Rattler," Uncle Dave and Dorris do a wisecracking and yodeling takeoff on "Away Out on the Mountain," and DeFord returns to do "Evening Prayer Blues," which he had recorded years before. He ends a little early and Judge Hay encourages him: "Keep it up, you're doing fine. Give us a little of that 'Memphis Blues.'" DeFord obliges, and Stone does his final Prince Albert commercial ("PA rolls up easy, too; you get seventy cigarettes in a tin.") The whole cast comes out on stage for a chorus of "Comin' 'Round the Mountain" something akin to the "Walkabout" in old minstrel shows. As they fade out, Stone invites listeners to tune in to other NBC shows, the Benny Goodman program and Bob Crosby and His Bobcats.

Hay later admitted that they had "not attempted to produce the show, in the accepted sense of the word. We had to be snatched off the air at the end of our thirty minutes, but with that exception the half hour went over pretty well." Hay and Stone were probably not quite sure what the network wanted or how much they could rely on national trends. Would the fantastic popularity of the new blockbuster film *Gone with the Wind* presage an interest in the fiddle and banjo music of the Old South? Would the concern over the war in Europe, which had broken out in September, suggest an interest in nostalgia, a desire for simpler times, a new sentimentalism? Was there a huge secret audience out in the rural areas that listened to Benny Goodman and Jack Benny only because nothing else was available to them and who would be eager to embrace a show with more rural, "country" values and traditions? On this first show, Hay and Stone seemed to be trying to cover all their bases. They put the spotlight on their newest star, Roy Acuff, but surrounded him with a sampling of the most traditional acts on the Opry. Macon, Wilkerson, and Bailey had been regulars on the program since its very first year. Conspicuous through their absence were the newer, smoother acts like the Missouri Mountaineers, the Golden West Cowboys, and Zeke Clements. (Bill Monroe had not yet joined the cast at the date of the first show.) This pattern was generally followed during the next several weeks: Acuff, Uncle Dave Macon, one of the hoedown bands—each doing two or even three numbers. DeFord Bailey was soon dropped, replaced by the "citybilly" singing of Ford Rush, whom Hay soon dubbed the High Sheriff. (Rush also took over the Artists Service Bureau when David Stone left shortly after.) Rush did popular cowboy and western songs, such as "Carry Me Back to the Lone Prairie" and "Beautiful Texas," in a smooth, relaxed voice that was quite a change from Acuff's straining mountain style. Other members who got shots on the network portion in late 1939 included Pee Wee King, the McGee Brothers, the Missouri Mountaineers, Bill Monroe, the Stacey Sisters (Nola and Marie), the Delmore Brothers (as special guests), and Robert Lunn. By 1941 Macon had been dropped from the Prince Albert portion, supposedly because non-Southern listeners found it hard to understand what he was singing about, with his strong Tennessee dialect and accent. Hay also found it necessary to work more and more from scripts; he had clearly been ad libbing a lot during the early shows. By 1941 things were sounding much slicker. He was even involving some of the performers in the ads for Prince Albert. In general, the PA segment did become less earthy than the first show, and Hay's concern about preserving the original sound of the Opry was well founded.

That October 14 broadcast was a watershed in many ways, and the start of a number of dramatic changes for the Grand Ole Opry. By 1943 the Prince Albert segment won a slot on the full coast-to-coast NBC network in a hookup that included 125 stations. On June 28, 1940, the Republic film that had been so long in the planning was released nationally under the name *Grand Ole Opry*. It featured Roy Acuff, Judge Hay, and Uncle Dave Macon—along with an old vaudeville team called the Weaver Brothers and Elviry. As World War II began, groups like Pee Wee King's traveled to military bases around the states as part of the Camel Caravan. And though wartime restrictions hobbled commercial recordings, some Opry shows were even recorded off the air and sent around the world on Armed Forces Radio Service transcriptions.

Suddenly the Opry was finding its nationwide audience, and George Hay was seeing his efforts of fifteen years come to fruition. When he had begun it back in the 1920s, Hay had called his creation "a good-natured riot." Now, in 1940, in a brochure designed for potential advertisers, he reflected on how far things had come since then. "The Grand Ole Opry has stood one of the exacting tests . . . Time," he wrote. "It is unique in radio, a strange slice of America—the homespun voice of America speaking to the homespun heart of America, through radio." The Grand Ole Opry was now poised to fulfill the wish of Uncle Jimmy Thompson—to throw its music out across the Americee. And along the way, it would take its place in the mainstream of American popular culture.

Appendix 1
Judge Hay's Valediction

One of the best-remembered features on the early Opry was the colorful, classic rhetoric of Judge Hay as he emceed the show. While the paucity of on-air recordings from the 1930s prevents us from looking at this in detail, many fans remember one feature of the Judge's spiel. This was an odd little poem he recited, usually as a hoedown band was playing the show off the air at the end of the Opry broadcast. It went:

> The tall pines pine,
> The pawpaws pause,
> And the bumble-bee bumbles all day;
> The eavesdropper drops,
> And the grasshopper hops,
> While gently the ole cow slips away.

Though many fans have assumed that Hay wrote the poem, it was in fact the work of a popular late-nineteenth century poet, songwriter, and musician named Ben E. King. He was a native of St. Joseph, Michigan (born 1857), but was living in Bowling Green, Kentucky, when he died suddenly in 1894. He was a child prodigy of sorts, playing the piano and touring, as well as writing songs that became popular, like "The Maiden's Prayer" (not the Bob Wills number but an earlier one that was a sheet music hit) and the sentimental "If I Should Die To-Night."

King also wrote a great amount of popular poetry, much of it about riverboats amd river lore and much of it in an Uncle Remus-like black dialect. Shortly after his death, a friend and singer named Nixon Waterman brought together some of the best work under the title *Ben King's Verse* (1894). The introduction proclaimed that King, "now so suddenly dead, was the drollest mimic and gentlest humorist of our region." The book proved to be immensely popular, running through fourteen editions by 1908.

King's wordplay and sense of style would have appealed to Judge Hay, and since many of his poems had entered the recitation repertoire, it is possible that Hay had learned them from childhood. The poem above is entitled "The Cow Slips Away" and was used as the last poem in the collection. It was probably King's most popular piece of verse, but running a close second was "The Pessimist" or "The Sum of Life," which reads in part:

> Nothing to do but work,
> Nothing to eat but food,
> Nothing to wear but clothes,
> To keep one from going nude.
>
> Nothing to breathe but air,
> Quick as a flash 'tis gone,
> Nothing to fall but off,
> Nowhere to stand but on.
>
> Nothing to sing but songs,
> Ah, well, alas! alack!
> Nowhere to go but out,
> Nowhere to come but back.

Appendix 2
The Opry Roster, 1925–1940

Acuff, Roy and His Smoky Mountain Boys. The coming of this popular singer is discussed in chapter 15; he and his band continued to appear on the program after 1940. **1938:** weekly from 3/5 to 12/31. **1939:** 1/7 to 7/8, 7/22 to 12/30.

Aladdin Lamp Program. This was apparently an anthology segment of the Opry that only lasted four weeks. **1929:** 12/23; **1930:** 1/26, 2/9, 2/16, 2/23.

Allen, Bennie. Apparently a banjoist, but nothing else is known about this performer. **1927:** 11/12.

Alsup, Richard D. A guitarist associated with the fiddler Julius Robinson (see chapter 5) and possibly from the Cedar Glades area east of Nashville, in Wilson County. (See also the Gladeville Trio, W. M. Rucker, M. G. Smith, J. J. Lovell, and Emmet Crouch, whose names are also associated with Alsup.) **1928:** 4/14, 7/7.

Andrews Brothers. Close-harmony duet act brought onto the show to replace the Delmore Brothers. (See chapter 16 for more details.) **1939:** 2/18 to 5/20; 6/3 to 6/24; 7/8 to 7/22; 8/27; 9/2; 9/30 to 10/28; 11/11 to 12/2. This act also appeared after 1940.

Andrews, Tom. Left-handed guitarist and singer for the Binkley Brothers Dixie Clodhoppers. Before he joined that band, he occasionally appeared as a soloist or with members of the Gully Jumpers. (See also: Roy Hardison, Paul Warmack, Odie Collins, and The Gully Jumpers.) **1927:** 5/7, 5/21, 6/11, 11/5, 11/30.

Anderson, T. H. Guitarist possibly associated with fiddler Odie Callis. **1928:** 7/7; 10/27.

Ard Sisters. No information available. Appeared weekly in 1935 from 3/23–4/27.

Armstead, Virgil. Associated with O. L. Kelley. **1927:** 12/10.

Arrington, Charles B. Fiddler for Warmack's Gully Jumpers. He also made some solo appearances in **1927:** 11/5 and 12/31; **1928:** 1/14, 2/25, 3/31, 5/5, 5/26. Also appeared with Tom Andrews and T. J. Givens, with R. E. Hudgens, the Wilkerson Brothers, and the Gully Jumpers. He was the fiddler on the first version of "Tennessee Waltz," recorded by the Gully Jumpers in 1928.

Bailey, DeFord. Harmonica player and first black star of the Opry. See details about his life in chapter 7. **1926:** 6/19, 6/26 weekly–12/4; **1927:** 1/8, 1/15, 1/29, 2/5, 2/19, 5/14, 5/21, 5/28, 6/4, 6/18, 7/23–8/20, 9/10, 9/17, 10/1, 10/15,

10/29–12/3, 12/17, 12/24. **1928:** 1/7, 1/28–5/12, 5/26–9/15, 9/29, 10/6, 10/13, 10/27–12/8. **1929:** 2/23–9/28, 10/19–12/28. **1930:** every week. **1931:** 1/3–9/5, 9/26–12/26. **1932:** 1/2–6/25, 7/9–11/5, 11/19–12/31. **1933:** every week. **1934:** every week. **1935:** 1/5–3/16, 4/27–12/7, 12/21–12/28. **1936:** 1/4–2/22, 3/7–6/20, 7/4–12/26. **1937:** every week. **1938:** 1/1–8/6, 8/20–11/19, 12/3, 12/24. **1939:** 1/7–2/18, 3/4, 3/25–4/15, 4/29, 5/20–6/3, 6/24, 7/1, 7/8, 7/22, 8/19, 9/2, 9/23, 10/14, 10/21, 10/28, 11/29, 12/2, 12/23. This artist also appeared after 1939.

Bailey, Harry. Leader of an early band called the Southern Serenaders, one of a number of regional string bands that the show experimented with in its first year. **1926:** 3/20, 4/10.

Baker, W. M. Fiddler during the first three years of the show. Sometimes accompanied by a Miss Nell Clark and later by a Mrs. Wakefield. **1926:** 2/6. **1927:** 7/30, 8/13, 8/27, 11/19, 12/17. **1928:** 1/28, 3/10, 7/7, 9/8, 10/13, 11/7.

Bandy, Henry. Well-known display fiddler from Petroleum, Kentucky. He rode the train to be on the Opry in the earliest days. For more details, see chapter 5. **1926:** 3/13, 4/17, 4/23, 5/1, 5/22, 6/26, 7/10, 10/23. **1928:** 1/7, 3/3, 4/14, 6/16, 8/25.

Bate, Dr. Humphrey. This genial harmonica-playing physician led the band that was the cornerstone of the early Opry, the Possum Hunters. He was called "the dean of the Opry," and his band routinely opened the shows on Saturday night. He and his circle are discussed at length in chapter 3. In addition to occasional appearances in late 1925 on WSM, Bate was present on the following dates: **1926:** 1/30, 2/6, 2/20–4/10, 5/1–7/3, 7/17, 7/31, 10/5, 10/30, 12/4. **1927:** 1/8, 1/22, 2/5, 2/19, 3/5, 4/30–5/14, 5/28, 6/18, 7/30, 8/13, 8/27, 9/10, 10/29, 11/26, 12/10. **1928:** 1/7, 1/21, 2/18, 2/25, 3/10, 3/24, 4/7, 4/21, 5/5, 5/19, 6/2, 6/16, 6/30, 7/28, 8/11, 8/25, 9/1, 9/8, 9/22–10/6, 10/20, 11/3, 11/17, 12/15, 12/29. **1929:** 1/2, 1/26, 2/9, 2/23, 3/9, 3/23, 4/6, 4/20, 5/4, 5/18, 6/1, 6/15, 6/22–9/28, 10/12–12/28. **1930:** every week. **1931:** 1/3–9/5, 9/26–12/26. **1932:** 1/2–6/25, 7/9–11/5, 11/19–12/31. **1933:** every week. **1934:** every week. **1935:** 1/25–12/7, 12/21, 12/28. (On June 12, 1936, Dr. Humphrey Bate died, but his band continued on as the Possum Hunters well into the 1960s.) **1936:** 1/4–2/22, 3/7–6/20, 7/11–10/24, 11/7–12/26. **1937:** every week. **1938:** every week. **1939:** 1/7–11/4, 12/16–12/30.

Bauitt, T. H. No information. Appeared once, 9/5/36.

Belmont Brothers. Local brother duet who made one appearance, 10/9/37.

Big Yank Southerners. This band, which appeared on the show for about five months in 1934, is a mystery. They were probably sponsored by Big Yank overalls and named after them. A tentative identification is a band from Imboden, Arkansas, led by Ernest (Red) Williams, who played a "cello bass." Other members included Leon Pinter (banjo), Red Meredith (fiddle) and Paul Gregory (guitar). **1934:** 2/17–7/21.

Bingham, George and His Hogwallow Band. No information. One appearance, 3/2/29.

Binkley Brothers and Their Dixie Clodhoppers. This band, led by brothers Amos and Gale Binkley, is discussed in detail in Chapter 8. They appeared only infrequently on the early years of the show, since they were also appearing on WLAC, WSM's prime rival in Nashville. 1926: 11/13. 1927: 1/8, 1/15, 2/5, 4/30, 5/21, 5/28, 6/4, 7/30. 8/20, 9/17, 10/29, 11/12, 12/17, 12.24. 1928: 1/21, 2/11, 2/18, 3/3, 3/17, 3/31, 4/14, 4/28, 5/12, 5/19, 5/26, 7/14, 7/21, 8/4, 8/18, 9/1, 9/22, 10/13, 11/17, 12/1, 12/15, 12/29. 1929: 3/9, 4/6, 11/30. 1931: 10/3. 1932: 2/6, 2/20, 3/5, 3/19, 4/2, 4/16, 4/30, 5/14, 6/11, 6/25, 7/9, 7/23, 8/6, 8/20, 9/3, 9/17, 10/1, 10/15, 10/29, 11/26, 12/24. 1933: appeared every other week throughout the year. 1934–1938: Appeared every other week throughout each year. 1939: 1/28, 2/11, 3/11, 3/25, 4/8, 4/22, 5/6, 6/3, 6/10, 6/17, 7/1, 7/15, 7/29, 8/5.

Bluegrass Serenaders. Though they may have been the first band to use the term "bluegrass" in their name, this group was an old-time string band from Gallatin, Tennessee, northeast of Nashville. They appeared three times. 1926: 1/6, 6/12. 1927: 1/22.

Blunkall, Marshall. Guitarist who accompanied Mitchell Crowder. 1928: 6/23.

Bone, Henry. Harmonica player from West Tennessee who later (1930) performed with and recorded with the Perry County Music Makers. Sole appearance was 2/18/28, with Iris Carrol.

Boult, Reber. A baritone singer who performed with Bob Cason. Sole appearance was 1/8/27.

Bowers, M. H. String band fiddler associated with W. B. Kingery, W. B. McKay, Tom Givens, and M. R. Hughes. Sole documented appearance 3/5/27.

Brady, A. J. Leader of a "barn dance team" from Adairsville, Kentucky; sole appearance 3/6/26.

Broach, Miss Nettie Mae. Apparently a pianist; sole appearance 10/8/27.

Brook Brothers. No information. 1928: 6/30.

Campbell, Claiborne. Associated with Roy Hardison, Carter Greer, and a Mrs. Wakefield. Appearances in 1928: 1/7, 7/28, 8/11, 9/22.

Carlton Sisters. Duet singers who appeared for one month. 1939: 1/7, 1/14, 1/21.

Carlton, Doc. Played the musical saw with a bow. This was a favorite novelty act in vaudeville in the 1920s, but this is the only recorded use of the instrument on the Opry. 1931: 12/5, 12/19, 12/26. 1932: 1/9.

Carmack, Ben. No information. 1929: 8/25.

Carroll, Iris. Associated with harmonica player Gentry Bone. 1928: 2/18.

Carthage Fiddlers. String band headed by harmonica player Jerry Gardenshire and including Robert King (f), T. K. Fort (g), and J. F. Reed (g). 1926: 3/13, 4/3, 5/1.

Carthage Quartet. A gospel group, possibly African American, that specialized in "spirituals." 1926: 6/19, 7/10. 1927: 3/5.

Cartwright, Allen. No information. 1927: 12/3. 1928: 2/18.

Carver, J. B. A fiddler from Hermitage, Tennessee. He was a familiar figure at mid-South fiddling contests in the '20s. A favorite partner was Elmer Coffee (bj). 1926: 7/10.

Carver, Lorenzo D. Kentucky fiddler associated with Vernie K. Edgens and Irving R. Edgens. **1927:** 8/6.

Cason, Bob. Probably a pianist who accompanied vocalist Reber Boult. **1927:** 1/8.

Champions. No information. **1939:** 4/15, 4/22, 4/29, 5/13–7/17.

Charlie the French Harp King. A harmonica player whose real name was Charles Melton. He owned a barbershop in downtown Nashville, supposedly the one in which Uncle Dave Macon first met the Leow's theater scout who started him on his career. **1926:** 1/9, 10/30. **1929:** 2/16.

Chesterfield Four. Vocal quartet; no other information. **1926:** 2/13.

Chuck & Ray. A close-harmony duet team that was for a time competition to the Delmore Brothers. Charles Haines and Ray Ferris came to WSM from Chicago radio and later returned to WLS. **1933:** 6/17–9/9.

Claiborne, Marshall. A well-known one-armed fiddler from Hartsville who was a familiar fixture in area fiddling contests. He was a runner-up to one of the Ford contests that Uncle Jimmy Thompson won. Often accompanied by E. D. Haines. **1926:** 4/3, 4/17, 4/23.

Clark, H. P. Associated with M. G. Smith band. **1928:** 7/14.

Clements, Zeke. Versatile singer, yodeler, and songwriter who was one of the first to bring western-style music to the Opry. He first appeared with Curly Fox in 1932 and after a short hiatus formed a band called the Bronco Busters in 1934. His later career included a stint with the Walt Disney studios, where he provided vocals for Bashful, one of the Seven Dwarfs. **1932:** 9/24, 10/8–11/5, 11/19–12/10. **1934:** 8/4, 8/11, 8/25–12/29. **1935:** 1/5, 1/12, 1/19, 2/2, 2/9. **1939:** 9/16, 10/14, 12/2, 12/9. This artist also appeared on the show after 1939.

Cline, Mrs. C. R. Though she has been described as playing a "zither," this native of Westmoreland, Tennessee, in fact played a hammer dulcimer—the only time such an instrument was featured on the show until the 1980s. Her specialty tunes were "Airplane Ride" and "Chippy Get Your Hair Cut." Her husband occasionally accompanied her on the guitar. **1928:** 3/24, 4/28, 6/2, 6/16, 6/30, 7/21, 8/4, 8/11, 8/25, 9/8, 9/22, 9/29, 10/27, 11/24, 12/8, 12/22. **1929:** 1/12, 4/6. **1933:** 4/1, 4/15, 4/29, 5/13, 5/27, 6/10. **1934:** 2/24, 3/3, 3/10, 3/17, 3/24, 3/31.

Cole, Leon. Appears to have started on the show as a duet partner with the Hawaiian guitarist Grady Moore, who had recorded extensively with Sid Harkreader. By late 1937 and for the first half of 1938, he teamed up with Red Hawn for another duet act. He apparently was an organist who played on WSM and other venues around Nashville. **1937:** 9/18, 9/25, 10/2, 11/6. **1938:** 1/15–6/25.

Collins, Dr. N. P. Unknown fiddler. **1928:** 9/15.

Collins, Odie. Member of Paul Warmack's Gully Jumpers (see chapter 8), though he did not record with them. **1927:** 5/28, 6/18, 11/5–11/27. **1928:** 5/7, 5/21, 6/11.

Condor, Alvin. A well-known banjo player from Perry County, Tennessee. He was a member of the Weems String Band, whose recordings for Columbia of "Davy Davy" and "Greenback Dollar" are regarded as two of the premier sides of the 1920s. Condor also recorded for Victor with Ad Lindsay. He made two Opry appearances, both with fiddler Dick Weems. 1927: 4/30, 10/29.

Craig, Francis and His Orchestra. For many years this group functioned as WSM's staff band. They were a pop band, a dance band with jazz overtones, but for several weeks in 1929 they had regular slots on the Opry. 1929: 2/2, 3/2–3/30, 4/20, 4/27.

Crook Brothers. One of the most enduring string bands on the Opry. The Crook Brothers Barn Dance Orchestra is discussed in detail in chapter 8. 1926: 7/24, 8/7, 12/4. 1927: 2/5, 5/14, 5/21, 6/4, 7/23, 9/10, 9/17. 1928: 2/4, 3/17, 4/21, 4/28, 5/12, 5/26, 6/16, 7/14, 7/28, 8/11, 8/25, 9/8, 9/29, 11/3, 11/17, 12/1, 12/15, 12/29. 1929: 1/12, 1/26, 2/9, 2/23, 3/9, 3/23, 4/6, 4/20, 5/4, 5/18, 6/1–9/28, 10/19–12/28. 1930: every week. 1931: 1/3–9/5, 9/26–10/31, 11/7–12/26. 1932: 1/2–6/25, 7/9–8/13, 8/27, 9/3, 9/10, 10/8, 10/22, 11/5, 11/19, 12/3. 1933: every other week. 1934: 1/6–6/16, 6/30–12/29. 1935: 1/5–12/7, 12/21, 12/28. 1936: 1/4–2/22, 3/7–6/20, 7/4–12/26. 1937: every week. 1938: 1/1–7/9, 7/23–8/20, 9/3–12/31. 1939: 1/7–2/11, 3/25, 4/8–4/22, 5/13, 5/20, 6/3, 6/17–7/15, 7/29–9/2, 9/16–10/14, 11/4–12/30. This band appeared on the the show after 1939 as well.

Crouch, Emmet. Associated with the bands of Julius Robinson and M. G. Smith. 1928: 4/18.

Crowder, Mitchell. Apparently the patriarch of a well-known family of fiddlers from the Winchester-Fayetteville area of southern Tennessee. He appeared with recording artist Whit Gayden and Marshall Blunkall. 1928: 6/9, 6/23.

Cukelek, Buford Jones. Associated somehow with Alton E. Wheeler. 1927: 10/8

Culver, Harold. No information. 1931: 6/20, 7/4.

Curtis, Cliff. Harmonica player who did duets with John Brittain. 1926: 6/12, 6/26.

Dawsen, Nolen. Early leader of "barn dance team" on 1/23/26. Though he was one of the very first Opry performers, little else is known about him.

Deason, J. W. No information except that he was listed as "leader of a barn dance orchestra"; one appearance, 1926: 3/27.

Delmore Brothers. This close-harmony brother duet was probably the most popular and influential act on the show during the mid-1930s. Details of their career can be found in chapter 13. 1933: 4/29–6/17, 7/15, 7/29, 8/12, 8/26, 9/9, 9/23–12/30. 1934: 1/6–2/17, 5/12–12/29. 1935: every week. 1936: 1/4–2/22, 3/7–6/13, 6/27–12/26. 1937: every week. 1938: 1/1–9/17.

De Moss, Perry. Fiddler associated with banjoist J. J. Lovell, 1926: 6/19.

Dixie Four. A local gospel quartet that appeared in 1934 from the first January show until the end of April. They also made two appearances in 1935, 5/4 and 5/11.

Dixieliners. This all-star string band consisted of Arthur Smith (fiddle) with the McGee Brothers, Sam and Kirk. Details about them are found in chapter 12. From 1934 to 1937 the band was listed as "Arthur Smith and His Dixieliners"; at other times it was listed simply as "The Dixieliners." 1932: 4/30–6/25, 7/9–11/19, 11/19–12/31. 1933: 1/7–6/24, 7/8, 7/22, 8/5, 8/19, 9/2, 9/16, 9/30–12/30. 1934: every week. 1935: 1/5–12/7, 12/21, 12/28. 1936: 1/4–2/22, 3/7–5/9, 5/23–6/20, 7/11, 7/25–12/26. 1937: every week. 1938: 1/1–1/22, 4/30, 5/14–8/6, 8/20–11/5, 12/17, 12/24, 12/31. 1939: 1/7, 1/14.

Dixie Serenading Band. No information. 1929: 4/20.

Dixie Volunteers. A very early band, possibly a brass ensemble. Listed as under the direction of Tom Ridings. 1926: 1/30.

Dugger, Brent. No information except that he was associated with Newt Emerson. 1928: 7/14.

Eagen, Jack. Vocalist; no other information. 1926: 1/30.

Earl, Bob. No information. 1927: 1/8.

Edgens, Irving R. and Vernie R. Backing musicians for Lorenzo Carver. 1927: 8/6.

El Chico Spanish Review. No information. They appeared in the midst of the Opry schedule one time. 1937: 2/6.

Elks Quartet. No information; probably a barbershop-style quartet. One appearance. 1927: 1/29.

Emerson, Newt. Associated with Brent Dugger, otherwise no information. 1928: 7/14.

Evening Star Quartet. Reportedly an African American group from the Nashville area. Appeared once. 1926: 10/30.

Farmer, Harvey. No information. 1927: 11/12.

Fields And Martin. Hawaiian guitar duo. 1926: 11/13.

Fitzgerald, Uncle Will. Harmonica player; no other information. 1928: 4/10, 6/30.

Ford & Junior. Veteran pop-country singer Ford Rush, working with his son. 1939: 9/23, 10/21–11/18. See also entries under Ford Rush.

Ford & Slim. Ford Rush with a different partner. 1939: 7/15.

Four Boys. No information. They had a six-week tenure on the show. 1933: 3/18–5/16.

Fox, Curly. Famed fiddler, best known for his "Black Mountain Rag" and "Listen to the Mockingbird," as well as numerous recordings. He first came to the Opry in 1932, working with Zeke Clements. He later returned in 1937, leading a band under his own name (Curly Fox and His Foxhunters) and teaming with his wife, singer Texas Ruby. 1932: 9/24, 10/8–11/5, 11/19–12/10. 1937: every week after 8/7. 1938: 1/1–2/26. This artist also appeared on the show after 1939.

Frezenda, Louis. Hollywood personality associated with Will Rogers and Douglas Fairbanks; probably in an Opry slot through an early network hook-up. 1927: 8/27.

Fruit Jar Drinkers. Classic Opry mainstay, led by fiddler George Wilkerson. They are discussed in detail in chapter 8. While Wilkerson appears under his own name in certain listings, this entry only lists those that use the term "Fruit Jar Drinkers." From 1927–1932, the listing read "G. W. Wilkerson and His Fruit Jar Drinkers"; after that, it read simply "Fruitjar Drinkers." The band remained active on the Opry into the 1960s. **1927:** 12/17, 12/24. **1928:** 1/21. **1929:** 1/12, 1/26, 2/9, 2/23, 3/23, 4/13, 5/4, 5/11, 5/26, 6/1, 6/15, 6/29, 7/13, 7/27, 8/10, 8/24, 9/7, 9/21, 10/19, 11/12, 11/16, 11/30, 12/14, 12/28. **1930:** 1/25, 2/8, 2/22, 3/8, 3/22, 4/5, 4/19, 8/3, 5/17, 5/30, 6/14, 6/28, 7/12, 7/26, 8/9, 9/23, 9/6, 9/20, 10/4–12/27. **1931:** 1/3–9/5, 9/26–12/26. **1932:** 1/2–6/25, 7/9–11/5, 11/19–12/31. **1933:** 1/7–2/18, 3/4–12/30. **1934:** every week. **1935:** 1/5–6/8, 7/6–12/7, 12/21, 12/28. **1936:** 1/4–2/22, 3/7–6/20, 7/4–10/10, 10/24–12/26. **1937:** every week. **1938:** 1/1–8/6, 8/20–12/31. **1939:** 1/7–1/21, 2/4–4/29, 5/13–12/9, 12/23. This band also performed on the show after 1939.

Gardenshire, Jerry. Harmonica player; see entry for Carthage Fiddlers.

Garvin, Tom. Fiddler who appeared with banjo player Hugh Peay. **1927:** 5/7, 9/10. 9/17.

Gayden, Whit. Well-known trick and imitative fiddler from West Tennessee. He recorded two titles for Victor in 1930, "Coon Hunt" and "Hen Cackle Piece." **1928:** 5/12, 5/26, 6/9, 6/23, 7/7, 7/14, 7/21, 8/4.

Georgia Wildcats. The band of famed fiddler Clayton McMichen. By this time they were specializing in a mixture of western swing, pop, and old-time tunes and were about to start recording for Decca. For a few weeks in 1936 they were associated with comedian Honey Wild. **1936:** 9/5, 9/12, 9/19, 10/3–10/31. **1937:** 1/2.

Gill, Clarence and Grady. Another in the long line of early harmonica acts. Each apparently played harmonica; where they were from is not known. **1927:** 9/17, 10/1, 10/15, 11/5, 12/3. **1928:** 1/28, 3/3, 5/5, 9/15.

Gilliam, Art. No information. **1927:** 2/26.

Givens, Tom. The banjo player who is heard on the four Crook Brothers Victor recordings from 1928. He played off and on with the Fruit Jar Drinkers and other early ensembles, who included at various times Tom Garvin, Hugh Peay, R. E. Hudgens, W. B. Kingery, W. B. McCay, and M. H. Bowers. The following list refers to only those appearances where he is singled out by name. **1927:** 3/5, 5/7, 6/18, 6/25, 9/30, 12/31. **1928:** 1/14, 2/25, 3/31, 5/5, 5/26.

Gladeville Trio. The regular band headed by Julius Robinson, a veteran fiddler from the Cedar Glades region near Lebanon. Robinson was well known at regional fiddling contests and taught several favorite tunes to younger fiddlers in the neighborhood, including Sid Harkreader. The basic personnel for the trio also included S. W. Robinson and William Rucker. For a time, they seemed poised to become regulars on the show but for some reason faded away. Gladeville still exists as a community deep in the cedar glades. **1927:** 2/19, 4/30, 10/29. **1928:** 5/5–6/2, 6/16.

Golden West Cowboys. Pee Wee King's band, as discussed in chapter 15. **1937:** 6/26, 7/10, 7/24 and weekly through the end of the year. **1938:** every week.

1939: 1/7, 1/21–7/8, 9/9–12/30. This band also appeared on the show after 1939.

Greer, Carter. Fiddler associated with Roy Hardison. No other information. **1928:** 7/28, 8/11, 9/22.

Gully Jumpers. Another of the classic hoedown bands that formed the foundation of the show. It was led by automobile mechanic Paul Warmack, and in the listings it appeared both as "the Gully Jumpers" and "Paul Warmack and His Gully Jumpers," in no particular pattern. The basic personnel for the band through the 1920s and 1930s was Warmack (m.), Charles Arrington (f.), Roy Hardison (b.), and Bert Hutcherson (g.). It was this line-up that recorded for Victor in 1928. **1927:** 12/24; see other entries under "Paul Warmack." **1928:** no entries under "Gully Jumpers;" see the many entries under "Paul War-mack." **1929:** 1/5, 1/19, 2/2, 2/16, 3/2, 3/16, 3/30, 4/13, 4/27, 5/11, 5/26–9/28, 10/12–12/28. **1930:** 1/4–6/7, 6/21–12/27. **1931:** 1/3–9/5, 9/26–12/26. **1932:** 1/2–6/25, 7/9–11/5, 11/19–12/21. **1933:** every week. **1934:** every week. **1935:** 1/5–12/7, 12/21, 12/28. **1936:** 1/4–2/22, 3/9–5/9, 5/23–6/20, 7/4–10/3, 10/17–12/26. **1937:** every week. **1938:** 1/1–7/30, 8/13, 9/3–10/8, 10/22–12/3, 12/17, 12/24, 12/31. **1939:** 1/7–3/4, 3/25–4/8, 4/22–6/3, 6/17–8/19, 12/9–12/30. This band also appeared on the show after 1939.

Hackley, Ken and His Cowboys. Well-known vaudeville act. They made one Opry appearance. **1935:** 2/16.

Haines, Happy Jack. Vaudeville entertainer who played piano and sang. He made a couple of appearances in the very earliest days of the show. **1926:** 1/2, 1/23.

Hale, Theron and His Daughters. A popular family band that consisted of fiddler Theron Hale (from Pikeville, Tennessee) and his daughters, Elizabeth and Mamie Ruth. They are discussed in detail in chapter 8. At first, only Mamie Ruth's name appeared, as Hale's accompanist, but later Elizabeth was added. This band also recorded at the 1928 Victor Opry session. In later years, after his daughters had grown and married, Hale continued to play (and even record) with fellow Opry members like Sam McGee. He died in Nashville in 1954. **1926:** 10/30, 11/13. **1927:** 1/8, 1/22, 2/5, 2/19, 3/5, 5/7, 9/17, 10/1, 11/19, 12/17, 12/31. **1928:** 2/11, 3/17, 4/21, 5/26, 6/9, 9/8, 9/15, 10/13, 11/10, 11/24, 12/8, 12/22. **1929:** 1/5, 1/19, 2/2, 2/16, 3/2, 3/6, 3/30, 4/13, 4/27, 5/16, 5/26–9/28, 10/12–11/23, 12/7–12/28. **1930:** every week. **1931:** 1/3–9/5, 9/26–12/26. **1932:** 1/2–3/12, 3/26–6/25, 7/9–9/3, 9/10, 9/17, 9/24, 10/15, 10/29, 11/26, 12/10–12/31. **1933:** 1/7, 1/21, 2/4, 2/18, 3/4, 3/8, 4/6, 4/15, 4/29, 5/13, 5/27, 6/10, 6/24, 7/8, 7/22, 8/5, 8/19, 9/2, 9/16, 10/7–12/30. **1934:** 1/6–5/26.

Hardison, Roy. A journeyman banjo player who played with a number of groups in the early years and seems to have been something akin to a staff musician. He eventually settled in with the Gully Jumpers. This entry deals only with appearances where Hardison is mentioned by name. He apparently began on the show on 11/30/26, when he accompanied fiddler W. G. Hardison, probably his father. During 1927 and 1928, he appeared with a number of special Opry guests (i.e., not regulars), such as J. F. Reid, Whit Gayden, W. M. Baker, Mrs. Wakefield, Carter Greer, and Claiborne Campbell. After that: **1927:** 5/7, 5/21, 5/28, 6/11–6/18, 7/30, 8/15, 8/27, 11/5, 11/9, 10/10, 12/17. **1928:** 1/28, 2/4, 3/10, 5/12, 7/7, 7/28, 9/8, 10/13, 11/17.

Harkreader, Sid. One of the all-time Opry greats and a native of Wilson County, Tennessee. Sid Harkreader became a versatile fiddler, guitarist, and singer on the early Opry. He was one of the first performers to try to make a living solely by his music and was for many years the recording and traveling partner of Uncle Dave Macon. He recorded under his own name for Vocalion (in 1924 and 1925) and for Gennett and Paramount. His own partners included guitarist Hick Burnett, John P. Holder, Jimmy Hart, Blythe Poteet, and Grady Moore, and some of these appear in the following listings. Harkreader also appeared on many of the performances by Uncle Dave Macon. **1926:** 7/25. **1927:** 7/23. **1929:** 5/11, 5/26. **1930:** 4/5, 4/12; **1931:** 1/10, 1/24, 5/2, 5/16, 5/30, 6/13, 6/27, 7/11, 7/25–8/29. **1935:** 7/6–12/7, 12/21, 12/28. **1936:** 1/4–2/22, 3/7–6/20, 7/11–8/8, 8/22, 9/12–12/12. **1936:** 9/19. This artist also appeared on the show after 1939.

Harmonica Club. A group from Scottsville, Kentucky, High School. **1927:** 5/7.

Harper, Raymond. Guitarist associated with the early Gully Jumpers. **1927:** 6/18.

Harris, Bob. A Kentucky banjoist who performed with Henry Bandy. **1928:** 1/7.

Hart, Jimmy. Versatile guitarist and singer from Nashville, associated with Harkreader and later with the Crook Brothers. He seems to have been a sort of utility infielder for the early show. The following dates single him out as principal performer. **1931:** 1/10, 1/31, 5/2, 5/30, 6/13, 6/27, 7/11, 7/25–8/29.

Henson, Bernard. No information. **1939:** 6/10.

Hicks, Al. Singer and bandleader. He made numerous appearances on the show in 1939, but no other information is available. **1927:** 3/25, 4/8, 5/6, 5/13, 5/27, 6/3, 6/10, 6/24–8/27.

Hilltop Harmonizers. A band that appeared not only on the Opry but also on early morning shows on WSM. It was essentially a string and vocal band, often accompanied by an organ. At its core were three young musicians from Ashland, Kentucky: Big Foot Keaton, Bob Shortridge, and Curley Wellman. They had gained their experience with a West Virginia band called the Mountain Melody Boys, which had done a six-month stay at the Village Barn in New York and had broadcasted over network radio. They were recruited to the Opry as a group by Curt Poulton, the former Vagabond, who became their leader. Joining them on bass was the comedian Jimmy Heaberlin from Ohio. They later became the band for Salt & Peanuts and billed themselves as the Boys from Kentucky. Their singing was modeled on the Sons of the Pioneers. **1936:** 1/4–9/5, 9/19–12/26. **1937:** 1/2–9/4, weekly. **1938:** 10/15, 11/5, 11/26.

Holder, John P. Guitar player associated with Sid Harkreader and R. B. Shelton. **1929:** 5/11, 5/26.

Honey & Daney. Probably a blackface comedy team; full stage names are Money Honey and Dandy Daney. No other information. **1939:** 7/15–9/16, 9/30.

Horner, W. M. Fiddler who made appearances on two occasions in 1932: 1/16, 2/13.

Horton, Charlie. No information. 1928: 1/7.

Hot Cops. No information, but possibly a group associated with veteran singer Ed McConnell. 1929: 4/6, 4/13.

Hudgens, R. E. Guitar player from Nashville who performed with Tom Givens, Hugh Peay, Tom Garvin, and Charlie Arrington. 1927: 5/7, 6/25, 11/5, 12/31. 1928: 1/14, 2/25, 3/31.

Hughes, M. R. No information. Associated with W. B. Kingery. 1927: 3/5.

Hutcherson, Bert. One of the most popular and influential guitarists on the early Opry. A regular member of the Gully Jumpers, he is discussed in chapter 8. However, he also worked as a solo act, or occasionally with mandolin player Paul Warmack as "Paul and Bert, the Early Birds." He also played a Hawaiian style guitar, using a slide on raised-up strings. Among the fans who listened and learned from him was Little Roy Wiggins, who used some of the Hutcherson style to form his own legendary "ting-a-ling" sound with Eddy Arnold in the 1940s. The following refer only to appearances where Hutcherson is singled out by name. 1927: 10/1. 1928: 1/28, 3/24, 4/7, 4/21, 4/28, 5/12, 5/26, 6/2, 6/9, 6/23, 7/7, 7/21, 8/14, 9/11, 9/15, 9/29, 10/13, 12/8, 12/22. 1929: 1/5, 1/19, 2/2, 2/16, 3/16, 3/30, 4/13, 4/27, 5/11, 5/26, 6/1, 6/15, 6/22, 7/6, 7/20, 8/3, 8/17, 8/31, 9/14, 9/28, 10/12, 10/26, 11/9, 11/23, 12/7, 12/21. 1930: every other week. 1931: every other week–6/6. This artist also performed on the show after 1939.

Ingram L. H. Member of Julius Robinson's Gladeville Trio. 1927: 3/5.

Jack & Billy. Probably Jack Shook in an early act. 1930: 4/5–11/22.

Jack and His Buddies. An early incarnation of the band that later became known as the Missouri Mountaineers. It was here a trio featuring guitarist Jack Shook, along with Dee Simmons and Nap Bastien. 1935: 6/22–9/21.

Jack Shook and His Missouri Mountaineers. Popular and versatile band discussed in chapter 15. They brought a touch of modern cowboy music to the Opry in the mid-1930s. Though they never recorded commercially, surviving air checks reveal a smooth, polished sound resembling the Sons of the Pioneers. 1935: 1/26–6/29, 7/13–7/27, 8/17–12/7, 12/21, 12/28. 1936: every week. 1937: every week. 1938: every week. 1939: every week. This artist also appeared on the show after 1939.

Jackson, Jack. Nicknamed "the Strolling Yodeller." A Lebanon, Tennessee, native, Jackson started out as a popular soloist for WSM's rival station WLAC and as a singer for the Binkley Brothers Dixie Clodhoppers. He was about the only Nashville singer in those days who could do Jimmie Rodgers material, and his shows drew sacks of mail. In 1928 he recorded with the Binkley Brothers for Victor (sharing label credit with them) and in 1929 recorded four solo sides for Columbia. He later quit the business and opened a welding shop in Lebanon. 1929: 1/5–1/19. 1932: 12/31. 1933: 1/7–1/21, 6/24–12/9, 12/30. 1934: 1/6–4/14, 5/5–5/26.

Jamup & Honey. A blackface comedy team discussed in chapter 14. See also the
   entry on Honey Wild. **1939:** 1/7, 1/21–2/11, 2/25, 3/11, 3/18, 4/1, 4/15,
   5/6–5/27, 6/10.

Johnson City High School Orchestra. Just why this improbable act appeared on the
   Opry is a mystery. **1927:** 4/16.

Jones, Colman. A banjo player from West Tennessee who performed with Arthur
   and Homer Smith. **1927:** 8/13.

Jones, Mrs. Eva Thompson. The niece of fiddler Uncle Jimmy Thompson. She
   worked as a local piano teacher and staff musician for WSM and accompanied her uncle, but she was once listed under her own name. **1927:** 1/29.

Jordan, D. String band musician associated with J. T. Lawhorn and R. W.
   Lawhorn. **1927:** 6/18, 7/30. 8/27.

Judge, The. A mystery entry. It might well be George D. Hay himself doing some
   kind of act on the Ory. Whoever it was, his performances ran weekly in 1929
   from 2/9–4/27.

Junior Strings. No information. 1/15/27.

Kelly, O. L. Associated with Virgil Armstead; no other information. **1927:** 12/10.

Kincaid, Bradley. A famous folk singer. Kincaid was a household word in the 1930s
   and made only one documented appearance on the Opry before 1940, that on
   10/16/37. In 1946 he briefly became a full-time member of the show.

Kingery, W. B. Guitarist who worked with several early string bands and was associated with W. B. McCay, Tom Givens, J. T. Lawhorn, and the Tomberlain
   family. **1927:** 3/5, 7/30, 8/6, 8/13, 8/20, 12/3, 12/24, 12/31. **1928:** 1/21, 3/17,
   4/14.

Kuhn, Vincent. Vocalist. **1927:** 6/18.

Lakeland Sisters. WSM's answer to the popular WLS act the Girls of the Golden
   West. Ann and Mary Lakeland were one of the first Opry groups to use western costumes and spent about a year and a half as regulars on the show. **1937:**
   1/23 weekly throughout the year. **1938:** 1/1 weekly–6/4.

Land, J. T. Mandolin player associated with several early string bands, including
   those with Ewing and Allen Cartwright. **1928:** 2/18.

Lasses & Honey. Blackface comedy team organized by veteran minstrel man Lasses
   White. See chapter 14 for details. During their tenure on the show, they
   appeared almost every week. **1934:** 4/21–6/30, 10/6–11/3, 11/17–12/29.
   1935: 1/5–6/8, 10/25–12/28. **1936:** 1/4–2/22, 3/7–5/30.

Lawhorn, J. T. Banjo player for several early string bands, including those of R. W.
   Lawhorn, D. Jordan. **1927:** 6/18, 7/30, 8/27.

Leffew, Tom. Versatile mandolin player associated with the early Fruit Jar
   Drinkers. **1927:** 5/7, 5/21, 6/4, 11/12.

Lovell, J. D. Guitar player associated with the band of M. G. Smith and that of
   Julius Robinson. **1927:** 2/19, 7/14, 7/23, 8/6. **1928:** 4/14.

Lunn, Robert. The famed "Talking Blues Man" discussed in detail in chapter 14.
   For some four and a half years he appeared almost weekly on the show and
   after 1937 was sponsored by the Strikalite Match Company. **1934:** 3/31–6/30,

7/14–12/29. **1935:** 1/5–12/7, 12/21, 12/28. **1936:** 1/4–2/22, 3/7–4/18, 5/2–6/20, 7/11–11/21, 12/5–12/26. **1937:** weekly throughout. **1938:** 1/1–6/4.

McConnell, Ed. A veteran vaudeville entertainer. He was not especially country but appeared on the early Opry for several years, at times under the aegis of the Aladdin Lamp Program. **1928:** 11/10–12/29. **1929:** 1/5, 2/2, 3/2–4/27.

Mcdonald, Aires. No information. **1928:** 4/28.

McGee, Kirk. The younger brother of Sam McGee. Kirk was a member of Dixieliners (chapter 12) and a versatile instrumentalist and singer. The following dates reflect occasions when he was singled out in the listings, performing with his brother or with his cousin Blythe Poteet. Starting in 1935, most of these appearances are by "the McGee Brothers." **1929:** 5/4, 5/18. **1935:** 10/12–12/7, 12/21, 12/28. **1936:** 1/4–2/22, 3/7–5/9, 5/23–6/20, 7/11, 7/25–12/26. **1938:** 1/8, 1/22–6/11, 6/25–7/9, 8/20, 8/27, 9/17, 10/1, 10/15, 10/22, 10/29. **1939:** 1/21–3/18, 4/1–5/6, 5/20–10/21, 11/11–12/30. He also appeared on the show after 1939.

McGee, Sam. Virtuoso guitarist and comic singer. Sam was Kirk McGee's older brother; member of Dixieliners (see chapter 12); and frequent recording partner for Uncle Dave Macon. The following dates do not include those with the Dixieliners nor others where he is not singled out in the listings. After 1935 he is normally listed as one of the McGee Brothers. **1927:** 12/24. **1928:** 12/22, 12/29. **1929:** 4/27, 5/18. **1935–1939:** see entries for Kirk McGee. He also performed on the show after 1939.

McKay, W. B. String band player associated with W. B. Kingery and Tom Givens. **1927:** 3/5, 7/30.

Macon, Dorris. Youngest son of Uncle Dave Macon, who accompanied him on guitar and vocals for much of his career. See entry for Uncle Dave Macon.

Macon, Uncle Dave. The first real star of the Opry. This Warren County, Tennessee, native who was described in one early listing as a "banjoist and character singer." By the time he first came to the show, in 1925, Macon was fifty-five years old and already had a national reputation as a recording and vaudeville star. During the late 1920s, he appeared on the show only occasionally, spending most of his time touring and recording. By the early 1930s, when those venues had declined, he became a regular and soon was the most popular performer on the show. Listings before 1930 show Macon as accompanied either by Sid Harkreader or Sam McGee. On one occasion (8/8/31) he was accompanied by "His Tennessee Moonshiners," and on another (6/4/27) by the McGee Brothers and fiddler Mazy Todd. After 1930 his son Dorris Macon is usually listed as his accompanist (on guitar and harmony vocals). As described in chapter 6, Macon had appeared several times on WSM even before the formal barn dance program began. He and Uncle Jimmy Thompson shared the spotlight on the first scheduled program on December 26, 1925. The following list picks up from there. **1926:** 5/1, 5/15, 5/22, 5/29, 6/5, 6/12, 6/19, 6/26, 7/3–7/17, 8/7, 10/23. **1927:** 6/4, 12/24, 12/31. **1928:** 3/31, 12/22, 12/29. **1929:** 4/27, 5/18, 8/10. **1930:** 1/11–3/29, 4/5, 4/12, 7/5, 8/16,

9/13, 10/25, 11/8, 12/6, 12/13, 12/20. **1931:** 2/7, 5/30, 6/6, 6/12, 7/4, 8/8, 8/15–9/5, 9/26–12/26. **1932:** 1/2–2/13, 3/5, 3/19–6/25, 7/9–11/5, 12/3–12/31. **1933:** 1/7–5/20, 6/3–12/30. **1934:** 1/6–7/7, 7/28–8/25, 9/8–12/29. **1935:** 1/5–7/27, 8/3–12/7, 12/21, 12/28. **1936:** 1/4–2/22, 3/7–5/9, 5/23–6/20, 7/4–12/26. **1937:** every week except for 9/11. **1938:** 1/1–7/9, 7/23–8/20, 9/3–9/17, 10/1–12/31. **1939:** 1/7–4/29, 5/13, 5/20, 6/3–6/17, 7/1–7/22, 8/5–8/27, 9/9–9/30, 10/14, 10/21. Both Uncle Dave and Dorris appeared on the show after 1939.

Mangrum, Uncle Joe. This blind fiddler from Paducah, Kentucky, often accompanied by accordion player Fred Shriver, became a regular on the show for three years, 1929–31. His career is discussed in detail in Chapter 5. **1928:** 6/30, 8/25, 9/15, 12/8, 12/22. **1929:** 1/12, 1/26, 2/9, 2/23, 3/9, 3/30, 4/6, 4/20; every other week–11/16. **1930:** 1/25, 2/8, 3/8, 3/22, 4/5, 4/19, 5/3, 5/17, 5/30, 6/14, 6/28, 7/12, 7/26, 8/9, 8/23, 9/6, 9/20, 10/4, 10/18, 11/1, 11/15, 11/29, 12/13, 12/20. **1931:** every other week. **1932:** 1/2, 1/9, 1/16.

Marshall, Jimmy and Mac. Fiddle and guitar duo; no other information. **1927:** 9/17. **1928:** 1/28.

Miller, William. Hawaiian Guitar. **1926:** 5/29.

Mingo Mountaineers. Unknown string band that may be related to Mingo Ramblers. **1935:** 5/18 and 12/21.

Mingo Ramblers. Unknown string band; one appearance. **1932:** 1/30.

Mitchell, Fulton. A fiddler who was leader of the Old Hickory Orchestra in the earliest days of the BARN DANCE. He was also a familiar fiddler at regional contests. **1926:** 1/30, 7/24, 8/7, 9/17.

Monroe, Bill. The legendary father of bluegrass (see chapter 15). Monroe began his long career on the Opry on 11/4/39 and appeared weekly throughout the remainder of that year. He continued to appear on the show after 1939.

Moore, Grady D. A Nashville instrument maker and repairer, an excellent Hawaiian guitar player, and sometime partner with Sid Harkreader. Moore recorded for Paramount in the late 1920s. **1927:** 5/14. **1934:** (as Grady Moore's Hawaiians) 1/6 weekly through the end of April.

Myer, Mrs. Eugene. Pianist who accompanied the more formal vocalists. **1927:** 2/26.

Nap & Dee. Founding members of the Missouri Mountaineers, Nap Bastien and Dee Simmons. For much of 1934 and 1935, however, they appeared as a duet act under their own names. **1934:** 3/31–12/29. **1935:** 1/5–1/19, 6/22–9/21.

Oklahoma Cowboys. This may have been the band of Ken Hackley, who brought a taste of western garb to the early Opry. **1930:** 12/6, 12/13. **1932:** 4/23, 5/14.

Old Hickory Orchestra. String band directed by Fulton Mitchell, from the Old Hickory community north of Nashville. **1926:** 8/7.

Osborne, James (Jim). Piano player. No other information available. **1927:** 9/19, 10/1, 10/15.

Peay, Hugh. Banjo player from Old Hickory area, associated with Tom Givens and R. E. Hudgens. **1927:** 5/7, 9/10, 9/17.

Pharris Band. Family string band featuring Willie, Floyd, and "Mrs. Pharris." 1928: 3/3, 3/31, 5/5, 5/26.

Pickard, Obed and the Pickard Family. Early vocal stars discussed in chapter 9. Obed Pickard, from Ashland City, north of Nashville, began as a soloist (billed as "The One-Man Orchestra") and then gradually added his family to the act. Most of the listings below appear as "Obed Pickard." 1926: 5/8, 6/5, 6/12, 7/10, 7/24, 7/31, 9/25, 10/5, 10/23, 10/30, 12/4. 1927: 1/8, 2/5, 2/19, 5/14–6/4, 6/18, 7/23–8/27, 9/10, 10/1, 10/15, 10/29–12/17, 12/31. 1928: 1/7–2/4, 2/18–5/19, 6/23, 9/15, 9/22. 1932: 10/29, 11/5, 11/19–12/31. 1933: 1/7–4/15. 1939: 5/6.

Poach, J. W. Harmonica player associated with W. M. Smith band. 1927: 12/24, 12/31. 1928: 1/21, 3/17, 4/14.

Polk, Marshall. Vocalist. 1926: 6/26.

Poplin, W. Ed and His Barn Dance Orchestra. Lewisburg, Tennessee, band, led by mail carrier Ed Poplin and profiled in chapter 8. Though they played during some early years, their heyday was in the mid-1930s, when they were regulars for several years. Under the name Poplin-Woods Tennessee String Band, they recorded a handful of sides in 1928 for Victor. 1927: 12/17. 1928: 3/3, 4/21, 5/19, 6/30, 7/28, 8/25, 10/13, 11/10, 12/15. 1929: every other week throughout. 1930: every other week throughout. 1931: every other week throughout. 1932: every other week throughout. 1933: every other week throughout. 1934: every other week throughout. 1935: every other week–11/30; 12/28. 1936: every other week throughout. 1937: every other week–10/2.

Porch, Whitman. Associated with Mac Smith; no other information. 1927: 9/10, 11/5, 12/3.

Possum Hunters. See Dr. Humphrey Bate.

Poteet, Blythe. Journeyman guitarist and singer. He appeared with his cousin Kirk McGee and toured with the Delmore Brothers. Recorded for Gennett with Kirk McGee in late 1920s. 1929: 5/4, 5/18.

Poulton, Curt. One of the original members of the Vagabonds (see chapter 11) and leader of the Hilltop Harmonizers. He was a versatile fixture at the station throughout the 1930s. In the dates below, the 1935 and 1936 entries list him as "Curt Poulton and His Guitar," suggesting solo performances. The 1937 dates list him as "Curt Poulton and the Sunbonnet Girls," an act consisting of Poulton, his wife Vervia (Betty), Mrs. John Duke, and Mary Dinwiddie. They also performed as a pop act called the Dream Shadows. 1935: 4/13–12/7, 12/21, 12/28. 1936: 1/4–2/22, 3/7–6/20, 7/4–12/26. 1937: 1/2, 1/9, 1/16, 2/6–9/4.

Powell, C. L. No information. 1938. 7/30.

Presley, Frank. Banjoist and fiddler. 1927: 6/18.

Preston, Azillee. Mandolin player in an unnamed string band with Alton E. Wheeler (piano) and Buford Jones (ukelele). 1927: 10/8.

Ragsdale, H. G. An early proponent of the doghouse bass in Opry hoedown bands. He for years was a regular member of George Wilkerson's Fruit Jar Drinkers.

Before Wilkerson formally named the band, Ragsdale appeared in the listings as part of a band that included Tom Leffew and Wilkerson. 1927: 5/7, 5/21, 6/4, 6/18.

Rambo, S. W. Harmonica player who did solo work and performed in an unnamed band with J.T. Lane and the Cartwright Brothers. 1927: 12/3. 1928: 2/18.

Ray-O-Vac Twins. No information. Possibly a network feed. 1928: 2/11.

Reed, J. Frank. Fiddler from Donelson, Tennessee; worked with banjoist A. C. Dukes. 1926: 7/17, 7/31.

Reid, J. F. See Whit Gayden.

Rick and Family. No information for this group that appeared regularly during the spring and summer of 1932: 4/23, 4/30, 5/14–6/18.

Roberts, Jack. Fiddler who led a band that made numerous appearances on the show in 1927 and 1928; often worked with Whitman (J. W.) Poarch (guitar) and W. M. Smith (banjo). 1927: 8/6, 8/13, 8/20, 9/10, 11/5, 12/3, 12/24, 12/31. 1928: 1/21, 3/17, 4/14.

Robinson, Julius H. Well-known fiddler. He was from the Cedar Glades region near Lebanon, due east of Nashville, and leader of the Gladeville Trio. Also associated with S. W. Robinson, Wilhelm Rucker, L. H. Ingram, and R. H. Alsup. The following dates specifically mention Robinson as opposed to the Gladeville Trio. 1927: 2/19, 3/5, 4/30, 10/29. 1928: 4/14, 7/7.

Rogers, Will. Famed American humorist. Rogers appeared during the Opry schedule one time, on 8/27/27. It may have been an early network feed. He was joined by Louise Fezenda and movie star Douglas Fairbanks.

Rose, Freddie. The famed songwriter. Rose came to WSM to start a non-Opry show called "Freddie Rose's Song Shop" and later became half of the Acuff-Rose Publishing Company. A pop songsmith who was learning quickly how to write country songs, he appeared on the Opry for several months as a performer, singing and playing the piano. 1934: 1/6–the end of April, 11/10–12/29.

Rubin, J. D. Associated with Dr. N. P. Collins. No other information. 1928: 9/15.

Rucker, Wilhelm M. Member of Gladeville Trio. 1927: 3/5. 1928: 2/19, 4/14.

Rush, Ford. Pop singer. For a time Rush was a member of the nationally known team of Ford and Glenn. Rush joined the show late in 1939 as a soloist and worked through the war years. 1939: 11/25, 12/9–12/30.

Sadler, Jack. Guitar player associated with the Fruit Jar Drinkers and the fiddler M. G. Smith. The following dates list him by name: 1927: 1/29. 1928: 5/28.

Salt & Peanuts. Comedy act featuring "Frank Salt" (Franklin Kurtz) and "Peanuts" (Margaret McConnell). They won fame over WMMN in Fairmont, West Virginia, often performing with the band that later became the Hilltop Harmonizers; in fact, they came to Nashville about the same time as the Harmonizers. They featured comic novelty tunes in their act. Their first tenure at the Opry was in 1934, from 2/3–6/31. They returned in late 1936 (12/25), and performed weekly from 1/2–3/16 in 1937. Both eventually died in retirement in Florida in 1976.

Sarie & Sally. Comedians whose sharp wordplay and rural situation comedy paved the way for artists like Minnie Pearl and Rod Brasfield. They are discussed in detail in chapter 14. For several years the team had a daily show on WSM in the late afternoon, but starting in 1935 they also had a regular slot on the Opry. They appeared almost every week from 1935 until 1939. **1935:** 1/26–7/20, 10/12–11/19, 11/23–12/7, 12/21, 12/28. **1936:** 1/4–6/20, 7/4, 7/11, 7/25–9/5, 9/19, 10/3–10/24, 11/7–12/26. **1937:** weekly except for 6/26 and 10/9. **1938:** 1/1–6/4, 6/18–12/31. **1939:** 1/7, 1/14.

Saxon Ramblers. Unknown string band. **1934:** 6/23.

Scottish Kilties Band. "From Border Chamber of Commerce." No other information. **1927:** 2/26.

Shelton, E. B. Harmonica soloist later associated with Sid Harkreader. **1928:** 1/28. **1929:** 5/26.

Shriver, Fred. Accordion player, accompanist to Uncle Joe Mangrum. See chapter 5 above and entries on Mangrum.

Silver String Hawaiians. No information; probably one of the numerous Hawaiian style bands that worked in Nashville at the time. **1926:** 7/31, 9/25, 10/5. **1927:** 1/8.

Sister Comedy Company. No information; linked somehow to the Smith Brothers. **1928:** 6/2.

Sizemore, Asher and Little Jimmie. Father-and-son duo, discussed in detail in chapter 9. They were one of the first Opry acts to make the big-time network shows. Little Jimmie, with his Shirley Temple–like bravado, made the act one of the most remembered from the prewar Opry. **1932:** 9/24, 10/1, 10/29, 11/26–12/31. **1933:** 1/7–2/4, 2/18–4/12, 6/10–12/30. **1934:** 1/6–1/20, 10/6–12/29. (In February, they appeared at 5:30 P.M., before the actual Opry, for several weeks.) **1935:** 1/5–4/6. **1936:** 12/19, 12/26. **1937:** 1/2–2/23. **1938:** 12/10–12/31. **1939:** 1/7–3/18, 4/22, 4/29.

Smith, Arthur and Homer. The fiddle and guitar duo before Fiddlin' Arthur Smith organized the Dixieliners. Though occasionally billed as "the Smith Brothers," the pair, in fact, were cousins. For a time in 1927 the two were also joined by banjoist Colman Jones, but he soon dropped out leaving the basic duo. They performed regularly on the show until February 1932. Listings with the McGee Brothers appear under the entry for the Dixieliners. **1927:** 7/16, 8/6, 8/13, 11/26, 12/10, 12/24. **1928:** 1/7–2/4, 2/18, 3/3, 3/17, 3/31, 4/14, 4/28–5/12, 5/26, 6/9, 7/7, 7/21, 8/4, 8/18, 9/1, 9/15, 9/29, 10/13, 10/27, 11/24, 12/8. **1929:** alternate weeks from 1/5–6/8, weekly from 6/22 to 9/28, weekly from 10/19–11/23, 12/7, 12/21. **1930:** alternate weeks from 1/4–9/27. **1932:** 2/13, 2/20. **1938:** 11/12–12/10 (without Homer Smith).

Smith, M. G. A popular fiddle player from Dickson County, Tennessee. Melvin Garfield Smith and his band were regulars on the show for three years, from 1926 to 1928. At first Smith appeared mainly with banjoist W. L. Totty, but by 1928 he had a band comprised entirely of Smiths: H. L. Smith, W. M. Smith, and C. M. Smith. At other times his band members included J. J.

Lovell, W. S. Williams, H. P. Clark, D. D. Alsup, and Emmet Crouch. After moving to Nashville, Smith taught Industrial Arts for many years at Hume-Fogg High School. Unfortunately he never recorded. **1926:** 2/13. **1927:** 2/19, 4/30, 5/7, 5/21, 5/28, 7/14, 7/21, 8/6, 9/10, 11/5, 11/12, 12/3, 12/10, 12/24, 12/31. **1928:** 4/14, 7/14, 8/11, 10/20.

Smith, Mac. String band performers with Jack Roberts and Whitman Poach. No other information. **1927:** 9/10, 12/24. **1928:** 1/21, 3/17, 4/14.

Smith, Slim. One of several "Slim Smith's" in early country music. This Smith seems to be the singer and guitarist who recorded several sides for Vocalion in 1939. Dates that specifically mention him by name are: **1939:** 10/14, 10/21, 11/4, 11/18, 12/2.

Smith County String Trio. Early string band from Chesnut Mound, Tennessee. **1926:** 5/22, 11/6.

Stacey Sisters. Another act trying out for the "girls' duet" slot; this group appeared in December 1939: **12/9–12/23.**

Stafford, Bann. Identified as a "jazz pianist." **1927:** 1/29.

Swan, John B, Fiddler; no other information. **1932:** 3/19.

Sweeney Sisters. No information. **1934:** 11/3–12/29. **1935:** 1/5–3/16.

Tecumech, Chief Kiutus. Probably a vaudeville act, associated with the Ray-O-Vac Twins. **1928:** 2/11; **1930:** 1/4.

Tennessee Guitar Trio. May have been a black string band from the Shelbyville area, headed by Coley Streeter. **1930:** 9/27.

Tennessee Songbirds. No information. **1939:** 2/4, 2/18, 2/25, 3/4, 3/18, 3/25, 4/18, 4/15, 5/6. 5/13, 5/20, 6/3, 6/10, 6/17, 6/24.

Tennessee Valley Boys. A western-swing styled string band organized by former Vagabond Herald Goodman. The personnel as of September 1938, when the band made its Bluebird recordings, included Goodman on vocal, Howdy Forrester and Arthur Smith on twin fiddles, Virgil Atkins on banjo, Billy Byrd on guitar, and Joe Forrester on bass. After spending most of 1938 at the Opry, the band later moved to Oklahoma. **1938:** 5/7–9/24, 10/22, 10/29, 11/5, 11/19–12/10. Howdy Forrester also appeared on the show after 1939.

Texas Drifter. The hobo song specialist Goebel Reeves, who traveled restlessly around radio stations in the South in the 1930s. He also recorded widely. **1938:** 7/23, 8/6.

Texas Ruby. Long-time partner to Curly Fox; occasionally appeared on her own in the listings. **1938:** 1/1–2/26. She also appeared on the show after 1939

Thompson, Uncle Jimmy. The patriarch of the Opry fiddlers. Thompson made his first WSM appearance on November 28, 1925, and appeared on the first scheduled "barn dance" show on December 26, 1925. His career is discussed at length in chapter 4. **1926:** 1/9, 1/16, 1/23, 1/30, 2/6–2/27, weekly throughout March, 4/10–4/23, 5/ 1–5/15, 7/3–7/24, 9/25, 11/27, 12/4. **1927:** 1/8, 1/25, 2/5, 2/19. **1928:** 12/29.

Thurman, Mac. Guitarist associated with Bob Harris; no other information. **1928:** 1/7.

Todd, Mazy. Best known for his recordings with Uncle Dave Macon (under the name Uncle Dave Macon and His Fruit Jar Drinkers). Todd was a well-known fiddler who ran a sawmill near Uncle Dave's home in Kittrell, Tennessee. His name appears in many lists of fiddlers in mid-South contests in the 1920s. In addition to his performing with Macon, he led his own "string trio," which appeared on the Opry infrequently from 1926 to 1932. 1926: 4/3, 10/30. 1927: 6/4, 11/26, 12/31. 1928: 3/10, 9/15. 1931: 6/27, 7/18, 7/25, 8/1. 1932: 2/20.

Tomberlain Family. This family string band, discussed briefly in chapter 5, hailed from the Murfreesboro-Lebanon area southeast of Nashville. The personnel included Waymon (W.L.) Tomberlain on banjo, George on fiddle, Robert on guitar, and Ernest on tenor banjo. W. L. was also associated with fiddler Jack Roberts and banjoist W.B. Kingery. 1927: 8/6, 8/13, 8/20, 12/3, 12/24, 12/31. 1928: 1/21.

Totty, W. L. Banjo player associated with the group of M. G. Smith; no other information. 1927: 2/19, 4/30, 5/21, 5/28, 7/23, 8/6, 11/12, 12/10.

Trout, J. R. Leader of an early "barn dance orchestra" from Gallatin, a town to the north of Nashville. 1926: 3/27.

Troy, Dale and His Orchestra. No information. 1927: 1/15.

Vagabonds. One of the most popular groups of the 1930s. This smooth-sounding vocal trio was accompanied by Curt Poulton's solo guitar, mixed old ballads like "Barbara Allen" with new love songs, and pioneered the sale of custom songbooks over the air. They also recorded extensively for Bluebird and toured widely. Their complex career is traced in chapter 11. 1931: 9/5, 9/26, 10/10–12/26. 1932: 1/2 weekly–6/25, 7/9 weekly–11/5, 11/19 weekly–12/31. 1933: 1/7 weekly–2/11, 2/25 weekly–6/10, 9/16 weekly–12/2, 12/16, 12/23, 12/30. 1934: 1/6 weekly–4/28, 5/12. 1937: 9/11 weekly through the end of the year. 1938: 1/1 weekly–6/4.

Virginia Ramblers Orchestra. No information. 1928: 7/14.

Wagon Wheel Orchestra. Apparently a western group modeled on the Sons of the Pioneers. No other information. 1936: 4/11.

Wakefield, Mrs. Fred. A piano player who worked with a number of early string bands, including those of W. M. Baker, Claiborne Campbell, and Roy Hardison. In the following dates, she is singled out by name. 1927: 12/17; 1928: 1/28, 3/10, 7/7, 8/11, 9/8, 9/22, 10/13, 11/17.

Walsh, Uncle. Comedian who appeared during the first four months of 1929, sometimes by himself and sometimes in partnership with "the Judge," probably George D. Hay. 1929: 1/5 weekly–4/27.

Warmack, Paul. A Nashville mechanic and mandolin player who for many years led the Gully Jumpers (see chapter 8). The group, which recorded for Victor at the 1928 session in Nashville, is chronicled under their own entry. The following lists those entries that singled out Warmack apart from (or before) the Gully Jumpers. With Bert Hutcherson, Warmack also had an early morning WSM show called "The Early Birds." 1927: 5/7, 5/21, 5/28, 6/11, 6/18, 8/13, 10/1, 10/15, 11/15, 12/3, 12/24, 12/31.

Weems, Dick. Famed fiddler from Perry County in West Tennessee. His group, the Weems String Band, which featured banjoist Alvin Condor, made two commercial discs for Columbia in 1928. The titles, "Davy Davy" and "Greenback Dollar," are today considered two of the finest string band sides of the era. Unfortunately, Weems only appeared (with Condor) twice on the Opry. 1929: 4/30, 10/29.

Wheeler, Alton E. No information; associated with Azillee Preston and Buford Jones Cukelek. 1927: 10/8.

Whitter, Henry. Pioneering guitarist, singer, and banjoist who recorded extensively in the early days. One-time partner of the influential mountain fiddler G. B. Grayson. 1930: 11/29.

White, James. No information. 1927: 10/8.

White, Lasses and His All-Star Minstrel Show. Veteran vaudeville star who came to the Opry in 1934. See account of him in chapter 14. 1934: 12/1 weekly–12/29.

Wilds, Honey. Famed blackface vaudeville star. Wilds recorded and toured widely and remained on the show through the 1940s. He is discussed at length in chapter 14. 1936: 6/13 weekly–6/27, 7/11 weekly–9/26, 10/3, 11/7 weekly–12/12.

Wild Cat Tom's Fiddlers. No information. 1926: 1/23, 2/20, 4/10.

Wilkerson, George W. The leader of the Fruit Jar Drinkers (see chapter 8). "Grandpappy " George Wilkerson appeared in early days as a fiddler backed by a guitarist (Jack Sadler or H. G. Ragsdale). For more entries, see under Fruit Jar Drinkers. 1927: 1/29, 5/7, 5/21, 6/4, 6/18, 11/12, 11/19, 12/17. 1928: 2/11, 2/25, 3/10, 3/31, 6/9, 6/23, 11/14.

Wilkerson Brothers. Probably not associated with George Wilkerson; worked some with Tom Givens and Charlie Arrington. 1928: 3/31, 5/5, 5/26.

Williams, W. S. Member of M. G. Smith band; no other information. 1928: 7/14.

Wills, Bob and His Texas Playboys. The famed western swing star. He made only one prewar appearance on the show, on 5/23/37. He also appeared in the 1940s.

Wilson, Dad's Boys. No information. 1935: 2/16.

Winchester String Band. Presumably from Winchester, Tennessee, about a hundred miles southwest of Nashville. No other information. 1926: 4/10.

Woodbury Trio. No information, but probably from Woodbury, Tennessee, in Cannon County, about fifty miles east of Nashville. 1/22/27.

Wright, O. L. One of first string bands on the Barn Dance, he led a group identified only as "Barn Dance Orchestra." 1926: 2/27.

York Quartette. Possibly a gospel quartet. 1932: 3/5.

Zahn, Chester. "Ukelele artist." 1926: 5/22.

Notes and Sources

In addition to the specific references listed below, a number of general histories of the Grand Ole Opry have been published, many of which include discussions of the period chronicled in this book. The first such work is George Hay's *A Story of the Grand Ole Opry*, published originally in Nashville by Hay in 1945 and updated and republished in 1953. Another early history comes from the Opry's former publicity director, William R. McDaniel and Harold Seligman: *Grand Ole Opry* (New York: Greenburg, 1952). For the Opry's fiftieth anniversary, the show asked veteran journalist Jack Hurst to write the text for a huge picture book called *Nashville's Grand Ole Opry* (New York: Abrams, 1975). In 1989 TV producer Chet Hagan published *Grand Ole Opry: The Complete Story of a Great American Institution and Its Stars* (New York: Owl, 1989). And Paul Kingsbury, then the editor of *The Journal of Country Music*, published the well-illustrated *The Grand Ole Opry History of Country Music* (New York: Villard, 1995). For a general overview of country radio and how the Opry related to it, see the standard history, Bill Malone's *Country Music U.S.A.*, 2d, revised edition (Austin: University of Texas Press, 1985), as well as Charles Wolfe, "Triumph of the Hills," in *Country: The Music and the Musicians*, ed. Paul Kingsbury and Alan Axelrod (New York: Abbeville, 1988, 1994).

Chapter 1

Many of the quotations in this chapter are taken from copies of the two Nashville newspapers of the mid-1920s, the *Tennessean* and the *Nashville Banner*, and are independently acknowledged in the text. Several sources (including Kirk McGee, Alcyone Bate Beasley, and Hay's daughter, Margaret Van Damm) have confirmed that Hay in fact wrote these early press releases for the papers. Additionally, Hay's own short book, *A Story of the Grand Ole Opry* (Nashville: privately published, 1945) has been an important source for the earliest days of the show—even though he constantly warns readers that he is not writing a formal history, but a memoir "from memory."

Other basic written sources include Powell Stamper's *The National Life Story* (New York: Appleton-Century-Crofts, 1968), a good history about the company that founded the Opry. An early study that utilized newspaper files as well as an interview with Eva Thompson Jones is Don Cummings pamphlet, "The Birth of the Grand Ole Opry" and an earlier manuscript version (in the files of the Country Music Foundation) called "Etiology of the Grand Ole Opry."

Biographical details of George Hay's life are drawn from interviews with his daughter, Margaret Hay Van Damm (1995–1997); from interviews with Harold Long, Mayor of Attica, Indiana (1997); from radio tape recollections by Hay at the Alexander and Jean Heard Library at Vanderbilt University; and from columns Hay wrote for *Pickin' and Singin' News*, especially issues of 9-30-54, 10-15-54, and 12-15-54. The quotation from Charlie Pickard is drawn from Ed Kahn, "Tapescript: Interview with Charlie, Ruth, and Lucille Pickard," *JEMFQ* 4, no. 12 (Dec. 1968): 134. A useful study of the Opry-National Life relationship is Richard Peterson, "The Early Opry: Its Hillbilly Image in Fact and Fancy," *Journal of Country Music* 4, no. 2 (Summer 1973): 39–51. Peterson's theories are more fully developed in *Creating Country Music* (Chicago: University of Chicago Press, 1997). Numerous personal interviews with early Opry performers listed in individual chapters below also help support many of the details presented here.

Chapter 2

Some of the details of Nashville in the 1920s are taken from interviews with individual musicians listed below and from a close scrutiny of the city's two newspapers. The quotation about the activity around the City Wharf comes from *The WPA Guide to Tennessee*, originally compiled by the Federal Writers Project and first published in 1939 but reprinted by the University of Tennessee Press in 1986. More general background on the city may be found in two studies by Don H. Doyle, *Nashville and the New South, 1880–1930* (Knoxville: University of Tennessee Press, 1985) and *Nashville Since the 1920's* (Knoxville: University of Tennessee Press, 1985). Also full of useful detail is Sarah Foster Kelley, *West Nashville: Its People and Environs* (Nashville: privately published, 1987). The quotation from James Aswell about Paradise Ridge comes from his anthology *God Bless the Devil*, a collection of WPA narratives first published in 1940 and reprinted in 1985 by the University of Tennessee Press. More details about the WOAN-WDAD relationship can be found in David Morton and Charles Wolfe, *DeFord Bailey: A Black Star in Early Country Music* (Knoxville: University of Tennessee Press, 1991). Background on the field recording industry comes from the author's personal files and from R. M. W. Dixon and John Godrich, *Recording the Blues* (New York: Stein & Day, 1970).

Chapter 3

The vast majority of the material in this chapter comes from a series of interviews with Alcyone Bate Beasley, the daughter of Dr. Humphrey Bate. She shared with me not only her memories and her contacts but also her huge archives and scrapbooks. Taped interviews during June 1975 provide most of the quotes; others come from later talks and telephone conversations. The two letters quoted at length were provided by Mrs. Beasley as well. Material about the early Gallatin Fiddlers' Carnival come from posters and correspondence on file at the Tennessee State Library and Archives in Nashville.

Chapter 4

Once again, the lion's share of material here comes from a series of personal interviews. The core of these was a long taped interview on 5-16-75 with Katherine Thompson, Uncle Jimmy's daughter-in-law, at her home in Greenbrier, Tennessee. The description of the feed store dance comes from veteran country star Johnnie Wright, who grew up near the area. Don Cummings's "Birth of the Grand Ole Opry" has some firsthand information about Eva Thompson Jones; he was apparently the only historian to interview her. Bill Harrison did some of the early interviews around Laguardo. Other members of the Thompson family who shared their memories include Dwight Manners, Boston; Mary Irwin, Nashville; Fred and William Thompson, Greenbrier. Other interviews were with Jug Steward, Laguardo; Mr. and Mrs. Jim Thompson, Laguardo; Frazier Moss, Cookeville; Sam Kirkpatrick and Bert Norther, Laguardo; Virginia Braun, Lebanon. A more detailed account of Uncle Jimmy's life can be found in Charles Wolfe, *The Devil's Box: Masters of Southern Fiddling* (Nashville: Country Music Foundation/Vanderbilt University Press, 1997).

Chapter 5

Details about the Skillet Lickers' concert at the Ryman come from newspaper coverage in the *Tennessean* and the *Banner*. Material on Joe Mangrum is drawn from interviews with Alcyone Bate Beasley, Kirk McGee, as well as Hay's memoir and Mangrum's various obituaries (January 13, 1933). Data on Henry Bandy came from Alcyone Bate Beasley and from researcher Guthrie Meade. More information on Bandy, as well as four of his rare test recordings, are found on the LP *Fiddle Music of Kentucky*, Shanachie Records. Much of the Uncle Bunt Stephens material comes from the extensive newspaper coverage of his participation in the Ford contest and from Hay's memoir. Additional details are drawn from Don Robertson, "Uncle Bunt Stephens: Champion Fiddler," *The Devil's Box* (quarterly), 12 (May 1970). Sid Harkreader's sketch is informed by three personal interviews, dated 6-17-77, 5-21-80, and 5-80, recorded at Harkreader's apartment in Nashville. A good discussion of his early recording career is Norm Cohen, "Fiddling Sid Harkreader," *JEMF Quarterly* 6, no 28 (winter 1972): 188–193. Also important is the slender but fascinating monograph, "Fiddlin' Sid's Memoirs," ed. Walter Haden, JEMF Special Series (Los Angeles: JEMF, 1971). Personal interviews with Nonnie Presson, Bulow Smith, and Mrs. Jewell Haynes have also contributed to an understanding of the subject.

Chapter 6

Many details in this chapter came from a series of personal, taped interviews with four of Uncle Dave Macon's sons. The most extensive of these was with Arch Macon, at his home near Murfreesboro, Tennessee, on 12-5-74 and 6-4-77. Also important was a pair with Dorris Macon at his home in Woodbury, Tennessee, on 6-6-77 and 3-11-79. Eston Macon was interviewed numerous times, but only the session of 7-8-82 was taped. Harry Macon was interviewed in 1978. Macon's former sideman Kirk McGee spoke at length about him on tape on 6-17-77, and Roy Acuff shared his memories on 9-19-77. The description of the 1935 recording session in New Orleans is taken from Alton Delmore's *Truth Is Stranger Than Publicity* (1975; new edition 1997, Country Music Foundation/Vanderbilt University Press). Much of the data about Macon's early life is given in more detail in Charles Wolfe's monograph, *Uncle Dave Macon* (Murfreesboro, Tenn.: Rutherford Country Historical Society, 1996). This contains a general history of the family and a title-only discography. I have also greatly benefited from conversations with Paul Ritscher, Stu Jamieson, John Doubler (the Macon great grandson), Cordell Kemp, Sam McGee, David Cobb, Grant Turner, and Bill Knowlton.

Chapter 7

Some of the material on DeFord Bailey comes from a series of personal interviews at Bailey's apartment in May and June 1975, as well as conversations with Dick Hulan, James Talley, and Alcyone Bate Beasley during the same time. Background on black country music can be found in Tony Russell's *Blacks, Whites and Blues* (New York: Stein & Day, 1970), and a convenient modern anthology on the issue is *From Where I Stand: The Black Experience in Country Music*, a 4-CD set produced through Warner Bros. and the Country Music Foundation (1998).

A much more detailed account of Bailey's life, and the source for most of the quotes and details presented here, is David Morton and Charles Wolfe, *DeFord Bailey: A Black Star in Early Country Music* (Knoxville: University of Tennessee Press, 1991). A selection of Morton's "living room tapes" featuring Bailey's harmonica, banjo, and guitar playing is found on *The Legendary DeFord Bailey* (Tennessee Folklore Society, TFS 122).

Chapter 8

The 1938 press release Hay quoted from is in the Grand Ole Opry collection at the Jean and Alexander Heard Library at Vanderbilt University. The census figures on Nashville are taken from U.S. census reports and from atlases in the author's collection. The quote from Judge Hay about calling the surviving members of the bands together in 1950 comes from a conversation with Lucy Gray.

The quotation from "Cradle of Copperheads" by Jesse Stuart comes from copies of the original manuscript made available to me from Harold Richardson, Stuart's biographer. Details and quotes about the Fruit Jar Drinkers are taken from interviews with Claude Lampley's daughter, Lucy Gray, in 1996 and 1997. Also useful is Gray's self-published booklet *The Fruit Jar Drinkers* (Nashville, 1989). The account of Hay chewing out Uncle Dave Macon for using the FJD name came from Kirk McGee. The home recordings that constitute the bulk of the FJD recorded legacy are housed in the files of the Country Music Foundation in Nashville.

The Crook Brothers story began with personal interviews with Herman Crook at his home in East Nashville on 2-19-73, on 3-20-73, and on an undated third interview. Details about Lewis Crook are drawn from a study by James E. Akenson, "Lewis Crook: Learning and Living Country Music," *JEMFQ* 20, no. 74 (Fall/Winter 1994), 84–93. The 1940s air checks described are in the vaults of the CMF and were done by Neal Matthews Sr.

The Binkley Brothers material is drawn largely from extensive interviews with singer Jack Jackson, recorded at his home in Lebanon on 9-19-73, as well as with Alcyone Bate Beasley and Lucy Gray.

Theron Hale sources include personal interviews (6-73) with his daughter Elizabeth at her home in Nashville; with Sam McGee, with Blythe Poteet, and with Alvin C. Young.

Material on the Poplin-Woods band comes from personal interviews with Louise Woods, daughter of Ed Woods, at her home in Belfast, Tennessee, in 1996.

Chapter 9

The description of the 1934 picnic concert is taken from an unpublished manuscript by Hay in the files of the Country Music Foundation. It was apparently designed to be part of one of the editions of *The Story of the Grand Ole Opry* but was never used. Kirk McGee also shared his memories of this in a personal interview, 6-17-77. The quotation from Vito Pellettieri comes from Jack Hurst's *Nashville's Grand Ole Opry* (New York: Abrams, 1975). Information on the Pickard Family comes from Hay's book, as well as from various comments in *Pickin' and Singin' News*, various issues, 1954. Other Pickard information is in the files of the Southern Folklife Collection, University of North Carolina, Chapel Hill. A summary of these interviews with the Pickard children, as well as a discography, is found in Ed Kahn, "Tapescript: Interview with Charlie, Bubb, and Lucille Pickard," *JEMFQ* 4. no. 12 (December 1968). Asher and Jimmie Sizemore are discussed in more detail in Charles Wolfe, *Kentucky Country: Folk and Country Music of Kentucky* (Lexington: University Press of Kentucky, 1981).

Chapter 10

Most of the data in this chapter is drawn from the original Victor "session sheets" made available at the Country Music Foundation. More details of the field recording sessions in general are in Brian Rust, *The Victor Master Book Vol.* 2 (Stanhope, N.J.: Walter C. Allen, 1970). Information about early recordings in Nashville are from data in the author's files, from personal interviews with the Jimmy Thompson family, and from city directories. Other details are from personal interviews with session participants Jack Jackson, DeFord Bailey, Louise Woods, Elizabeth Hale, and Herman Crook.

Chapter 11

Details from the biographies of the Vagabonds is drawn largely from personal interviews with Mrs. Curt (Vervia) Poulton, Nashville, done in June 1977. Mrs. Poulton also had a large collection of scrapbooks, photos, and flyers that she made available to me. Other information, including the day in the life of the Vagabonds, is taken from the first of their songbooks, *Old Cabin Songs for the Fiddle and Bow* (Nashville: Old Cabin, 1932). The quote about the two classes of musicians is from Alton Delmore, *Truth Is Stranger Than Publicity*, revised edition (Nashville: Country Music Foundation/Vanderbilt University Press, 1997). The *Variety* quote is from an undated clip in the Poulton scrapbook.

Chapter 12

The material about Sam and Kirk McGee and Arthur Smith is based on numerous personal interviews. Significant ones with Sam McGee (all done at his home near Franklin, Tennessee) occurred on 4-6-73, 4-9-73, 5-27-73, 6-27-73, 2-74, and 7-20-75. Important ones with Kirk McGee, done in his office and at his home in Franklin, date from 8-29-74, 6-17-77, and 1980; Paul Ritscher also made available tapes of numerous conversations he had had with Kirk McGee in the period 1977–1982. Barry Poss also made available tapes he recorded with Lavonne Brown and Kirk McGee. More details on Sam McGee's own career can be found in Charles Wolfe, "Sam McGee," in *Three Tennessee Singers*, ed. Thomas Burton (Knoxville: University of Tennessee Press, 1977).

While the McGees provided much material on Arthur Smith, more comes from personal interviews done with his daughter Lavonne Brown at Hixson, Tennessee; with Blythe Poteet, at Franklin, Tennessee; with Grady Stringer and Floyd Pruett, Dickson, Tennessee; with Howdy Forrester, Nashville. Quotes from Alton Delmore come from his book *Truth is Stranger Than Publicity,* revised edition (Nashville: Country Music Foundation/Vanderbilt University Press, 1997). For more details about Smith's post-Opry career, see Charles Wolfe, *The Devil's Box: Masters of Southern Fiddling* (Nashville: Country Music Foundation/Vanderbilt University Press, 1997), 113–51.

Chapter 13

The most detailed account of the Delmore Brothers' career, and the source for all the quotes in this chapter, is Alton's incomplete autobiography *Truth Is Stranger Than Publicity,* originally published in 1977 (Country Music Foundation) and republished in a revised edition in 1997 (Nashville: Country Music Foundation/Vanderbilt University Press). The data on the popularity of the duo's Bluebird records comes from a press release in the Opry collection at the Jean and Alexander Heard Library at Vanderbilt. More information is drawn from personal interviews recorded with Lionel Delmore (Alton's son) at his home in Fairview, Tennessee, in May 1977. Bill Harrison, of Limestone County, Alabama, also shared his memories of conversations he had had with Alton during the singer's last years.

Chapter 14

Hay's memories of Lasses White come from his Opry memoir, as well as from unpublished chapters from that work found in manuscript at the Country Music Foundation in Nashville. The song parodies and details of songs are from the 1935 and 1936 editions of *Lasses White's Book of Humor and Song* ([Nashville]: privately printed: 1935 and 1936) Other details are from original sheet music to "Nigger Blues" (Dallas, 1916), and "Pray for the Lights to Go Out" (Little Rock, 1916). Information on George "Honeyboy" Evans is from Leonard's book *Masquerade in Black,* as well as conversations with Robert Cogswell.

Material on Sarie & Sally comes from personal interviews recorded with Edna Wilson in 1989, as well as a number of interviews done by Paul Ritscher from 1988–1992 in Nashville. Mrs. Wilson also allowed us to copy many of her old scripts and scrapbooks in which she had chronicled her career.

An outline of Robert Lunn's career can be found in Hay's memoir, as well as in the liner notes to his Starday LP *The Original Talking Blues Man,* Starday SLP-228 (1962).

The history of Chris Bouchillon and the "Talking Blues" comes from personal interviews with members of the Bouchillon family, Greenville, South Carolina, in 1991.

Chapter 15

The long description of the Opry picnic and early tours is taken from an unpublished passage of Hay's memoir, in the files of the Country Music Foundation in Nashville. Quotes from his daughter Margaret are from a personal interview done in May 1997. Material on the Andrews Brothers comes from author's files and from material in various issues of *Rural Radio* magazine. Those issues also helped clarify the chronology of Hay's return to the show and who was hired when. Information on advertising rates is drawn from advertising rate sheets in the Grand Ole Opry collection at the Heard Library at Vanderbilt University. Material from WLAC comes from a promotional picture book from 1939, in author's files. Quotes about the Golden West Cowboys come from an oral history interview with Pee Wee King in the CMF files in Nashville. The discussion of the music played on the air comes from a series of airchecks made in Virginia in the late 1930s, provided by Kip Lornell and the Blue Ridge Institute at Ferrum, Virginia. More detail about King is found in Charles Wolfe, *Kentucky Country: Folk and Country Music of Kentucky* (Lexington: University Press of Kentucky, 1981). See also Wade Hall, *Hell-Bent for Music: The Life of Pee Wee King* (Lexington: University Press of Kentucky, 1996).

Chapter 16

Data and quotes from Roy Acuff come from personal interviews with him in Nashville on 9-19-77 and 3-18-82. Letters and other documents are in the Roy Acuff room at the Country Music Foundation in Nashville, contributed by Elizabeth Schlappi. I have also used material from personal interviews done with Beecher Kirby (Oswald) at his home in Madison in the spring of 1995. Independent researcher Gayle Wardlow has also discussed with me at length his own research into Acuff's early recordings.

Material on Bill Monroe is from personal interviews with Monroe in Murfreesboro and Nashville, April 1975, September 1991, and May 1995. There is also some interesting material about Monroe's early days on the Opry in Hay's unpublished chapters of his Opry memoir.

Details of the first Opry network feed come from a copy of the transcribed show, in the archives of the Country Music Foundation, Nashville.

Discography

The following compact discs contain reissues of vintage recordings made by many of the artists discussed in this book.

Acuff, Roy. *The Essential Roy Acuff*. Columbia Legacy CK 48946. A good cross-section of the singer's career, including the original "Great Speckle Bird."

Bailey, DeFord. *The Legendary DeFord Bailey: Country Music's First Black Star*. Tennessee Folklore Society TFS 122. Recordings, including taped recollections, done in the 1970s by the early Opry's "harmonica wizard."

Macon, Uncle Dave. *Go 'long, Mule*. County CD-3505. A cross-section of Macon's best 1920s recordings, including several with His Fruit Jar Drinkers.

Macon, Uncle Dave. *Travelling Down the Road*. County CD-115. Later 1930s recordings from the Bluebird era.

McGee Brothers. *Sam McGee*. Document 8036. An import set from Austria containing most of the original recordings done by Sam as a soloist and by Sam with his brother Kirk.

McGee, Sam. *Grandad of Country Guitar Players*. Arhoolie 5012. Recordings from the 1960s on both banjo and guitar.

Various artists. *Nashville: The Early String Bands, vols. 1 and 2*. County CD 3518 and 3519. By far the best sampler of the sounds of the early Opry in the late 1920s. Included are original recordings by Theron Hale, Sid Harkreader, the Binkley Brothers, Paul Warmack and the Gully Jumpers, Uncle Jimmy Thompson, Uncle Dave Macon, Dr. Humphrey Bate, DeFord Bailey, the Crook Brothers, Uncle Joe Mangrum, and others. Detailed annotations.

Index

CHARLES K. WOLFE, Professor of English at Middle Tennessee State University, is among the foremost historians of country music and other forms of American popular culture. He is the author of more than a dozen highly acclaimed books, including *The Devil's Box: Masters of Southern Fiddling* (with a foreword by Mark O'Connor), published by Vanderbilt University Press in collaboration with the Country Music Foundation, which won the Belmont Award for the best book on country music published in 1997. Wolfe has also produced or annotated over fifty recorded albums of music, for which he has received three Grammy nominations. Another of his books, *The Life and Legend of Leadbelly*, published by Harper-Collins, won the 1993 Deems Taylor ASCAP Award.